Edward Berdoe

Browning Studies

Being Select Papers by Members of the Browning Society

Edward Berdoe

Browning Studies
Being Select Papers by Members of the Browning Society

ISBN/EAN: 9783337014179

Printed in Europe, USA, Canada, Australia, Japan

Cover: Foto ©ninafisch / pixelio.de

More available books at **www.hansebooks.com**

BROWNING STUDIES

BEING

SELECT PAPERS BY MEMBERS

OF THE

BROWNING SOCIETY

EDITED, WITH AN INTRODUCTION

BY

EDWARD BERDOE, M.R.C.S., &c.

AUTHOR OF "THE BROWNING CYCLOPÆDIA," "BROWNING'S MESSAGE TO HIS TIME," &c., &c.

NEW YORK: MACMILLAN AND CO.
LONDON: GEORGE ALLEN
1895

INTRODUCTION.

WHEN the Browning Society was founded fourteen years ago, the works of the great poet were read by comparatively few general readers in England, although they had long been familiar to the American public and had secured a great number of earnest students who united themselves into societies and reading clubs for the discussion of a literature which even then was voluminous. At that time it was considered in England an affectation of erudition to pretend to any wider acquaintance with Browning's works than was involved in knowing the *Pied Piper of Hamelin, How they Brought the Good News from Ghent to Aix*, and having a nodding acquaintance with *Rabbi Ben Ezra.*

To have owned to familiarity with *Paracelsus* or *The Ring and the Book* subjected one to the gibes and sneers of smart people, who thought it clever to call *Pacchiarotto* a "pack o' rot." To confess that *Sordello* interested and even delighted one entailed the certainty of having to listen to the ancient wheeze about Douglas Jerrold, who once essayed to read the poem, and having done so took medical opinion about the state of his reason. Everybody had a cheap joke about Browning, and if people knew nothing else of the poet, they could at least raise a laugh against those who pretended to know him.

Reviewers, in the intervals between criticising a society novel and a volume of minor poetry, knocked off a column or so on Browning, and conclusively settled that he could write neither grammatically nor intelligibly, and that having no "form" his works could not possibly be poetry.

There is no more remarkable fact in the history of literature, and no greater disgrace to English criticism, than the treatment meted out to Robert Browning for half a century. Here was the greatest

English poet since Shakespeare living amongst us, pouring out treasures of thought and disseminating germs of "wholesome ferment"
for other minds, as Mr. Lowell has happily said, and England would
have none of him.

"Ye British Public who like me not"

he complained, after writing for thirty-five years; after giving the
world *Men and Women*, *Pippa Passes*, *Paracelsus*, *Christmas Eve and
Easter Day*, and other priceless literary treasures which will never die
while the English language affords them a home. The British Public
who unceasingly bragged of the Shakespeare of whom it knew little,
and the Spenser and Dryden and the rest of whom it knew practically
nothing, ridiculed the idea that Browning could be of the regal caste
of poets because he spoke a language that was not of the sort it was
accustomed to. Browning mixed no water with his ink, as Goethe
said our modern poets do; there was often little music in his words,
and the sense was at times rather hard to grasp; and so our strong,
robust, gloriously sane poet "came to his own and his own received
him not"; he spoke vigorous, pregnant words warm from his great,
loving heart, and 'poured for us wine' to brace our souls in the degen-
erate days when men were giving up God for the Unknowable, and
their faith in Christianity for belief in "something not ourselves
which makes for righteousness"; he taught us a pure religion,
reasonable and manly, robust and in harmony with the science of
the age, and few would listen and fewer still would heed. Yet the
age had such need of him! The cancer of salacity, the poison-germs
of impurity infected our literature, and were being disseminated as
never had been known before. The age was a frivolous, listless,
lackadaisical time, when such thought as could be tolerated by our
youth was growing daily more pessimistic, less reverent and earnest;
well-educated, happily placed men and women began to ask if life
were worth living; and for want of anything to stir their pulses
after exhausting their energies in devising new modes of breaking
the Ten Commandments one after another, bethought themselves of
importing a so-called Buddhism, and cultivating melancholy and
atheism. Christianity was declared to be "played out," and no
longer to be credited by men and women who had passed a science
examination or studied Huxley.

Just when such sentiments as these became popular, even with those who had no qualifications for any such difficult task, Browning had reached the zenith of his glory, and a few lovers of the man and his work decided upon the rather risky scheme of founding a society in his honour, or rather for the promulgation of his teaching. It is not to be understood, however, that all lovers of Browning are either Christians or Theists. Some of the most able and esteemed founders of the Browning Society had no sympathy with either his Theism or Christian teaching. It was in the year 1881, on October 28th, that the Browning Society was inaugurated at University College, London, with the address by the Rev. J. Kirkman, M.A., "On the Characteristics of Browning's Philosophy and Poetry," which occupies the first place in this volume. The Vice-Presidents of the Society were the Rev. H. R. Haweis, M.A., Miss Anna Swanwick, and Lady Mount-Temple. The Committee consisted of Mr. Sidney Ball, M.A., Oxford ; Professor Corson, M.A., Cornell ; Mr. F. J. Furnivall, M.A., Cambridge ; Rev. Professor E. Johnson, M.A., London ; Rev. J. Kirkman, M.A., Cambridge ; Miss Mary A. Lewis, Miss Elinor M. Lewis, Mr. J. T. Nettleship, Mr. Hume C. Piment, M.A., Cambridge, and Mr. James Thomson ; with Miss E. H. Hickey as Honorary Secretary. The object of the Society, as declared in the Founders' prospectus dated July, 1881, was set forth as follows :—

"This Society is founded to gather together some, at least, of the many admirers of Robert Browning, for the study and discussion of his works, and the publication of Papers on these, and extracts from works illustrating them. The Society will also encourage the formation of Browning Reading Clubs, the acting of Browning's dramas by amateur companies, the writing of a Browning Primer, the compilation of a Browning Concordance or Lexicon, and generally the extension of the study and influence of the poet.

"Without entering on the vext question of who is the greatest living poet, Mr. Browning's admirers are content to accept the general verdict that he is both one of the greatest, and *the* most thought-full. They find as his leading note that which Prof. Spalding declared was Shakspere's :

"The presence of a spirit of active and inquiring thought through every page of his writings, is too evident to require any proof. It is exerted on every object which comes under his notice ; it is serious when its theme is lofty ; and when the subject is familiar, it is content to be shrewd. He has impressed no other of his own mental qualities on all his characters ; this quality colours every one of them. . . . Imagination is active, powerfully and unceasingly, but she is rebuked

by the presence of a mightier influence ; she is but the handmaid of the active and
piercing understanding; and the images which are her offspring serve but as
the breeze to the river, which stirs and ripples its surface, but is not the power
which impels its water to sea."—*Letter on the Authorship of the " Two Noble
Kinsmen."* 1833, p. 20-1. (N. Sh. Soc. reprint.)

" That this very fullness of thought in Mr. Browning, with its
lightning darts, abrupt transitions, is hard to take in, difficult to
follow, is matter of course. That the thought is more worthful to
him than its expression, the heart of oak than its bark, has made
some men refuse to try and penetrate through the rough covering to
the strength beneath. But Æschylus is often obscure; some passages in Shakspere still puzzle the best critics. Browning's themes
are the development of Souls, the analysis of Minds, Art, Religion,
Love, the relation of Man and Nature to God, of Man to Man and
Woman, the Life past, present, and to come. If on some of these
great themes Browning's thoughts have not been easily apprehended,
may this not come from want of faithful study, default of deadened
minds ? At any rate the Browning student will seek the short-
coming in himself rather than in his master. He will wish, by
conference with other students, by recourse to older scholars, to
learn more of the meaning of the poet's utterances; and then,
having gladly learnt, 'gladly wol he teche,' and bring others under
the same influence that has benefited himself. To this end *The
Browning Society* has been founded.

" The Society will consist of all Subscribers of 21*s.* a year. It will
meet once a month from October to June (except in December), on
the 4th Friday of every such month, at 8 p.m., at University
College, Gower Street, W.C., for the hearing and discussion of a
Paper or Address on some of Browning's poems or his characteristics.
The Society's best Papers, and Reports of its Discussions, will be
printed either in full or in a *Monthly Abstract* sent to all members, as
funds allow. Till July 7, 1882, the Society will be managed by a
Committee of its Founders and Promoters. At that day's Meeting,
after the experience of the first Session, the Constitution of the
Society will be settled, and its Officers elected for the ensuing year.

" The Committee are anxious to appoint as *Local Honorary Secre-
taries* those students of Browning in or out of London who will undertake either to get up Browning Reading Clubs in their respective
districts,—after the example of Professor Corson, who has directed

one in his University (Cornell) for the last four years,—or otherwise promote the study of Browning in their neighbourhood as opportunity offers.

"The Society may not be a large or permanent one. It appeals only to thoughtful men and women willing to study Browning's works. It exists, and will begin its Meetings next autumn. It has promises of some Papers for its first Session, but desires more. Its few present members hope that some, at least, of the many to whom Browning's works have been a help and strength, will join them in their endeavour to know him better, and bring more minds under his influence.

" To remove misunderstandings that have arisen, the Committee state that any one joining the Society is not in any way pledged to indiscriminate admiration of BROWNING, but is only supposed to hold that the poet is profound enough in thought, noble enough in character and feeling, eloquent and interesting enough in expression, to deserve more thorough study, and a far wider circle of readers, than he has yet had. The Committee wish for frankness of expression in all Papers, &c. ; and they give notice from the first, that every writer in the Society's publications is to be held as speaking for himself or herself alone, without any responsibility whatever on the Committee's part."

In the "Forewords" to "A Bibliography of Robert Browning, 1833–1881," by Dr. Furnivall, published in Part I. of the *Browning Society's Papers*, 1881, the writer says that after the Alphabetical List and the Chronological one of the poet's works in their order of time, which he presented to the Society (including a number of most valuable notes by Mr. Shepherd and Mr. Carson), it would be necessary to have *A Subject-Index to Browning's Works*, and a short statement of the story and purpose of each of these works. He particularly desired the publication of a *Browning Primer*. All these desirable objects were achieved by the Browning Society in due order. It is impossible to praise too highly the splendid work done by Dr. Furnivall in his Bibliography of Browning, forming the whole of Part I. and more than 50 pp. of Part II. of the Society's Papers. This work is indispensable to the Browning student, and was a purely literary labour of love on the author's part, as he candidly stated in his Forewords that personally "he did not care for the special Christian or doctrinal side of Browning's work, yet he felt the worth of his teaching as a man and thinker, and admired his imaginative power, his strength and subtlety." This was a peculiar and interesting feature of the Browning Society, and one which endears it to the recollections of those who were its most active members, that it was a platform on which we could all meet—Christians, both Protestant and Catholic, atheists, agnostics, and indifferents—and each find something in Browning which appealed to the best that was in us, making us all feel stronger, more earnest and real, and truer to our better selves. Mr. James Thomson, the atheist, author of *The City of Dreadful Night*, could recognise and reverence Browning's Christianity. In his paper on the "Genius of Robert Browning," read at the third meeting of the Society, January 27, 1882, he said: "Finally, I must not fail to note as one of the most remarkable characteristics of his genius, his profound, passionate, living, triumphant faith in Christ, and in the immortality and ultimate redemption of every human soul in and through Christ. . . . Thoroughly familiar with all modern doubts and disbeliefs, he tramples them all under foot, clinging to the Cross; and this with the full co-operation of his fearless reason, not in spite of it, and by its absolute surrender or suppression." Mr. Cotter Morrison, Mr. Moncure Conway, Miss Eleanor Marx, Bishop Westcott, Canon Farrar, the Hon. Roden Noel, Miss Beale the distinguished Principal of the Ladies' College, Cheltenham, the Rev. Mr. Haweis, Mr. Nettleship the painter, and a host of other leaders of all shades of religious opinion, met with us and contributed to the common store of Browning knowledge; one and all, like wanderers in a Brazilian forest, found something to delight him or her, and though not every one chose the same precious or beautiful object, not one was disappointed, not one but left the meeting the richer for some treasure of high and pure thought. Surely never since Shakespeare's days came amongst us English folk so potent a genius as Robert Browning, who could blend into one by the spell of his love and power so many and so various shades of thought. Yet ours was no slavish hero-worship, no uncritical compact to worship Browning at all hazards; we criticised him freely, expressed our opinions unmistakably, and, if report be true, greatly to the amusement and satisfaction of the poet himself, who once having been asked to explain the meaning of one of his dark sayings, bade the querist "Ask the Browning Society: they could tell, he couldn't!" Dean Church used to say that "Browning went into polite society in his shirt-sleeves and made faces at it." We often felt that was so, and very often, no doubt, when we had been hotly debating to whose side some particular arrow was directed, the poet was chuckling his *De te fabula*. We only quarrelled in the Society when certain folk of one or other party tried to monopolise Browning all to themselves, to stow away the master into their own little pocket and walk off with him. It was quite a natural thing to do, for we were for the most part very ordinary folk, and few of us had the warm generosity of Mr. Thomson to reverence and admire what we did not happen to believe; but after a little reflection we yielded to Browning's loftier spirit, and felt very much ashamed of being so little in the presence of one so great. I think we must have been useful to one another. The unbeliever must have felt that there was something in Christianity after all, when such a genius as that of Browning could accept it as devoutly as a mediæval saint; and the Christian no doubt often felt that the all-embracing love of the poet was a good deal wider and much more divine than the narrow bounds of some of our creeds.

But we were not by any means all theological in our meetings. We talked and thought of Browning as a musician; as a landscape painter; as an interpreter of Greek life and character; as a poet of science; as a dramatist; as an historian; as a philosopher; as a lover. Yet in the twelve years of our existence we had but entered the borders of the Browning-land, and when we broke up the Society in 1893, although we had done so much, we felt that had time and means permitted, we could have carried on our work profitably and pleasantly for another decade or two. We accomplished however all we set out to do. We had acted all the really actable plays, had published thirteen volumes of papers and discussions, with many beautiful photographs of pictures referred to in the poems. Mrs. Sutherland Orr had published her useful Handbook to the works of the poet; Mr. Nettleship had written his invaluable Essays; Miss Hickey had contributed her "Notes on Strafford"; Mr. Arthur Symonds had given us his "Introduction to the Study of Browning"; Miss Wilson and Miss Defries had each published her "Primer of Browning" and the present writer his "Browning Cyclopædia," and written the "Biographical and Historical Notes" to the poet's complete works; all this was the direct outcome of the Society's activity. But beyond this, as due chiefly to the interest awakened in Browning's works by our efforts, an enormously increased demand arose for the poems themselves. Many volumes of essays and other explanatory works had helped to spread the light and set thousands studying a poet now no longer neglected nor unloved by English people. All this would have come in time, Society or no Society; but it is certain that the time was greatly hastened in the twelve years of its existence.

Although the poet never wrote for profit, and never craved for praise from the unthinking and unappreciative world, he could have been no other than solaced and gratified by the recognition of his efforts for the pleasure and instruction of the world; and when the time came, when all too soon he left us, it must have cheered him to know that no longer could he complain that "the British Public liked him not," and in his own last words he could "greet the unseen with a cheer."

His work was done, the clouds had broken; "right was not worsted, nor did wrong triumph."

As the publications of the Browning Society are now for the most part out of print, it has been thought advisable to offer to the public this volume of Selected Papers by authors whose reputation suffi-ciently guarantees their importance, and whose treatment of their special subjects largely contributed to the success of the Society for whose benefit they were written. Should the general appreciation of these Selected Papers warrant it, a second series will follow in due course.

EDWARD BERDOE.

CONTENTS.

CONTENTS.

INTRODUCTORY ADDRESS TO THE BROWNING SOCIETY.

BY THE REV. J. KIRKMAN, M.A., QUEEN'S COLL., CAMBRIDGE.

Friday, October 28, 1881, *at University College, London.*

AMONG the honours and penalties to which the higher order of genius is doomed may be reckoned reverential students, enthusiastic advocates, purblind detractors; then reviews and volumes of criticism; lastly, a *Society* for the special study of a man's works. To all this has Mr. Browning now come. We do ourselves the honour of meeting to-night to inaugurate the *Browning Society*. The words have been already printed, "It exists." And I call to mind some words of the other great Poet of our Golden Age, singing of Nature and considering everywhere her secret meaning in her deeds, and

> "Finding that of fifty seeds
> She often brings but one to bear."

What might some infant have been! What might it not have been! Of the infants cast up on the shore of the living, Blake says,

> "Some are born to sweet delight:
> Some are born to endless night."

The possibility of a child

> "Whose exterior semblance doth belie its soul's immensity,"

as Wordsworth says, might have developed into *a critic* to save poets from a short mortality of fame, or a curse to deluge mountain-tops in the region of mind with merciless floods of words. Thus this *Society*, while hitherto *in ovo*, has already undergone ridicule and the killing frost of indifference. Nevertheless it makes an attempt *to be;* and possibly may develop into a worthy successor of the *Lyncœi* of the sixteenth century. When its requiem shall be sung, after a long or short life, that life will have been one of noble intentions and efforts, at least in full harmony with the merits and requirements of the case, and suited to the customs of the age in which we eclectic ones live both to learn and teach. Let us unanimously resolve that it shall not exist in vain; but shall deserve both guineas and gratitude for the benefits it shall

B

dispense.   Although we cannot and would not shoulder Browning up
into a factitious popularity that would be sure to become extinct like
fireworks, we may be instrumental in organizing, developing, and cultivating, the recognition, which is the first element in our *raison d'être*,
that Browning is undoubtedly the profoundest intellect, with widest
range of sympathies, and with universal knowledge of men and things,
that has arisen as a poet since Shakespeare.   In knowledge of many
things he is necessarily superior to Shakespeare, as being the all-receptive
child of the century of science and travel.   In carefulness of construction, and especially in the genius of constructing *drama*, he claims
not comparison with Shakespeare.   But his truly Shakespearian genius
pre-eminently shines in his power to throw his whole intellect and
sympathies into the most diverse individualities ; to think and feel as
one of them would, although undoubtedly glorified by Browning's
genius within.   Goethe's canon is, "The Poet should seize the particular,
and he should, if there be anything sound, thus represent the universal."
In this Browning is infallible : but he is, as Shakespeare often is, perceptible through the visor of his assumed individuality.   Notice the great
number of persons, the wide range of characters and specialities, through
which he speaks.   Browning rightly and proudly enough scorns the
interpretation of being made to speak his own soul when he utters the
soul of another.   "With this same key Shakespeare unlocked his heart.
Did Shakespeare ? If so, the less Shakespeare he." (*Pacchiarotto* volume,
p. 63.)   The fullest poem in which his chief characteristics of throwing
himself into the individuality of another, of unfolding the history of a
human soul, and of making the human subjective modes called time and
eternity inseparable, so that the struggling and emotions and efforts or
desires of a life, or a day, or a thought, for any mind, prove it like "a
pin-point rock " founded in earth but pointing heavenwards, is *Sordello*.
In lesser degrees of detailed unfolding, most of his poems are acts or
scenes in some "soul's development."   I said, his profound acquaintance with men and things was Shakespearian.   I should have emphatically said, with men, *women*, and things.   Browning's women are as
wonderful a class almost as Shakespeare's.   He understands women
with perfecter intuition and less uniform rose-colour than Richter, of
whom Browning often reminds us.   Anthony can no more say of *any*
woman,   "She is cunning past *man's* thought." (*A. & C.* i. 2.)

I do not attempt to attract the notice of the Eumenides by specially
referring to Browning's women now.

    Browning is our nearest to Shakespeare.   Comparisons may flit and
pass : but we take him on his indisputable merits, not blindly, but

proudly and gratefully. Some one told Goethe that the Germans disputed whether he or his contemporary Schiller were the greater poet. His worthy reply was, "They ought to be very thankful that they have two such fellows to dispute about." But let me add what De Quincey says on resembling Shakespeare, when he pays that tribute to Richter : " If a man could reach Venus or Mercury, we should not say he has advanced to a great distance from the earth : we should say he is very near to the Sun. So also, if in anything a man approaches Shakespeare, or does but remind us of him, all other honours are swallowed up in that : a relation of inferiority to him is a more enviable distinction than all degrees of superiority to others ; the rear of his splendours a more eminent post than the supreme station in the van of all others." (De Quincey, ' On Richter.' Vol. xiii. 119, 120.)

We have to consider to-night both Browning and the *Browning Society* as correlative, but not as coincident. For the keynote has been given to me of " Characteristics of Browning's Poetry and Philosophy." But this is too ambitious. We cannot scamper over the whole field of Browning's works, with the rapidity of him who brought the good news from Ghent to Aix. It is only an open question for some of us, as yet, how far these *characteristics* conceal or reveal the Poetry and Philosophy : as bees, when they are too numerous, swarm all over the hive, while the regular work of honey-making is in abeyance. I wished more modestly to have taken for title, " *Browning made easy.*" I am still somewhat fondly of opinion that that title would have been suitable. A friend said to me, " If you could manage that, you would have a tremendous following. A man ought to be *born* with a faculty for understanding Browning : so, if he is not, you must try to create it." Another said that title would be undignified. But it raises the question, on which I hope there will be some discussion, whether we are more to address ourselves to the select circle of ourselves who do already love and value Browning far beyond the measure of conventional acknowledgment, and desire to help each other to study him more and know him better ; or whether we are not rather to appeal to the far larger circle of those who may wisely be attracted to discover and appreciate him for themselves. I venture to suggest that, for various reasons the latter attempt will secure a measure of the former, rather than *vice versâ*. For the two chief notorious facts that we can never lose sight of, are : 1st, the intense devotedness, the intellectual reverence, and profound personal indebtedness, of Browning's admirers ; and 2nd, the vast prevalence of indifference, dislike or depreciation, which prevents him from being the popular teacher he deserves to be to this generation, and might be with infinite advantage. I hardly know a greater pain and

bitterer disappointment caused by facts in the history of literature, than
that given by the acknowledgment registered in that sad and abhorred
line, which Milton's archangelic haughtiness would have made him
scorn to write :
                        " You, British public, you who love me not."
Let us, with Uncle Toby's recording angel, let fall a tear on that repeated line, as we have written it down, and blot it out for ever. The
regret over this, which is however by no means so fully the fact as he
may have been led to feel from isolated symptoms, is akin to that one
feels over Bacon and Jeremy Taylor ignoring the existence of their
greater contemporary and superior, Shakespeare.   Yet, our special business is with reference to this love and indifference, to help the light to
conquer more of the darkness, and the love to overcome the indifference.
If the unanswerable plea for the indifference to Browning be his extreme
obscurity, " dark with excess of light," and painfully rapid succession
of thoughts, and general difficulty in following thro' the involved tangle
of endless sentences, subtlety of perpetual suggestiveness, which can
only be overcome and turned into pleasure by very intellectual and
persevering readers ; this is a legitimate object for our Society to deal
with.   And we may, with respect to it, gather hope to-night from
the pleasing paradox (if you will notice the list of Members, and
especially the four caryatides which support the entablature of this
Society), of the great proportion of *clergymen* and *ladies !*   About
2 to 1 on the whole.   The poet has no need to be ashamed of his
clients ; nor they of themselves, in the intellectual ranks likely to
influence lower mortals.   Still, in the face of this, no one can fairly
reiterate the pretty old class slander that we (of those two species)
are emphatically those in whom emotion dominates over intellect and
judgment.   Speaking for myself, probably also herein for my peers,
this suggests one of the most practical hints we have to offer ; that *our*
elective affinities are determined by a man's *best works ;* and are not
dissolved by those which are less worthy of his greatest self.

   Wherefore, as the all-important subject of *classification* has already
been mentioned by the Chairman, *we must first divide Browning's works
into two great classes.* I don't think either of the two volumes of *Selections*
has done this wisely.   And I anticipate that probably my division may
be repudiated by some present, or counted unworthy and trivial.   Nevertheless, it is possible that the lapse of time may only strengthen this
roughly reasonable classification.   First, *those works which may be
understood and enjoyed.*   Second, *those which never will be:* such
as the involved narratives and subtle disquisitions, the store of headaches, and volumes of cobwebs strung with innumerable pearls glittering

in a light beyond our ordinary powers of vision. This division corresponds loosely with that between his earlier and later works ; although by no means accurately or entirely, of course. With respect to such a rather daring distinction, I presume most humbly to suggest that blind adulation and indiscriminate commendation of all that our great teacher has writ, because he has writ it, is no rational allegiance to him on the part of such sincere disciples as we are ; and in proportion as it should threaten to prevail, must lower the standard of this Society. I believe it was Coleridge who said, "The affections are monarchical, but the intellect is democratic." Nor ought we to be embarrassed by the fact that Browning is still alive. May he long live : on into his aftermath, the

"rare afterbirth of peeping blooms sprinkled its wealth among,"

similar to the glorious season of 40 or less years ago. We can hardly help feeling that if Browning would *take our advice*, we should "make him all he ought to be." But at least we will study, while he laughs kindly on us.

Now, I have claimed somewhat of the function of a *foolometer* to-night ; or, as Bacon said, to think with the learned and speak with the vulgar : and in that capacity may state one case that represents thousands. An intelligent man hears Browning praised. He finds *Red Cotton Night-Cap Country*, or *Prince Hohenstiel-Schwangau* or *Pacchiarotto* within reach. He says, "I read it once and could not make cap or *queue* of it. I thought I had read it *too fast*. I read it again, with no more success, and thought I had read it *too slowly*. I read it a third time *aloud*, dropped pieces of my broken teeth on the carpet in the process, and gave up Browning in despair." There is great reasonableness in that. *He began in the wrong class.* So is a well-disposed convert lost. He had perhaps never heard of *Rabbi Ben Ezra*, or *Christmas Eve*, or *Saul*. This case has been related, as you are aware, in some Periodical ; and we have frequently met with such cases ourselves. Moreover, it illustrates the fact of some one of the later volumes lying near, while probably the three volumes of earlier compositions were returning unto dust on the book-shelf. If the cruel difference between *Christmas Eve and Easter Day*, for instance, and *Pacchiarotto* or *P. Hohenstiel-Schwangau*, does prevail to any reasonable degree between the earlier and later works, therein is a mystery and a titanic grief on which least shall be said and most felt. Some find compensation in the theory that Browning has insisted on enlarging our conception of what must be included under the designation of *Poetry* ; and that he has, with the indisputable right of genius acting by its own instinctive laws, created an expansion beyond the accepted manners of his predecessors, as the Natural School did beyond the mechanical formality of Pope. Then some new name is wanted. It is infinitely too serious to be doggerel, in spite of all the wantonness and fun of quaint rhyming and punning; yet so often apparently deficient in the conscientious elaborating and perfecting which he condescends to affirm in his short prefaces. It won't come under any *definition* that I know. Where we cannot understand we must wonder. I believe that is the philosophical attitude of spirit in any such emergency. The charge of *obscurity* has been so admirably met by Mr. Swinburne in the Browning digression in his noble Introduction to George Chapman's Poems, that there is no need to refute it further. But as to the cognate charge of *ruggedness*, I am inclined, instead of blaming, to glory in Browning's writings as a protest of the grandest kind against the popular demand that everything is to be *smooth* and *sweet* now-a-days. Sweetness and smoothness, the combination which now threatens to emasculate both literary and religious productions, both writing, speech, and action, while still the serpents are gliding under the grass and the roses where there ought to be some burr-thistles too, is no equivalent to Swift's "sweetness and light." Even the polished poet-prophet Isaiah (c. xxx. 10) stoutly resisted it. And Browning evidently shares this feeling with us; as he has but too vigorously perhaps asserted in *Pacchiarotto*, and so felicitously shown in *Date and Dabitur*. It may be better in these oily days of minds as well as railway-trains advancing without friction, to be somewhat rugged with Browning, Isaiah, Carlyle, &c., than ever smooth with the more popular prophets of lies and delusions.

At this date it requires a downright effort of the mind to realize that *Paracelsus* was published 46 years ago, *Sordello* in 1840, *Christmas Eve and Easter Day* in 1850: and here we are now recommending them and the earliest streams that flowed down to the level of our intelligence from the sunlit mountains of his. It was, in a great measure, through omitting altogether Vol. iii. of the *Dramatic Works*, and taking only the two volumes and *Dramatis Personæ*, that we succeeded in Hampstead in a course of Lectures fifteen years ago, and quickened a good number to appreciate Browning, before he suddenly rose to more general recognition, as he has since that time. This must still be more or less the plan to be pursued. And plenty will remain to be done. But it is one thing to give a lecture on some difficult work; it is quite another thing to get Browning's best works known, loved, enjoyed, and quoted as household words of daily intellectual resource, like Tennyson. I would rather take my chance with *Sordello* than with *The Ring and the Book*. We were, at any rate, among the "few who must like" the incidents in that development of a soul. Taking *Sordello* as the severest part of

our happy task, we felt that it does not share so much of those features
which mark the poems published since 1868, at which I stand aghast
and bewildered. *Sordello* is far more *quotable;* rhyme tends to make
the sentences shorter; and they never run out as cable to the length of
a whole page or more, as in *The Ring and the Book.* I have not time
to speak especially upon *Sordello,* with its innumerable beauties, its
luxuriant excesses, as of vegetable and animal life in an American
forest. It comprises a wider grasp, deeper fathoming, and higher
scaling, in the development of a soul, than *Paracelsus.* But most of
Browning's poems might have the sub-title of Incident or Incidents in
the development of a soul. The task laid upon our attention by fulness
and rapidity of thought is peculiarly in *Sordello* a stimulating difficulty to
be dealt with, and ends in satisfaction and enhanced degrees of pleasure.
Ruskin says, in reference to *The Bishop ordering his tomb in S. Prazed's
Church,* "The worst of it is that this kind of concentrated writing needs
so much *solution* before the readers can fairly get the good of it, that
people's patience fails them, and they give up the thing as insoluble :
though truly it ought to be to the current of common thought like
Saladin's talisman, dipped in clear water, not soluble altogether, but
making the element medicinal." ('M. P.' vol. iv. 379.) All that Ruskin
has said on Browning ought to be quoted in full. There are, however,
other features besides *concentration* in Browning's later works about
which time would not allow me to speak otherwise than inadequately
now. Some one will have the delight of exhibiting his great gift of
humour, which is one that allies him so truly with Shakespeare ; and
which, inextricably interwoven with seriousness, Carlyle, in reference to
Richter, describes as the last finish and perfection of the human faculties.
Often Browning reminds us of Richter also in his sudden and surprising
illustrations. Let future speakers take a text for vindication of those
twenty years of personal rule that were the ruin of France ; or extract
the "pleasure" that is supposed to be an ingredient in reading poetry,
the gentleness and the sweetness, from *Pacchiarotto :* while some of us,
who cannot bear that Jupiter should frown so, or Apollo gather such
black clouds around his glory,

"For fear creep into acorn-cups and hide us there,"

lest there should be a ray or a shadow of allusion to such minds
as our own. Not only the later poems, however, but perhaps every
poem of Browning's "must be read three times to be understood." You
must always "image the whole, then execute the parts." Coleridge says
he read the 'Pilgrim's Progress' three times, first as a theologian,
secondly with devotional feelings, thirdly as a poet. ('Table Talk,' p. 89.)
Whether thrice or more, there is an order in which Browning must be

read by one who has to be *charmed* into appreciating him. The first sign of that order is the separation already insisted on, between those poems and extracts which may be read with pleasure and infinite advantage, and those which I fear no power nor a score of Browning Societies will ever make *popular*, or acceptable with ordinary minds backed by only ordinary leisure in these rapid days, and an average degree of perseverance. *Albeit there is, even in our day*, a higher *merit* than popularity : although you cannot get more than one in a thousand to own as much.

It may sound foolish to put poems *in rank* like modern symmetrical bouquets of flowers or buds : but it is an old philosophy, still essential, to advance from the easy to the difficult, if poetry is to be a serious and elevating enjoyment for the head and the heart. We may even applaud the judgment of that selection which takes *From Ghent to Aix*, and the *Pied Piper* as suitable for Penny Readings. And I may add, *Date and Dabitur* is an admirable little gem for children to learn by heart, and many children I am concerned with know it well. But for adults, *begin with Rabbi Ben Ezra*, one of the very noblest modern religious moral poems, swallowing up in light that miserable shadow of the faithless coldness of the times cast in the doubt, "Is life worth living?" If a man does not value that, let him alone : he is no better than one of the dolls Jean Paul made for his children with a Sultana raisin put in for a soul. Why has not our glorious poet given us more like that? Minerva leaps from the brain with all the varieties of Proteus, as we pass to quite other poems. They say, in our less classical times, poets have poems born, as ladies have beautiful children ; and for inscrutable reasons the last may not be as beautiful as the last-but-one. *Rabbi Ben Ezra* and *Prospice* are as two guiding angels of subdued effulgence which conduct a man to *Childe Roland*. This is such an absolutely unique effort of genius, constructed every line and word even with such happy art, that I won't speak about it now, as I am under the responsibility of giving it a separate treatment as my favourite poem. Then *Abt Vogler*, for a person having any music in his soul. And *Caliban*, the identical Caliban of Shakespeare, the hairy ancestor of all theologians and philosophers, with his keen eyes, perched on a rock's edge, of Sir Noel Paton ; the Caliban in his speculating spirit into which Browning has thrown himself as completely as into *Protus* or *Johannes Agricola*, without a single flash of thought incongruous to that undeveloped piece of humanity, who gives us a treasury of the natural history in the island, and of unconscious felicities as piercing as his own eyes, as well as of that natural philosophy beyond which we ourselves could never have

emerged, if such a guiding star had never risen on us as Tennyson's, that
"Nothing is which errs from law ; "
nor S. John's sunlight that "God is love." No preacher ever gave
a grander sermon on a Scripture text than *that* is on Psalm l. 21.
Following so reluctantly this idea of successive arrangement, or even
taking *intelligibility* as the great merit, yet if it be
"Weakness to be wroth with weakness,"
take *Christmas Eve*, which is intelligible enough ; and if enjoyed on
Saturday, Dec. 24, by the time Lent-lilies are out the weaker brethren
might venture into *Easter Day*, which is more abstruse. Any one can
understand *Saul*, and the *Arabian Physician*, the *Boy and the Angel*, and
Holy Cross Day : and then Paracelsus, which is not at all difficult to
any one who can at all harmonize with Browning's marvellously versatile
genius in his striking selection of subjects, and can become accustomed
to his glorious plenitude of thought with lesser degrees of his abstruse-
ness. This is low ground indeed to take : but we must not forget that
the prejudice to be overcome is against the extreme difficulty of following
him without headaches, and with a chance of real enjoyment. Suppose
we offered ourselves as guides to Switzerland, with similarly graduated
guarantees that *enjoyment* may be had from flowers, forests, and valleys,
as well as intellectual elevation from sublime mountains and wondrous
glaciers ! These poems named above ought to convince any one (out of
Colney Hatch) that he is sitting at the feet of a wonderful poet, who
will richly repay all further efforts bestowed on a fuller acquaintance.
And we who have patiently to labour in teaching and raising others,
and cannot expect them at once to follow us in all our intellectual
soaring with eagles' wings (or Icarus-wings) must forbearingly sympathize
with those limited abilities and pardonable aversions, that can never
appreciate (and more than a small minority of readers never will) such
poems as *P. Hohenstiel-Schwangau* and *Pacchiarotto*, or even *The Ring
and the Book*, or *Sordello*. The thing to maintain is that such incomparable poetry as is steadily gaining its deserved popularity, or *will*
through the impetus of this Society, is not more widely different from
the other class, is not less in amount comparatively, or lower in
comparative excellence of artistic finish, than Wordsworth's 'Ode on
Immortality' is compared with his wearisome drivelling pedlars, or the
valued and unvalued portions of many another poet's writings.

I will now conform to my title by drawing attention to three of the
greatest *characteristics* of Browning's poetry and philosophy, which have
hitherto received either utterly inadequate recognition or none at all.
First, Music : second, Art : third, Christianity.

1. *Take Music First.* He is a born musician, and a cultivated musician.

as to the history, the laws, and the compositions, of music. No other poet has ever ventured to occupy such a position.

> " His magic may not copied be :
> For in that circle none durst walk but he."

The spiritual transcendentalism of music, the inscrutable relation between the seen and the eternal, of which music alone unlocks the gates by inarticulate expression, has never had an articulate utterance from a poet before *Abt Vogler.* This is of a higher order of composition, quite nobler, than the merely fretful rebellion against the earthly condition imposed here below upon heavenly things, seen in *Master Hugues.* In that and other places, I am not sure that persons of musical *attainment,* as distinguished from musical *soul and sympathy,* do not rather find a professional gratification at the technicalities, as

> " those lesser thirds so plaintive,
> sixths diminished, sigh on sigh . . .
> those commiserating sevenths . . ."
>   *(A Toccata of Galuppi's.)*

as curiosities, and phenomena of music being reduced *to words* at all ; as again the five parts of a fugue,

> " What with affirming, denying,
> Holding, risposting, subjoining, . .
> So your fugue broadens and thickens
> Greatens and deepens and lengthens. ."
>   *(Master Hugues.)*

or the peculiarities of composers, &c., than get conducted to " the law within the law." But in *Abt Vogler,* the understanding is spell-bound, and carried on the wings of the emotions, as Ganymede in the soft down of the eagle, into the world of spirit. Compare what any one else has written on music. Cowper's

> " With easy force it opens all the cells where memory slept."

Wordsworth's fiddling

> " in the street that from Oxford has borrowed its name."

Dryden's Odes, so overpraised ; even the Poet Laureate's

> " little sharps and trebles."

The beautiful utterances of Richter alone approach to the value of Browning's on music. Well does he deserve remembrance for the remark, that " Music is the only language incapable of expressing anything impure," and for many others. They all, comparatively, speak *from outside;* Browning speaks *from inside,* as if an angel came to give all the hints we could receive,

> " of that imperial palace whence we came."

He speaks of music as Dante does of Heaven, Hell, and Purgatory,

because he has been there. Even the musical Milton, whose best
line is,

> " In linked sweetness long drawn out." (*L'Allegro*.)

whose best special treatment of music is in the occasional Poem, '*At a
solemn music*,' has given us nothing of the nature of *Abt Vogler*. It
should be perfectly learnt by heart; and it will be ever whispering
analogies to the soul in daily life. Because, of course, the mystery of
life and the mystery of music make one of the most fundamental transcendental harmonies breathed into our being. We may even correlate
Shakespeare here. For the 5th Act of '*M. of Venice*,' which comes
nearest, gives us briefly the mighty secret, which is so marvellously
organised in *Abt Vogler*. This requires a treatment by itself, and a
sympathetic notice of all the "curiosa felicitas," the many revelations
subordinate to the one keynote, "It is all triumphant art, but art in
obedience to laws." *The Heretic's Tragedy* has been but slightingly
noticed, and for 'the demoniac malignity of persecution' generally condemned; less noticed in its ecclesiastical aspect, or its solemn moral retribution, in such strange surprise reasserting its forgotten omnipotence in
the dead stagnation of corrupt ages: for its musical value quite unnoticed.
It deserves a Handel to compose fit music for it, as a most solemn
oratorio. Yet one *Review* placidly notices *this*, among the poems which
make the reader shudder, by the physical or moral horrors they set before
him, as "culminating in the burning alive of a man before a slow fire."

We might observe his equal sympathy with Hephzibah tune in the
little chapel, and the organ in S. Peter's at Rome swallowing up the
sense of time:

> " Earth breaks up, time drops away;
> In flows heaven with its new day
> Of endless life." (*C. E.* 10.)

A curious instance of his adopting classical mythology long seemed to
me a case of imagination at the expense of accuracy, until I hit upon
the explanation:

> " Like some huge throbbing-stone, that poised a-joint
> Sounds to affect on its basaltic bed,
> Must sue in just one accent," &c., 10 *lines*. *Sordello*, ii. 450-460.

I suppose the allusion is to the stone upon which Apollo laid his lyre
while he was at work rebuilding Megara; and which was henceforth
capable of giving only a sound similar to that of the lyre. *Uhland* has a
sonnet on the legend. While speaking of Browning's most musical genius
it sounds very paradoxical, when it is perpetually dinned into our ears
that he is not a master of *rhythm*. One discriminating Review ('B. Q.'
Nov. '47) says "he is neither a deep thinker nor a musical writer. He
is certainly not a born singer: he wants the melody and the grace of

which verse should be made.   At the same time he occasionally pours
forth a strain of real melody.   He is rather a thinker than a singer. . ."
Yet see the generosity of a reviewer who believes but feebly in the
existence of either *Bells* or *Pomegranates*, concluding his estimate of all
Browning's poetry by quoting THE WHOLE OF *How they brought the good
news from Ghent to Aix.*   I venture the opposite opinion, that however
reckless or defiant he may be in the elaboration of form, he has a far
wider and more commanding versatility of rhythm than Tennyson.   The
rhythm of *Ghent to Aix* has admirably caught the rapidity of galloping
for very life.   *As I ride* has just the wavy motion of a creature's
back.   Ruggedness is sometimes as essential to the subject as smoothness at other times.   I may allude to the gentle flowing of

> "Thus the Mayne glideth, Where my love abideth ; "

at which soothing undertones Paracelsus' darkness passes

> "Like some dark snake that force may not expel,
> Which glideth out to music sweet and low."

The subdued tone of calm, so exquisitely pathetic, of that plaint,

> "I hear a voice, perchance I heard,
> Long ago but all too low. . ."   (*Paracelsus*, p. 41.)

and the sweet melancholy deliberateness of the song there, where you
must obey the four beats of each line in order *to read* it properly, as
when there are only four words, or even three, in a line.

> "Lost, | lost | yet | come | . . .
> "Re- | proach | to | thee | "

This time-test also applies to the beautiful legend of *The Boy and the
Angel.*   Or compare the three couplets descriptive of Hell, Purgatory,
and Heaven, so happily distinct :

> "Dante, pacer of the shore
> Where glutted hell disgorgeth filthiest gloom, }
> Unbitten by its whirring sulphur-spume ; }
> Or whence the grieved and obscure waters slope }
> Into a darkness quieted by hope ; }
> Plucker of amaranths grown beneath God's eye }
> In gracious twilights where His chosen lie."   } *Sordello*, i. 366-372.

The *cortège* of the *Grammarian's Funeral* steps to the tune of that noble
requiem of a Scaliger or some Prince of bookworms, as much as the
iambic lightness of the *Pied Piper* with its variations suits its own subject.   Compare the two parts of *Holy-Cross Day ;* with the humour, the
scorn of the first, and the placid dignity of a sublime faith in *Ben Ezra's
Song of Death.*   This poem, on other grounds, has been most blindly
depreciated.   It is *a capital test-poem* of a gift which little minds eminently lack, but which is very characteristic of *genius* (and its brother
madness), *the ability for sudden transitions.*   Some persons have no con-

ception of the natural ability to laugh one moment, and to be perfectly solemn and reverential the next; nor can they discern (*e. g.* 'C. Rev.' Feb. '67) the artistic power of the contrast given by

> " the festering squalor of the Ghetto "

as background for the indestructible trust in the ancient writings of the Hebrew prophets. They shrink less from the facts than from the tragical record of them. Browning may well retort in the language of Dryden (Preface to Fables): " *Prior læsit* is justification sufficient in the civil law " : or better still in Milton's paraphrase of Sophocles :

> " 'Tis you that say it, not I.   You do the deeds,
> And your ungodly deeds find me the words."   *Electra*, 624-5.

We may add to this branch of the subject such secondary marks of rhythmical structure as *time*-beats, with noble indifference, or freedom of a bird's wings in the air, as to *syllables* in the ordinary five-feet lines. Even the rhyme he has imposed on himself so unaccountably in the long epic of *Sordello* is no fettering whatever.   He simply revels in his inexhaustible wealth of rhyming, one, two, or three-syllable rhymes. Nevertheless we cannot help feeling a greater steadiness and measure in the earlier compositions.   Compare *Paracelsus* with any of the more recent narratives wherein lines are the mere warp for the terribly subtle woof of metaphysical analysis.   Care rather marks the first period, and recklessness the second.   But for a poet who spurns the thought of the number of syllables in a line, I presume to take exception (*salvâ reverentiâ*) to the irksome mannerism of i' and o' for *in* and *of*. I counted, *Colenso*-like, or *Furnivall*-like, the number of i' and o' cases in *The Ring and the Book*, and other poems, but have mislaid my bag of winnowed chaff.   Why should we be ashamed of English prepositions, more than of the *enclitic* δε which *ends* a line the Scaligers might object to even over their coffins ?   The breathless rapidity of the thought for which *little words* shaken out of a pepper-box are rather a nuisance, is no doubt the cause.

> " Words have to come : and somehow words deflect
> As the best cannon ever rifled do."   *H.-Schw.* p. 147.

But all words were perhaps rather a nuisance to Browning's angelic velocity of thought,

> " Until . . Language the makeshift grew
> Into the bravest of expedients too."   *Sordello*, ii. 179.

Another peculiarity on which my fastidiousness stumbles, so that I can hardly pick up myself *in time* for the sentence, the sense, or the line, is the most strange and immoderate use of the—dash—.   It is sometimes equal to a parenthesis ; to a stop ; sometimes to apposition ; sometimes silently suggestive that more might be said ; sometimes I cannot gauge

its value. I do not know its proper name, or recognized value, in
English Grammar; in Browning it is but dust amidst gold. However,
it affronts one scores of times daily, in the outrageous, senseless pro-
fusion of employment, in books, in the daily press, in notice bills,
before a name, after a complete sentence, anywhere, everywhere; a plague
that has worried me in correcting print till I have made a pact that it
shall not be used for me : fretting one sometimes,

> " As its mates do, the midge and the nit,—
> Through minuteness to wit. The gravamen's in that ! " *Instans Tyrannus.*

2. *Art.* It is an omission hitherto that no art-critic has given us a fit
notice of, or more than slight allusions to, Browning's poetry on Art.
Browning's Italian soul in his " myriad-minded " genius could not but
throw itself much into Art. And his Art-poems are as great contribu-
tions to our understanding of the moral principles, and the religious
principles, of Art, as Ruskin's poetical-prose is. His business is, as Fra
Lippo says, " to paint the souls of men." Painting, Music, Verse, are
but three cognate languages, of which the last may even be sometimes
most inadequate to its high object. *Art* covers the three.

> " Poet and painter are proud in the artist list enrolled."

In the sketch of the Florentine monk not only do we have most powerfully conceived the religious obligations of art, and the desperate attempt
at compromise between the highest efforts of genius and the irregularities
of the lower nature, as if the one could pay off arrears with God for the
other, or as if every artist were a double personality, doomed to the
Mezentian punishment that S. Paul takes as the type of the two laws
striving within : but also, because of these features, one great inward
contradiction of spirit traces so sad an account of all that highly over-
strung humanity which includes so many bright names ; suns darkened
with sunspots on their discs ; Bacon, Turner, Byron, Handel ; painters,
musicians, poets, philosophers. I mention this, because the essential
Browning in the art-poems is not only, nor so much, the art-critic, but
the exponent of *the religious aspect of art,* the conscience in discord or
harmony, of the relation to God in his art as well as in his life, in
Rafael, Giotto, Andrea del Sarto, and in the Florentine painters all, as
truly as in *Paracelsus.* As to judging of pictures, " Poets, and men of
strong feeling in general, are apt to be among the very worst judges
of painting. The slightest hint is enough for them. . .   Thus Wordsworth writes many sonnets to Sir G. Beaumont and Haydon, none to
Sir Joshua or to Turner." (*Ruskin.* ' M. P.' iii. 138-9.) But " Browning
is unerring in every sentence he writes of the Middle Ages ; always vital,
right, and profound : so that in the matter of art, there is hardly a principle connected with the mediæval temper that he has not struck upon,

in those seemingly careless and too rugged lines of his. (Quotation from
S. Praxed's Church.) I know no other piece of modern English, prose
or poetry, in which there is so much told, as in these lines, of the
Renaissance spirit, — its worldliness, inconsistency, pride, hypocrisy,
ignorance of itself, love of art, of luxury, and of good Latin. It is nearly
all that I said of the central Renaissance in thirty pages of the ' Stones
of Venice ' put into as many lines, Browning's being also the antecedent work." ('M. P.' iii. 377-379.) This subject, which is too technical
to be more than just touched now, is however of vital importance, as
lying at the root of our whole estimate of Browning. When we consider that he is ever making incandescent, visible, and illuminating, as
by powerful electric current, the dark line of *conscience* running through
all the workings of genius, and asserting painting, music, and poetry to
be but three allied forms of one spirit, the Art of Expression or
Intimation from soul to soul :

> (" Art was given for that :
>   God uses us to help each other so,
>   Lending our minds out." *Fra Lippi*.)

how far are we authorized in applying the moral philosopher's test *to his
own art ?* Are we to consider all his poems finished works of art, each
in proportion to its ideal ? Certainly not by the test of *smoothness*, or
finish as many would call it. For there is an *art-canon* in that capital
verse,

> " Grand rough old Martin Luther
>   Bloomed fables, flowers on furze :
>   The better the uncouther :
>   Do roses stick like burrs ? "

The poems already named, *Ben Ezra, Abt Vogler, Childe Roland,
Paracelsus, Caliban, Holy Cross Day, The Heretic's Tragedy*, no one
could deny to be carefully-wrought works of art. There is further quite
a revelation, especially for the " pickers up of learning's crumbs," in the
numerous *alterations*, which must needs suggest carefulness of recon-
sideration, and elaboration, in some poems ; in the niceness which could
change lepidoptera to coleoptera in *Easter Day*, 6 ; and especially in
that industrious collection of changes made by the devotedness of Mr.
Furnivall and others from *Sordello*. But if, on this theory, which he
himself has gauged in the Dedication of *Sordello*, we are to consider all
the *later* works equally works of art, each according to its kind, free of
mere defiance of stupid criticism, free of entanglement in the webs of
his own extraordinary facilities : then, it may be, we have even yet
much to learn, as I have already hinted, about the elasticity, compre-
hensiveness, possible development and even generosity, to be allowed to
the word *Poetry*, adorning as it does the brows of gods and men, the

heads of chirping cicale and many drowsy insects secular and religious. I would presume to deprecate as untrue rather than ungenerous Mr. W. Bagehot's comparisons of grotesque with pure art and ornate. *Holy Cross Day* is chosen, with *Caliban*, to illustrate "not the *success* of grotesque art but the nature of it." Under which of the three epithets are we to range *criticism* which concludes an estimate of Browning with three-fourths of the *Pied Piper* as " the best and most satisfactory instance " ? *Caliban* is selected, to be called "not a normal type but an abnormal specimen." I wish this were true. Why, Shakespeare's Caliban is a higher type of humanity, as possible to rise, than Trinculo who has sunk into low habits as vile as the bog. I fear there are whole tribes of Calibans, not only in still-vext Bermoothes. There is a Caliban in each of us. Browning could not have painted that picture without the touch of Caliban which makes the whole world kin. Ask Mr. Charles Darwin about this !

    3. *Christianity.* I must claim for Browning the distinction of being pre-eminently the greatest Christian poet we have ever had. Not in a narrow dogmatic sense, but as the teacher who is as thrilled-through with all Christian sympathies as with artistic or musical. A man whose very genius is to identify himself, for the nonce, with each human soul he enters, and makes to speak to us, must necessarily find his profoundest, fullest harmony in souls alive with Christian faith and experience, questions and conflicts. I hold very light that solicitude to know and tabulate what his own system of truth is. I cannot sympathize with the intrusive deduction as to what Browning himself is. " The longer I live," says Jean Paul, " the more I find I have to determine *to unlearn systems.*" " Je länger ich lebe, desto mehr verlern' ich das Gelernte, nämlich die Systeme." (December, 1820. ' Wahrheit aus J. P.'s Leben,' ii. 140.) He could not adopt a character, and would not select it, unless he could become one with it by inward affinity. How can you get at Shakespeare who is as truly Falstaff as he is King Lear ; Iago as much as Othello? He is humanity. So is Browning religion : with all forms of art, philosophy, and experience as her ministers. It would be astounding to observe how utterly ignored he is in this his deepest innermost being (as far as it is revealed to us as his very self) were it not that we are fully, however painfully, aware, of the petty antipathies, the poor miserable sufficiency of intelligence, and the feeble reiterations of truisms or sentimentalities, that myriads of sincere Christian people allow in their favourite religious literature. Well may *M. Arnold* say that poetry is a monument of a nation's strength, religious poetry of a nation's weakness. What do the childlike worshippers of Keble, Cowper, Dr. Watts, know of *Browning*, or

even of *Blake ?* The Church never did know its most glorious sons, since it first stoned the prophets, till now that it extols the vapid, thin, milk-and-water runlets called religious poetry. How much might be burnt with impunity to make a light to read *Christmas Eve and Easter Day* by? Browning himself, by-the-bye, speaks in that. The incomparable sermon on the charity that dare not condemn any school of religious thought, lest it lose eternal hold on the *salvation of the Vest;* the preference, worthy of the firmest believer in Christian doctrine, for Zion Chapel or superstitious Rome over the negative vacuum of the learned skeptic, and the splendid consummation of *E. Day* so closely resembling the well-known crisis in Faust : these are the grandest special tributes poet ever brought to Christianity.

In this spiritual relation, and also for another reason, I may observe here, we might arrange an impressive little selection of *descriptive* pieces; descriptive of objects in nature. First and foremost of these would be the sublime description of the lunar rainbow (*Ch. Eve,* 6 and 7), although the actual detail has been called in question of " the seven proper colours chorded." I could hardly believe that so infallible an observer as he is would run so flagrant a risk, if this were indeed beyond the bounds of possibility. There, the transition from apparition to imagination,

" Whose foot shall I see emerge ? "

is worthy of Moses or Ezekiel. I have never seen it noticed how this finally merges into what rather belongs to the *aurora borealis.* We must have seen the pictures, many of us have seen the reality, " of the sight, Of a sweepy garment vast and white, With a hem that I could recognize." This is most beautifully interwoven with the account of the woman who touched the hem of Christ's garment ; and is retained as the emblem of saving correspondence with heaven, throughout the poem, and in several other places. It may be worth while to observe how similarly Goethe employs the same emblem for Faust, as the corporeal Helena vanishes and her clothes pass into clouds. (2 Part, Act iii. Sc. 4.) Then the astonishingly graphic description of the sunset sky with its black and ruddy ripples infinite over the whole dome of heaven, in *Easter Day,* 15. How often have we seen that sky since, as not even Ruskin had opened our eyes to observe!

It is *Paracelsus* as *alter Luther,* who is unfolded, aspiring, failing, attaining ; not the charlatan that any one may despise. However utterly different from Tennyson's two sonnets on Lazarus in 'In Memoriam,' the strange experience of the *Arab Physician* is no less magnificent a monument in honour of John xi. The finely-introduced comparison of the blue-flowering borage, and the involuntary dominance of that

C

overwhelming thought which is like the moon heaving along the tide before the sun rises in the morning as light :

> " The very God! think Abib: dost thou think?
> So the All-great were the All-loving too ! "

is of the very highest order both of meditation and of composition. Closely resembling that is the dazzled bewilderment of Cleon in the blaze of nobler truth than Athens ever taught, which he cannot reject and yet cannot receive. These are two admirably pourtrayed instances of the way in which Christian truth *wrought* in the minds of the intellectual, while it simply *converted* simpler minds to the faith. Which of us ever preached such a sermon on doing God's will, as *The Boy and the Angel?* It is having revealed to us the working of a human soul to the truest advantage of our own, if we go with John to the close of his century of a life of love, to that " thought extracted from a world of thinking" (*Bp. Gambold*), God is love ; or listen to the persiflage of *B. Blougram ;* or point the rebuke to the lust of gold with the *Legend of Pornic ;* or arouse the listless indolence of dilettanti professing Christians by the unexpected moral of *The Statue and the Bust.* The most beautiful of all his lyrical romances is *Saul.* In a word, the religious poetry, as I may perhaps call it, as distinct from the art-poetry and the metaphysical-narrative, ought to *startle* Christian people into elevation and gratitude. It is a fact that cannot be slurred over, that our two great poets maintain their dominion over the affections of their countrymen, *not by sheer power of thinking*, mere granite depths and height of *mind ;* but by the relation of their main convictions to Christian truth, to holy and eternal emotions, to the moral workings of the heart and conscience ; whether in *Paracelsus*, or the *Artist*, or *Fifine*, or *In Memoriam*. Intellectual subtlety and pre-eminence, on Shelley's ground of denial and antipathy, could not attain, not to say retain, the hold they have upon us. It is the *high priest of religious life* whose beautiful garment is fringed with *Bells and Pomegranates* (Exod. xxviii. 33, 34). The emblem is first taken from Aaron's robe : although I don't see that noticed anywhere. Take away the *religious* tissue from Browning's tapestry, with its vast variety of figures, and almost every one would be a *caput mortuum.* But lest the designation *Christian* should seem too exclusive, we may say that his whole soul is orbed round the central thought of *God*, and man's relation to God. He is as suffused with the thought of God, as Spinoza was : or

> " As saffron tinges flesh, blood, bones, and all."

Not only in *Pope Theocrite*, but in *Instans Tyrannus, Andrea del Sarto* as much as *Saul, The Grammarian*, and on to the arraignment of the soul before the last judgment-seat in *Easter Day*, the relation to God is the consummated impression left. And this is the inmost secret of another element that has received more attention. Because God is ever revealing and hiding Himself, beaming out and withdrawing behind impenetrable cloud, therefore all mental workings are traced on towards eternity, never ending in to-day and to-day's thought. Time and eternity are not "lumped together." Only bunglers lug in *eternity,* and scatter the huge word about "like lumps of marl on a barren moor, encumbering what it is not in their power to fertilize." But they are interwoven, or so subtly interlinked, that the soul's working is a sort of golden chain traced from its anchoring in the hidden depths of the soul, onwards towards the throne of God. It is intimated as running into the infinite, though not in all cases tracked along the same distance thitherward. This is one chief secret of Browning's being the poet not only of religious, but of thoughtful, persons; and of the intense sympathy we have with him; and of his being essentially an exponent of the best movements of English mind in this age. Without that he could not be so. Shelley might have become so, had he lived as Browning suggests; but he did not. Still, it is by no means necessary to agree with Browning's over-specialized religious views. Certainly all here present cannot do so.

Finally: among the objects which I anticipate as of real value to us who gratefully reverence Browning, because we feel so deeply indebted to the

"Poet whose thoughts enrich the blood of the world,"

and also to those whose mere ignorance of him without prejudice has left them hitherto strangers to his wealth, are such as these:

A separate treatment of special poems which need a key; being enigmatical, as *Childe Roland;* or

"a pomegranate full of many kernels,"

as *Sordello;* or requiring a pilot through the metaphysical high seas, as *The Ring and the Book.* Treatises on his humour: his attitude towards science: the poems of a class, as *Music, Painting, Art:* or the *Love Poems,* as Mr. Nettleship has already written. (Although, I can almost wish sometimes *Love* had never been specialized for poets, or cast her sun-suffused cloud around their clear minds; were it not for such glow as of that beautiful and touching invocation, *Ring and Book, Part I.*) And next, short introductions to such poems as hardly require a separate treatment, giving the "Argument" as it is called. And then a Lexicon of names, remote allusions, learned things fetched from some-where in the universe where he has been, and other mortal foot hath ne'er or rarely been. A devoted admirer of Jean Paul did that very inadequately for *his* writings ; and the explanations of English allusions are highly amusing.   Then the organizing of readings, or courses of lectures, with reasonably competent lecturers.   And a *digest of Reviews,* which are the queerest milestones along the course of Browning's popularity that a traveller on his own Rosinante could pass or imagine. These would be real helps, worthy of the dignity of a living poet free of all that emasculating popularity which Carlyle so vigorously deprecates, worthy of ourselves, and worthy of the sensible practical object we have in view.

There will still remain that which no such helps can impart, for

> " Therein the patient must minister to himself ; "

the soul's own intense sympathy with his teacher ; his keen enjoyment and noblest pleasure under " love's intellectual law ; " the enriching of his memory and ennobling of his moral being, the survey of life, and growth towards attaining the attitude of *Prospice.*   No one can read Browning without being immensely benefited, both in his intellect and his heart.   Coleridge was not the last to complain, " The indisposition, nay the angry aversion *to think,* even in persons who are most willing to attend, is the fact that ever forces itself on my notice afresh . ."   So, after all our efforts, there will still remain a large number to whom we can wave the hand for farewell :

> " Vex not thou the poet's mind
> With thy shallow wit:
> Vex not thou the poet's mind,
> For thou canst not fathom it."

But not he more than Milton need disdain the condition to which all teachers a head taller than their fellows are subject,

> " And fit audience find though few."

Were he shallow instead of subtle, and had he dabbled in summer pools instead of fathoming the depths of the soul and eternity, he would have had the sickening incense of steaming popularity in his nostrils. But

> " I love him, on this side idolatry, as much as any ".

Or, to throw a last arrow feathered with his own words at him, we may reverentially contemplate him as

> " Still loftier than the world suspects,
> Living and dying."

ON "PIETRO[1] OF ABANO"

AND THE LEADING IDEAS OF "DRAMATIC IDYLS," SECOND SERIES 1880.

BY THE REV. J. SHARPE, M.A.

(Read at the 2nd Meeting of the Browning Society.   Friday, Nov. 25, 1881.)

Structure of the Poem.   (Dram. Idyls, II, p. 63—111.)

				(first lines)
p. 63.	Part i.	Stanzas i—v.		
p. 68.	„ ii.	„ vi—xxii.		'Now as on a certain evening.'
p. 82.	„ iii. scene (1)	„ xxiii—xxxiii.		'Presently the young man.'
p. 92.	scene (2)	„ xxxiv—xlv.		'Gone again—what, is he?'
p. 102.	scene (3)	„ xlvi—li.		''Tis my own soul soars now.'
p. 107.	„ iv.	„ lii—liv.		'What was changed?'
	Epilogue.	„ lv—lvi.		'When these parts Tiberius.'

---

[1] Peter of A'bano—*Petrus de A'pono* or *Aponensis,* or *Petrus de Padua*—was an Italian physician and alchemist, born at Abano near Padua in 1246, died about 1320. He is said to have studied Greek at Constantinople, mathematics at Padua, and to have been made Doctor of Medicine and Philosophy at Paris. He then returnd to Padua, where he was Professor of medicine, and followed the Arabian physicians, especially Averroes. He got a great reputation, and charged enormous fees. He hated milk and cheese, and swooned at the sight of them. His enemies, jealous of his renown and wealth, denounst him to the Inquisition as a magician. They accused him of possessing the Philosopher's Stone, and of making, with the Devil's help, all money spent by him come back to his purse, &c. His trial was begun; and had he not died naturally in time, he would have been burnt. The Inquisitors orderd his corpse to be burnt; and as a friend had taken that away, they had his portrait publicly burnt by the executioner. In 1560 a Latin epitaph in his memory was put up in the church of St. Augustin. The Duke of Urbino set his statue among those of illustrious men; and the Senate of Padua put one on the gate of its palace, beside those of Livy, &c. His best known work is his *Conciliator differentiarum quæ inter philosophos et medicos versantur;* Mantua, 1472, and Venice, 1476, fol., often reprinted.   Other works are: 1. *De venenis, eorumque remediis,* tr. into French by L. Boet; Lyons, 1593, 12mo; 2. *Geomantia;* Venice, 1505, 1556, 8vo; 3. *Expositio problematum Aristotelis;* Mantua, 1475, 4to; 4. *Hippocratis de medicorum astrologia libellus,* in Gr. and Lat.; Venice, 1485, 4to; 5. *Astrolabium planum in tabulis ascendens, continens qualibet hora atque minutæ æquationes demorum cœli,* &c.; Venice, 1502, 4to; 6. *Dioscnides, digestus alphabetico ordine;* Lyon, 1512, 4to; 7. *Heptameron;* Paris, 1474, 4to; 8. *Textus Mesues noviter emendatus,* &c.; Venice, 1505, 8vo; 9. *Decisiones phyrionomicæ,* 1548, 8vo; 10. *Quæstiones de febribus;* Padua, 1482; 11. *Galeni tractatus varii a Petro Paduano, latinitate donati;* MS. in S. Mark's Library, Venice; 12. *Les éléments pour opérer dans les sciences magiques;* MS. in the Arsenal Library, Paris —*Nouvelle Biographie Universelle.*   Paris, 1855, i. 29–31. —F.

Part i, stanzas i—v. *Description of Peter.*

PETRUS APONENSIS is a magician. He has boundless power and knowledge; he uses both for the good of men: yet he not only fails to win gratitude, but is met with curses, insult, and persecution. If he works under some disguise in the hope of earning gratitude, the moment he is detected he is denounced as a wizard, and driven away by those whom he has benefited. Why is it that a man at once so powerful, wise, and beneficent, should yet fail to win in return even a little gratitude, not to say love? In the answer lies the idea which this poem is intended to illustrate.

'Si vis amari, ama,' said Hecaton. (Sen. Ep. i. 9.) Love is won only by love, and love involves self-sacrifice. Men cannot love Peter, for they see that he does not love them. Though his acts are beneficent, they are no proofs of love, for they cost him nothing; they are wrought by a word and by magic power, not by any sacrifice. Thus, as Democritus said, 'he who loves none, will be loved by none.'

Part ii, stanzas vi—xxii, p. 68. 'Now as on a certain evening.' *The clever Greek.*

As Peter is entering his house he is stopped by a young man, a Greek, clever, and imbued with the spirit of Greek philosophy. He tells Peter that he does not believe the vulgar stories current concerning him. He has a boon to beg, that Peter will gratify the purest of ambitions, to make him a great poet, so that he may make his kind wise, free, and happy. This he purposes to do by fictions suited to the ignorant crowd, by apparent truths which to them seem good; by gratifying their low aims, he will use them for his own ends.

He illustrates his meaning by reference to architecture. The king who has the palace built seeks his own glory, the workmen seek merely for wages, but the architect uses the low aims of both to display his own power, and has in the end all the credit. Human fame, however, is nothing compared with the consciousness of power; nay, even persecution is nothing to the sage who is conscious that he and he only is the real ruler of the world.

The clever Greek anticipates an objection which Peter might raise: 'If I grant your wish how can I be sure that you will not turn out ungrateful like the rest?' He replies, 'The vulgar story that you cannot touch milk means that you cannot win 'the milk of human kindness,' human love: now touch my heart and love is yours; the higher you lift me the more I shall love you.' Peter replies that he has often been deceived by such promises; no one yet has ventured to risk anything to save him from persecution. Still he will try again. He throws the

Greek into a trance by magic art, and shows him in three scenes what the future would be, if he were to give the Greek the power he asks.

Peter evidently represents the wise man of the Platonic philosophy. Plato omitted the benevolent affections from his psychological analysis, and Peter has no love for the men whom he benefits. Plato said that the just man will be scourged, racked, and finally crucified, and all because he preferred *being* to *seeming*. So Peter, who does not condescend to disguise his want of feeling, is met with insult and persecution. The clever Greek is the very opposite. He chooses to *seem* rather than to be, and prospers accordingly. (See Plato, *Republic*, book i.)

The clever Greek addressed Peter on the ground of the Platonic philosophy, 'dosed him with the fair and good.' He assumed a fundamental principle of Greek philosophy, viz. truth for the few wise, fiction for the ignorant many. Greek philosophy was vicious at the core: it was based upon pride; self-love was its leading motive. In Peter, self-love took the form of the pride of intellect and conscious power; his reward was that he 'knew himself the mighty man he was.' He is satisfied with the judgment, 'admirationem incutit.' In the Greek, self-love takes a coarser form.

In neither case is self-love inconsistent with benevolence. Peter exemplifies this in a private station, the Greek in public life. (See *Butler*, sermon xi.) But how different is his conduct from that of true love. He would raise men by being raised above them; true love sinks that it may raise. He would make men happy by indulging their delusions, while he uses them for his own ends; true love imparts truth, and raises others to its own level.

Part iii, stanzas xxiii—li, p. 82. 'Presently the young man.'
The Parasite, the Councillor, and the Pope.

In the visions, the Greek is seen in three stages of his upward-downward career; first he wins wealth, next political power, and lastly spiritual power. At each stage Peter appears and asks for his reward, gradually diminishing his demands. First he asks for a home with the Greek; next for a remote and hidden sanctuary; lastly, that the Greek will edit his literary remains. On the two former occasions the Greek puts off his request upon the plea that his ambition is not yet fully gratified, he acknowledges the debt; but at last as Pope he can rise no higher, and then he refuses to pay. As the Greek has risen higher in the world, he has sunk morally lower; when Peter has raised him to the full height of his ambition, the very acknowledgment of a debt of gratitude is withheld.

Thus the career of the Greek exemplifies the truth, that love is won only by love; love is not won by the gratification of desires. What is called 'cupboard love' by children is no love, but selfishness disguised. Peter has gratified every wish of the Greek, but failed to touch his heart.

In the *first scene* the Greek shows some regard to conscience, but stifles it by reasoning. Poisons are often useful medicines; so may evil actions be beneficial. The wise man scorns riches and power; yet no one will believe this unless he first wins and then rejects them. He feels therefore justified in the acquisition of wealth by the evil arts of the parasite.

In the *second scene* the Greek's idea of vice betrays a lower moral condition. As we put off silk to climb a tree, so must we lay aside virtue if we would rise in the world. It is hopeless to try and reform the masses, their vices should rather be used as helps by clever men. A horse allows a man to mount him by an ocular delusion, and goes all the better for it; so by making use of the delusions of the crowd the clever man will seize the reins of government, yet greatly to the good of his fellow men.

In the *third scene* the Greek has so far fallen that he puts forth no excuses. He is cleverness without conscience, bare shameless selfishness, gratifying its ambition in that sphere where love and humility should reign.

Thus the small seed of selfishness which lay at the root of ancient philosophy has developed its inevitable consequences.

Part iv, stanzas lii—liv, p. 107. 'What was changed.'
The Awakening.

When the Greek awakes from the vision his judgment is that at length he knows cheese from chalk, *i. e.* being from seeming, true love from self-love. Peter's ultimate fate was not martyrdom; he had not the love which is needed for self-sacrifice. The future of the Greek is only hinted at; cleverness uncurbed by conscience will give him all that earth can give, but there is no record of his gaining it.

The leading idea of the volume.

The introductory verses contrast the difficulty we find in assigning the cause of bodily disease, with the assurance and positiveness with which we pass judgment upon a human soul. In such a complicated unity as the human soul, many motives are working at once, and actions may be due to motives of a character exactly opposite to the character of the action.

The idyls present us with six actions of this kind.

Yet though the difficulty of fixing the motive is clearly recognized, each idyl gives us the means of ascertaining the motive.

I. The *first idyl* deals with patriotic action. Miltiades and Themistocles are recognized types of patriotism. We do not hesitate to ascribe their conduct at Marathon and Salamis to pure love of the fatherland. But can this be sustained in the light of subsequent history? In the attack on Paros, Miltiades used the power of his country to gratify his own vindictive feelings. Themistocles was guilty of Medism, and lived as a pensioner of his country's foe. How then can we be sure that at Marathon they fought for pure love of country, and not to gratify ambition, to win power or wealth? The true patriot is Echetlos, who refused to tarnish the lustre of his patriotism by any honour or reward[1]; but Echetlos is mythical, Miltiades and Themistocles are historical.

II. The *second idyl* deals with an act of courage.

As pure patriotism is found only in the mythical Echetlos, so pure courage exists only in the imagination.

Clive dared certain death rather than tell a lie. Here was an act of heroic courage. Clive faced death fearlessly; but in that very moment he felt a pang of fear, fear of disgrace if his enemy had spared his life. In that case he would have been compelled to escape disgrace by suicide. His friend replies that this would have been an act of courage, to dare to confront God. Soon after, Clive committed suicide. Was this due to courage or to fear?

As on the previous occasion Clive would have committed suicide to escape disgrace, so it is probable his suicide was due to a desire to escape the trouble and disgrace which clouded his latter days. The Clive of the friend's imagination is pure courage; the real Clive is also moved by fear. Clive can charge a battery, but he cannot face a sneer; he is bold toward God, but a coward toward his fellow men.

Some passages of Aristotle's Ethics illustrate the courage and fear of Clive (Eth. iii. 6). The courageous man fears disgrace. No man is more able than he to endure terrible things, but death is the most terrible of all things. The brave man, however, has to deal only with the most honourable kinds of death, as in war. Suicide is an act of cowardice; for the suicide does not undergo death because it is honourable, but in order to avoid evil. For the sake of what is honourable, the brave man bears and performs those things which belong to courage.

There is a contrast between the bully and Clive. Clive fears man, but not God; the bully fears God, and not man. When the bully sees Clive's resolute adherence to truth in the face of death, he thinks that

---

[1] Compare Hervé Riel's refusal of any reward for saving the French fleet, save a holiday to see his wife.—F.

Clive would rather go to God's presence with truth upon his lips, than save his life by a lie. Such trust in God and in retribution overpowers him; he dares disgrace among his fellows rather than face the judgment of God. Clive the courageous had no such courage. Moral courage, the special courage of the soldier of Christ, was wanting in the fearless Clive.

We may note how Mr. Browning *more suo* sees the 'soul of goodness in things evil.' This moral courage was displayed by a man who was apparently an utter blackguard, and, like all bullies, a coward at heart.

Thus acts of moral courage are due to fear of God; acts of physical courage may be due to fear of man.

III. The *third idyl* deals with love for an animal.

Love produces the deeds of hate. Hoseyn is on the point of catching up Muléykeh, when he tells Duhl the secret of her speed, and loses his mare. After refusing a high price, he gives the mare away for nothing to a thief. What could have urged him to act so? Love for his mare: he would rather lose her than have her surpassed; the animal's spirit would never be the same if once conquered; her fame as invincible would have perished. No one who really loved the mare would keep her at such a cost.

(Cynics might say there was a touch of pride at being the owner of an animal never beaten.)

IV. The *fourth idyl* deals with acts of benevolence not due to feelings of benevolence. Both Peter and the Greek benefited mankind; the motive of both was self-love, not love for others. Peter was moved by pride, the Greek by ambition. Peter acts openly and is persecuted; the Greek dissembles and prospers.

" On the great theatre of public life . . . it is much rather the astute statesman, earnest about his ends but unscrupulous about his means, equally free from the trammels of conscience and from the blindness of zeal, who governs, because he partly yields to the passions and prejudices of his time." (Lecky, *Morals,* i. 1.)

V. The *fifth idyl* deals with an act of love and power; but the power is that of hate, not love, and the motive is not the good of the sufferer but the desire to annoy. It is written in Cant. viii. 6, that 'Love is strong as death.' But the opposite of love, hate in its worst form, is stronger than death. 'Corruptio optimi pessima.' Wedded love is best. But Satan cannot love; hence his married life produces the deadliest hate.

VI. The *sixth idyl* deals with an act of love. Pan and Luna are opposite extremes. Pan is half a brute; Luna is purity and modesty.

Pan by a stratagem gets possession of Luna. Does she faint? Does she flee? Neither; she follows him, 'by no means spurning him.' To what motive shall we attribute her conduct? Certainly not to any want of modesty. Rather to love. Love awakens love. Pan's feelings are such as are described by Seneca, Ep. i. 9, 'Ipse per se amor, omnium aliarum rerum negligens, animos in cupiditatem formæ non sine spe mutuæ caritatis accendit.' Pan is not actuated by brute passion, but by Luna's beauty, and the hope of mutual love. This wins her. The godlike element dominates in Pan; bristles and horns count for nothing.

In these idyls we have seen ambition work deeds of patriotism, fear act like courage, love like hate; self-love, ambition, and pride have wrought deeds of benevolence; hate has effected the work of mercy; purity has acted like immodesty.

Hence it is evident, that in judging of the quality of an action, we must pay regard to the motive, and not merely to the outward character of the act. Motive as well as Intended Action is the proper subject of moral intuition. (See Sidgwick, *Method of Ethics*, iii. 1.)

In the closing lines the poet rejects the foolish notion of some of his admirers, that the variety of subjects treated in the idyls is due to the fact that a poet naturally breaks forth into song upon any subject which touches him. Rather his poems are like rocks, hard, forbidding, with few flowers; yet hidden in them is a seed of eternal truth, which time will develop, and posterity will recognize.

One such pine seed I will point out: a living thought which lies hid in the rugged mass of Pietro of Abano.

Students of Browning are aware that when he has illustrated a principle by some apparently trivial example, his method is to apply the principle in the highest sphere of thought.

If God were only Almighty, Allwise, Beneficent, that is, if He were Peter upon an infinite scale, He would fail to win the love of mankind, as Peter did. If God were to grant every wish of man, as Peter granted every wish of the clever Greek, man would not feel even gratitude, much less love Him; just as the Greek failed to love Peter, and at last even denied the debt. For love is won only by love; and love involves self-sacrifice. If God would win the love of man, He must sacrifice Himself; as in the Epistle of Karshish, 'thou must love me who have died for thee.' This is the Christian's faith, 'We love Him because He first loved us.' Here, as so often in Browning, reason leads to the Incarnation of God.

BROWNING'S PHILOSOPHY.

By JOHN BURY, Trin. Coll., Dublin.

(Read at the 6th Meeting of the Browning Society, Friday, April 28, 1882.)

I start with the distinction which Browning has himself drawn in his Essay on Shelley between the objective and the subjective poet. The former is he who is impelled to embody his perceptions with reference to the many below; the latter to embody them with reference to the One above him, "the supreme Intelligence which apprehends all things in their absolute truth,—an ultimate view ever aspired to, if but partially attained, by the poet's own soul. Not what man sees, but what God sees—the Ideas of Plato, seeds of creation lying burningly on the Divine Hand—it is towards these that he struggles."

We are tempted to ask, Is Browning himself an objective or a subjective poet? The dramatic form of such a large majority of his works might induce some on superficial consideration to decide that he belongs to the former class. But lovers of Browning who go beyond the external form will recognize, along with his objectivity, that power "to lift his fellows, with their half-apprehensions, up to his own sphere, by intensifying the import of details and rounding the universal meaning," which marks the subjective poet. Whilst he supplies us with "the fresh and living swathe," whilst he represents to us separately and analytically the facts of experience, he is not carelessly content to be ignorant of laws for recombining them, but seeks to bring them under a universal and harmonizing synthesis. In this view then he is at once a subjective and objective poet; he has in fact transcended the one-sided standpoints of both classes, and if he does not succeed in striking the highest notes of the greatest singers of either, yet he has attained to a fuller and more steadfast view of the universe and its problems, because on the one side his objective faculty both moderates the extravagance of spiritual intuition and gives it solid as well as airy material for its use, and on the other side his subjective faculty supplies wings to soar above the immediate world of experience and demonstrate its affinity to something higher. And this is just the poet that men seemed to be in need of. Considering that the poet's function is to find and show us Truth, the objective poet tries to fulfil this function by presenting to us in poetical dress nature and life as they immediately seem to be; the subjective poet by transcendent acts of insight apprehends transcendent Truth, he rises as on the waves of Abt Vogler's music to heights which many indeed of his hearers, borne along with him, may catch sight of for a moment, but when they sink again to the common chord, and are bereft of his assistance, they are liable to apprehensions that the vision may have been an illusive dream. We want then a poet who will use understanding as well as insight, and instead of taking a giant leap—a lead which few can follow—from the objectivity of experience to an absolute Truth like Plato's Ideas, will condescend to help those Jacobs not endowed with his own wings of spiritual intuition up the several steps of a ladder. This is what Browning does; he supplies mediating links between experience and the absolute Truth. It is this discursive reasoning element in Browning which makes us associate philosophy with him more than with most poets, for they are content to see; he seeks to explain.

The aim of this paper is to give in a connected form the general bearings of his philosophical teaching. In the belief that the thoughts of a philosopher often illustrate, and so help us to pierce more clearly, the perceptions of a poet, I had intended to draw some parallels as I went along between Browning and Hegel. But when I came to write, I found that the compass of a single essay would not admit of it, and so I shall merely indicate some general points of comparison with Hegel, after I have first exhibited Browning's doctrines.

But, to begin, I must insist on the *necessity* of clearly comprehending Browning's *theory*, in order to understand what are the practical conclusions which he draws: especially, does he believe in immortality of the individual. And supposing such immortality to be the high hope upon which he has fixed his eyes, and at the same time the corner-stone on which he has raised the towers of philosophical optimism over the turf of doubt, yet inasmuch as doubt is our lot as the sparks fly upward, inasmuch as we are still of the turf turfy, we are forced to pause and consider whether this corner-stone is firm and deeply enough sunk to bear up the edifice, or whether it is but a turf-clod which, chancing to be a little concreter and denser, has presented the illusive appearance of rock. When we have redescended the turrets that we have mounted under Browning's guidance, and "stand on alien ground"; when we sink to the common chord of this life—sorrow that is hard to bear, and doubt that is slow to cure—we cannot but question the objective permanence of the heights that we "rolled from into the deep"; we feel sober acquiescence very difficult; it is hard to find our resting-place. Is the poet in possession of a point or peak that can fix the wandering star of immortality? has he found a real spark on earth that reflects the ideal "ball of blaze" in heaven? Or, dropping meta-phor, has he established a tenable basis for this great hope, if indeed he holds it, without any aid from that unfortunate dogmatism which is so often made to serve for reasoned truth?

Such questions as these will seem of course irrelevant to orthodox Christians, but it is not for "maw-crammed," "crop-full" Christians, who never feel doubt, that Browning writes; it is for men and women, whom indeed he endeavours to make Christian in the widest sense of the word, but not by forcing dogma down their throats by

"method abundantly convincing, | But scarce to be swallowed without
As I say, to those convinced before, | By the not-as-yet-convinced." [wincing

Let us try then to see Browning's "scheme of the weal and woe," that we may, if we can, understand the hope of Caponsacchi, and see the possibility of "worlds not a few" wherein our hopes shall be realized, and their impersonations, our Evelyn Hopes, be revived for us.

I. BROWNING'S POINT OF VIEW: INDIVIDUAL.

Philosophers, strictly so called, set themselves the problem of ex-plaining the universe, the spheres of Abstract Thought, of Nature, and of Spirit, whose inner bond they try to discover; and this bond con-stitutes the metaphysics of their system. But history tells us that every system that has yet been elaborated has, in a generation or two, when weighed in the balance, been found wanting, and been superseded by a new system which its author in turn fancied was the "key to all the knowledges"; but soon gates were found with locks of too complicated wards for it, and a new key must be forged. This is the natural con-sequence of the growth and progress of the human spirit, its increase of knowledge and civilization; and new philosophical schemes must arise till the end of things. But great world-schemes are universal, not indi-vidual, and philosophers like Epictetus or Epicurus speak to individuals more than Plato or Aristotle. Individuals, though they may grasp a system with eagerness, as giving them a wide and satisfactory view of the mysteries of mind and nature, must go back into the individual again and ask, What is the meaning of this *for me ?* And this question the universal systems do not solve; and when they try, cannot solve quite adequately or self-consistently: this is a question on which poets give us deeper hintings, on which music gives us momentary revelations.

It were possible to class human souls in genera and species, classes and varieties, yet none the less each individual soul is individual, and life has a different meaning for each. No spiritual kernel can get free of the nut-shell it is bounded in, though it count itself a king of infinite space. The coefficients of refraction vary with the media: the "natural fog" of a good pastor's mind augments his truths to double their size, and the pearl of price lies on a professor's table "dust and ashes levigable." It is from the individual that Browning starts:

"Meantime I can but testify . God's care for me—no more, can I— It is but for myself I know;	The world rolls witnessing around me Only to leave me as it found me." (*Chr. Eve.*)

As Mr. Arnold expresses it

"Thou hast been, shalt be, art alone." (*Switzerland.*)

The human world is a collection of units, each by himself and for himself; and, because they coexist, *externally* dependent on one another: it is like a sea studded with "pin-point rocks." Each man's mind is like a

"convex glass Wherein are gathered all the scattered points . Picked out of the immensity of sky,	To reunite there, be our heaven on earth, Our known unknown, our God revealed to man." (*Ring and Book,* iv. 57.)

But there are two sides to an individual's *Weltanschauung*, the individual and the universal. From the individual side he considers the universe as his own world; from the universal he looks upon himself as a single unit of that world. Now it is the individual side that comes prominently forward in Browning; but to understand it we must take it in its context; and as the universal side, being less obtrusive, is very likely to escape notice, I shall occupy myself first and principally with it, and afterwards take it in connection with the individual side.

II. BROWNING'S FIRST PRINCIPLE, OR GOD.

Browning's first principle or absolute Truth is Love: that which abideth one and the same, the subject and substance of all change, the permanence by which alone change is possible, whose sum ever "remains what it was before," in short, God or Truth; for, as he tells us in *Fifine,* "falsehood is change," and "truth is permanence." In the whole realm of thought, including the laws of nature and the course of history, and especially the lots of souls, Browning has essayed to pierce through the phenomenal exterior, and the abiding reality that he reaches and brings back tidings of is Love: Love is the Truth.

It is naturally asked, How does Browning arrive at this first concrete principle? how does he support the claims of Love as that in terms of which the universe is to be ultimately explained? The answer is, he derives it from experience. His poems are dramatic pictures of life drawn in such a way as to let us detect Love as the permanent spiritual unity underlying the manifold changing variety of circumstances, which are merely the modes in which Love's power compels it to reveal itself. Hence most of his works have two sides: (1) they contribute severally to establish the great tenet of his teaching, that Love is God; (2) they at the same time exhibit conclusions deducible from this hypothesis; and thus (3) the doctrine itself may be looked upon as the pervading and unifying fluid, which gives to all his poems, as a whole, an organic life.

It is, perhaps, scarce necessary to remark that this procedure of Browning is most strictly philosophical. Such an objection as that he himself imports Love into the circumstances would tell as much or as little against all science. Theory is as necessary to interpret facts as facts are to support theory.

III. HOW LOVE MANIFESTS ITSELF IN THE WORLD: POWER AND KNOWLEDGE.

Love is a mere verbal abstraction unless it be conscious of itself; and in order to be conscious of itself, it must reveal itself to itself. Its very nature and essence is to manifest itself; until it do so, it is only a potential idea, not an actual reality. The conditions of its revelation, Browning shows us, are given by its two modes, *Power* and *Knowledge* (or Intellect). Power is the mode of Love's manifestation in Nature; Knowledge is Love's recognition of itself through the medium of Power. But it is better to quote some of Browning's own expositions of these principles from the individual point of view.

"Man, therefore, stands on his own stock
Of love and power as a pin-point rock,
And, looking to God who ordained divorce
Of the rock from his boundless continent,
Sees, in his power made evident,
Only excess by a million-fold
O'er the power God gave man in the mould.
For, note: man's hand first formed to carry
A few pounds' weight, when taught to marry
Its strength with an engine's, lifts a mountain,—
Advancing in power by one degree;
And why count steps through eternity?
But love is the ever-springing fountain:
Man may enlarge or narrow his bed
For the waters play, but the water-head—
How can he multiply or reduce it?
As easy create it, as cause it to cease;
He may profit by it, or abuse it,
*But 'tis not a thing to bear increase
As power does:* be love less or more
In the heart of man, he keeps it shut
Or opes it wide, as he pleases, but
Love's sum remains what it was before."
(*Chr. Eve.*)

Here is shown the function of Power: to it are due all apparent changes and quantitative variations of Love. Though Knowledge is not in these lines expressly mentioned, yet it is implied in man, who recognizes Love and Power. Love being the substance, and therefore also the end and purpose of life, Knowledge is the means whereby it perfects and fulfils itself—

> "why live
> Except for love—how love unless they know?" (*R. & B.*, Pope.)

Truth and Beauty are merely Love revealed as an object to man's Knowledge:

"all thou dost enumerate	Inextricably round about.
Of power and beauty in the world,	Love lay within it and without
The mightiness of love was curled	To clasp thee." (*Easter Day.*)

Again,

> "the truth in God's breast
> Lies trace for trace upon ours impressed," &c. (*Chr. Eve.*)

But the fault in men is not to recognize that beauty and truth are manifestations of Love. When Fra Lippo Lippi says—

> "Or say there's beauty with no soul at all—
> (I never saw it—put the case the same—)
> If you get simple beauty and nought else,
> You get about the best thing God invents:
> That's somewhat: and you'll find the soul you have missed,
> Within yourself, when you return him thanks"—

he means that beauty is always an apparition of Love; for the *soul* is the faculty of Love, as distinguished from *mind* the faculty of Knowledge, and from Power. And if any one, though loving the beauty, fail consciously to detect a latent soul, yet the effect it works on his own soul proves the secret presence of Love.

When Love is once free and flowing, having set itself free by means of Power, it manifests itself in advancing stages from "the extreme of the minute" up to the mind of man "recognized at the height"— progressive forms of Beauty. I can only refer—the passage is far too long to quote—to the last speech of Paracelsus, which describes in marvellously vivid poetry the evolution of God, through the stages of nature and spirit. I entreat especial attention to this passage.

As power is thus the vesture, "the suits and trappings" of Love, it follows that Browning considers the natural world—space, our surroundings, our bodies, "this dance of plastic circumstance"—to possess its significance as the sphere wherein Love shows itself and learns to know itself, and which belongs most of all to man, who is the clearest "facet of reflection of God"; it is the stage on which he is to "love in turn and be beloved," and be initiated in Godship; it is "machinery just meant to give thy soul its bent."

D

"Man appears at last. So far the seal
Is put on life; one stage of being
  complete,
One scheme wound up: and from the
  grand result
A supplementary reflux of light
Illustrates all the inferior grades,
  explains
Each back step in the circle. Not
  alone

For their possessor dawn those qualities,
But the new glory mixes with the heaven
And earth; man, once descried, imprints
  for ever
His presence on all lifeless things: the
  winds
Are henceforth voices, wailing or a shout,
A querulous mutter or a quick gay laugh;
Never a senseless gust, now man is
  born," &c.   (*Paracelsus.*)

The lower forms of creation are perfect each in its place, each has its
" due facet of reflection " too, each is a mode of the life that God made
be, but their very perfection is due to their inferiority in the scale. It is
as if we conceive nature developing from an atom-point of force, like a
spiral cone which winds round and round in ever-widening circles; but
all except the last are shut in, fixed and confined in their positions;
the last alone has an end-point and room for further progress : man is

"Lower than God who knows all and
  can all,
Higher than beasts which know and
  can so far
As each beast's limit, perfect to an end,
Nor conscious that they know, nor
  craving more ;
While man knows partly, but conceives beside,

Creeps ever on from fancies to the fact,
And in this striving, this converting air
Into a solid he may grasp and use,
Finds progress, man's distinctive mark
  alone,
Not God's, and not the beasts' : God is,
  they are,
Man partly is, and wholly hopes to be."
              (*Death in the Desert.*)

This distinction is one of the striking features of Browning's teaching :
man's perfection consists in his imperfection, and his consciousness
thereof.   He is not like a

> "lark emballed by its own crystal song,
>   Or rose enmisted by that scent it makes!"   (*Ar. Apol.*)

These, indeed, God hath pronounced to be very good ; they are good in
their degree; but there are degrees higher; and the use of the lower
degrees is, that they are modes of Love for man's love to recognize.
Man realizes Love by knowledge ; by knowledge, for example, of what
"love can do in the leaf and stone."   But the essence of his manhood
is " the passion that leaves the ground to lose itself in the sky."   The
spark "that disturbs our clod" is the pledge of our divinity.   The
beasts "partake" and "receive," but think not of the provider and
effecter: we indeed receive gifts too, we are confined in our cistern, we
are finite, we are dust as well as they ; but then we can, while they
cannot, look from the gift

> "to the giver,
> And from the cistern to the river,
> And from the finite to infinity,
> And from man's dust to God's divinity."

And so in Art,

> "the incomplete
> More than completion matches the immense."

Witness Michael Agnolo, witness Andrea del Sarto. Giotto's Bell-tower's incompletion constitutes its greatness.

As closely connected with this point of view, I pass to what I consider another great feature of Browning's philosophy.

IV. THE IMPLICATION OF OPPOSITES: NECESSITY OF FALSEHOOD AND EVIL.

The Truth of Love, in order to assert itself, requires a medium of negation or falsehood, in contrast with which it may shine out and show itself to be the Truth. If there were not falsehood or show, there would be no means for Truth's revelation. For if Truth existed alone, pure and unclouded, its end is already obtained, and there is no room for process or progress; in fact, there would be no meaning in the term "truth." As Jacob Böhme showed, Yes would have no meaning if there were not the possibility of saying No. Pure truth with no falsehood we could not distinguish from pure falsehood with no truth. Sludge, the Medium, was not altogether wrong when he said,

> "Don't let truth's lump rot stagnant for the lack
> Of a timely helpful lie to leaven it!"

On the one hand, "everybody can, will, and does cheat;" on the other, "every cheat's inspired, and every lie quick with a germ of truth." And Ogniben said, "There is truth in falsehood, falsehood in truth." To use an illustration that is common to Hegel and Browning, it is as little possible to see in absolute unlimited light as in absolute unlimited darkness; vision is only possible when one is tempered by the other:

> "Clouds obscure—
> But for which obscuration all were bright?
> Too hastily concluded! Sun-suffused,
> A cloud may soothe the eye made blind by blaze,—
> Better the very clarity of heaven." (*R. & B.*, Pope, p. 71.)

And in *Aristoph. Apol.*, p. 90, we read:

> "No sun makes proof of his whole potency,
> For gold and purple in that orb we view;
> The apparent orb does little but leave blind
> The audacious, and confused the worshiping.
> But, close on orb's departure, must succeed
> The serviceable cloud,—must intervene,
> Induce expenditure of rose and blue,
> Reveal what lay in him, was lost to us."

Thus we have the *raison d'être* of evil and falsehood and pain; without them, good and truth and pleasure were not possible.

> "The evil is null and nought, silence implying sound."
> "Why rushed the discords in, but that harmony should be prized?"

Even a heaven cannot be conceived without at least the possibility of pain and ill.

The virtue of a sheathed flower may be drawn forth by a "thundrous midnight." Mistake for man is "midway help till he reach fact indeed," and error is in the world in order that he may look above its scope and "see the love." Care and doubt are symbols and pledges of the love that is his soul, pledges of his alliance with Divinity:

> "Irks care the cropful bird? frets doubt the maw-crammed beast?"

"For mankind springs salvation by each hindrance interposed." Hear Paracelsus's regrets—

> "In my own heart love had not been made wise
> To trace love's faint beginnings in mankind.
> To know, even hate is but a mask of love's,
> To see a good in evil, and a hope
> In ill-success; to sympathize, be proud
> Of their half-reasons, faint aspirings, dim
> Struggles for truth, their poorest fallacies,
> Their prejudice and fears and cares and doubts."

I may quote two out of many pertinent passages in *Sordello*:—

> "Where the salt marshes stagnate, crystals branch;
> Blood dries to crimson; Evil's beautified
> In every shape. Thrust Beauty then aside
> And banish Evil! Wherefore? After all,
> Is Evil a result less natural
> Than Good?" (Book 6.)

And—

> "Venice seems a type
> Of Life—'twixt blue and blue extends, a stripe,
> As Life, the somewhat, hangs 'twixt nought and nought:
> 'Tis Venice and 'tis Life: as good you sought
> To spare me the Piazza's slippery stone
> Or keep me to the unchoked canals alone,
> As hinder Life the evil with the good
> Which make up Living, rightly understood." (Book 3.)

I could fill pages more with quotations to the same effect. On the use of doubt does Browning everywhere especially insist (cf. e. g. *Rabbi Ben Ezra*). It is a kind of spiritual purgatorio for souls *di farsi belle*. Even pessimism is not to be condemned without qualification; for it implies a high standard of good in the pessimist.

But it is in *Fifine* that far the longest and fullest exposition of this principle is to be found. I refer particularly to the simile of the swimmer in the ocean, one of the very greatest of Browning's many great similes.

Here I would make an observation on this poem, which is the subject of so much contention. The view that some hold that the arguments in it are, most of them, sophisms, and some of them truths, seems to me mistaken. The lesson of *Fifine* is really of the same kind, and taught by the same method, as that of *Blougram's Apology*. All that the Bishop so brilliantly urges to show the utility of doubt, in fact its indispensability as a moment in enlightened faith, is *perfectly true;* the falsehood consists in making it a maxim for conduct in a different sense from its theoretical validity. Doubt is valuable, nay, necessary as a MEANS to enlightened faith; and this very statement confutes the Bishop's indifferent life, because he is content to rest in doubt as if it were an *end*. From God's point of view, doubt and evil are good as means to good; but from man's point of view—as practiser, not theorist —doubt and evil in themselves must be always evil, because imperfect. So in *Fifine :* all Don Juan's arguments are theoretical truths propounded clearly and splendidly; we are taught to see that flirtation with a Fifine and temporary inconstancy may be productive of good, may be a "midway help" to a deeper-grounded and abiding constancy, an assistance to finding reality in falsehood; for certain natures it may perhaps be the only road to truth and love. But the falsity consists in converting this theoretical optimism into a rule of life to excuse fickle affections. Blougram and Don Juan fall into the same sophism through not recognizing the true relations of theory and practice (cf. Butler, *Analogy*, Pt. I. cap. vii.).

V. LOVE AND KNOWLEDGE COMPLEMENTARY.

Of every real fact of experience Love, Power, and Knowledge are elements (cf. sect. iii, p. 263). Although one may be present in apparently much larger proportion—so large as to monopolize the attention —yet the others too must be there in some measure, for all three are essential elements of reality, and mutually imply one another. (Power, indeed, which is the negative element, need not be specially considered, because either longing love or eager knowledge implies its presence in equal amount.)

This consideration has brought Browning to most important results in psychological analysis. It is the inharmonious blending of these elements that puts souls out of tune. Excess of Love accompanied by defect of Knowledge, and excess of Knowledge accompanied by defect of Love, are equally disastrous. Aprile and Paracelsus failed through holding to these opposite abstractions. Aprile would love infinitely : the failure of his life was due to leaping at the end without recognizing and employing the indispensable means; and an end pursued in ignorance of, and abstraction from, the necessary means, is an imaginary and false end. Paracelsus would know infinitely : the failure in his life consisted in mistaking the means for the end, in assuming knowledge to be the throne, whereas it is but the steps. We call the object of knowledge Truth or Reality ; but since the only abiding True and Real behind its show and appearance is Love, Truth and Love are ultimately identical. Men go astray by separating these that are properly inseparable. Blind desire pursues Love as if it were independent of Knowledge, and fails to find it, like Aprile ; and Knowledge pursues Truth as if it were independent of Love, and can find no Truth—except the truth of failure—like Paracelsus. It may be observed that these two characters, the Italian and the German, may be looked on as respectively the types of the Romanic and German nations.

With slight variation of the point of view :—Knowledge is Love's recognition of itself ; but if the human soul, the individual pin-point of Love, does not recognize Love in its object, but calls it merely truth or fact, then it does not *know* in the highest sense of the word, it has only a half-truth ; and half-truths, besides being defective, are false because taken to be whole truths. Perfect love would be also perfect knowledge, and perfect knowledge perfect love. This shows us the meaning of that great line in *Paracelsus*,

"I, you and God, can comprehend each other,"

where "I, you" are Aureole and Aprile, who have learned by failure, and God is the ideal union of the two things which they had witlessly separated ; he is the "perfect Poet," for poets are those who knowing love, and loving know, with whom mind and soul are not, as in ordinary men, separated energies, but are a harmonious unity.

But of the two, Love is the prior, the superior : a loving worm were diviner than a loveless god. Goethe cries (in *Werther*), "Was ich weiss, kann jeder wissen—mein Herz habe ich allein." (What I know, can every one know : my Heart is mine alone.)

Let no one say that it must be a poor palette on which there are only three colours ; for in different combinations and proportions they produce infinite variety of shades. These three principles—Love, Knowledge, Power—are the fundamental chord of the universe, and Love is the keynote ; each of these is "everywhere in the world—loud, soft, and all is said." Man's problem is to harmonize them in his soul, which he can do but incompletely until by the process of evolution he has become, as God, a perfect musician ; in the mean time let him seize and hold as earnests of ultimate everlasting music all passing revelations vouchsafed to him—moonbeams made marble.

VI. COMPARISONS WITH HEGEL.

Before proceeding to consider Browning's views on Christianity and Immortality, and the significance of the Universe for the Individual, I stop to draw some comparisons with Hegel. The philosopher finds a first principle and a method of applying it wherewith he interprets the universe; the poet does not set himself directly to interpret the universe, but to interpret human souls; yet inasmuch as they are part and parcel of the whole, and must be studied by the light of the whole in which they are set, their interpretation equally involves a theory of the universe. Of course this is only applicable to poets like Browning, not equally to those who, like Shakspere, give us characters and their accompanying problems without interpreting or solving them. Browning mediates them for us; not only gives them to us reflected from a glass of his own, but also supplies a light, which he had to take care should be of such intensity and colour as would illuminate every variety—in short, he had to metaphysicize.

The few glimpses in not very detailed outline of the universal side of Browning's *Weltanschauung*, which we find in his poems, and which I have here attempted to collect, brought me to think that if he was a philosopher proper he would have been a Hegelian—at least the universal side of his philosophy would have been Hegelian.

To begin with the idea of God or the Absolute. Both Hegel and Browning show us that God is "over us, under, round us, every side," at our gates, and no mystical intellectual or spiritual intuitions like those of Schelling or Shelley are necessary to reach him. We have found God when we have recognized and realized the identity of Being and Thought, of Love and Knowledge. Power corresponds to Hegel's principle of negation—the moving, differentiating element in the world. Knowledge (Thought) tends to integrate Love (Being), which Power had differentiated, and it is ever bringing back the manifold centrifugal productions of Power to the centrality of Love, and thus progressing in the realization of a unity in which Power, and the accompanying Falsehood and Evil, will be a suspended moment.

A great service that Hegel performed for philosophy was his method; and the spirit of this method pervades Browning's reasoning. It depends on recognizing that when we think anything, we implicitly think what it is not; and when we think a definite quality, we implicitly think its opposite—e. g. good and evil, bright and dark. Thus affirmation involves negation, and identity involves difference. We have already called attention to the prominence of this truth in Browning: it is the essence of Hegel.

Good is positive, and must be ultimately victorious, with Hegel as with Browning. Hear Walt Whitman's lines on reading Hegel : "Roaming in thought over the Universe, I saw the little that is Good steadily hastening towards immortality, And the vast all that is call'd Evil I saw hastening to merge itself and become lost and dead."

The development of Hegel's pure, bare, undiluted Being through successive stages up to the complicated forms of State, Religion, Philosophy, is like the mounting of waves towering higher and higher, "one crowd but with many a crest"; and as the waves must fall in order to rise to a greater height, so the march of the Idea is a series of self-negations involving self-affirmations. But the poet has not to do, as the philosopher has, with a systematic history of the progress of the Universal Principle. By seeing into souls, Browning has obtained his notion of God, which is accordingly of an ethical nature, not merely logical. With him the absolute Idea is Love, which as a negative, self-revealing force phenomenally in Nature is Power, and, becoming conscious of itself *in individuals* as spirit, moves in a continually advancing process of reconciliation of its absolute noumenal permanence (Love) with its phenomenal mode of manifestation (Power).

An obvious objection (admitting of an obvious enough answer) that might be made against Browning's principle may be noticed. It may be said that Love has no meaning except as characterizing the relations of sentient beings; that to set it up seriously as a first universal principle, not only supplies no explanation, but is unwarranted,—either mystical or absurd; that it can be analyzed into simpler elements—its evolution traced back, for example, to Hegel's Being. This objection, although if Browning were a pure philosopher it would apply so far as to demand from him definite explanation and logical analysis, is really shallow. Browning knows, like all philosophers, that Time is phenomenal, and that an absolute Principle by its very notion is independent of Time, contains in itself the possibility of Time :

"Time's wheel runs back or stops: Potter and clay endure." (*R. Ben Ezra.*)
     "Till earth's work stop and useless time run out." (*Death in Desert.*)

But the distinction between First and Final Cause depends on Time; and as the latter is a far fuller idea than the former, it is more adequate to express God, who is indifferent to the distinction : consequently Browning is strictly justified in conceiving God as Love, because he has found in the world Love as an abiding reality, to whose perfection the world's movement is tending as an *End*. But the proximate reason for the form which his universal principle takes is his individual and ethical (poetical), not universal and metaphysical (philosophical), standpoint.

A main point on which I wish throughout to insist is that Browning realizes the defect and falseness of one-sidedness, and never halts at half-truths : he always gives them their proper place in relation to each other and a higher unity. This, as is well known, is a great characteristic of Hegel.

VII. PERSONAL GOD : CHRISTIANITY : INDIVIDUALS.

Browning is generally spoken of as holding the doctrine of a personal God : the orthodox are glad, and the unbelieving shrug their shoulders. But it is plain that a *personal* God (in any meaning of the word " personal " that is intelligible to us) is inconsistent with the tenor of Browning's teaching. For God is not limited by time, as we have seen above, nor by space (compare *Ring and Book*, Pope, l. 1317, " There (which is nowhere) speech must babble thus ! In the absolute immensity—"), and thus personality applied to him in our sense has no meaning : personal is a completely inadequate and therefore misleading term—"speech must babble thus ! " Even supposing—a supposition which seems to me to have no basis, and to be due to superficial study—Browning does teach a personal God, his God is at all events a Being of a glorious kind whom we could feel glad to worship, far different from the diabolical God or divine Devil whom many are still taught to praise and pray to.

This may enable us to comprehend his attitude to Christian Dogma, of which there have also—even more so—been false ideas abroad.

If, as he holds, Love is God, then the greatest crisis in Love's conscious development as human spirit is when it first knows itself explicitly as Love,—that is, when man first recognizes that God, in whom he lives, moves, and has his being, is Love. But this recognition is the soul of Christianity ; this gives it a divinity different in kind and not merely in degree from all other religions : its main dogma is true, though disfigured by so many false wraps. Historical questions about parthenogenesis, resurrection, ascension, are quite irrelevant to this truth, and owe all their significance to the false conception of a personal God. Browning's view transcends and includes the one-sidedness of the Churches and the Göttingen professor. Relative historical falseness or myth in the Christian creed is consistent with the absolute truth of the dogma : the professor clung to the former and rejected the latter, and thereby, to use an expressive German proverb, " schüttete das Kind mit dem Bade aus "; the preachers holding the dogma insist on the historical truth of the myth.

This view of Christianity is practically that of Hegel. But it is his individualism, so to speak, that gives Browning's view its peculiar character. Throughout the preceding remarks I have purposely dwelt more on his conceptions of the evolving world and mankind as a collection of units, than on his view of the individual in himself and for himself—purposely because, the latter being more prominent, readers of Browning are much less likely to overlook it.   We must now turn to the individual side of his *Weltanschauung.*   The tendency nowadays among English scientific thinkers is to look on the human individual as a passing accidental mode of the universal energy, who contributes to the progress of humanity, but has no further significance.   From an empirical standpoint this is true; but, like all empiricism, it is one-sided, and Browning teaches us that the individual has a worth and meaning in and for himself independent of his worth and meaning for the world: he comes and goes, and serves the world while he stays, but the world also serves him, is meant to try him and turn him forth "sufficiently impressed": he is related to *it* indirectly as a particular member of a multitude, but as an individual he is directly related to the Absolute, and possesses universal value.   He has a signifi-cance in time and space, as a unit helping in the process of the universe ; but he has also a primary significance for himself that is independent of these limitations; and since this latter significance, being absolute, is superior and logically prior to the former, which is only relative, it must legislate morality (cf. *Statue and Bust*, and monologue of Caponsacchi in *Ring and Book*, l. 1812, &c.).   A man's highest boast is—

> "not even while the whirl was worst,
> Did I,—to the wheel of life,
> With shapes and colours rife,
> Bound dizzily,—mistake my end, to slake thy thirst."

This would be the place to speak of—I can now only refer to—the autonomy of the Will, an important and often-noticed element in Browning's teaching; for the right of an individual will to autonomy depends upon its universal value.

And here I must again call attention to the incomplete and unsatis-fying character of man's work, for to the individual this is a gauge of his universality.   His individuality goes out beyond its work, and is like a space without bound which the work, at least in this cramped life, can never fill: the soul's "lone way" is limitless, and its home is not here.

This union of individualism and universalism in Browning is perhaps most strikingly set forth in *Rabbi Ben Ezra*, and in the Epilogue of Three Speakers, which shows its bearing on Christianity, and is, I think, the decisive passage as to Browning's view.   The simple universalism of David, who worships with the *senses* in a temple made with hands, and the particularism of Renan, who is sceptical because historical difficulties give pause to the *understanding*, are superseded by the individualism of the Third Speaker, whose *reason* transcends the simple conviction of David and the intellectual doubt of Renan, by seeing that both are reconcilable when transformed into parts of a higher view : as an individual personality, Christ was God (self-conscious Love); as a particular unit in the world he was man, subject to the laws of the world's machinery. It is for the individual that his personality and divinity have their significance : progressive humanity and scientific history concern themselves only with the phenomenal effects produced by his teaching independently of his personality.

And thus Browning's view is on the one side consistent with all Herbert Spencer's philosophy, whose result is to show that egoism and altruism (the interests of the individual and of society) are in gradual process of conciliation ; but he gives prominence to another side also, in which virtue and vice have an inward significance for the individual, apart from the evolution of the world.

In Browning are the germs of a religion that transcends ecclesiastical Christianity and Comte's Positivism, and includes the truth of both.

In connection with his individualism should be considered his original views of the relations of men and women, which I can but barely touch on. An individual's soul has two sides : the potential and the actual, the divine and the human, reality and show. But the inner side can be revealed to the object of sexual love, and so even in this world to a certain extent actualize its divinity :

> "Was there nought better than to enjoy ?
> No feat which, done, would make time break,
> And let us pent-up creatures through
> Into eternity, our due ?
> No forcing earth teach heaven's employ ?"—*Dis aliter visum.*

Thus an individual receives a revelation of Love from another of opposite sex (sex, it must not be forgotten, is only phenomenal), and this person might be called a Personal God, as the vehicle of the revelation of the Absolute God. It is this love alone that can reach to the inner pent-up side of the soul, else unrevealed and "locked fast," but let loose by "love for a key." Shelley reached this view by spiritual intuition (witness *Epipsychidion*), and Dante said of Beatrice, "Che lume fia tra 'l vero e lo 'ntelletto"; but Browning, combining the reason of the philosopher with the instinct of a poet, first worked it consistently out. See on this subject *Fifine, Dramatic Lyrics* passim, *James Lee's Wife, The Worst of it, Dis aliter visum, Too Late, Youth and Art, Statue and Bust*, &c., but above all, *One Word More.* This two-sidedness of souls is the leading idea running through the Pacchiarotto volume.

VIII. IMMORTALITY.

As a consequence of his individual point of view, Mr. Browning has reached a higher standpoint than the vague pantheism of, for example, Mr. Tennyson's *In Memoriam*, in the same way as the German Transcendentalists, beginning with Kant, got beyond the pantheism of Spinoza. The universe exists for the individual as much as the individual for the universe: he is immortal. But immortality in Browning's poems has a different significance from that which it ordinarily conveys. (*Personal* immortality is as inadequate a term as personal God.) It does not imply memory in the sense of an unbroken chain of consciousness—which has significance only in time—nor yet an absorption into unconsciousness: it implies a state inconceivable to us, limited as we are by phenomenal conditions,—a state which may involve other manifestations in other worlds not a few. There is indeed one way, according to Browning, in which it is possible for some to approximate to a conception and gain a foretaste of this state which may be called heaven—namely by music. Music, as Hegel says, frees from the limit of space—and also partially suspends time. Past and future seem mixed into one present ideal emotion:—"Presences plain in the place; or, fresh from the protoplast," "or else the wonderful Dead who have passed through the body and gone" are not wanting "in the glare and glow." It is our completest revelation of God: earth attains to heaven; there is no more near nor far. Mr. Herbert Spencer has well spoken of cadences as the comments of the emotion on the propositions of the intellect. Thus in music ideas and emotions, love and knowledge, are fused in a perfect mixture, that is, an anticipation of the absolute union of love and knowledge—the goal to which both the individual and the universe tend.

As I said before, while Shakspere sets us problems, Browning tries to give us solutions, or at least grounds for hoping that there are solutions that are not merely negative. Hamlet's last words are, "The rest is silence"; Romeo and Othello "look their last" and "die upon a kiss"; but with Browning silence means sound, and in the hand of the dead Evelyn Hope lies a leaf, earnest of a future.

To some this belief in "silence implying sound" will appear very consoling; others will find more comfort in an eternal night in which "silence is more than all tunes." But it is not consolation or pathos that Browning offers (and for this reason in certain moods we find Mr. Swinburne's or Mr. Matthew Arnold's poems more solacing): his message to us is to remember that our aspirations, our ways of life and manners of thought, our seeking after Love, and our love for Beauty, are all so much gain for the individual soul, and have an eternal value *for it*, quite beyond the passing delight or the good contributed thereby to the world without. "There shall never be one lost good! what was, shall live as before."

> "All we have willed or hoped or dreamed of good shall exist;
> Not its semblance, but itself," &c.

Take this in connection with *Rabbi Ben Ezra*, verses 23, 24, 25.

Thus each individual beauty or affection on earth has an import for eternity through its influence on an individual's soul,

> " a sunset-touch,
> A fancy from a flower-bell, some one's death,
> A chorus-ending from Euripides ; "

and with a chorus-ending from Euripides I conclude, as expressing a truth that Browning has ever in view—the correlation of Love and Beauty as of *absolute* significance :

> ὅ,τι καλὸν φίλον ἀεί.

P.S. It has been objected that there is inconsistency in conceiving God as concrete and self-conscious Love, and at the same time refusing the predicate "personal." I think the question may be one of words more than the objectors suspect. On the one hand, God is manifested in the individual as *his* (the individual's) *personality*, and in this sense God may be called personal; on the other hand, as a universal, God is impersonal : but these sides are mutually complementary, and each is as inadequate as the other to express the Absolute, which, while it contains in itself the conditions of both, is indifferent to the distinction, and so neither of the adjectives (personal and impersonal) can accurately be predicated of it, though of course *personal* is the higher conception of the two, as is indicated by the histories of Philosophy and Religion. We are not entitled to speak of the Absolute as personal because it contains the conditions of personality, just as its containing the conditions of space does not entitle us to speak of it as extended. In short, to arrive at the notion of God we must raise the notion of *person* to a universal : we thereby suspend the essence of *person* in a new and higher notion, and thus not only is "personal" a wrong predicate to apply to God, but *universal person* is a false description, because it sets the two terms of the notion abstractly side by side, and so implies that they are still contradictory and unreconciled, whereas in the concrete notion of God (the Idea) they are suspended moments of a higher unity. (Note : the opposition of *abstract* and *concrete* must not be taken to imply such a contrast, for example, as of Thought and Life; it is the contrast—cf.

sect. v.—of a one-sided with a complete view, of the grasping of thought which seizes but a part with the grasp which holds the whole. Thus in the very example instanced, to look upon Life as concrete is an abstract point of view, because Life expresses only one side of the whole of Thought.)

Now I have tried to show that Browning, while insisting—as his purposes demanded—chiefly on the individual side, nevertheless does not neglect the universal side. He does not conceive Love as bound up with personality (personality rather expresses the form in which Love knows itself in the individual), but conceives it as the unity that underlies and forms the connecting bond of both sides, and it is consequently his expression of God. It is not my object to criticize, but merely to exhibit, what I consider to be Browning's teaching; and the purpose of this note is to defend my reading of Browning against the charge of formal inconsistency.

I may add, as it is in the interests of ethics more than of metaphysics, that the Personality of God is so obstinately clung to, that this conception is even more plainly untenable from an ethical than from a metaphysical standpoint; for, thus viewed, "personal God" becomes a contradiction in terms, since it expresses God as co-ordinated with other persons,—superior indeed in degree, but *qua* person co-ordinate. Such a personal Being may be a fine abstract ethical ideal, but is not God. The Christian religion first obtains its true significance when this remnant of anthropomorphism, the doctrine of a personal God, is laid aside.

In general such objections seem due to the respectable but unfounded prejudice that it is blasphemy to deny personality of God. The retort might be made, that it is they who blaspheme, in limiting God by the category of personality. Mr. Herbert Spencer well speaks of the "erroneous assumption that the choice is between personality and something lower than personality; whereas the choice is rather between personality and something higher."

THE IDEA OF PERSONALITY,

AS EMBODIED IN ROBERT BROWNING'S POETRY

BY HIRAM CORSON, LL.D.,
PROFESSOR IN THE CORNELL UNIVERSITY, U.S.A.

(Read at the 8th Meeting of the Browning Society, June 23, 1882.)

> " Subsists no law of Life outside of Life.
>
> . . . .
> The Christ himself had been no Lawgiver,
> Unless he had given the *life*, too, with the law."

THE importance of Robert Browning's poetry, as embodying the profoundest thought, the subtlest and most complex sentiment, and, above all, the most quickening spirituality of the age, has, as yet, with the exception of a few special and devoted students, received but a niggardly recognition. There are, however, many indications in the poetical criticism of the day, that upon it will finally be pronounced, though late, the verdict which has so long been its due. And the recent founding of a Society in England "to gather together some, at least, of the many admirers of Robert Browning, for the study and discussion of his works, and the publication of papers on them, and extracts from works illustrating them," is an earnest that something ere long will be done towards paying, in part, at least, a long-standing debt.

Mr. Browning's earliest poem, *Pauline* (he calls it, in the Preface to the reprint of it, in 1868, "a boyish work," though it exhibits the great basal thought of all his subsequent poetry), was published in 1843, since which time he has produced the largest body of poetry produced by any one poet, in English literature ; and the range of thought and passion which it exhibits is greater than that of any other poet, without a single exception, since the days of Shakspere. And he is the most like Shakspere in his deep interest in human nature, in all its varieties of good and of evil. Though endowed with a powerful, subtle, and restless intellect, he has, throughout his voluminous poetry, made the strongest protest that has been made in these days, against mere intellect. And his poetry has, therefore, a peculiar value in an age like the present—an age exhibiting "a condition of humanity which has thrown itself wholly on its intellect and its genius in physics, and has done marvels in material science and invention, but at the expense of the interior divinity." It is the human heart, that is, the intuitive, the non-discursive side of man, with its hopes and its prophetic aspirations, as opposed to the analytic, the discursive understanding, which is to him a subject of the deepest and most scrutinizing interest. He knows that its deepest depths are "deeper than did ever plummet sound;" but he also knows, that it is in these depths that life's greatest secrets must be sought. The philosophies excogitated by the insulated intellect, help nothing toward even a glimpse of these secrets. In one of his later poems, that entitled *House*, he has intimated, and forcibly intimated, his sense of the impossibility of penetrating to the Holy of Holies of this wondrous human heart, though assured as he is that all our hopes in regard to the soul's destiny are warmed and cherished by what radiates thence. He quotes, in the last stanza of this poem, from Wordsworth's sonnet on the Sonnet, "With this same key Shakspere unlocked his heart," and then adds, "*Did* Shakspere? If so, the less Shakspere he!"

Mrs. Browning, in the Fifth Book of her *Aurora Leigh*, has given a full and very forcible expression to the feeling which has caused the highest dramatic genius of the present day to seek refuge in the poem and the novel. "I will write no plays; because the drama, less sublime in this, makes lower appeals, defends more menially, adopts the standard of the public taste to chalk its height on, wears a dog-chain round its regal neck, and learns to carry and fetch the fashions of the day, to please the day; . . . 'Tis that, honouring to its worth the drama, I would fear to keep it down to the level of the footlights. . . . The growing drama has outgrown such toys of simulated stature, face, and speech, it also, peradventure, may outgrow the simulation of the painted scene, boards, actors, prompters, gaslight, and costume; and *take for a worthier stage, the soul itself, its shifting fancies and celestial lights, with all its grand orchestral silences to keep the pauses of the rhythmic sounds.*"

Robert Browning's poetry is, in these days, the fullest realization of what is expressed in the concluding lines of this passage: he has taken for a worthier stage, the soul itself, its shifting fancies and celestial lights, more than any other poet of the age. And he has worked with a thought-and-passion capital greater than the combined thought-and-passion capital of the richest of his poetical contemporaries. And he has thought nobly of the soul, and has treated it as, in its essence, above the fixed and law-bound system of things which we call nature; in other words, he has treated it as supernatural. "Mind," he makes the Pope say, in *The Ring and the Book*,—and his poetry bears testimony to its being his own conviction and doctrine,—"Mind is not matter, nor from matter, but above." With every student of Browning, the recognition and acceptance of this, must be his starting-point. Even that which impelled the old dog, in his poem entitled *Tray* (*Dramatic Lyrics*, First Series), to rescue the beggar child that fell into the river, and then to dive after the child's doll, and bring it up, after a long stay under water, the poet evidently distinguishes from matter,—regards as "not matter nor from matter, but above:"

> "And so, amid the laughter gay,
> Trotted my hero off,—old Tray,—
> Till somebody, prerogatived
> With reason, reasoned : 'Why he dived,
> His brain would show us, I should say.
>
> John, go and catch—or, if needs be,
> Purchase that animal for me!
> By vivisection, at expense
> Of half-an-hour and eighteen pence,
> How brain secretes dog's soul, we'll see!'"

In his poem entitled *Halbert and Hob* (*Dramatic Lyrics*, First Series), quoting from Shakspere's *King Lear*, "Is there a reason in nature for these hard hearts?" the poet adds, "O Lear, That a reason *out* of nature must turn them soft, seems clear!"

Mind is, with Browning, *supernatural*, but linked with, and restrained, and even enslaved by, the natural. The soul, in its education, that is, in its awakening, becomes more and more independent of the natural, and, as a consequence, more responsive to higher souls and to the Divine. *All spirit is mutually attractive*, and the degree of attractiveness results from the degree of freedom from the obstructions of the material, or the natural. Loving the truth implies a greater or less degree of that freedom of the spirit which brings it into *sympathy* with the true. "If ye abide in My word," says Christ (and we must understand by "word" His own concrete life, the word made flesh, and living and breathing), "if ye abide in My word" (that is, continue to live My life), "then are ye truly My disciples ; and ye shall know the truth, and the truth shall make you free" (John viii. 32).

In regard to the soul's *inherent* possessions, its microcosmic potentialities, Paracelsus is made to say (and this may be taken, too, as the poet's own creed), "Truth is *within* ourselves ; it takes no rise from outward things, whate'er you may believe : there is an inmost centre in us all, where truth abides in fullness ; and around, wall upon wall, the gross flesh hems it in, this perfect, clear perception—which is truth.

E

A baffling and perverting carnal mesh blinds it, and makes all error ; and, *to know*, rather consists in opening out a way whence the imprisoned splendour may escape, than in effecting entry for a light supposed to be without."

All possible thought is *implicit* in the mind, and waiting for release —waiting to become *explicit*. "Seek within yourself," says Goethe, "and you will find everything ; and rejoice that, without, there lies a Nature that says yea and amen to all you have discovered in yourself." And Mrs. Browning, in the person of Aurora Leigh, writes : "The cygnet finds the water ; but the man is born in ignorance of his element, and feels but blind at first, disorganized by sin in the blood,—his spirit-insight dulled and crossed by his sensations. Presently we feel it quicken in the dark sometimes ; then mark, be reverent, be obedient,— for those dumb motions of imperfect life are oracles of vital Deity attesting the Hereafter. Let who says 'The soul's a clean white paper,' rather say, a palimpsest, a prophet's holograph defiled, erased, and covered by a monk's,—the Apocalypse by a Longus ! poring on which obscure text, we may discern perhaps some fair, fine trace of what was written once, some off-stroke of an alpha and omega expressing the old Scripture."

This "fair, fine trace of what was written once," it was the mission of Christ, it is the mission of all great personalities, of all the concrete creations of Genius, to bring out into distinctness and vital glow. It is not, and cannot be, brought out,—and this fact is emphasized in the poetry of Browning,—it cannot be brought out, through what is born and resides in the brain : it is brought out, either directly or indirectly, by the attracting power of magnetic personalities, the ultimate, absolute personality being the God-man, Christ, θεάνθρωπος.

The human soul is regarded in Browning's poetry as a complexly organized, individualized divine force, destined to gravitate towards the Infinite. How is this force, with its numberless checks and counter-checks, its centripetal and centrifugal tendencies, best determined in its necessarily oblique way? How much earthly ballast must it carry, to keep it sufficiently steady, and how little, that it may not be weighed down with materialistic heaviness? How much certainty must it have of its course, and how much uncertainty, that it may shun the "torpor of assurance,"[1] and not lose the vigor which comes of a dubious and obstructed road, "which who stands upon is apt to doubt if it's indeed a road."[2] "Pure faith indeed," says Bishop Blougram, to Gigadibs, the literary man, "you know not what you ask ! naked belief

[1] *The Ring and the Book*, The Pope, v. 1853.
[2] *Bishop Blougram's Apology*, vv. 198, 199.

in God the Omnipotent, Omniscient, Omnipresent, sears too much the
sense of conscious creatures, to be borne. It were the seeing him, no
flesh shall dare. Some think, Creation's meant to show him forth : I
say, it's meant to hide him all it can, and that's what all the blessed
Evil's for. Its use in time is to environ us, our breath, our drop of
dew, with shield enough against that sight till we can bear its stress.
Under a vertical sun, the exposed brain and lidless eye and disim-
prisoned heart less certainly would wither up at once, than mind,
confronted with the truth of Him. But time and earth case-harden us
to live; the feeblest sense is trusted most : the child feels God a
moment, ichors o'er the place, plays on and grows to be a man like us.
With me, faith means perpetual unbelief kept quiet like the snake
'neath Michael's foot, who stands calm just because he feels it writhe." [1]

There is a remarkable passage to the same effect in *Paracelsus*, in
which Paracelsus expatiates on the "just so much of doubt as bade him
plant a surer foot upon the sun-road."

And in *Easter Day :*

> " You must mix some uncertainty
> With faith, if you would have faith *be*."

And the good Pope in *The Ring and the Book*, alluding to the absence
of true Christian soldiership, which is revealed by Pompilia's case,
says : " Is it not this ignoble *confidence*, cowardly hardihood, that dulls
and damps, makes the old heroism impossible? Unless . . . what
whispers me of times to come? What if it be the mission of that age
my death will usher into life, to *shake this torpor of assurance from our
creed*, re-introduce the *doubt* discarded, bring the formidable danger back
we drove long ago to the distance and the dark?"

True healthy doubt means, in Browning, that the spiritual nature is
sufficiently quickened not to submit to the conclusions of the insulated
intellect. It *will* reach out beyond them, and assert itself, whatever be
the resistance offered by the intellect. Mere doubt, without any resistance from the intuitive, non-discursive side of our nature, is the dry-rot
of the soul. The spiritual functions are "smothered in surmise."
Faith is not a matter of blind belief, of slavish assent and acceptance,
as many no-faith people seem to regard it. It is what Wordsworth
calls it, "a passionate intuition," and springs out of quickened and
refined sentiment, out of inborn instincts which are as cultivable as
are any other elements of our complex nature, and which, too, may be
blunted beyond a consciousness of their possession. And when one in
this latter state denies the reality of faith, he is not unlike one born
blind denying the reality of sight.

[1] *Bishop Blougram's Apology*, vv. 650-671.

A reiterated lesson in Browning's poetry, and one that results from his spiritual theory, is, that the present life is a tabernacle-life, and that it can be truly lived only as a tabernacle-life; for only such a life is compatible with the ever-continued aspiration and endeavour which is a condition of, and inseparable from, spiritual vitality.

Domizia, in the tragedy of *Luria*, is made to say,

> "How inexhaustibly the spirit grows!
> One object, she seemed erewhile born to reach
> With her whole energies and die content,—
> So like a wall at the world's edge it stood,
> With naught beyond to live for,—is that reached?—
> Already are new undream'd energies
> Outgrowing under, and extending farther
> To a new object;—there's another world!"

The dying John in *A Death in the Desert*, says,

> "I say that man was made to grow, not stop;
> That help he needed once, and needs no more,
> Having grown up but an inch by, is withdrawn:
> For he hath new needs, and new helps to these.
> This imports solely, man should mount on each
> New height in view; the help whereby he mounts,
> The ladder-rung his foot has left, may fall,
> Since all things suffer change save God the Truth.
> Man apprehends him newly at each stage
> Whereat earth's ladder drops, its service done;
> And nothing shall prove twice what once was proved."

Browning has given varied and beautiful expressions to this idea, throughout his poetry.

● The soul must rest in nothing this side of the infinite. If it does rest in anything, however relatively noble that thing may be, whether art, or literature, or science, or theology, even, it declines in vitality— it torpifies. However great a conquest the combatant may achieve in any of these arenas, "striding away from the huge gratitude, his club shouldered, lion-fleece round loin and flank," he must be "bound on the next new labour, height o'er height ever surmounting—destiny's decree!"[1]

But this tabernacle-life, which should ever look ahead, has its claims which must not be ignored, and its standards which must not be too much above present conditions. Man must "fit to the finite his infinity" (*Sordello*, p. 203). Life may be over-spiritual as well as over-worldly. "Let us cry, 'All good things are ours, nor soul helps flesh more, now, than flesh helps soul!'"[2] The figure the poet employs in the *Ring and the Book* to illustrate the art process, may be as aptly applied to life itself—the greatest of all arts. The life-artist must know

---

[1] *Aristophanes' Apology*, p. 35, American ed.   [2] *Rabbi Ben Ezra*

how to secure the proper degree of malleability in this mixture of flesh and soul. He must mingle gold with gold's alloy, and duly tempering both effect a manageable mass. There may be too little of alloy in earth-life as well as too much—too little to work the gold and fashion it, not into a ring, but ring-ward. "On the earth the broken arcs; in the heaven a perfect round" (*Abt Vogler*). "Oh, if we draw a circle premature, heedless of far gain, greedy for quick returns of profit, sure, bad is our bargain" (*A Grammarian's Funeral*).

An Epistle containing the strange Medical Experiences of Karshish, the Arab Physician, is one of Browning's most remarkable psychological studies. It may be said to polarise the idea, so often presented in his poetry, that doubt is a condition of the vitality of faith. In this poem, the poet has treated a supposed case of a spiritual knowledge "increased beyond the fleshly faculty—heaven opened to a soul while yet on earth, earth forced on a soul's use while seeing heaven," a spiritual state, less desirable and far less favourable to the true fulfilment of the purposes of earth-life, than that expressed in the following lines from *Easter Day*:—

> "A world of spirit as of sense
> Was plain to him, yet not *too* plain,
> Which he could traverse, not remain
> A *guest in* :—else were permanent
> Heaven on earth, which its gleams were meant
> To sting with hunger for full light," etc.

The Epistle is a subtle representation of a soul conceived with absolute spiritual standards, while obliged to live in a world where all standards are relative and determined by the circumstances and limitations of its situation.

The spiritual life has been too distinctly revealed for fulfilling aright the purposes of earth-life, purposes which the soul, while in the flesh, must not ignore, since, in the words of Rabbi Ben Ezra, "all good things are ours, nor soul helps flesh more, now, than flesh helps soul." The poem may also be said to represent what is, or should be, the true spirit of the man of science. In spite of what Karshish writes, apologetically, he betrays his real attitude throughout, towards the wonderful spiritual problem involved.

It is, as many of Browning's Monologues are, a double picture—one direct, the other reflected, and the reflected one is as distinct as the direct. The composition also bears testimony to Browning's own soul-healthfulness. Though the spiritual bearing of things is the all-in-all, in his poetry, the robustness of his nature, the fullness and splendid equilibrium of his life, protect him against an inarticulate mysticism. Browning is, in the widest and deepest sense of the word, the healthiest of all living poets; and in general constitution the most Shaksperian.

Perhaps the most comprehensive passage in Browning's poetry, expressive of his ideal of a complete man under the conditions of earth-life, is found in *Colombe's Birthday*, Act IV.   Valence says of Prince Berthold,

"He gathers earth's *whole good* into his arms, standing, as man, now, stately, strong and wise—marching to fortune, not surprised by her : one great aim, like a guiding star, above—which tasks strength, wisdom, stateliness, to lift his manhood to the height that takes the prize ; a prize not near—lest overlooking earth, he rashly spring to seize it—nor remote, so that he rests upon his path content : but day by day, while shimmering grows shine, and the faint circlet prophesies the orb, he sees so much as, just evolving these, the stateliness, the wisdom and the strength, to due completion, will suffice this life, and lead him at his grandest to the grave."

Browning fully recognizes, to use an expression of his *Fra Lippo Lippi*, fully recognizes "the value and significance of flesh."   A healthy and well-toned spiritual life is with him the furthest removed from asceticism.   To the passage from his *Rabbi Ben Ezra* already quoted, "all good things are ours, nor soul helps flesh more, now, than flesh helps soul," should be added what David sings to Saul in the poem entitled *Saul*.   Was the full physical life ever more beautifully sung ?

✱   "Oh ! our manhood's prime vigour ! no spirit feels waste,
Not a muscle is stopped in its playing, nor sinew unbraced.
Oh, the wild joys of living ! the leaping from rock up to rock,
The strong rending of boughs from the fir-tree, the cool silver shock
Of the plunge in a pool's living water, the hunt of the bear,
And the sultriness showing the lion is couched in his lair.
And the meal, the rich dates yellowed over with gold dust divine,
And the locust-flesh steeped in the pitcher, the full draught of wine,
And the sleep in the dried river-channel where bulrushes tell
That the water was wont to go warbling so softly and well.
How good is man's life, the mere living ! how fit to employ
All the heart and the soul and the senses for ever in joy !"

Though this is said in the person of the beautiful shepherd-boy, David, whoever has lived any time with Browning, through his poetry, must be assured that it is also an expression of the poet's own experience of the glory of flesh.   He has himself been an expression of the fullest physical life : and now, in his one and seventieth year, since the 7th of last May, he preserves both mind and body in a magnificent vigour. If his soul had been lodged in a sickly, rickety body, he could hardly have written these lines from *Saul*.   Nor could he have written *Caliban upon Setebos*, especially the opening lines : "Will sprawl, now that the heat of day is best, flat on his belly in the pit's much mire, with elbows wide, fists clenched to prop his chin.   And, while he kicks both

feet in the cool slush, and feels about his spine small eft-things course,
run in and out each arm, and make him laugh: and while above his
head a pompion-plant, coating the cave-top as a brow its eye, creeps
down to touch and tickle hair and beard, and now a flower drops with
a bee inside, and now a fruit to snap at, catch and crunch,—he looks
out o'er yon sea which sunbeams cross and recross till they weave a
spider-web (meshes of fire, some great fish breaks at times), and talks
to his own self, howe'er he please, touching that other, whom his dam
called God."

There's a grand passage in *Balaustion's Adventure: including a
transcript from Euripides,* descriptive of Herakles as he returns, after
his conflict with Death, leading back Alkestis, which shows the poet's
sympathy with the physical. The passage is more valuable as revealing
that sympathy, from the fact that it's one of his additions to Euripides :

> " there stood the strength,
> Happy, as always ; something grave, perhaps ;
> The great vein-cordage on the fret-worked brow,
> Black-swollen, beaded yet with battle-drops
> The yellow hair o' the hero !—his big frame
> A-quiver with each muscle sinking back
> Into the sleepy smooth it leaped from late.
> Under the great guard of one arm, there leant
> A shrouded something, live and woman-like,
> Propped by the heart-beats 'neath the lion-coat.
> When he had finished his survey, it seemed,
> The heavings of the heart began subside,
> The helping breath returned, and last the smile
> Shone out, all Herakles was back again,
> As the words followed the saluting hand."

It is not so much the glory of flesh which Euripides represents in
Herakles, as the indulgence of appetite, at a time, too, when that
indulgence is made to appear the more culpable and gross.

This idea of "the value and significance of flesh," it is important to
note, along with the predominant spiritual bearing of Browning's
poetry. It articulates everywhere the spiritual, so to speak—makes it
healthy and robust, and protects it against volatility and from running
into mysticism.

Shelley's poetry is wanting in this articulation.

This much I wished to say introductory to my special subject.
After reading closely all B.'s poetry, much of it many times over, I
asked myself the question, What great idea or ideas do I feel to be the
most strongly enforced in his Poetry? and the spontaneous reply to
myself was, The idea of Personality as a quickening, regenerating power,
and of Art as an intermediate agency of Personality. These two ideas
I endeavour to set forth in this paper.

I. *The Idea of Personality as embodied in Browning's Poetry.*

A cardinal idea in Browning's poetry is the regeneration of men through a personality who brings fresh stuff for them to mould, interpret, and prove right,—new feeling fresh from God—whose life reteaches them what life should be, what faith is, loyalty and simpleness, all once revealed, but taught them so long since that they have but mere tradition of the fact,—truth copied falteringly from copies faint, the early traits all dropped away. (*Luria.*) The intellect plays a secondary part. Its place is behind the instinctive, spiritual antennæ which conduct along their trembling lines, fresh stuff for the intellect to stamp and keep—fresh instinct for it to translate into law.

"A people is but the attempt of many to rise to the completer life of one." (*A Soul's Tragedy.*)

Only the man who supplies new feeling fresh from God, quickens and regenerates the race, and sets it on the King's highway from which it has wandered into byways—not the man of mere intellect, of unkindled soul, that supplies only stark-naked thought. Through the former, "God stooping shows sufficient of His light for those i' the dark to rise by." (*R. and B., Pompilia.*) In him men discern "the dawn of the next nature, the new man whose will they venture in the place of theirs, and whom they trust to find them out new ways to the new heights which yet he only sees." (*Luria.*) It is by reaching towards, and doing fealty to, the greater spirit which attracts and absorbs their own, that, "trace by trace old memories reappear, old truth returns, their slow thought does its work, and all's re-known." (*Luria.*)

> "Some existence like a pact
> And protest against Chaos" (*Sordello*, p. 168).
>
> . . . "The fullest effluence of the finest mind,
> All in degree, no way diverse in kind
> From minds above it, minds which, more or less
> Lofty or low, move seeking to impress
> Themselves on somewhat ; but one mind has climbed
> Step after step, by just ascent sublimed.
> Thought is the soul of act, and, stage by stage,
> Is soul from body still to disengage,
> As tending to a freedom which rejects
> Such help, and incorporeally affects
> The world, producing deeds but not by deeds,
> Swaying, in others, frames itself exceeds,
> Assigning them the simpler tasks it used
> To patiently perform till Song produced
> Acts, by thoughts only, for the mind : divest
> Mind of e'en Thought, and, lo, God's unexpressed
> Will dawns above us!" (*Sordello*, p. 168, 169).

A dangerous tendency of civilization is that towards crystallization— towards hardened, inflexible conventionalisms which "refuse the soul its way."

Such crystallization, such conventionalisms, yield only to the dissolving power of the spiritual warmth of life-full personalities.

The quickening, regenerating power of personality is everywhere exhibited in Browning's poetry. It is emphasized in *Luria*, and in the Monologues of the Canon Caponsacchi and Pompilia, in the *Ring and the Book;* it shines out, or glints forth, in *Colombe's Birthday*, in *Saul*, in *Sordello*, and in all the Love poems. I would say, *en passant*, that Love is always treated by Browning as a *spiritual* claim; while *duty* may be only a worldly one. *See* especially the poem entitled *Bifurcation*. In *Balaustion's Adventure: including a transcript from Euripides*, the regenerating power of personality may be said to be the leavening idea, which the poet has introduced into the Greek play. It is entirely absent in the original. It baptizes, so to speak, the Greek play, and converts it into a Christian poem. It is the "new truth" of the poet's *Christmas Eve.*

After the mourning friends have spoken their words of consolation to the bereaved husband, the last word being, "Dead, thy wife—living, the love she left," Admetos "turned on the comfort, with no tears, this time. *He was beginning to be like his wife.* I told you of that pressure to the point, word slow pursuing word in monotone, Alkestis spoke with; so Admetos, now, solemnly bore the burden of the truth. And as the voice of him grew, gathered strength, and groaned on, and persisted to the end, we felt how deep had been descent in grief, and *with what change he came up now to light*, and left behind such littleness as tears."

And when Alkestis was brought back by Herakles, "the hero twitched the veil off: and there stood, with such fixed eyes and such slow smile, Alkestis' silent self! It was the crowning grace of that great heart to keep back joy: procrastinate the truth until the wife, who had made proof and found the husband wanting, might essay once more, hear, see, and feel him *renovated* now—*able to do, now, all herself had done, risen to the height of her:* so, hand in hand, the two might go together, live and die." (Compare with this the restoration of Hermione to her husband, in *The Winter's Tale*, Act V.)

A good intellect has been characterized as the chorus of Divinity. Substitute for "good intellect," "an exalted magnetic personality," and the thought is deepened. An exalted magnetic personality is the chorus of Divinity, which in the great Drama of Humanity, guides and interprets the feelings and sympathies of other souls and thus adjusts their attitudes toward the Divine. It is not the highest function of such a personality to *teach*, but rather to *inform*, in the earlier and deeper sense of the word. Whatever mere doctrine he may promulgate, is of inferior importance to the spontaneous action of his concrete life, in which the True, the Beautiful, and the Good, breathe and live. What is born in the brain dies there, it may be; at best, it does not, and cannot of itself, lead up to the full concrete life. It is only through the spontaneous and unconscious fealty which an inferior does to a superior soul (a fealty resulting from the responsiveness of spirit to spirit), that the former is slowly and silently transformed into a more or less approximate image of the latter. The stronger personality leads the weaker on by paths which the weaker knows not, upward he leads him, though his steps be slow and vacillating. Humility, in the Christian sense, means this fealty to the higher. It doesn't mean self-abasement, self-depreciation, as it has been understood to mean, by both the Romish and the Protestant Church. Pride, in the Christian sense, is the closing of the doors of the soul to a great magnetic guest.

Browning beautifully expresses the transmission of personality in his *Saul*. But according to Browning's idea, personality cannot strictly be said to be transmitted. Personality rather evokes its *like* from other souls, which are "all in degree, no way diverse in kind."—*Sordello*, p. 168.

David has reached an advanced stage, in his symbolic song to Saul. He thinks, now, what next he shall urge "to sustain him where song had restored him?—Song filled to the verge his cup with the wine of this life, pressing all that it yields of mere fruitage, the strength and the beauty: beyond, on what fields, glean a vintage more potent and perfect to brighten the eye and bring blood to the lip, and commend them the cup they put by?" So once more the string of the harp makes response to his spirit, and he sings :

> "In our flesh grows the branch of this life, in our soul it bears fruit.
> Thou hast marked the slow rise of the tree,—how its stem trembled first
> Till it passed the kid's lip, the stag's antler ; then safely outburst
> The fan-branches all round ; and thou mindest when these, too, in turn
> Broke a-bloom and the palm-tree seemed perfect ; yet more was to learn,
> E'en the good that comes in with the palm fruit. Our dates shall we slight,
> When their juice brings a cure for all sorrow? or care for the plight
> Of the palm's self whose slow growth produced them? Not so! stem and branch
> Shall decay, nor be known in their place, while the palm-wine shall staunch
> Every wound of man's spirit in winter. I pour thee such wine.
> Leave the flesh to the fate it was fit for! the spirit be thine!
> By the spirit, when age shall o'ercome thee, thou still shalt enjoy
> More indeed, than at first when inconscious, the life of a boy.
> Crush that life, and behold its wine running! each deed thou hast done
> Dies, revives, goes to work in the world ; until e'en as the sun
> Looking down on the earth, though clouds spoil him, though tempests efface,
> Can find nothing his own deed produced not, must everywhere trace
> The results of his past summer-prime,—so, *each ray of thy will*,

Every flash of thy passion and prowess, long over, shall thrill
Thy whole people, the countless, with ardour, till they too give forth
A like cheer to their sons: who in turn, fill the South and the North
With the radiance thy deed was the germ of."

In the concluding lines is set forth what might be characterized as the apostolic succession of a great personality—the succession of those " who in turn fill the south and the north with the radiance his deed was the germ of."

What follows in David's song gives expression to the other mode of transmitting a great personality—that is, through records that "give unborn generations their due and their part in his being," and also to what those records owe their effectiveness, and are saved from becoming a dead letter.

"Is Saul dead? In the depth of the vale make his tomb—bid arise
A grey mountain of marble heaped four-square, till, built to the skies,
Let it mark where the great First King slumbers: whose fame would ye
    know ?
Up above see the rock's naked face, where the record shall go
In great characters cut by the scribe,—Such was Saul, so he did;
With the sages directing the work, by the populace chid,—
For not half, they'll affirm, is comprised there! Which fault to amend,
In the grove with his kind grows the cedar, whereon they shall spend
(See, in tablets 'tis level above them) their praise, and record
With the gold of the graver, Saul's story,—the statesman's great word
Side by side with the poet's sweet comment. The river's a-wave
With smooth paper-reeds grazing each other when prophet-winds rave :
So the pen gives unborn generations their due and their part
In thy being! Then, first of the mighty, thank God that thou art!"

What is said in this passage is applicable to the record we have of Christ's life upon earth. Christianity has only to a very limited extent been perpetuated through the letter of the New Testament. It has been perpetuated chiefly through transmissions of personalities, through apostolic succession, in a general sense, and through embodiments of his spirit in art and literature—"the stateman's great word," "the poet's sweet comment." Were it not for this transmission of the quickening power of personality, the New Testament would be, to a great extent, a dead letter. It owes its significance to the quickened spirit which is brought to the reading of it. The personality of Christ could not be, through a plastic sympathy, moulded out of the New Testament records without the aid of intermediate personalities.

The Messianic idea was not peculiar to the Jewish race—the idea of a Person, gathering up within himself, in an effective fullness and harmony, the restorative elements of humanity, which have lost their power through dispersion and consequent obscuration. There have been Messiahs of various orders and ranks, in every age,—great personalities that have realized to a greater or less extent (though there has been but one, the God-Man, who fully realized), the spiritual potentialities in man, that have stood upon the sharpest heights as beacons to their fellows. In the individual, the species has, as it were, been gathered up, epitomized, and intensified, and he has thus been a prophecy, and, to some extent, a fulfilment of human destiny.

"A poet must be earth's *essential* king," as Sordello asserts, and he is that by virtue of his exerting or shedding the influence of, his essential personality. "If caring not to exert the proper essence of his royalty, he, the poet, trifle malapert with accidents instead—good things assigned as heralds of a better thing behind"—he is "deposed from his kingly throne, and his glory is taken from him." Of himself Sordello says: "The power he took most pride to test, whereby all forms of life had been professed at pleasure, forms already on the earth, was but a means of power beyond, whose birth should, in its novelty, be kingship's proof. Now, whether he came near or kept aloof the several forms he longed to imitate, not there the kingship lay, he sees too late. Those forms, unalterable first as last, proved him her copier, not the protoplast of nature: what could come of being free by action to exhibit tree for tree, bird, beast, for beast and bird, or prove earth bore one veritable man or woman more? Means to an end such proofs are: what the end?"

The answer given involves the great Browning idea of the quickening power of personality: "Let essence, whatsoe'er it be, extend—never contract!"

By "essence" we must understand that which "constitutes man's self, is what Is," as the dying John, in *A Death in the Desert*, expresses it—that which backs the active powers and the conscious intellect, "subsisting whether they assist or no."

"Let essence, whatsoe'er it be, extend—never contract!" Sordello says. "Already you include the multitude;" that is, you gather up, in yourself, in an effective fullness and harmony, what lies scattered and ineffective in the multitude; "then let the multitude include yourself;" that is, be substantiated, essenced with yourself; "and the result were new: themselves before, the multitude turn *you*" (become yourself). • "This were to live and move and have, in them, your being, and secure a diadem you should transmit (because no cycle yearns beyond itself, but on itself returns) when the full sphere in wane, the world o'erlaid long since with you, shall have in turn obeyed some orb still prouder, some displayer, still more potent than the last, of human will, and some new king depose the old."

This is a most important passage to get hold of in studying Browning.

It may almost be said to gather up Browning's philosophy of life in a nutshell.

There's a passage to the same effect in *Balaustion's Adventure*, in regard to the transmission of the poet's essence.   The enthusiastic Rhodian girl, Balaustion, after she has told the play of Euripides, years after her adventure, to her four friends, Petalé, Phullis, Charopé, and Chrusion, says,

"I think I see how . . . you, I, or any one, might mould a new Admetos, new Alkestis.   Ah, that brave bounty of poets, the one royal race that ever was, or will be, in this world !   They give no gift that bounds itself, and ends i' the giving and the taking : theirs so breeds i' the heart and soul of the taker, so transmutes the man who only was a man before, that he grows god-like in his turn, can give—he also : share the poet's privilege, bring forth new good, new beauty from the old.   As though the cup that gave the wine, gave too the god's prolific giver of the grape, that vine, was wont to find out, fawn around his footstep, springing still to bless the dearth, at bidding of a Mainad."

II. *Art as an Intermediate Agency of Personality.*

If Browning's idea of the quickening, the regeneration, the rectification of personality, through a higher personality, be fully comprehended, his idea of the great function of Art, as an intermediate agency of personality, will become plain.   To emphasize the latter idea may be said to be the ultimate purpose of his masterpiece, *The Ring and the Book*.

The complexity of the circumstances involved in the Roman murder case, adapts it admirably to the poet's purpose—namely, to exhibit the swervings of human judgment in spite of itself, and the conditions upon which the rectification of that judgment depends.

This must be taken, however, as only the articulation, the frame-work, of the great poem.   It is richer in materials, of the most varied character, than any other long poem in existence.   To notice one feature of the numberless features of the poem, which might be noticed, Browning's deep and subtle insight into the genius of the Romish Church is shown in it more fully than in any other of his poems,—though special phases of that genius are distinctly exhibited in numerous poems : a remarkable one being *The Bishop orders his Tomb at St. Praxed's Church*.   It is questionable whether any work of any kind has ever exhibited that genius more fully and distinctly than *The Ring and the Book* exhibits it.   The reader breathes throughout the ecclesiastical atmosphere of the Eternal City.

To return from this digression, the several monologues of which the poem consists, with the exception of those of the Canon Caponsacchi,

Pompilia, and the Pope, are each curious and subtle and varied exponents of the workings, without the guidance of instinct at the heart (*Sordello*, p. 179), of the prepossessed, prejudiced intellect, and of the sources of its swerving into error. What is said of the "feel after the vanished truth" in the monologue entitled *Half Rome*—the speaker being a jealous husband—will serve to characterize, in a general way, " the feel after truth " exhibited in the other monologues : " honest enough, as the way is : all the same, harbouring in the *centre of its sense* a hidden germ of failure, shy but sure, should neutralize that honesty and leave that feel for truth at fault, as the way is too. Some prepossession such as starts amiss, by but a hair's-breadth at the shoulder-blade, the arm o' the feeler, dip he ne'er so brave ; and so leads waveringly, lets fall wide o' the mark his finger meant to find, and fix truth at the bottom, that deceptive speck."

The poet could hardly have employed a more effective metaphor in which to embody the idea of mental swerving. The several monologues all going over the same ground, are artistically justified in their exhibiting, each of them, a quite distinct form of this swerving. For the ultimate purpose of the poet, it needed to be strongly emphasized. The student of the poem is amazed, long before he gets over all these monologues, at the Protean capabilities of the poet's own intellect. It takes all conceivable attitudes toward the case, and each seems to be a perfectly easy one.

These monologues all lead up to the great moral of the poem, which is explicitly set forth at the end, namely, " that our human speech is naught, our human testimony false, our fame and human estimation, words and wind. Why take the artistic way to prove so much ? Because, it is the glory and good of Art, that Art remains the one way possible of speaking truth, to mouths like mine, at least. How look a brother in the face and say, Thy right is wrong, eyes hast thou yet art blind, thine ears are stuffed and stopped, despite their length : and, oh, the foolishness thou countest faith ! Say this as silvery as tongue can troll—the anger of the man may be endured, the shrug, the disappointed eyes of him are not so bad to bear—but here's the plague, that all this trouble comes of telling truth, which truth, by when it reaches him, looks false, seems to be just the thing it would supplant, nor recognizable by whom it left : while falsehood would have done the work of truth. But Art, —wherein man nowise speaks to men, only to mankind,—Art may tell a truth obliquely, *do the thing shall breed the thought*," that is, bring what is *implicit* within the soul, into the right attitude to become *explicit* —bring about a silent adjustment through sympathy induced by the concrete ; in other words, prepare the way for the perception of the truth—"do the thing shall breed the thought, nor wrong the thought missing the mediate word;" meaning, that Art, so to speak, is the word made flesh,—*is* the truth, and, as Art, has nothing directly to do with the explicit. "So may you paint your picture, twice show truth, beyond mere imagery on the wall,—so, note by note, bring music from your mind, deeper than ever the Andante dived,—so write a book shall mean beyond the facts, suffice the eye and save the soul beside."

And what is the inference the poet would have us draw from this passage? It is, that the life and efficacy of Art depends on the personality of the artist, which "has informed, transpierced, thridded and so thrown fast the facts else free, as right through ring and ring runs the djereed and binds the loose, one bar without a break."[1] And it is really this fusion of the artist's soul, which kindles, quickens, *informs* those who contemplate, respond to, reproduce sympathetically within themselves the greater spirit which attracts and absorbs their own. The work of Art is apocalyptic of the artist's own personality. It *cannot* be impersonal. As is the temper of his spirit, so is, *must* be, the temper of his Art product.[2] *Titus Andronicus* could not have been written by Shakspere. Even if he had written it as a burlesque of such a play as Marlow's *Jew of Malta*, he could not have avoided some revelation of that sense of moral proportion which is omnipresent in his Plays. But there's no Shakspere in *Titus Andronicus*. Are we not certain of what manner of man Shakspere was from his Works (notwithstanding that critics are ever asserting their impersonality)—far more certain than if his biography had been written by one who knew him all his life, and sustained to him the most intimate relations? We know Shakspere, or, he *can* be known, if the requisite conditions are met, better, perhaps, than any other great author that ever lived—know, in the deepest sense of the word, in a sense other than that in which we know Dr. Johnson, through Boswell's Biography. The moral proportion which is so signal a characteristic of his Plays could not have been imparted to them by the conscious intellect. It was *shed* from his spiritual constitution.

By "speaking truth" in Art's way, Browning means, inducing a right *attitude* toward, a full and free *sympathy* with, the True, which is a far more important and effective way of speaking truth than delivering truth *in re.* A work of Art, worthy of the name, need not be true to fact, but must be true in its spiritual attitude, and being thus true, it will tend to induce a corresponding attitude in those who do fealty to

[1] *The Ring and the Book.*
[2] 'And long it was not after, when I was confirmed in this opinion, that he who would not be frustrate of his hope to write well hereafter in laudable things, ought himself to be a true poem."—*Milton's Apology for Smectymnuus.*

it   It will have the influence, though in an inferior degree, it may be,
of a magnetic personality. Personality is the ultimate source of spiritual
quickening and adjustment. Literature and all forms of Art are but the
intermediate agencies of personalities. The artist cannot be separated
from his art. As is the artist so *must* be his art. The *aura*, so to
speak, of a great work of Art, must come from the artist's own personality. The spiritual worth of Shakspere's *Winter's Tale* is not at all
impaired by the fact that Bohemia is made a maritime country, that
Whitsun pastorals and Christian burial, and numerous other features
of Shakspere's own age, are introduced into pagan times, that Queen
Hermione speaks of herself as a daughter of the Emperor of Russia, that
her statue is represented as executed by Julio Romano, an Italian painter
of the 16th century, that a puritan sings psalms to hornpipes, and, to
crown all, that messengers are sent to consult the oracle of Apollo, at
Delphi, which is represented as an island ! All this jumble, this galli-
maufry, I say, does not impair the spiritual worth of the play. As
an Art-product, it invites a rectified attitude toward the True and
the Sweet.

If we look at the letter of the trial scene in *The Merchant of Venice*,
it borders on the absurd ; but if we look at its spirit, we see the
Shaksperian attitude of soul which makes for righteousness, for the
righteousness which is inherent in the moral constitution of the universe.

The inmost, secretest life of Shakspere's Plays came from the
personality, the inmost, secretest life, of the man Shakspere. We
might, with the most alert sagacity, note and tabulate and aggregate
his myriad phenomenal merits as a dramatic writer, but we might still
be very far from that something back of them all, or rather that
immanent something, that mystery of personality, that microcosmos,
that "inmost centre, where truth abides in fullness," as Browning
makes Paracelsus characterize it, "constituting man's self, is what Is,"
as he makes the dying John characterize it, in *A Death in the Desert*,
that "innermost of the inmost, most interior of the interne," as Mrs.
Browning characterizes it, " the hidden Soul," as Dallas characterizes it,
which is projected into, and constitutes the soul of, the Plays, and which
is reached through an unconscious and mystic sympathy on the part
of him who habitually communes with and does fealty to them. That
personality, that living force, coöperated spontaneously and unconsciously with the conscious powers, in the creative process ; and when
we enter into a sympathetic communion with the concrete result of
that creative process, our own mysterious personalities, being essentially
identical with, though less quickened than, Shakspere's, respond,
though it may be but feebly, to his. This response is the highest result

of the study of Shákspere's works. The dramas are really means to
this end.

It is a significant fact that Shaksperian critics and editors, for
nearly two centuries, have been a *genus irritabile*, to which *genus*
Shakspere himself certainly did not belong. The explanation may
partly be, that they have been too much occupied with the *letter*,
and have fretted their nerves in angry dispute about readings and
interpretations; as theologians have done in their study of the sacred
records, instead of endeavouring to reach, through the letter, the personality of which the letter is but a manifestation more or less imperfect.
To *know* a personality is, of course, a spiritual knowledge—the result
of sympathy, that is, spiritual responsiveness. Intellectually it is but
little more important to know one rather than another personality. The
highest worth of all great works of genius is due to the fact that they
are apocalyptic of great personalities.

Art says, as the Divine Person said, whose personality and the
personalities fashioned after it, have transformed and moulded the
ages, "Follow me!" Deep was the meaning wrapt up in this command : it was, Do as I do, live as I live, not from an intellectual
perception of the principles involved in my life, but through a full
sympathy, through the awakening, vitalizing, actuating power of the
incarnate Word.

Art also says, as did the voice from the wilderness, inadequately
translated, "*Repent* ye, for the kingdom of heaven is at hand."
(Μετανοεῖτε ἤγγικε γὰρ ἡ Βασιλεία τῶν οὐρανῶν.) Rather, be transformed, or, as De Quincey puts it, "Wheel into a new centre your
spiritual system; *geocentric* has that system been up to this hour—
that is, having earth and the earthly for its starting-point; henceforward
make it *heliocentric* (that is, with the sun, or the heavenly, for its
principle of motion)."

The poetry of Browning everywhere says this, and says it more
emphatically than that of any other poet in our literature. It says
everywhere, that not through knowledge, not through a sharpened
intellect, but through repentance, in the deeper sense to which I have
just alluded, through conversion, through wheeling into a new centre
its spiritual system, the soul attains to saving truth. Salvation with him
means that revelation of the soul to itself, that awakening, quickening,
actuating, attitude-adjusting, of the soul, which sets it gravitating toward
the Divine.

Browning's idea of Conversion is, perhaps, most distinctly expressed
in a passage in the Monologue of the Canon Caponsacchi, in *The Ring
and the Book*, wherein he sets forth the circumstances under which his

F

soul was wheeled into a new centre, after a life of dalliance and elegant folly, and made aware of "the marvellous dower of the life it was gifted and filled with." He has been telling the judges, before whom he has been summoned, the story of the letters forged by Guido to entrap him and Pompilia, and of his having seen "right through the thing that tried to pass for truth and solid, not an empty lie." The conclusion and the resolve he comes to, are expressed in the soliloquy which he repeats to the judges, as having uttered at the time : "So, he not only forged the words for her but words for me, made letters he called mine : what I sent, he retained, gave these in place, all by the mistress messenger ! As I recognized her, at potency of truth, so she, by the crystalline soul, knew me, never mistook the signs. Enough of this— let the wraith go to nothingness again, here is the orb, have only thought for her !" What follows admits us to the very *heart* of Browning's poetry—admits us to the great Idea which is almost, in these days, strange to say, peculiarly his—which no other poet, certainly, of this intellectual, analytic, scientific age, with its "patent, truth-extracting processes," has brought out with the same degree of distinctness—the great Idea which may be variously characterized as that of soul-kindling, soul-quickening, adjustment of soul-attitude, regeneration, conversion, through *personality*—a kindling, quickening, adjustment, regeneration, conversion, in which *thought* is not even a coefficient. As expressed in Sordello, "Divest mind of e'en thought, and, lo, God's unexpressed will dawns above us !" (p. 169). "Thought?" the Canon goes on to say, "Thought? nay, Sirs, what shall follow was not thought : I have thought sometimes, and thought long and hard. I have stood before, gone round a serious thing, tasked my whole mind to touch and clasp it close, . . . God and man, and what duty I owe both,—I dare to say I have confronted these in thought : but no such faculty helped here. I put forth no thought,—powerless, all that night I paced the city : it was the first Spring. By the *invasion I lay passive to*, in rushed new things, the old were rapt away ; alike abolished—the imprisonment of the outside air, the inside weight o' the world that pulled me down. Death meant, to spurn the ground, soar to the sky,—die well and you do that. The very immolation made the bliss ; death was the heart of life, and all the harm my folly had crouched to avoid, now proved a veil hiding all gain my wisdom strove to grasp. . . . Into another state, under new rule I knew myself was passing swift and sure ; whereof the initiatory pang approached, felicitous annoy, as bitter-sweet as when the virgin band, the victors chaste, feel at the end the earthy garments drop, and rise with something of a rosy shame into immortal nakedness : so I lay, and let come the proper throe would thrill into the ecstasy and out-throb pain. I' the gray of the dawn it was I found myself facing the pillared front o' the Pieve—mine, my church : it seemed to say for the first time, 'But am not I the Bride, the mystic love o' the Lamb, who took thy plighted troth, my priest, to fold thy warm heart on my heart of stone and freeze thee nor unfasten any more? This is a fleshly woman,—let the free bestow their life blood, thou art pulseless now!' . . . Now, when I found out first that life and death are means to an end, that passion uses both, indisputably mistress of the man whose form of worship is self-sacrifice—now, from the stone lungs sighed the scrannel voice, 'Leave that live passion, come be dead with me!' As if, i' the fabled garden, I had gone on great adventure, plucked in ignorance hedge-fruit, and feasted to satiety, laughing at such high fame for hips and haws, and scorned the achievement : then come all at once o' the prize o' the place, the thing of perfect gold, the apple's self : and, scarce my eye on that, was 'ware as well of the seven-fold dragon's watch. Sirs, I obeyed.[1] Obedience was too strange,— this new thing that had been *struck into me by the look of the lady*,— to dare disobey the first authoritative word. 'Twas God's. I had been *lifted to the level of her*, could take such sounds into my sense. I said, 'We two are cognizant o' the Master now ; it is she bids me bow the head : how true, I am a priest ! I see the function here ; I thought the other way self-sacrifice : this is the true, seals up the perfect sum. I pay it, sit down, silently obey.' "

Numerous and varied expressions of the idea of conversion set forth in this passage, occur in Browning's poetry, evidencing his deep sense of this great and indispensable condition of soul-life, of being born anew (or from above, as it should be rendered in the Gospel, ἄνωθεν, that is, through the agency of a higher personality), in order to see the kingdom of God—evidencing his conviction that "the kingdom of God cometh not with observation : for lo ! the kingdom of God is within you." In the poem entitled *Cristina*, he says, or the speaker is made to say,

" Oh we're sunk enough here, God knows ! but not quite so sunk that moments,
 Sure tho' seldom, are denied us, when the spirit's true endowments
 Stand out plainly from its false ones, and apprise it if pursuing
 Or the right way or the wrong way, to its triumph or undoing.
 There are flashes struck from midnights, there are fire-flames noondays kindle,
 Whereby piled-up honours perish, whereby swollen ambitions dwindle,
 While just this or that poor impulse, which for once had play unstifled,
 Seems the sole work of a life-time that away the rest have trifled."

And again, when the Pope in *The Ring and the Book* has come to the decision to sign the death-warrant of Guido and his accomplices, he

---

[1] He means the entreaty of Pompilia, to rescue her from her husband, Count Guido Franceschini, and take her to Rome, to the Comparini, her putative parents.

says : "For the main criminal I have no hope except in such a *suddenness of fate*. I stood at Naples once, a night so dark I could have scarce conjectured there was earth anywhere, sky or sea or world at all : but the night's black was burst through by a blaze—thunder struck blow on blow, earth groaned and bore, through her whole length of mountain visible : there lay the city thick and plain with spires, and, like a ghost disshrouded, white the sea. *So may the truth be flashed out by one blow, and Guido see, one instant, and be saved.* Else I avert my face, nor follow him into that sad obscure sequestered state where God *unmakes but to remake* the soul he else made first in vain ; which must not be. Enough, for I may die this very night : and how should I dare die, this man let live ? Carry this forthwith to the Governor ! "

Browning is the most essentially Christian of living poets. Religion with him is, indeed, the all-in-all ; but not any particular form of it as a finality. This is not a world for finalities of any kind, as he constantly teaches us : it is a world of broken arcs, not of perfect rounds. Formulations of some kind he would, no doubt, admit there must be, as in everything else ; but with him all formulations and tabulations of beliefs, especially such as "make square to a finite eye the circle of infinity,"[1] are, at the best, only *provisional*, and, at the worst, lead to spiritual standstill, spiritual torpor, "a ghastly smooth life, dead at heart."[2] The essential nature of Christianity is contrary to special prescription, do this or do that, believe this or believe that. Christ gave no recipes. Christianity is with Browning, and this he sets forth again and again, a *life*, quickened and motived and nourished by the Personality of Christ. And all that he says of this Personality can be accepted by every Christian, whatever theological view he may entertain of Christ. Christ's teachings he regards but as *incidents* of that Personality, and the records we have of his sayings and doings, but a fragment, a somewhat distorted one, it may be, out of which we must, by a mystic and plastic sympathy, aided by the Christ spirit which is immanent in the Christian world, mould the Personality, and do fealty to it. The Christian must endeavour to be able to say, with the dying John, in Browning's *Death in the Desert*, "To me that story,—ay, that Life and Death of which I wrote 'it was'—to me, it is." ·

If there were any elements in Christ's nature not potentially in our own, those elements would not be of any service to us. Our own natures can be quickened only by what is identical with them.

The poem entitled *Christmas Eve* contains the fullest and most explicit expression, in Browning, of his idea of the personality of Christ as being the all-in-all of Christianity.

---

[1] *Christmas Eve.*   [2] *Easter Day*, 17th v. from end.

"the truth in God's breast
Lies trace for trace upon ours impressed:
Though He is so bright and we so dim,
We are made in His image to witness Him
And were no eye in us to tell,
Instructed by no inner sense,
The light of Heaven from the dark of Hell,
That light would want its evidence,—
Though Justice, Good, and Truth, were still
Divine, if, by some demon's will,
Hatred and wrong had been proclaimed
Law through the worlds, and Right misnamed,
No mere exposition of morality
Made or in part or in totality,
Should win you to give it worship, therefore:
And if no better proof you will care for,
—Whom do you count the worst man upon earth?
Be sure, he knows, in his conscience, more
Of what Right is, than arrives at birth
In the best man's acts that we bow before:
And thence I conclude that the real God-function
Is to furnish a motive and injunction
For practising what we know already.
And such an injunction and such a motive
As the God in Christ, do you waive, and 'heady,
High-minded,' hang your tablet votive
Outside the fane on a finger-post?
Morality to the uttermost,
Supreme in Christ as we all confess,
Why need *we* prove would avail no jot
To make Him God, if God he were not?
Where is the point where Himself lays stress?
Does the precept run ' Believe in Good,
In Justice, Truth, now understood
For the first time'?—or ' Believe in ME,
Who lived and died, yet essentially
Am Lord of Life'?[1] Whoever can take
The same to his heart and for mere love's sake
Conceive of the love,—that man obtains
A new truth; no conviction gains
Of an old one only, made intense
By a fresh appeal to his faded sense."

If all Christendom could take this remarkable poem of *Christmas Eve* to its heart, its tolerance, its Catholic spirit, and, more than all, the fealty it exhibits to the Personality who essentially is Lord of Life, what a revolution it would undergo! and what a mass of dogmatic and polemic theology would become utterly obsolete! The most remarkable thing, perhaps, about the vast body of Christian theology which has

[1] " Subsists no law of life outside of life."

*   *   *   *   *

" The Christ himself had been no Lawgiver,
Unless he had given the *life*, too, with the law."
Mrs. Browning's *Aurora Leigh*.

' een developed during the eighteen centuries which have elapsed since Christ was in the flesh, is, that it is occupied so largely, it might almost be said, exclusively, with what Christ and his disciples *taught*, and with fierce discussions about the manifold meanings which have been ingeniously extorted from the imperfect *record* of what he taught. British museum libraries of polemics have been written in defence of what Christ himself would have been indifferent to, and written with an animosity towards opponents which has been crystallized in a phrase now applied in a general way to any intense hate—*Odium Theologicum.*

If the significance of Christ's mission, or a large part of it, is to be estimated by his teachings, from those teachings important deductions must be made, as many of them had been delivered long before his time. As a mere teacher or moralist, he could not have maintained any important place in history.

Browning has something to say on this point, in this same poem of *Christmas Eve*—

> " Truth's atmosphere may grow mephitic
> When Papist struggles with Dissenter,
> Impregnating its pristine clarity,
> —One, by his daily fare's vulgarity,
> Its gust of broken meat and garlic ;
> —One, by his soul's too-much presuming
> To turn the frankincense's fuming
> And vapors of the candle starlike
> Into the cloud her wings she buoys on.
> Each that thus sets the pure air seething,
> May poison it for healthy breathing—
> But the Critic leaves no air to poison ;
> Pumps out by a ruthless ingenuity
> Atom by atom, and leaves you—vacuity.
> Thus much of Christ, does he reject?
> And what retain? His intellect?
> What is it I must reverence duly?
> Poor intellect for worship, truly,
> Which tells me simply what was told
> (If mere morality, bereft
> Of the God in Christ, be all that's left)
> Elsewhere by voices manifold ;
> With this advantage, that the stater
> Made nowise the important stumble
> Of adding, he, the sage and humble,
> Was also one with the Creator."

Browning's poetry is instinct with the essence of Christianity—the *life* of Christ. There is no other poetry, there is no writing of any form, in this age, which so emphasizes the fact (and it's the most consoling of all facts connected with the Christian religion), that the Personality, Jesus Christ, is the impregnable fortress of Christianity. Whatever assaults and inroads may be made upon the original records by Göttingen professors, upon the august fabric of the Church, with its creeds and dogmas, and formularies, and paraphernalia, this fortress will stand forever, and mankind will forever seek and find refuge in it.

The poem entitled *Cleon* bears the intimation (there's nothing directly expressed thereupon), that Christianity is something distinct from, and beyond, whatever the highest civilization of the world, the civilization of Greece, attained to before Christ. Through him the world obtained "a new truth—no conviction gained of an old one merely, made intense by a fresh appeal to the faded sense."

Cleon, the poet, writes to Protos in his Tyranny (that is, in the Greek sense, Sovereignty). Cleon must be understood as representing the ripe, composite result, as an individual, of what constituted the glory of Greece—her poetry, sculpture, architecture, painting, and music, and also her philosophy. He acknowledges the gifts which the King has lavished upon him. By these gifts we are to understand the munificent national patronage accorded to the arts. "The master of thy galley still unlades gift after gift; they block my court at last and pile themselves along its portico royal with sunset, like a thought of thee."

By the slave women that are among the gifts sent to Cleon, seems to be indicated the degradation of the spiritual by its subjection to earthly ideals, as were the ideals of Greek art. This is more particularly indicated by the one white she-slave, the lyric woman, whom further on in his letter, Cleon promises the King he will make narrate (in lyric song we must suppose) his fortunes, speak his great words, and describe his royal face.

He continues, that in such an act of love,—the bestowal of princely gifts upon him whose song gives life its joy,—men shall remark the King's recognition of the use of life—that his spirit is equal to more than merely to help on life in straight ways, broad enough for vulgar souls, by ruling and the rest. He ascribes to the King, in the building of his tower (and by this must be understood the building up of his own selfhood), a higher motive than work for mere work's sake,—that higher motive being, the luring hope of some *eventual rest* atop of it (the tower), whence, all the tumult of the building hushed, the first of men may look out to the east.[1]

---

[1] Tennyson uses a similar figure in *The Two Voices*. The speaker, who is meditating whether "to be or not to be," says:

> "Were this not well, to bide mine hour,
> Though watching from a ruined tower
> How grows the day of human power."

The ruined tower is his own dilapidated self-hood, whence he takes his outlook upon the world.

By the eventual rest atop of the tower, is indicated the aim of the Greek civilization, to reach a calm within the finite, while the soul is constituted and destined to gravitate forever towards the infinite—to " force our straitened sphere . . . display completely here the mastery another life should learn " (*Sordello*, p. 23). The eventual rest in this world is not the Christian ideal. Earth-life, whatever its reach, and whatever its grasp, is to the Christian a broken arc, not a perfect round.

Cleon goes on to recount his accomplishments in the arts, and what he has done in philosophy, in reply to the first requirement of Protos's letter, Protos, as it appears, having heard of, and wonderingly enumer-ated, the great things Cleon has effected; and he has written to know the truth of the report. Cleon replies, that the epos on the King's hundred plates of gold is his, and his the little chaunt so sure to rise from every fishing-bark when, lights at prow, the seamen haul their nets; that the image of the sun-god on the light-house men turn from the sun's self to see, is his; that the Poecile, o'er-storied its whole length with painting, is his, too; that he knows the true proportions of man and woman, not observed before; that he has written three books on the soul, proving absurd all written hitherto, and putting us to ignorance again; that in music he has combined the moods, inventing one; that, in brief, all arts are his, and so known and recognized. At this he writes the King to marvel not. We of these latter days, he says, being more *composite*, appear not so great as our forerunners who, in their simple way, were greater in a certain single direction, than we ; but our composite way is greater. This life of men on earth, this sequence of the soul's achievements here, he finds reason to believe, was intended to be viewed eventually as a great whole, the individual soul being only a factor toward the realization of this great whole—toward spelling out, so to speak, Zeus's idea in the race. Those divine men of old, he goes on to say, reached each at one point, the outside verge that rounds our faculty, and where they reached, who could do more than reach ? I have not chanted, he says, verse like Homer's, nor swept string like Terpander, nor carved and painted men like Phidias and his friend ; I am not great as they are, point by point; but I have entered into sympathy with these four, running these into one soul, who, separate, ignored each other's arts. The wild flower was the larger—I have dashed rose-blood upon its petals, pricked its cup's honey with wine, and driven its seed to fruit, and show a better flower, if not so large.

And now he comes to the important questions in the King's letter— whether he, the poet, his soul thus in men's hearts, has not attained the very crown and proper end of life—whether, now life closeth up, he faces death with success in his right hand,—whether he fears death less than he, the King, does himself, the fortunate of men, who assigns the reason for thinking that he does that he, the poet, leaves much behind, his life stays in the poems men shall sing, the pictures men shall study, while the King's life, complete and whole now in its power and joy, dies altogether with his brain and arm, as *he* leaves not behind, as the poet does, works of art embodying the essence of his life which, through those works, will pass into the lives of men of all succeeding times. Cleon replies that if in the morning of philosophy, the King, with the light now in him, could have looked on all earth's tenantry, from worm to bird, ere man appeared, and if Zeus had questioned him whether he would improve on it, do more for visible creatures than was done, he would have answered, "Ay, by making each grow conscious in himself: all's perfect else, life's mechanics can no further go, and all this joy in natural life is put, like fire from off thy fingers into each, so exquisitely perfect is the same. But 'tis pure fire—and they mere matter are; it has *them*, not they *it*: and so I choose, for man, that a third thing shall stand apart from both, a quality arise within the soul, which, intro-active, made to supervise and feel the force it has, may view itself and so be happy. But it is this quality, Cleon continues, which makes man a failure. This sense of sense, this spirit consciousness, grew the only life worth calling life, the pleasure-house, watch-tower, and treasure-fortress of the soul, which whole surrounding flats of natural life seemed only fit to yield subsistence to; a tower that crowns a country. But alas! the soul now climbs it just to perish there, for thence we have discovered that there's a world of capability for joy, spread round about us, meant for us, inviting us; and still the soul craves all, and still the flesh replies, "Take no jot more than ere you climbed the tower to look abroad! Nay, so much less, as that fatigue has brought deduction to it." After expatiating on this sad state of man, he arrives at the same conclusion as the King in his letter: "I agree in sum, O King, with thy profound discouragement, who seest the wider but to sigh the more. Most progress is most failure! thou sayest well."

And now he takes up the last point of the King's letter, that he, the King, holds joy not impossible to one with artist-gifts, who leaves behind living works. Looking over the sea, as he writes, he says, "Yon rower with the moulded muscles there, lowering the sail, is nearer it than I." He presents with clearness, and with rigid logic, the *dilemma* of the growing soul; shows the vanity of living in works left behind, and in the memory of posterity, while he, the feeling, thinking, acting man, shall sleep in his urn. The horror of the thought makes him dare imagine at times some future state unlimited in capability for joy, as this is in *desire* for joy. But no! Zeus has not yet revealed such a state; and alas! he must have done so were it possible!

He concludes, "Live long and happy, and in that thought die, glad for what was! Farewell." And then, as a matter of minor importance, he informs the King, in a postscript, that he cannot tell his messenger aright where to deliver what he bears to one called Paulus. Protos, it must be understood, having heard of the fame of Paul, and being perplexed in the extreme, has written the great apostle to know of his doctrine. But Cleon writes that it is vain to suppose that a mere barbarian Jew, one circumcised, hath access to a secret which is shut from them, and that the King wrongs their philosophy in stooping to inquire of such an one. "Oh, he finds adherents, who does not. Certain slaves who touched on this same isle, preached him and Christ, and, as he gathered from a bystander, their doctrines could be held by no sane man."

There is a quiet beauty about this poem which must insinuate itself into the feelings of every reader. In tone it resembles the *Epistle of Karshish, the Arab physician.* The verse of both poems is very beautiful. No one can read these two poems, and *Bishop Blougram's Apology*, and *The Bishop orders his Tomb at St. Praxed's Church*, and not admit that Browning is a master of blank verse in its most difficult form—a form far more difficult than that of the epic blank verse of Milton, or the Idyllic blank verse of Tennyson, argumentative and freighted with thought, and, at the same time, almost chatty, as it is, and bearing in its course exquisitely poetical conceptions. The same may be said of much of the verse of *The Ring and the Book*, especially that of the monologues of the Canon Caponsacchi, Pompilia, the Pope, and Count Guido Franceschini. But this by the way.

Cleon belongs to a grand group of poems, in which Browning shows himself to be, as I've said, the most essentially Christian of living poets —the poet who, more emphatically than any of his contemporaries have done, has enforced the importance, the indispensableness of a new birth, the being born from above (ἄνωθεν) as the condition not only of soul vitality and progress, but also of intellectual rectitude. In this group of poems are embodied the profoundest principles of education—principles which it behoves the present generation of educators to look well to. The acquisition of knowledge is a good thing, the sharpening of the intellect is a good thing, the cultivation of philosophy is a good thing; but there's something of infinitely more importance than all these—it is, the rectification, the adjustment, through that mysterious operation we call sympathy, of the unconscious personality, the hidden soul, which co-operates with the active powers, with the conscious intellect, and, as this unconscious personality is rectified or unrectified, determines the active powers, the conscious intellect, for righteousness or unrighteousness.

The attentive reader of Browning's poetry must soon discover how remarkably homogeneous it is in spirit. There are many authors, and great authors too, the reading of whose collected works gives the impression of their having "tried their hand" at many things. No such impression is derivable from the voluminous poetry of Browning. Wide as is its range, one great and homogeneous spirit pervades and animates it all, from the earliest to the latest. No other living poet gives so decided an assurance of having a *burden* to deliver. An appropriate general title to his works would be, "The Burden of Robert Browning to the 19th century." His earliest poems are the least articulate, but there can be no question about their *attitude*. We know in what direction the poet has set his face—what his philosophy of life is, what soul-life means with him, what regeneration means, what edification means in its deepest sense of building up within us the spiritual temple. And if he had left this world after writing no more than those poems of his youth, *Pauline* and *Paracelsus*, a very fair *ex-pede-Herculem* estimate might have been made of the possibilities which he has since so grandly realized.

THE RELIGIOUS TEACHING OF BROWNING.

BY DOROTHEA BEALE.

(Read at the 10th Meeting of the Browning Society, on Friday, October 27, 1882.)

THERE are those who judge others, as the world does, by their faults and failures, who seem to think that in these the true character comes out; and there are those who, knowing that they have within themselves a high ideal, of which they fail, believe that the true character comes out in the best that we know of any one.

> "What I aspired to be.
> And was not, comforts me."

So they judge a thinker by his noblest works . Wordsworth by his *Ode to Duty* rather than by *The Idiot Boy;* Milton by his *Areopagitica* rather than his *Divorce* tracts; Shakspere by his *Hamlet.* Thus we love Browning for his great thoughts, for his high enthusiasm, for his faith in God, and man and woman. We come to him for his philosophy, and we care not to dwell upon the shortcomings, of which he is doubtless more conscious than we are, upon the superficial faults, which every one can see; rather would we bring to light the hidden treasures. We thank him for the comfort and strength he has given us. We know that he has enriched our sympathies, cheered us under failure and disappointment, and helped us to understand the meaning of life. But I think what draws most of us to him is this: we are struggling with the waves of doubt—storm-tost and ready to sink—and as we look at him, we see him with a smile on his face, calmly floating, his head above the waves, his body supported therein. He quietly tells us our safety is to do the same. He[1] teaches that to bury ourselves in the things of earth is death; to try to rise out of the conditions in which God has placed us may end in a Soul's Tragedy; to use the visible to sustain and teach, this is our wisdom during our life here, ere the disembodied Psyche can float up into more ethereal regions, and revel in the sunlight; and so he conciliates philosophy and religion.

He is ever cheerful and consoling, so that we turn to him in our

---

[1] See *Fifine.*

trouble. Are we oppressed with pessimism, discontented with all that is? He tells us this is the witness to our own nobility, and to a future immortality.

> " Progress is man's distinctive mark alone,
> Not God's, and not the beasts' : God is, they are,
> Man partly is, and wholly hopes to be." (*Death in the Desert.*)

> " 'Tis not what Man Does which exalts him, but what man Would do." (*Saul.*)

> "for mankind springs
> Salvation by each hindrance interposed ;
> They climb." (*Sordello.*)

> " They are perfect—how else? they shall never change ;
> We are faulty—why not? we have time in store." (*Pictures in Florence.*)

> " He said, 'What's time? Leave Now for dogs and apes !
> Man has Forever.'" (*Grammarian's Funeral.*)

Do we cry out that we are tired of battling with the waves, and does it seem a weary quest ever to be following the light, never reaching it? He tells us that gradual development is the condition of our spiritual health, *i. e.* of life.

> "——this gift of truth
> Once grasped, were this our soul's gain safe, and sure
> To prosper as the body's gain is wont,—
> Why man's probation would conclude."

Do we complain of error? He tells us this is partial truth, that the imperfect must precede the perfect, that disappointment and darkness is an earnest of real success.

> " God's gift was that man should conceive of truth
> And yearn to gain it, catching at mistake." (*Death in the Desert.*)

> " Imperfection means perfection hid,
> Reserved in part, to grace the after time." (*Cleon.*)

> " And what is our failure here but a triumph's evidence
> For the fulness of the days? Have we withered or agonized?
> Why else was the pause prolonged, but that singing might issue thence?
> Why rushed the discords in, but that harmony should be prized?"
> (*Abt Vogler.*)

> " If I stoop
> Into a dark tremendous sea of cloud,
> It is but for a time ; I press God's lamp
> Close to my breast ; its splendour soon or late
> Will pierce the gloom." (*Paracelsus.*)

> "Love, wrong, and pain, what see I else around?
> Yea, and the resurrection and uprise
> To the right hand of the throne.
>   *   *   *   *   *
> If ye demur, this judgment on your head—
> Never to reach the ultimate, angels' law ;
> There, where law, life, joy, impulse are one thing."
> (*Death in the Desert.*)

Do we doubt the goodness of God when we see some hideous evil? He tells us that only through the contest with evil can man pass to power and glory.

> "Why comes temptation, but for man to meet
> And master, and make crouch beneath his foot;
> And so be pedestalled in triumph? Pray,
> 'Lead us into no such temptations, Lord'?
> Yea, but, O thou, whose servants are the bold,
> Lead such temptations by the head and hair,
> Reluctant dragons, up to who dares fight,
> That so he may do battle, and have praise."
>
> *(The Ring and the Book.)*

Do we find in old age the sights and sounds by which the soul learned truth fading in the darkness, the active powers failing? This is an earnest not of death, but of life. God is taking away the earthly sight that the "celestial light" may so much the more shine inward. He is withdrawing us into some quiet retreat, that we may "ponder on the entire past"; the evening shades are gathering that we may sleep and wake refreshed.

> "Lie bare, to the universal prick of light!
> Is it for nothing we grow old and weak,
> We whom God loves?" *(Death in the Desert.)*

> "Ponder on the entire past
> Laid together thus at last,
> When the twilight helps to fuse
> The first fresh with the faded hues,
> And the outline of the whole,
> As round eve's shades their framework roll,
> Grandly fronts for once thy soul.
> And then, as 'mid the dark, a gleam
> Of yet another morning breaks,
> And, like the hand which ends a dream,
> Death, with the might of his sunbeam,
> Touches the flesh, and the soul awakes,
> Then————." *(Flight of the Duchess.)*

> "So, still within this life,
> Though lifted o'er its strife,
> Let me discern, compare, pronounce at last.
>   •   •   •   •   •
> So, better, age, exempt
> From strife, should know than tempt
> Further. Thou waitedst age: wait death nor be afraid."
>
> *(Rabbi Ben Ezra.)*

> "And stung by straitness of our life made strait
> On purpose to make sweet the life at large,
> Freed by the throbbing impulse we call death,
> We burst there, as the worm into the fly,
> Who, while a worm still, wants his wings." *(Cleon.)*

The lovers of Browning's poetry wonder that any one can ask the question, Is he a religious poet? True, he has not written religious epics as Dante and Milton, and there are but few poems which are definitely on religious subjects, but the unseen is ever present to him. He is ever seeking to interpret the seen by the unseen, to justify the ways of God to man. He is ever conscious of the double life, of a Divine presence,

> "The spiritual life around the earthly life :
> Which runs across some vast distracting orb
> Of glory on either side that meagre thread." (*An Epistle*.)

> "God glows above
> With scarce an intervention presses close
> And palpitatingly His soul o'er ours!
> We feel Him, nor by painful reason know." (*Luria*.)

So we are never shut in by the visible universe ; it is to us the veil, the sacrament of the invisible, the infinite, the καλόν καγαθὸν. Yet is the Infinite no mere pantheistic presence, but the Father of spirits, manifested first and pre-eminently in the soul of man, His child, who, because he *is* a son, is heir of all things. Thus does the Christian teaching interpenetrate all his thoughts. Yet to the religious consciousness of some Browning does not speak. There are childlike souls who have ever looked up to God in simple loving faith, over whose being the storms of doubt have never swept, who have not known what it is to sit in the midst of a thick darkness, a darkness that may be felt ; an unquestioning faith is theirs, and they have never had to wrestle with the problems of life. To such Browning may appear non-religious, yes, even irreligious, as did Job to his friends, because he cannot receive truth from the outside ; it must be looked at from his deepest consciousness, an external revelation is not enough ; it is not put in the forefront, because to him it is the outcome, the complement of that which is known by the intuitions of the soul ; for though we may believe a person, we cannot believe in a person because some one tells us he did wonderful works—we must be united by inward sympathies,

> "Whereby truth, deadened of its absolute blaze,
> Might need love's eye to pierce the o'erstretched doubt."
> (*Death in the Desert.*)

We know the Divine through the Spirit bearing witness with our spirit ; in other words, the kingdom of heaven is within.

Thus Browning seems to me a prophet whom God has given to our storm-tost age, a pilot who has learnt by long experience the hidden rocks and sandbanks on which the vessel of faith may be wrecked, now that the old anchor chains are burst asunder. An infallible Church, an infallible Book, an infallible Pope, all these have failed us—failed us that, rejecting the stones of the desert, we may learn that man doth not live by bread alone, but by the word of God doth man live. I will take a few typical poems familiar to most of us, to establish my position

His ideal of what a *poet* is called to be is given in his picture of a Contemporary.

> " I only knew one poet in my life,
> And this or something like it was his way."

And then we read of one who walked about in the haunts of men,

> " Scenting the world, looking it full in face,
> Trying the mortar's temper 'tween the chinks."

Watching common sights and common people, and seeing, not the outside shows, but the real thing behind, and thus awakening the conscience, and exercising a kingship by right Divine. Judging not according to the appearance, but righteous judgment.

> " My father, like the man of sense he was,
> Would point him out to me a dozen times.
> ' St, St,' he'd whisper, ' the Corregidor.' "

> " If any beat a horse, you felt he saw ;
> If any cursed a woman, he took note,
> Yet stared at nobody—you stared at him,
> And found, less to your pleasure than surprise,
> He seemed to know you, and expect as much."
> *(How it strikes a Contemporary.)*

His reward was to know he was

> " Doing the king's work all the dim day long,"

whilst the tongue of scandal was busy with his life—a life which the low and sensual cannot believe in. At last dying on

> " The neat low truckle bed " ;

alone haply, as far as man could see, but waited on by unseen hosts.

And mark, though no audible voice spoke to the poet, though no vision of glory appeared, yet he *knew*, he *felt* the king's approval.

> " But never word or sign that I could hear
> Notified to this man about the street
> The king's approval of those letters.
>   *   *   *   *
> Was some such understanding 'twixt the two ? "

" Hereby we know that we know Him, because we love **Him** and keep His commandments."

The consciousness of the priesthood of the true poet breathes through the whole of *Sordello ;* his sin was that he was unfaithful almost unto the end to the spirit within him, that he was content to enjoy, to receive, when he was heir to the kingship over humanity, the crown of which is a crown of thorns. His claim to the throne had to be made good by the power of self-sacrifice, by dying to self, that he might find a larger life in those for whom he lived, and this at last redeems

the erring one. What grander picture can be drawn of a poet than that
of the ideal Sordello,

> " the complete Sordello, Man and Bard,
> John's cloud-girt angel, this foot on the land,
> That on the sea, with, open in his hand,
> A bitter-sweetling of a book."

In the consciousness of an unseen presence then, in the faith that
there is a reality behind the shows of earth, a meaning in this wondrous
kosmos, and that each lives and dies nobly who faces the sphinx and
gives an answer to the riddle of life ; in the faith that though here we
know *in part*, we shall one day truly know, Browning addresses himself
to his task.

And what is it which calls out first in us the sense of poetry ? Ask
the great poets of the world. It is the sight of suffering. The real must
be unsatisfying ere we seek for the ideal. The great epics and dramas
have all been tragic ; each has his own vision of Prometheus, agonizing
humanity. If there is one poem into which Browning has thrown all his
artistic power, I think it is *Saul*. How grand is the stage on which we see
the suffering Titan ! the black tent in the midst of the sand " burnt to
powder "; the blinding glare without, darkness within. There he endures
in the desert, through which flow no refreshing streams to quench the
thirst of his soul ; he who once had " heard the words of God, had seen
the vision of the Almighty," is now blinded by the glory, and he knows
not the love which his own heart has cast out. There he hangs, upon
his cross.

> " He stood, as erect as the tent-prop, both arms stretched out wide,
> On the great cross-support in the centre that goes to each side.
> He relaxed not a muscle, but hung there, as caught in his pangs,
> And waiting his change, the king-serpent all heavily hangs
> Far away from his kind, in the pine, till deliverance come
> With the spring-time ;—so agonized Saul, drear and stark, blind and dumb."

To him, doubly shut out from the light of heaven, comes youth and
beauty and innocence personified in David. He comes like a ministering
angel, the dew of heaven in his " gracious gold hair," with bright lilies
telling of life and hope—

> "Just broken to twine round thy harp-strings, as if no wild heat
> Were now raging to torture the desert."

Then he sings the simple songs of the shepherd lad, the beauty and
peace of nature, the felt harmony and love in all things.

> " God made all the creatures, and gave them our love and our fear,
> To give sign we and they are His children, one family here."

Next he passes on to the tale of human joys and sorrows ; but there
is no response till he comes to that which gives to man's life a meaning,
the consciousness of a glory beyond.

"Then here in the darkness Saul groaned,
  And I paused, held my breath in such silence, and listened apart ;
  And the tent shook, for mighty Saul shuddered, and sparkles 'gan dart
  From the jewels that woke in his turban at once with a start
  All its lordly male-sapphires and rubies, courageous at heart ;
  So the head ; but the body still moved not, still hung there erect."

He tries another theme. He tells of the joyous sense of life and
vigour, once felt by the warrior king ; bids him follow again the story
of the past, and thence believe in the love of God.

           " Let one more attest
      I have lived, seen God's hand thro' a lifetime, and all was for best."

Then he shows him in the lives of others the ennobling of the soul
through suffering.

   " Such result as, from seething grape-bundles, the spirit-strained true."

From the vantage-ground of the past he would have him contemplate
the present suffering ; through sorrow he had been crowned.

           " Then Saul, who hung propped
      By the tent's cross-support in the centre, was struck by his name.
                One long shudder thrilled
      All the tent till the very air tingled, then sank, and was stilled
      At the king's self, left standing before me, released and aware."

But this only awakens the king to consciousness, it cannot restore
him. Can he live by the thought that his life may enter into the
being of humanity, that though he perish he may pour out palm wine
for the life of posterity ; can he be sustained by the enthusiasm of
humanity ? No ! the wretched despise themselves ; only in the consciousness of a larger life and love, sustaining, fulfilling them, can they
hope to bless others. They must be conscious of a love, not small
enough for them to possess, but large enough to possess them ; of an
ocean in which they and all may be baptized, of a boundless love in
which we may all live and move ; a spiritual presence, which, brooding
over the dead soul, awakens it to a responsive life. And it is upon
the revelation of the Divine love first revealed within the soul that
our poet rests the salvation of humanity. The love which David feels
kindling, glowing, burning in himself towards this sufferer, what is it
but the Spirit bearing witness with his spirit to the deeper depths of the
Divine love ?

           " Shall the creature surpass the Creator,—the end, what began ?
      Would I fain, in my impotent yearning, do all for this man,
      And dare doubt, He alone shall not do it, who yet alone can."

As man's love yearns to utter itself, though it cannot, so must the
Divine love, and God can. Man cannot utter through the feeble body,
in the bonds of time, the infinite love which he yet feels within, but the
Infinite, the Eternal, God is uttering it in all creation, in every soul of

man who feels and responds to the music of heaven. This it is which restores life to the dying soul, whilst to the prophet, the Divine incarnation becomes a fact realized in the inner consciousness; it is a truth antecedent to and resting upon a deeper foundation than any external evidence, it is a truth in Plato's sense; it is a Divine, an eternal idea, which *must* be realized in time, be one day revealed to redeem the world. So he passes on from the *must be* to the *shall be;* this was the argument of the risen Lord, ἔδει παθεῖν τὸν χριστόν.

"Then the truth came upon me. No harp more—no song more! outbroke
    *   *   *   *   *   *   *
I believe it! 'Tis thou, God, that givest, 'tis I who receive.
    *   *   *   *   *   *   *
Would I suffer for him that I love? So wouldst thou—so wilt thou!
So shall crown thee the topmost, ineffablest, uttermost crown,
And thy love fill infinitude wholly, nor leave up nor down
One spot for the creature to stand in!
    *   *   *   *   *   *   *
He who did most shall bear most; the strongest shall stand the most weak.
'Tis the weakness in strength that I cry for! my flesh that I seek
In the Godhead! I seek and I find it. O Saul, it shall be
A Face like my face that receives thee: a Man like to me,
Thou shalt love and be loved by, for ever: a Hand like this hand
Shall throw open the gates of new life to thee! See the Christ stand."

And in the consciousness of this Divine presence, the Divine love comes in like a flood upon his soul, it overflows into creation, all vibrates to the music of heaven, and trembles in the glow of its surpassing glory; the earth is transformed, there seems no longer an inanimate, for the life of God Himself breathes through all.

"And the stars of night beat with emotion and tingled and shot
Out in fire the strong pain of pent knowledge: but I fainted not,
For the Hand still impelled me at once and supported, suppressed
All the tumult, and quenched it with quiet and holy behest,
Till the rapture was shut in itself and the earth sank to rest."

And as we read we feel the poet has given us a higher idea of inspiration; no outside voice is heard now; the revelation is not by the voice of nature through sense and understanding, but through the heart; the love of God possesses the soul, the heart of God is felt beating with the heart of man; it is a moral revelation. In the depths of man's being is felt the quickening spirit, the true enthusiasm, and he rises to a new life; there is the revelation to the human consciousness of the Divine in man,—the central truth of Christianity.

But the pessimist may turn to the reverse; it may be said, if the intuitions of the noble tell of self-sacrifice and love, what about the degraded creeds that men have held? are not these all the outcome, the utterances of humanity too, though on a lower plane? Mr. Browning has not shrunk from facing this question. As in the poem of *Saul* we have intuitions, which enable us to grasp Divine truth, in *Caliban* we have a teaching from the text, "Thou thoughtest that I was altogether such an one as thyself." He refuses to recognize as man, one without moral consciousness. He does not believe that there is any such monster born of woman, or, if such lives, he has descended from the human to the animal kingdom, by starving or poisoning the spirit. His creed, derived from the experience of his own wickedness, needs but to be expressed to be rejected. Caliban is a monster, for *he* is not a man who has no aspirations, who is content to lie and kick in the mud, who is a slave of impulse. His god, Setebos, is only a monstrous Caliban.

In these two poems I think Browning has sought to illustrate the deep truth that according to our moral standard are we able to receive Divine light and truth into our being. Let him not, however, be misunderstood. It is not historical propositions about Divine truth with which he is dealing—these, as St. James says, devils may believe—but the faith which lifts us out of the region of the phenomenal and transitory and imperfect into the real, the eternal, the inwardly true.

But it may be said, if God be indeed love, if man's utmost joy is to enter into the full recognition of that love (which is eternal life), why are we left to grope our way in the dim light? why does God not open for us the portals of the grave, let us look beyond, and then, with light and truth in our minds, return to lead our life here.

Bearing in mind the neo-platonic psychology which underlies Browning's thought, and is fully expressed in the *Death in the Desert*, we may say that as in *Saul* we have the truly human, the man in whom the soul predominates, and in *Caliban* the bestial type, so in the *Epistle of Karshish* we have the spiritual, the supernatural man, and his theology.

The scene of the drama is a land desolated by war, dangerous from robbers and beasts of prey, barren and dreary, as it seems; yet in it are content to journey, or to live, two men—one to whom the soul's life perishes with the body, who therefore spends his time in studying how best

> "To coop up and keep down on earth a space
> That puff of vapour from God's mouth, man's soul;"

the other, to whom this life is but a shadow of the true.

We have in Lazarus the study of a soul that has seen things as they are, whose life has therefore passed out of the sphere of the phenomenal into that of the real. He has seen the "consuming fire" of the Divine glory, and "the elements have melted with fervent heat." Sensitive only to that transcendent light, the things of earth seem but as shadows, and the path of life a

> " meagre thread
> Which runs across some vast, distracting orb
> Of glory."

Faith has passed into sight, and the human will is effaced in the Divine.

> " Indeed the special marking of the man,
> Is prone submission to the heavenly will—
> Seeing it, what it is, and why it is."

But therefore is the moral discipline of life over for him; he can will only God's will. But in the order of God's education it is necessary we should walk first by faith, afterwards by sight; should work out the moral law ere we recognize it as Divine, else we could not know God as good, and there could be no personal life, only the absorption of the human will in the infinite. Virtue can take root only in the darkness; we need to live in a world opaque for us. If, whilst enduring the agony, we could see the joy set before us, how could our spiritual nature attain its full growth! No; we must utter the cry "lama sabachthani" ere we can say, "It is finished." "Clouds and darkness must be round about Him," that we may learn that "righteousness and judgment are the habitation of His seat." We must do right not only because we know God wills it, but we must know that God wills it because it is right. We are to yield not a "prone submission," a satisfied assent, but the gladness of a full consent. There may be submission to the Almighty, but there can be concord only with the All-good.

And it seems that Lazarus has lost his characteristics as a man, because for him the work of this life is over; he has anticipated the next stage of existence ere he has entered on it, and so there is discord.

> " The law of that is known to him as this,
> His heart and brain move there, his feet stay here,
> So is the man perplext.
>
>   *   *   *   *   *
>
> ' It should be ' baulked by ' here it cannot be.' "

This life, too, has lost with its educative power its interest; for to enjoy we must ever be seeking the unattained, ever advancing.

> "He listened not, except I spoke to him,
> But folded his two hands, and let them talk,
> Watching the flies that buzzed.
>
>   *   *   *   *
>
> Sayeth he will wait patient to the last
> For that same death, which must restore his being
> To equilibrium, body loosening soul,
> Divorced even now by premature full growth."

And he is no longer able to help others. We must *feel* their difficulties ere we can meet them; there must be a measure of stupidity in us; one may be too clever to be a teacher. He despairs of unfolding spiritual realities, as we of explaining sight to the blind.

> "How can he give his neighbour the real ground,
> His own conviction."
> "Hence I perceive not he affects to preach
> The doctrine of his sect."

In conclusion the poet leads us to feel that we must learn by degrees to use the heavenly treasure, not demand our inheritance ere we have attained our majority; that the all-sufficient gospel is this—to know that the heart of God beats in sympathy with the heart of man.

> "So All-great were the All-loving too—
> So, through the thunder comes a human voice,
> Saying, 'O heart I made, a heart beats here!
> Face My hands fashioned, see it in Myself!
> Thou hast no power, nor may'st conceive of Mine :
> But love I gave thee, with Myself to love,
> And thou must love Me who have died for thee!'"

We have said that Browning deals especially with the problems which force themselves most upon our age, and answers them as a poet, by appealing to our deepest consciousness, to our sense of what must be, to our moral intuitions.

Perhaps in none are we made more conscious of his deep spiritual sympathies than in the companion poems, *Easter Day* and *Christmas Eve.* Browning knows people better than they know themselves. Which of us has not at some time professed to hold a creed, and thought perhaps we did believe, what in the depths of our hearts we abhorred? So he faces the superficial thinker, and makes him know himself. Does the agnostic approach with a smiling countenance, saying, " I am content with this world's beauty, with science and art and law;" Browning leads him to an earthly paradise, where no voice of God is heard among the trees of the garden; he casts at his feet all the gifts of beauty, but they are gifts from no one; he places him in a tabernacle vast and glorious, and it becomes to him a prison-house, because there is no escape from it into a larger life; and as for human love, this too dies in the desert, it has no root, it is cut off from all that can feed its life; and at last the soul is made to feel the utter desolation of a life without God, to know what is eternal death, to understand that deepest utterance of man's heart, " This is life eternal, to know Thee; " to understand that the resurrection for man is this—to come into the full consciousness of union with God. Without it we pine and die amidst all the earth has to give; but, if we know it, streams water the desert, it rejoices and blossoms as the rose, the mountains and hills break forth into singing, and everything that hath breath praises God. And *Christmas Eve* is complementary to *Easter Day.* That has dealt most with the relation of the individual soul to the source of its life—to the centre of the universe,—realized within. This deals with the relation of the soul to the life of God manifested in others; it teaches us that when we can say only My Father, not Our Father, we cannot enter into the mind of God, nor pray aright; that if we are not quite in darkness, we are only in the moonlight; if we are touching the hem of Christ's garment, we have not entered with Him the transfiguring cloud; we are not wrapt in that glory, we are only on the verge of light. And as in *Easter Day*, he forces us to face the thoughts, and see whether we really feel what we supposed we did, he shows us we cannot do without God; as we found in the one, that the love of God glorifies nature, and alone draws us into loving sympathy; so in *Christmas Eve* we find that *same* love it is, which, being shed abroad in our hearts, enables us to love man, to lose sight of what is merely phenomenal and faulty, and to go down to those deeper depths, where we meet in truest sympathy in the sense of a common need, a common aspiration, a common love. We have been sentimentalizing perhaps about love, bestowing our charity in inverse proportion to people's nearness to us. Browning brings us, as it were, face to face with our complacent religious selves, and he bids us then follow, cling to Christ, say with our hearts, "Where Thou goest, I will go." Then we listen to those words, "Where two or three are gathered together, there am I"—present, with infinite compassion and love; not with the refined and cultivated and æsthetic, but with those who are in your eyes ugly and ignorant and narrow; in that miserable little Bethel, out of which you have dashed with contempt; present, because their souls are seeking Me, and longing for the light, and are therefore growing up into it, though their life does seem so dreary and dark to you; present with those you despise for utter want of æsthetic sense. Present in the great cathedral, with those too whom you regard as superstitious, because the emotions of their souls are expressed in the ascending incense, the thrilling music, the pictured forms. Yes, even with him who knows Me not as a living Presence, but desires truth; who has with toilsome steps climbed the mountain-tops, that he might dwell in a region of pure light, and who is starving amidst the snows; even to him I come breathing warmth and love, and therefore life. None are cast out of My Presence; if you cast out from your love any human soul, you must let go then of the hem of that garment from whence virtue goes out to all suffering humanity.

There is a musical trilogy which corresponds with the three poems on which I have previously dwelt. And here I may perhaps remark that I know of no modern poet at least, in whom art is so unified as in Browning; the scenery and sound so harmonized with the thought. He owes his excellence in this partly to his familiarity with Greek drama, especially with Æschylus. Comparing the three poems, we may say *Saul* corresponds to *Hugues of Saxe-Gotha ; Caliban*, the debased, the bestial, to the *Toccata of Galuppi ; Abt Vogler* to *Lazarus*, the glorified, spiritualized man.

The central poem, *Master Hugues of Saxe-Gotha*, represents the truly human, the soul seeking to interpret the perplexed music of earth, arguing, disputing, contending, in the faith that there is a meaning in all, though the final answer is delayed. The very sound is given of the perplexed intricate fugue, with its many melodies, crossing, interpenetrating, and moving on together.

> " One says his say with a difference ;
> More of expounding, explaining ;
> All now is wrangle, abuse, and vociference ;
> Now there's a truce, all's subdued, self-restraining,
> Five, though, stands out all the stiffer hence.
>
> Est fuga, volvitur rota,
> On we drift : where looms the dim port ?
> One, Two, Three, Four, Five, contribute their quota ;
> Something is gained, if one caught but the import—
> Show it us, Hugues of Saxe Gotha.
>
> So your fugue broadens and thickens,
> Greatens and deepens and lengthens."

And the same thought of the perplexities of life is repeated to the sight in the intricate mouldings of the roof. Our scene is a mediæval church, in which the musician lingers ; the dim lights are growing dimmer as the sexton extinguishes one after another, and the golden cherubs which reflect some of that feeble light are partly hidden by the cobwebs.

> " There I see our roof, its gilt moulding and groining
> Under those spider-webs lying.
>   *   *   *   *
> Is it your moral of Life?
> Such a web, simple and subtle."

The answer does not come, the meaning cannot be evolved, the vision of glory is only dimly seen through the symbols of earth.

> " So we o'ershroud stars and roses,
>   Cherub and trophy and garland ;
> Nothings grow somethings which quietly closes
> Heaven's earnest eye ; not a glimpse of the far land
> Gets through our comments and glozes."

And as the last candle by which he had been able to interpret the music, sinks in its socket, he stumbles down the dangerous staircase, out of the dark church into the moonlight silence, whither we cannot follow ; the lights of earth extinguished for him, the restless questioning over.

A Toccata of Galuppi's corresponds with *Caliban.* Here we have the low, sensuous, the fleshly school, with no outlook beyond the amusements of the immediate present; the scene, a ball-room in Venice. We hear the light foolish talk, scarcely lulled as the musician begins.

> " I can always leave off talking when I hear a master play ! "

For the roar of the fugue we have a music like the thin chirp of a cricket, wonderfully imitated in the monosyllabic verse, a sort of grown-up baby language, full of affectations ; a silly, inane music which brings before us a ghastly vision of dead men and women, for whom life had no meaning at all.

> " Did young people take their pleasure, when the sea was warm in May ?
> Balls and masks begun at midnight, burning ever to midday,
> When they made up fresh adventures for the morrow, do you say ?
>   *   *   *   *   *
> Then they left you for their pleasure, till in due time, one by one,
> Some with lives that came to nothing, some with deeds as well undone,
> Death stepped tacitly and took them, where they never see the sun."

And lastly there is *Abt Vogler*, the music of faith grand and mighty, which evokes the sense of spiritual presences,

> " Claiming each slave of the sound at a touch, as when Solomon willed
> Armies of angels that soar, legions of demons that lurk,"

building up a world of real harmony—a world true because ideal.

> " Ah, one and all how they helped, would dispart now, and now combine,
> Zealous to hasten the work, heighten their master his praise."

We are no longer shut in, as at Saxe-Gotha, in a church in which the lights are dying out one by one. We are watching a glorious cathedral grow before our eyes, and the glory is ever spreading, and the light is ever increasing, ascending higher and higher, until earth and heaven become one, and the bounds of space and time are lost in an eternal present.

> " For higher still and higher (as a runner tips with fire
> When a great illumination surprises a festal night),
> Outlining round and round Rome's dome from space to spire
> Up, the pinnacled glory reached, and the pride of my soul was in sight."

The lights are climbing from earth to the sky ; we see terrace above terrace shine forth, and the lights are spirits ascending heavenward, even as in Jacob's vision of the angels, ascending ere they descended, and forming, as they lose themselves in the sky, a vision of a Church triumphant, such as Dante beheld in Paradise.

> " And another would mount and march like the excellent minion he was,
> Ay, another and yet another, one crowd but with many a crest,
> Raising my rampired walls of gold as transparent as glass,
> Eager to do and die, yield each his place to the rest."

And the music ascends up and up, until the sense of effort is gone, for the highest pinnacle of earthly endeavour is reached, and then the soul sinks into the infinite and is lost, yet lives in the life and light of heaven.

> "The emulous heaven yearned down, made effort to reach the earth,
> As the earth had done her best, in my passion to scale the sky :
> For earth had attained to heaven, there was no more near nor far."

All is then seen not as it is to sense, but as it exists truly in the Divine idea, one day to come forth from the region of being to the region of consciousness. All the possibilities, which to us are not, but which truly are, the Divine ideas, one day to become existent in the visible.

> "Nay more ; for there wanted not who walked in the glare and glow,
> Presences plain in the place ; or fresh from the Protoplast,
> Furnished for ages to come, when a kindlier wind should blow,
> Lured now to begin and live."

All that too is seen as existing, which to us was, and is not, but which truly is.

> "Or else the wonderful dead who have passed through the body and gone,
> But were back once more to breathe in an old world worth their new."

And as the vision of the Infinite opens around, it becomes clear that no energy is lost, no true effort vain, for all life and energy are Divine,

> "evil is null, is nought, is silence implying sound."

The music of a holy life may die out on earth, but it exists for ever in the Eternal, the Unchanging, because it is the Divine idea.

> "All we have willed or hoped or dreamed of good shall exist ;
> Not its semblance, but itself ; no beauty, nor good, nor power
> Whose voice has gone forth, but each survives for the melodist,
> When eternity affirms the conception of an hour ;
> The high that proved too high, the heroic for earth too hard,
> The passion that left the ground, to lose itself in the sky,
> Are music sent up to God by the lover and the bard ;
> Enough that he heard it once : we shall hear it by and by."

But is it true, as some say, that the teaching of these earlier poems is superseded by that of the later, and so the poet has destroyed his own work ? To me it seems that in the later poems there is a more restful faith than in the earlier ; a belief less vehement, and therefore less struggling. Is there not a deep significance in the beautiful story of *Alcestis* (*Balaustion's Adventure*) ; a real consciousness which needs not proof in *Prospice*, in some passages of the *Ring and the Book*, in *A Wall*, and in the beautiful prologue and epilogue of *Fifine*. The vehement questionings of *La Saisiaz*, what are they but the cries of a present grief, which we all utter, as we see some loved friend pass out of sight. We cry to the whirlwind, "Wherefore? whereto?" No answer comes, but the heart replies.

> "Traversed heart must tell its story uncommented on : no less
> Mine results in 'Only grant a second life, I acquiesce

In this present life as failure, count misfortune's worst assaults
Triumph, not defeat; assured that loss so much the more exalts
Gain about to be. For at that moment did I so advance
Near to knowledge, as when frustrate of escape from ignorance?
Did not beauty prove most precious when its opposite obtained
Rule, and truth seem more than ever potent because falsehood reigned?
While for love—Oh how but, losing love, does whoso loves succeed
By the death-pang to the birth-throe—learning what is love indeed?
Only grant my soul may carry high through death her cup unspilled,
Brimming though it be with knowledge, life's loss drop by drop distilled,
I shall boast it mine—the balsam, bless each kindly wrench that wrung
From life's tree its inmost virtue, tapped the root whence pleasure sprung,
Barked the bole, and broke the bough, and bruised the berry, left all grace
Ashes in death's stern alembic, loosed elixir in its place!"

I grant that in the later poems he cares less to formulate. As we climb higher and our vision widens, that which once seemed the whole truth now takes its place as part only of a larger, more embracing unity. In our individual lives, as in the world's history, we follow the sun in his course; but horizons change, and we never reach the land of light; truth recedes, but it is to tempt us onward; the crystal spheres of the world's childhood are broken, and if for a moment the soul flutters down and stands panting upon some solid cliff, she rises thence having plumed her pinions for a longer flight; she returns again and again only to renew her strength, and at last, in all the might of a great trust in the All-good, she wings her flight into the infinite unknown. This utter trust is proved only when we can go forth, as the faithful of old, not knowing whither we go.

"truth is truth in each degree;
Thunderpealed by God to nature, whispered by my soul to me.
Nay, the weakness turns to strength and triumphs in a strength beyond:
'Mine is but man's truest answer—how were it did God respond?'
I shall no more dare to mimic such response in futile speech,
Pass off human lisp as echo of the sphere-song out of reach."
"Only a learner,
Quick one or slow one,
Just a discerner,
I would teach no one." (*Pisgah Sights.*)

The lesson taught in the earlier poem of *Saul* is repeated in the latest, that the Divine love shed abroad in our hearts is the witness for a Divine love which we can trust for ever and ever; and it is the strength of this inner consciousness, the witness of the Spirit, that has enabled the poet-seers of all ages to sing loud above the storm-waves their Gloria in excelsis.

"Soul that canst soar!
Body may slumber,
Body shall cumber
Soul-flight no more.

"Waft of soul's wing!
What lies above?
Sunshine and love."
(*Pisgah Sights.*)

ON SOME POINTS IN

BROWNING'S VIEW OF LIFE.

BY THE REV. PROF. B. F. WESTCOTT, D.D.

(A Paper read before the Cambridge Browning Society, Nov. 1882.)

[In the following Paper I have endeavoured to bring together what appear to me to be Browning's most characteristic teachings on some of the widest problems of life. My object will be fully gained if I can encourage others to study a poet whose works require and repay patient thought; and at least I have had the pleasure of acknowledging my own debt to one who sees and shows " the infinite in things."]

In my undergraduate days, if I remember rightly, I came across the description of a poet which speaks of him as one "who sees the infinite in things." The thought has been to me from that time forward a great help in studying the noblest poetry. The true poet does, I believe, of necessity, see the infinite in his subject; and he so presents his vision to his readers that they too, if their eyes are open, are enabled in some degree to share in its lessons.

The same gift belongs in a certain degree to the artist. But the range of the poet is unlimited; while the artist's choice of subject is conditioned by the requirement that its treatment shall come within the domain of the beautiful. The ground of this difference obviously lies in the different means which the poet and the artist use to express what they see with the eyes of the soul. The mode in which words and the melody of words (not to speak now of music) affect us is different in kind from the action of form and colour.

All life, all nature, is therefore the legitimate field of the poet, as prophet. There is an infinite, an eternal, meaning in all; and it is his office to make this intelligible to his students. No modern poet has more boldly claimed the fulness of his heritage of life than Browning. He has dared to look on the darkest and meanest forms of action and passion, from which we commonly and rightly turn our eyes, and he has brought back for us from this universal survey a conviction of hope.

He has laid bare what there is in man of sordid, selfish, impure, corrupt, brutish, and he proclaims in spite of every disappointment and every wound, that he still finds a spiritual power in him, answering to a spiritual power without him, which restores assurance as to the destiny of creation.

Such a survey and such a conviction command careful study; and I wish to indicate a few points in Browning's view of human life which have especially struck me—we can each see only a little of the poet's teaching—but before doing this it is necessary to emphasize this fact, that it is personal human life with which he characteristically deals by deliberate choice. " Little else," he tells us, " is worth study [than the development of a soul]. I at least, always thought so."[1] He recognizes rarely, and, as it were, at a distance, the larger life of humanity;[2] but the single soul in its discipline, its progress, its aspirations, its failures, is the main object of his study, analysis, and portraiture. It has been so from first to last, in *Paracelsus*, in *Sordello*, and in the latest Dramatic Idylls.

By this choice, as has been well pointed out,[3] Browning occupies a position complementary to that of Wordsworth. He looks for the revelation of the Divine as coming through the spiritual struggles of man and not through Nature. Both poets, however, agree in this, that they assert the sovereignty of feeling over knowledge, of that within us which they hold to have affinity with the heavenly and eternal, over that which must be earthly and temporal.[4] But Browning justifies the position with the fullest detail of illustration, as was natural from the current of contemporary thought which he has encountered. He never wearies of dwelling on the relativity of physical knowledge, on its inadequacy to satisfy man, on its subordinate action in the crises of moral growth. The key-note of his teaching, in a word, is not knowledge, but love.

A single passage in which he lays down the relation of love to life will serve as an introduction to the thoughts which follow :

> ". . . Life, with all it yields of joy and woe,
> And hope and fear, . . .
> Is just our chance o' the prize of learning love
> How love might be, hath been indeed, and is."[5]

---

[1] Dedication to *Sordello*.

[2] *By the Fireside*, L " Each of the many helps to recruit
        The life of the race by a general plan;
        Each living his own, to boot."
This thought lives in *The Boy and the Angel*.

[3] Particularly in a paper by M. A. Lewis in *Macmillan* for June, 1882.

[4] *The Ring and Book, The Pope*, 1003 ff.   [5] *A Death in the Desert*, p. 101.

This learning of love, this acquisition of the power of self-sacrifice, involves a long and painful discipline :

> "Life is probation, and this earth no goal,
>   But starting point of man. . . .
>   *   *   *   *   *
>   To try man's foot, if it will creep or climb,
>   'Mid obstacles in seeming, points that prove
>   Advantage for who vaults from low to high,
>   And makes the stumbling-block a stepping-stone.
>   *   *   *   *   *
>   Why comes temptation but for man to meet
>   And master, and make crouch beneath his foot,
>   And so be pedestalled in triumph ?"[1]

As Browning presents the great drama of the soul, thus significantly foreshadowed, several truths seem to me to come into prominence which I may call briefly the unity of life, the discipline of life, the continuity of life, the assurance of life. In other words, the poet teaches that life now must be treated as a whole ; that learning comes through suffering ; that every failure felt to be failure points to final achievement ; that the visible present is but one scene in an illimitable growth. These then are the points to which I wish to call attention.

I.

Our present life is to be taken in its entirety. The discipline of man is to be fulfilled, the progress of man is to be secured, under the conditions of our complex earthly being. These lets and limitations are not to be disparaged or overborne, but accepted and used in due order. No attempt must be made either to retain that which has been or to anticipate that which will be. Each element in human nature is to be allowed its proper office. Each season brings its own work and its own means. This conception is wrought out in many-sided completeness in *Rabbi Ben Ezra*, which is, in epitome, a philosophy of life. To quote a few lines is to do injury to the perfect structure of the whole ; but at least they will attract not only to the reading but to the study of it. Here are the lessons of advancing years :

> "Let us not always say,
>   'Spite of this flesh to-day,
> I strove, made head, gained ground upon the whole !'
>   As the bird wings and sings,
>   Let us cry, 'All good things
> Are ours, nor soul helps flesh more now, than flesh helps soul !'
>   *   *   *   *   *
>   Grow old along with me !
>   The best is yet to be,
> The last of life, for which the first was made :

---

[1] *The Pope*, 1435 f. ; 409 ff. ; 1184 ff.

> Our times are in His hand
> Who saith, ' A whole I planned,
> Youth shows but half ; trust God ; see all, nor be afraid.'
>   *　　　*　　　*　　　*　　　*
> So take and use thy work !
> Amend what flaws may lurk,
> What strain o' the stuff, what warpings past the aim !
> My times be in Thy hand !
> Perfect the cup as planned !
> Let age approve of youth, and death complete the same." [1]

The capacity for moral progress, thus recognized in the law of outward growth and decay, is indeed laid down by Browning to be the essential characteristic of man :

> ". . . Man . . .
> Creeps ever on from fancies to the fact,
> And in this striving . . .
> Finds progress, man's distinctive mark alone,
> Not God's, and not the beast's : God is, they are,
> Man partly is and wholly hopes to be . . .
>   *　　　*　　　*　　　*
> Getting increase of knowledge, since he learns
> Because he lives, which is to be a man,
> Set to instruct himself by his past self." [2]

Hence the mutability of things may become a help to his growth :

> " Rejoice that man is hurled
> From change to change unceasingly,
> His soul's wings never furled.
>   *　　　*　　　*　　　*
>   There's life's pact,
> Perhaps probation—do *I* know?
> God does : endure His act ! " [3]

The very infirmities of later years, incapacity to receive new impressions, dulness of sight by which far and near are blended together, have their peculiar office in revealing the lessons of life.　Thus the weird visitor, who has laid before the Duchess the trials and triumphs of the life to which she invites her, a life wholly given up that it may be received again in richer fulness, concludes :

> " So at the last shall come old age,
> Decrepit as befits that stage :
> How else would'st thou retire apart
> With the hoarded memories of thy heart,
> And gather all to the very least
> Of the fragments of life's earlier feast,
> Let fall thro' eagerness to find
> The crowning dainties yet behind?
> Ponder on the entire Past
> Laid together thus at last,

---

[1] *Rabbi Ben Ezra*, 12, 1, 32.　　[2] *A Death in the Desert*, p. 115.
[3] *James Lee*, vi. 14 f.

When the twilight helps to fuse
The first fresh with the faded hues,
And the outline of the whole,
As round eve's shades their framework roll,
Grandly fronts for once thy soul.
And then as, 'mid the dark, a gleam
Of yet another morning breaks,
And like the hand which ends a dream,
Death, with the might of his sunbeam,
Touches the flesh and the soul awakes,
Then——" [1]

The true human life will therefore present a just balance of powers in the course of its varied progress. To make this truth more impressive by contrast, Browning has worked it out in two pairs of characters, each stamped with a real nobility and yet seen to be essentially imperfect, Aprile and Paracelsus, Lazarus and Cleon.

The complementary aspirations and failures of Aprile and Paracelsus —the absorbing undisciplined desire to love, on the one hand, and to know, on the other—are plainly and fully portrayed by the poet himself, and it is sufficient to refer to the poem of *Paracelsus*. The correspondences between Lazarus and Cleon are less obvious.

In the strangely fascinating *Epistle of Karshish* Browning has drawn the portraiture of one to whom the eternal is sensibly present, whose spirit has gained prematurely absolute predominance :

" Heaven opened to a soul while yet on earth,
Earth forced on a soul's use while seeing Heaven : " [2]

and the result is not a man but a sign ; a being

" Professedly the faultier that he knows
God's secret, while he holds the thread of life." [3]

Lazarus therefore, while he moves in the world, has lost all sense of proportion in things about him, all measure of and faculty of dealing with that which sways his fellows. He has no power or will to win them to his faith, but he simply stands among men as a patient witness of the overwhelming reality of the divine : a witness whose authority is confessed, even against his inclination, by the student of nature, who turns again and again to the phenomenon which he affects to disparage.

In this crucial example Browning shows how the exclusive dominance of the spirit destroys the fulness of human life, its uses and powers, while it leaves a passive life, crowned with an unearthly beauty. On the other hand, he shows in his study of Cleon that the richest results of earth in art and speculation, and pleasure and power, are unable to remove from life the desolation of final gloom. Thus,

---

[1] *The Flight of the Duchess,* i. 270 (compare *Transcendentalism,* i. p. 322).
[2] *An Epistle,* i. 337.   [3] *Id.* 339.

over against the picture of Lazarus is placed that of the poet, who by happy circumstance has been enabled to gather to himself all that is highest in the civilization of Greece. Cleon enjoys every prize of present success, the homage of king and fisherman, the glory of artist and philosopher; and over all there is the oppressive shadow of an inevitable loss. Writing "to Protus in his tyranny," his judgment is, that he dare not accept the view

> "That imperfection means perfection hid,
> Reserved in part, to grace the after-time."[1]

The wealth of man's endowment, which is understood too late for use, seems to him to be rather a curse than a blessing, nourishing vain hopes, and showing what joy man is capable of feeling, and never can feel,

> "The consummation coming past escape,
> When [he] shall know most and yet least enjoy."[2]

The contrast is of the deepest significance. The Jewish peasant endures earth, being in possession of heaven: the Greek poet, in possession of earth, feels that heaven, some future state,

> "Unlimited in capability
> For joy, as this is in desire for joy,"

is a necessity for man; but no,

> "Zeus has not yet revealed it; and alas,
> He must have done so, were it possible!"

But we must not pause to follow out the contrast into details. It is enough to see broadly that flesh and spirit each claim recognition in connexion with their proper spheres, in order that the present life may bear its true result.

We must then, in other words, that we may live human lives, loyally yield ourselves to, and yet master the circumstances in which we are placed. This is an arduous task, but it is fruitful: "when pain ends gain ends too."[3] And the principle holds good not only in regard to the physical, but also in regard to the intellectual difficulties by which we are beset. For doubt, rightly understood, is just that vivid, personal questioning of phenomena, which breaks "the torpor of assurance,"[4] and gives a living value to decision. In this sense, and not as if doubt were an absolution from the duty of endeavour, we can each say,

> "I prize the doubt,
> Low kinds exist without,
> Finished and finite clods, untroubled by a spark."[5]

---

[1] *Cleon*, i. p. 417.   [2] *Id.* p. 422.
[3] *A Death in the Desert*, p. 99.   [4] *The Pope*, 1853.
[5] *Rabbi Ben Ezra*, 3; compare *Bp. Blougram's Apology*, pp. 381. 397; *Paracelsus*, iii. p. 143; *Easter Day*, § iv.

Nor is it difficult to understand that the circumstances which make
doubt possible answer to the necessities of our nature:

> " Sun-suffused
> A cloud may soothe the eye made blind by blaze—
> Better the very clarity of heaven :
> The soft streaks are the beautiful and dear.
> What but the weakness in a faith supplies
> The incentive to humanity, no strength
> Absolute, irresistible, comports?
> How can man love but what he yearns to help?"[1]

II.

In such a view of life, as is thus outlined, no room is left for
indifference or neutrality.   There is no surrender to an idle optimism.
A part must be taken and maintained.   The spirit in which Luther said
pecca fortiter finds a powerful expression in *The Statue and the Bust*:

> " Let a man contend to the uttermost
> For his life's set prize, be it what it will !
> *   *   *   *   *
> And the sin I impute to each frustrate ghost
> Is, the unlit lamp and the ungirt loin."[2]

And again in the concentrated and moving pathos of *The Lost Leader* :

> " Best fight on well, for we taught him—strike gallantly,
> Menace our heart ere we master his own ;
> Then let him receive the new knowledge and wait us,
> Pardoned in heaven, the first by the throne."[3]

The erring but generous adversary of the truth must be struck down
sooner or later; and he who has chosen the right side will not escape
the severity of reverses.   Such an one sums up his experience shortly :

> (" And so) I live, (you see),
> Go through the world, try, prove, reject,
> Prefer, still struggling to effect
> My warfare ; happy that I can
> Be crossed and thwarted as a man,
> Not left in God's contempt apart,
> With ghastly smooth life, dead at heart."[4]

Thus, in the midst of strenuous endeavour or of patient suffering,
the lesson of life, the lesson of love, is brought within man's reach.   It
is finally taught perhaps by a sudden appeal of distress (*Caponsacchi*) ;
or by human companionship (*By the Fireside*) ; or by a message felt to
be divine (*Easter Day*).

There are also sharper ways of enforcing the lesson.   One illustration I cannot forbear quoting, for it brings out the basis of Browning's
hopefulness, and combines two passages which in different ways, for
grandeur of imagery and for spiritual insight, are unsurpassed in
Browning—I will venture to say in literature.

---

[1] *The Pope*, 1644 ff.   [2] i. p. 309.   [3] i. p. 5,   [4] *Easter Day*, xxxiii.

I need not recall the character of Guido, which Browning has analyzed with exceptional power and evidently with the deepest interest. This, at last, is the judgment which the Pope pronounces on him :

> " For the main criminal I have no hope
> Except in such a suddenness of fate.
> I stood at Naples once, a night so dark
> I could have scarce conjectured there was earth
> Anywhere, sky, or sea, or world at all ;
> But the night's black was burst through by a blaze,
> Thunder struck blow on blow, earth groaned and bore
> Through her whole length of mountain visible :
> There lay the city thick and plain with spires,
> And, like a ghost disshrouded, white the sea.
> So may the truth be flashed out by one blow,
> And Guido see, one instant, and be saved." [1]

Degraded and debased, Guido is seen to be not past hope by the true spiritual eye. And what is the issue ? Up to the last, with fresh kindled passion, the great criminal reasserts his hate. He gathers his strength to repeat his crime in will. I grow, he says, one gorge

> " To loathingly reject Pompilia's pale
> Poison my hasty hunger took for food."

So the end comes. The ministers of death claim him. In his agony he summons every helper whom he has known or heard of—

> " Abate, Cardinal, Christ, Maria, God— "

and then the light breaks through the blackest gloom :

> " Pompilia, will you let them murder me ? " [2]

In this supreme moment he has known what love is, and, knowing it, has begun to feel it. The cry, like the intercession of the rich man in Hades for his five brethren, is a promise of a far-off deliverance.

In this case the poet shows how we may take heart again in looking on the tragedies of guilt. But there are wider and more general sorrows in life. There is the failure, the falling from our ideal, of which we are all conscious ; there is the incompleteness of opportunity, which leaves noblest powers unused. Browning states the facts without reserve or palliation :

> " All labour, yet no less
> Bear up beneath their unsuccess.
> Look at the end of work, contrast
> The petty Done, the Undone vast,
> This Present of theirs with the hopeful Past !
>
> " What hand and brain went ever paired ?
> What heart alike conceived and dared ?
> What act proved all its thought had been ?
> What will but felt the fleshy screen ? " [3]

---

[1] *The Pope*, 2116 ff.   [2] *Guido* (2), 2425 f.   [3] *The Last Ride together*, v. vi.

> "In this world, who can do a thing will not ;
> And who would do it, cannot, I perceive :
> Yet the will 's somewhat—somewhat, too, the power—
> And thus we half-men struggle." [1]

In dealing with the difficulties which are thus raised, Browning offers what appears to me to be his most striking message. Acknowledged failure is, he teaches, a promise of future attainment : unfruitful preparation is the sign of the continuity of life. And these two principles rest upon another : imperfection is the condition of growth :

> "Let the mere star-fish in his vault
> Crawl in a wash of weed, indeed,
> Rose-jacynth to the finger-tips :
> He, whole in body and soul, outstrips
> Man, found with either in default.

> "But what's whole can increase no more,
> Is dwarfed and dies, since here's its sphere." [2]

And hence comes (as may be noticed parenthetically) the contrast between works of art and living men :

> "They are perfect—how else? they shall never change :
> We are faulty—why not? we have time in store.
> The artificer's hand is not arrested
> With us—we are rough-hewn, nowise polished :
> They stand for our copy, and once invested
> With all they can teach, we shall see them abolished.

> "'Tis a life-long toil till our lump be leaven,
> The better ! what's come to perfection perishes." [3]

Perhaps we can all readily acquiesce in the fact of imperfection; but the consideration of failure is more complicated. Failure, as Browning treats it, may come in two ways. It may come from what he does not scruple to call "the corruption of man's heart," [4] or it may come from the want of necessary external help. The first form of failure is in various degrees universal. But as long as effort is directed to the highest, that aim, though it is out of reach, is the standard of hope. The existence of a capacity, cherished and quickened, is a pledge that it will find scope. The punishment of the man who has fixed all his thoughts upon earth, a punishment felt on reflection to be overwhelming in view of possibilities of humanity, is the completest gratification of desires unworthily limited :

> "Thou art shut
> Out of the heaven of spirit ; glut
> Thy sense upon the world ; 'tis thine
> For ever—take it ! " [5]

On the other hand, the soul which has found in success not rest but

---

[1] *Andrea del Sarto*, i. p. 364.   [2] *Dis aliter visum*, 28 f.
[3] *Old Pictures at Florence*, xvi. f.   [4] *A Legend of Pornic*, 20.
[5] *Easter Day*, xx.

a starting-point, which refuses to see in the first-fruits of a partial
victory the fulness of its rightful triumph, has ever before it a sustaining and elevating vision :

> " What stops my despair?
> This :—'tis not what man Does which exalts him, but what man Would do ! " [1]

> " All I could never be,
> All, men ignored in me,
> This, I was worth to God, whose wheel the pitcher shaped.

> Then welcome each rebuff
> That turns earth's smoothness rough,
> Each sting that bids nor sit nor stand but go !
> Be our joys three-parts pain !
> Strive, and hold cheap the strain ;
> Learn, nor account the pang ; dare, never grudge the throe !

> For thence—a paradox
> Which comforts while it mocks—
> Shall life succeed in that it seems to fail :
> What I aspired to be,
> And was not, comforts me ;
> A brute I might have been, but would not sink i' the scale." [2]

So far the cause of failure lies mainly in the man himself. He is
conscious of a potency, a promise unfulfilled, and he trusts to Him who
gave it for fulfilment. But the failure may lie in those for whom the
patriot, or the lover, or the poet works and suffers. Even so the
assurance is the same :

> " ' Paid by the World—what dost thou owe
> Me ? ' God might question : now instead,
> 'Tis God shall repay ! I am safer so." [3]

> " If you loved only what were worth your love,
> Love were clear gain, and wholly well for you ;
> Make the low nature better by your throes !
> Give earth yourself, go up for gain above ! " [4]

> " His [God's] clenched Hand shall unclose at last,
> I know, and let out all the beauty ;
> My poet holds the Future fast,
> Accepts the coming ages' duty,
> Their Present for this Past." [5]

Meanwhile the work, even as it has been accomplished, does not perish
from the earth. Of him who has striven faithfully, the words supposed
to be addressed by David to Saul are true in due measure :

> " Each deed thou hast done
> Dies, revives, goes to work in the world . . . so, each ray of thy will,
> Every flash of thy passion and prowess, long over, shall thrill
> Thy whole people, the countless, with ardour, till they too give forth
> A like cheer to their sons : who in turn fill the South and the North
> With the radiance thy deed was the germ of." [6]

---

[1] *Saul*, xviii.   [2] *Rabbi Ben Ezra*, 25, 6, 7.   [3] *The Patriot*, vi.
[4] *James Lee*, vii. 2.   [5] *Popularity*, iii.   [6] *Saul*, xiii.   Cf. *Sordello*, iii. p. 416.

III.

But while Browning recognizes the reality and the glory of this subjective immortality, he has shown elsewhere, in *Cleon*, that it is wholly inadequate to satisfy the heart of man.   He assumes, therefore, in these various studies of imperfection and failure, as prophetic of progress and attainment, the continuity of personal life through death.   In such a continuity of being he also finds the assurance of the full use of powers disciplined but not called into play on earth.

There is, perhaps, little in the literary history of the Renaissance to justify the picture which Browning has drawn, in *The Grammarian's Funeral*, of the perfect self-sacrifice of the scholar as realized then.   But the thoughts expressed in the poem find a partial embodiment at all times.   A large proportion of a student's labour must be in preparation for tasks which he cannot accomplish.   His material may remain for others; but the experience, the insight, the delicate tact, the accumulated enthusiasm which he has gained in long years, pass away with him.   The example, indeed, abides for us; but this is not all.   There will yet be, as we believe, a field for the exercise of every power which has been trained and not called into service.   What has been consecrated cannot be wasted :

> " Yea, this in him was the peculiar grace
> *   *   *   *
> That before living he'd learn how to live—
>   No end to learning :
> Earn the means first—God surely will contrive
>   Use for our earning,
> Others mistrust and say, ' But time escapes !
>   Live now or never ! '
> He said, ' What's time?   Leave Now for dogs and apes !
>   Man has Forever.'
>
> Was it not great?   did not he throw on God
>   (He loves the burthen)—
> God's task to make the heavenly period
>   Perfect the earthen ?
> Did not he magnify the mind, show clear
>   Just what it all meant?
> He would not discount life, as fools do here,
>   Paid by instalment." [1]

But the preparation and discipline of intellect is subordinate to the preparation and discipline of feeling.   The end of life is, as we have seen, the learning love—the learning God—and that in a large degree through human fellowship.   *Omne vivum ex vivo*—" life is the one source of life "—is an axiom true in the spiritual as in the physical order.   An intellectual result may be the occasion, but it cannot be the

---

[1] *A Grammarian's Funeral*, i. pp. 281 ff.

source of a moral quickening. Man's spirit enters into communion with the Spirit of God directly, or with the Spirit of God acting through men. A soul meets the soul which its nature needs, and receives its quickening influence; and this is its confession:

> " Life will just hold out the proving
>   Both our powers, alone and blended ;
>   And then, come the next life quickly !
>   This world's use will have been ended."[1]

And so again in the enjoyment of a perfect sympathy the poet can say:

> " My own, see where the years conduct !
>   At first, 'twas something our two souls
>   Should mix as mists do ; each is sucked
>   In each now ; on, the new stream rolls,
>   Whatever rocks obstruct." [2]

This happy issue, however, is not always gained. The soul may recognize its need and also that which will satisfy it, and yet fail to gain what is wanting. And what then? Is all the fruit of self-questioning and self-devotion and self-surrender to be lost? *Evelyn Hope* is the answer. The lover, by the side of the dead girl who could not have known his love, replies for us:

> " No, indeed ! for God above
>   Is great to grant, as mighty to make,
>   And creates the love to reward the love:
>   I claim you still, for my own love's sake !
>   Delayed it may be for more lives yet,
>   Through worlds I shall traverse not a few :
>   Much is to learn, much to forget
>   Ere the time be come for taking you.

> " So hush,—I give you this leaf to keep—
>   See, I shut it inside the sweet, cold hand !
>   There, that is our secret ; go to sleep !
>   You will wake, and remember and understand." [3]

IV.

Here we might well stop. We have followed in outline the thoughts which Browning offers to us on the unity of life, the discipline of life, the continuity of life, a unity which enables us to regard every condition of labour as contributing to its efficiency, a discipline which, through spiritual intercourse, fashions us to the Divine likeness, a continuity which abides through cycles of change passing all imagination. The unity, the discipline, the continuity rest upon and express that Divine Love, of which love in man is at once the offspring and the evidence. So we rise to the highest:

---

[1] *Cristina*, viii. Compare v.   [2] *By the Fireside*, xxvi.
[3] *Evelyn Hope*, iv. vii. Contrast *Too Late*, D.P. 57 ff.

" Do I find love so full in my nature, God's ultimate gift,
  That I doubt His own love can compete with it ? here, the parts shift ?
  Here, the creature surpass the Creator,—the end, what Began ?

     *   *   *   *   *   *

I believe it ! 't is Thou, God, that givest, 't is I who receive ;
  In the first is the last, in Thy will is my power to believe.

     *   *   *   *   *   *

Would I suffer for him that I love ?—so would'st thou—so wilt thou !
  So shall crown thee the topmost, ineffablest, uttermost crown—
  And thy love fill infinitude wholly, nor leave up nor down
  One spot for the creature to stand in." [1]

" So, through the thunder comes a human voice
  Saying : ' O heart I made, a heart beats here !
  Face, My hands fashioned, see it in Myself,
  Thou hast no power, nor may'st conceive of Mine,
  But love I gave thee, with Myself to love,
  And thou must love Me who have died for thee !" [2]

And what does the poet say of the end? For that which is evil
there is judgment of utter destruction ; for that which is good, purify-
ing. So it is that chastisement is often seen to come through the
noblest part of a character otherwise mean, because in that there is
yet hope :

" You were punished in the very part
  That looked most pure of speck,—the honest love
  Betrayed you—did love seem most worthy pains,
  Challenge such purging, as ordained survive
  When all the rest of you was done with ? " [3]

And on the whole :

" There shall never be one lost good ! What was shall live as before ;
  The evil is null, is nought, is silence implying sound ;
  What was good shall be good with, for evil, so much good more ;
  On the earth the broken arcs ; in the heaven a perfect round.

" The high that proved too high, the heroic for earth too hard,
  The passion that left the ground to lose itself in the sky,
  Are music sent up to God by the lover and the bard ;
  Enough that He heard it once ; we shall hear it by-and-by.

" And what is our failure here but a triumph's evidence
  For the fulness of the days ? " [4]

" My own hope is, a sun will pierce
  The thickest cloud earth ever stretched ;
  That, after Last, returns the First,
  Though a wide compass round be fetched ;
  That what began best, can't end worst,
  Nor what God blessed once, prove accurst." [5]

---

[1] *Saul*, i. ff. 93.   [2] *An Epistle*, i. 343.   [3] *The Pope*, 1229 ff.
[4] *Abt Volger*, ix. ff.   [5] *Apparent Failure*, vii.

These thoughts, which I have endeavoured to set forth and not to criticize, come to us in the words of our own time.   They are clothed in images which are familiar to our own experience.   Our hearts in the main, I believe, respond to them as interpreting the fulness of our lives, our trials, and falls, and aspirations; as expressing our trust through disappointment, and our ideal aims in spite of imperfection.   And, as it seems to me, they help us to understand better, that is, with a more real and vital intelligence, some parts of our Faith in which alone, as far as I can see, they find their solid foundation.

ONE ASPECT OF BROWNING'S VILLAINS.

By MISS E. D. WEST.

(Read at the 15th Meeting of the Browning Society, on Friday, April 27, 1883.)

A. General Statement of View.
B. Application thereof to Particulars.   **C. Epilogue.**

A. GENERAL STATEMENT OF VIEW.

AMONGST the most prominent characteristics of Mr. Browning's mind and art, there are two which seem at first sight wholly unlike the qualities which we might expect to find in any *one* man's work. What concord, we may ask, is there between these : a joyous, persistent faith in Good being somehow the final significance of all Creation ; and a delight in the employing of artistic powers in the delineation of evilest aspects of Humanity?

Should we not, beforehand, suppose that an optimistic thinker would, if also a painter or poet, incline naturally to let his art dwell on the pleasant and loveable features of the human world, averting his regard from sights and sounds repugnant to his disposition ; and that, conversely, an artist employing his powers frequently in depicting subjects connected with moral evil, would be likely, as a thinker, to lean towards a creed of pessimism, or some dark theology of terror? However, as we *do*, as a fact, find in the whole mass of the writings which bear Mr. Browning's name, a mingling of these seemingly discordant elements, it is natural that students of those writings should wish to inquire into the matter more closely, questioning whether that odd juxtaposition of mental traits is one of those accidents in character which cannot be accounted for, or whether the apparent incongruity is, after all, only apparent.

To me it seems that a closer consideration brings us very soon to cease to see any want of harmony between these characteristics of this poet ; brings us to discern a real connection between the optimism of his way of thinking, and the peculiar success which he has achieved in artistic portraiture of the psychology of human evil.

With a view to tracing some of the lines of this connection, I want to say something about Mr. Browning and his Villains this evening. (I do not aim at anything like a thorough analysis of any one of the characters I may name, but only at a glance at one especial aspect which they present. I presuppose that all persons here are so familiar with Mr Browning's poetical portraits as to need only reference to, rather than description of, any one of them which may concern our present subject.)

That the whole tone of Mr. Browning's "mind" *is* optimistic needs here no proving. Other Papers read before your Society have dwelt on that feature of his poetry. That character of it, indeed, while it has gained for him the gratitude of those who can become disciples to his philosophy, has detracted in other folk's estimate from the value of his work. To some it makes all that (as a thinker) he has produced appear only as the error of an enthusiast, recommended to their intellectual mercy by its singular beauty and nobility, and by the pathos of its contrast with the sternness of verifiable beliefs.

That Mr. Browning's *Art*, on the other hand, is very secure against any charges of a blind amiability, and an ignoring of the darker side of Nature, is what will be as readily admitted by most people. As a matter of fact, a large class of minds are repelled from attempting to penetrate into the thought of his poetry by the unloveliness of so many of its artistic themes, an unloveliness more harshly developed in his mature literary life than in his earlier.

If any of us have asked ourselves "In what department of Mr. Browning's work does he seem to reach his highest level as *artist ?*" I should imagine that the answer would be, that it is in his dealing with evil and repulsive aspects of humanity.

I do not speak here of his general attainments as *poet* (which word includes in one's meaning, commonly, all that a man is as thinker, feeler, and artist). A man's success as *poet* cannot be determined by any critics' tests. It lies in his power of affecting the readers' perceptions on all sides of their natures ; and the part of this poet's work of most value to us may be his portraying of "whatsoever things are pure, whatsoever things are lovely," inasmuch as this is the part of it which stimulates what is best in ourselves—that sense of "admiration, hope, and love" by which Wordsworth says "we live."

What I mean is, that we find his artistic or technical genius attaining in its dealing with things evil, a kind of perfection which seems forbidden to it elsewhere. In his dealings with the beautiful, Browning oftenest seems to choose suggesting, rather than presenting, to the reader's imagination the ideas which his own has in view. A voluntary restraint of artistic force seems to be then exercised, and we receive the impres-

sion of its being subordinated to some superior poetical necessity. We
may admit this without accounting it a defect; nay, rather, this sort of
incompleteness in the art which in words communicates to us ideas of
things beautiful, ennobles it—making it seem as the vision of "one who,
on seeing Beauty in this lower world, being reminded of the True, begins
to recover his wings; and, having recovered them, longs to soar aloft,
but, being unable to do so, looks upward like a bird."[1]

In his artistic treatment of *evil* (that is, "*evil*" in the sense of $\tau\acute{o}$
$\alpha i\sigma\chi\rho o\nu$, the opposite of $\tau\acute{o}$ $\kappa\alpha\lambda o\nu$) this tendency to avoidance of completeness seems to disappear. In minute elaboration of each detail of
his pictures of "horror, crime, remorse," we find him not inclined to
spare either his own energy or his reader's sensibility. He seems to
dwell with a keen satisfaction in his own workmanship, on his reproduction, not only of the aspects of large open crime, but of all forms of
secret motives base and unbeautiful in human hearts.

Browning's pictured world of humanity (unaccompanied by Browning's own comment of interpretation thereof), how far more remote does
it seem from conditions paradisaical, than the corresponding worlds of
Wordsworth's, or even of Tennyson's art!

In powerful portraying of evil another modern poet—the German
poet Robert Hamerling—does perhaps in some respects surpass Browning (in the element of gruesomeness, for instance). But to find a
fondness for the artistic painting of evil does not surprise us when the
man in whom we find it grounds his poetry upon the philosophy of
Schopenhauer, as does Hamerling.

Amongst Browning's English contemporaries there are, as we know,
other painters of evil whose portraits of character are each in their own
style as powerful and as horribly realistic; Dickens and Thackeray
having each his points of excellence in this, and George Eliot's work
being peculiarly remarkable for its dealing with not only the actual
presence and operation of evil in man, but its genesis and development
in them through different stages. But in this the writers here instanced
do not appear going against their own normal theory, inasmuch as the
two former do not definitely commit themselves to *any* theory of human
destiny, and *that* theory which George Eliot makes her own is one
which keeps to the facts of human life from birth merely to death—*and
there stops.*

What puzzles the student of Browning is the finding that the same
man who tells us so often in various forms of expression that finally
"*evil is null, is nought,*" has done so much to aid our imagination in
realizing how much and how manifold is the evil that *is* present with

---

[1] *Phædrus* of Plato.

us. Now, in what way may we account for the prominence given in Browning's writings to the portraiture of what is morally unbeautiful?

In some measure we may attribute this to the natural indulgence of one set of his faculties in work affording them exercise. Browning is at once a mystic and a mental mechanic (however mutually exclusive these characters may be considered as a general rule). He has needs, not only to let perceptions of ideas float into him through the eye of the soul, but also to handle mental things with the hands of a craftsman, taking to pieces and putting together again.

One of these dispositions in him, the mystical, receives its satisfaction in the mental sights of the Beautiful that reach it as " rays that shoot in meteor-light athwart our earth,"[1] as "gleams that sting with hunger for full light."[2] It is receptive of the ideas of Beauty that thus reach it, and does not seek to dominate over them.

But the other disposition in him is a sort of *Tubal-Cain* nature, which this apprehending of things that are above us leaves unemployed; it has the faculty for dealing with things over which it is superior, and which, not reverencing, it can use freely as its brass and iron, for its material to work upon. To these mechanic's-propensities of his he can only give the satisfaction of exercise by thus occupying them with things which, being devoid of spiritual beauty, do not engage his mystical faculty. To meet this requirement, he chooses sometimes the grotesque, sometimes the morally ugly, for his subject matter.

This is only a passing suggestion of one consideration which in some measure explains to us certain apparent incongruities in Robert Browning's art.

I go on to a second consideration about the matter, which last is what is intended to be the main theme of this Paper. And this is the peculiar *quality* of his dealings with evil in his poetry, which seems to indicate a real connection between his artistic work in that department and his work as a speculative thinker.

This quality is his recognition of the *individuality of the soul* in his wicked " dramatis personæ," and all that, according to his creed, follows upon that recognition.

I suppose many or most of us here this evening have, at some time or other, read that strangely-vivid prose-poem of J. H. Newman's, his sermon on " The Individuality of the Soul." If one chances, after a reading of this, to open a volume of Browning at some story of crime and malevolence, and the sayings and thoughts of the actors therein, one's mind passes from the one book to the other without perceptible break in its tone of mood. (I at least have found it so.)

---

[1] *Easter-Day.*   [2] *Ibid.*

This I mention merely to *define* the quality I mean better than any words of mine could do. That the coincidence of tone in the two men only extends a little way, one need hardly say. The point of resemblance is, that each brings his theories of mankind to bear upon his ideas of individual men.

This quality, seeming as it does to be essential in Browning's treatment of evil in his poetry, is in Shakspere's accidental—sometimes present, sometimes not. Though Shakspere does at all times recognize good and evil as present in the whole mass of humanity, and bases his tragedies on the struggle between them, as opposed forces in the earth, he does not care to strenuously pursue the idea into the personality of the wicked characters whom his art creates. Some of these are not realized by our imagination as persons who could conceivably have been at all less wicked than we actually find them in the *rôles* which respectively they fill, in the tales where they are met with. Appearing upon the scene as the agents required to bring about certain disastrous events or complications in the plots, there is not discernible in them any suggestiveness of irrelevant capacities. They seem as if their proper function in the world were the being a part of its evil force. Their wicked doings constitute their right to exist there, a right no less valid than that of the noblest and loveliest of the other characters in the story. If Cordelia, in being what she is, and doing what she does, perfects her natural destiny, Goneril and Regan, in their deeds and dispositions, seem as fulfilling no less perfectly theirs. And Iago seems, in Shakspere's view, a creature that has developed legitimately the powers that were inherent in it ; a being hateful indeed, but not culpable, inasmuch as it had only obeyed the natural laws of growth of its kind ; and so in like manner Richard the Third. Now, wherever this is the case in Shakspere, the tragic interest of the stories *stops short of the villain's own character.* Monsters such as these seem rather a part of the machinery to produce the tragedy than in themselves tragic figures. It is only when the dramatic character is presented to our imagination as a human being turned to evil through misuse of potentialities for good, that we can by an appropriation of the villain's *ego* (however swift and transient such exchange of personality may be) have a "real apprehension" of the character's individuality. If the villain in a tale is not made in the likeness of us men, we can as indifferently witness the spectacle of his wickedness as we could watch, for instance, the destructiveness of the "dragons of the prime, who tare each other in their slime." Is it not so?

Iago and the horrible sisters in *Lear* are not tragic to us *per se.* The totality of the action in the plays where they are found represents indeed one aspect or another of the huge war going on in our world between "evil" and "good," taking those words in their widest sense. In this war these *dramatis personæ* play their parts; but it does not enter within their own individual natures: their place in the drama appertains to them by right of what they *do*, not what they *are*. Their agency is required to effect the disasters necessary for the working out of the plot. And accordingly, when the consequences of their villainy have ensued, they, the agents, cease to be the objects on which our attention is supposed to be engaged in the story. What remains as the persistent idea, is the spectacle of the sorrows that have been brought upon the other actors in the tale, and the noble or beautiful manifestations of character which their misfortunes have evoked from them.

As to what becomes of the doer of all this we are not led to inquire. When once his fate has ceased to be connected with that of the persons he has injured, it becomes of no account. Does some swift death overtake him? Well, this is viewed rather as the world's riddance of a noxious reptile or beast, than as a punishment judicial or remedial. Is he left to live on unpunished? Well, his subsequent life vanishes, we know not whither, and we are not concerned to know. The ill that he has wrought remains, and the feeling that lingers on in our minds is the unending "*pity of it,*" and the pathos of its contrast with the happiness which he has destroyed.

Not only in Shakspere's tragedies, but in his happy-ending plays, do we find the same unconcern often for his villains as individual souls. They interrupt temporarily the happiness of the good folk, and then, when their machinations are frustrated, they are themselves made away with somehow. The inner life and the destiny of Cymbeline's wicked queen as an individual concerns us not, for instance, when once Imogen and Posthumus have been reunited; one might multiply examples of the like.

These observations are, it is true, inapplicable all round to Shakspere's villains (irrespective of his larger heroes of crime, like Lady Macbeth, in whose personality the interest of the plots of course centres). It is true that he shows us some who, being baleful forces in the tale, are that and more besides; who are *per se* subjects of tragic interest; who come before us as men of like passions with ourselves, their lives being marred through guilt which we their brethren have escaped. Their wickedness *itself*—I don't mean its *punishment*—has the pathos of failure rather than the triumph of a malign success. Edmund in *Lear* is an instance of this. That there was in him a "might-have-been" of good is discernible in that flash of conscience just before his death, his recognition of the justice of his doom, and forgive ness of Edgar, its instrument; and in the dimly-pathetic momentary desire to be the object of a human love, evinced when he looks back with a sort of satisfaction on the horrible parody of it which the two sisters, one of them murderess and suicide for his sake, had given him; and in the dying "I pant for life!"—life that might leave space and opportunity to "do some good despite mine own nature."

"It is," Hartley Coleridge says, "amazing how small a beam of light redeems a soul from the condemnation of utter darkness."

One must feel that the strife between good and evil is included in Edmund, as well as including him. He is not extra-human; his *ego* is the same in kind as ours; his life is ruined because the good element in him was too feeble to make its way against those adverse circumstances of his bastardy which only a strong force of virtue could have overcome. His existence contains for us (in Carlyle's phrase concerning a historical character) "a poetic Tragedy, which is made up of Fate and one's own deservings (*Schicksal und eigene Schuld*), full of the elements of pity and fear."

It seems to me that, broadly speaking, Browning's evil men and women belong to a class from which Shakspere's treatment of his Iago and his Lear's elder daughters excludes them. That is to say, his villains are not merely actors in a tragic drama, but within each of their own existences a soul's tragedy is enacted. They are represented, not as inherently evil, but as having become so, through failure to be otherwise. Our poet sets them in the position of morally responsible beings, whom he makes to incur from us, or from whoever fills the part of Chorus in the drama, not merely abhorrence of their evil, but condemnation of their guilt,—a condemnation mingled, it may be, with varying degrees of pity. Inquiry, explicit or implied, is made into the circumstances of their criminal actions—distinguishing what therein is error and what wickedness.

Granting the existence of this difference between the treatment of Browning's and Shakspere's villains, which I have here roughly stated, or rather suggested, we may ask ourselves, "Whence does it seem to arise?" We may find answer, I think, in observing the difference between the attitudes of mind of the two men towards questions lying outside the range of mundane experience.

Shakspere, innately a positivist, can let any phenomenon be to him as an ultimate fact, which he does not care to go beyond. Browning, born a speculator, cannot and will not forgo the attempt to get at what lies behind the visible things of the world's order. For the positivist artist, the spectacle of an Iago can rest as it is, if only it seem to him a true counterfeit of nature mirrored in his art. He is under no obligation to suggest any future destiny of the monster; or to ask himself under what law the existence of such is permitted; or how it is reconciled with other facts terrestrial.

That this agnostic attitude of Shakspere's mind, content to admit, without questioning, appearances which he received as facts, whether in harmony with or discordant with each other, is an attitude of a peculiar dignity and beauty, moral and artistic, is of course to be fully acknowledged. But it seems to me to be no less true, that from the opposite tendency in Browning's mind, which precludes him from such an attitude of thought, there results one distinct gain to his art, a gain not at all affected by the question as to whether his speculations into matters extra-mundane arrive at facts or fancies. Either way, the result of his attaining by his half-intellectual, half-emotional process to the faith that good will be, at the last, the issue of all that we see in the world around us, is, that this creed which (unproven though it be to him) he adopts as a working hypothesis, drives him into a region of deeper, more recondite psychology in his character-drawing.

In art, as well as in science, the starting with a hypothesis and patiently trying whether experience will tally with it, is a method conducive to thoroughness of observation, and likely also to lead to unlooked-for gains.

Bound by theoretical faith to maintain a creed of limitless hope for humanity (which faith finds utterance so exultantly in *Abt Vogler's* words, and in other poems), and bound at the same time by his habits of shrewd unvisionary insight into matters of fact, to take account of all blemishes and deficiencies in its present aspects, Browning becomes forced into a more thorough analysis of those repulsive appearances, by the necessity to find warrant for the holding of his optimistic beliefs. In dealing with the wicked souls in his art-world, he must leave no dark corner of them unsearched out, where, possibly, amongst the motives underlying their action, something might be discovered which could give them a conceivable place in the world of a God, whose "care subsisteth ever," who

> "By God's own ways occult
> May, *doth* I will believe, bring back
> All wanderers to a single track." [1]

Whose

> "Mercy every way
> Is infinite." [2]

In this thorough analyzing of evil appearances in humanity, the two Browning natures, the ethical and the artistic, co-operate. The same

---

[1] *Christmas Eve.*   [2] *Easter Day.*

methods work towards the ends of both. To place the character dealt with in a story in some imagined circumstances which stir it to its foundations, and by some violent disturbances upturn things in it which the ordinary conditions of life leave buried far below the surface ; this method obtains for the Artist the *stoff* which he delights to deal with— *stoff* of psychological phenomena, subtle, rare, and precious ; and for the Thinker, the traces of undeveloped good, which, however slight, serve in some degree as confirmatory of his creed of hope.

A former paper of your Society has noted how very remarkably the characteristic of *Personality* makes itself felt in Browning's dramatic figures.

That his work as a dramatist does produce this effect on our minds, seems to me to be due, in a measure, to the prevalence in it of the idea of some indication of good—potential at least—being discoverable in each and all of its dramatic characters, that is, wherever these characters are at all fully portrayed.

Is it possible for us, with our human faculties, to make *real* to our minds any clear image of Personality wholly dissociated from good? (that is, good, in the sense of some quality either claiming in some way our admiration, or mitigating our aversion). I doubt if ever men have found it so. It is noteworthy, with regard to this point, that the two great poets who have chiefly impressed upon the public imagination their conceptions of the Devil, have been apparently under necessity of choice between giving to their artistic idea of him the attribute of pure evil or the attribute of Personality (by the latter phrase I mean making us feel the character to be an *I*).

Milton elected to make his Satan a Being of very marked Personality ; the most salient characteristic of him is his seeming an *ego* to us ; and (what falls in with this theory) Milton did not attempt to make him purely evil to our imagination. His fallen archangel claims some sort of admiration from us by reason of his loftiness and dignity in rebellion. Goethe chose to let *his* Devil be essential evil ; and accordingly we find that Mephistopheles is to us an impersonal presence, whose *ego* we cannot grasp by our imagination ; the very triumph of Goethe's art being of course here, his thus making this manifestation of the Evil-Principle a thing impalpable, and therefore all the more horrible, as a sort of wind, only to be perceived by its effects.

A. H. Clough followed on Goethe's lines in the Devil of his poem of *Dipsychus*. Byron's " Lucifer" claims kindred with the Satan of the *Paradise Lost*, in appearing before us with a distinct Personality, and being not without a certain μεγαλοψυχία (greatness of soul) in his demeanour.

It is not a mere idle speculation to ask oneself, "What would Browning's treatment have been of a character whose external acts should be precisely those of Iago?" The probability is, that without at all lessening the amount of the active evil in the man, or the terrible efficaciousness of his malice, Browning would have dug and dug into the lower strata of his motives, conscious and unconscious, until, underlying the whole character, something should be got at which could link the apparent fiend on to Humanity, and bring him within the scope of our dramatic sympathy.

The Iago known to us is viewed from *without;* and nobody feels as if he were really known to us. Browning could not but have somehow got *within* him, and have looked from *his* evil soul's stand-point outwards. And it might be that then this villain's spiritual debasement might be felt by us to be a sadder tragedy than even the ruin wrought by him in the temporal lives of the Moor and Desdemona.

B. APPLICATION OF THE GENERAL VIEW TO THE PARTICULAR.

Let us see now if a glance at some few of Mr. Browning's wicked folk may verify, so far as it goes, the foregoing generalization. In a complete survey of his evil characters (which, however, this Paper does not at all pretend to be) they might be classified thus :—

1st. Those in whom the actual operation of good overcoming in some manner this or that force of evil in the soul, is made the theme of the narrative (as, for instance, "Halbert and Hob," "Ned Bratts," &c.).

Then 2ndly, Those in whom there are shown to us potentialities of good, warped or unused, or only so faintly or transiently in operation as barely to indicate to us their existence.

And 3rdly, Those in whom we (owing to the character's position amongst the dramatic figures in the poem, or other causes) miss the traces of that care for the destiny of the individual soul which commonly shows itself in Browning's dealings with it.

On the confines of these classes would be the mixed multitude of non-criminal characters who are more or less swayed by unworthy motives.

This classification of course should be looked upon only as arbitrary, for convenience of one's thinking. In Browning's art-world, as in real life, there are not hard and fast distinctions always traceable between varieties of sinners.

Concerning the first of these classes, there is small need for much expounding of the ethical significance. On the face of the story it is sufficiently plain for any reader to see.

Passing on to the second of the classes, we should find there Browning's two principal villains : Count Guido Franceschini of the *Ring and the Book*, and the devil-like " elder man " of the *Inn Album*, together with others.

What position do these here named occupy in the respective poems where we meet with them? It is primarily true to say that each of them is the agent through whom the tale becomes a tragedy. Subtract their operation from it, and very smooth and unheroic would be the course of all the other folks' lives therein. Without Guido, Caponsacchi would have remained to the end the gay, mundane ecclesiastic, undisturbed by thought or emotion ; and Pompilia would have expanded from gentle, ignorant girlhood to commonplace womanhood. The parson's beautiful daughter (in the *Inn Album*) would, without the advent of her seducer, have "vegetated on, lily-like," through some ordinary lot of life, never attaining to the sorrowful grandeur of soul to which the ruin of her peace raised her. But, in the characters of these two workers of evil as presented to us by Browning, is there not *significance beyond the actual parts which they play in the dramas ?* Does there not seem to be about them the same sort of inconsistency in evil which we find in veritable human beings? Does not Browning suggest to us all along that these villains' personality and their wickedness which is made known to us, are not co-extensive.

I am not disposed to attempt any whitewashing of these very black characters ; it is more to the purpose of anything I have been saying to accept them as intended by the man who created them for types of extreme human depravity. They are not the sort of sinners whom ordinary story-writers would select to invest with moral interest for a reader. There *are* waverings and balancings in human natures between good and evil of such a kind that the situation is easy enough to enter into by our ethical sympathy when it is presented to us in fiction ; and demands of this sort upon our sympathy are made by writers many of prose and verse. But to put forth demands so facile to respond to is precisely what Browning does not ever care to do. He requires in his readers qualities the same in kind as his own. They must be ready to grapple with not only intellectual difficulties, but with moral.

Here, in these two characters, he sets before us evil of the most repulsive sort, wholly unadorned by any of the, so to speak, heroic characteristics of crime. Greed of money, cold, deliberate lust, refinements in hatred and cruelty towards things weaker in any way than themselves—these are the traits which distinguish them ; the *Inn Album* scoundrel being, in his Mephistophilean polish and exquisite sapience in the social world's ways, even more revolting than the rougher Guido Franceschini.

Truly, if Browning maintains his hopeful theory about humanity, nobody can say that he shirks putting it to a very severe test. The adjective "shallow," which so currently affixes itself now to the noun "optimism," is hardly applicable to the theory as held by the thinker who admits thus the obligation to find room in it for the fact that humanity comprises existences so hateful as these.

The question cannot be evaded, and he shows no desire to evade it: "Is there in human nature, in these its concrete forms, potentiality of final deliverance from the evil in it, given only time enough for the work?" To this question his answer is affirmative; expressed, indeed, in no definite formula, but discoverable in and through his art, if we care to look for it there.

Do not understand me to view Browning in any way as a doctrinaire writer, using here his poetical work as a vehicle for his particular opinions on eschatology. It goes without saying that it is not the wont of the larger race of dramatists or novelists to make their art serve to "point their moral," after the manner of story-writers in temperance magazines, for instance. But, nevertheless, may not the matter stand thus—that while for each true artist the world, or portion of the world depicted by him in his books, is created for him by the involuntary operation of his genius, *that* art-world is to himself as the real world, full of problems which he may, if his tendencies so dispose him, set himself to investigate as directly as one would the problems arising out of the facts of real life? It is enough to say that Browning, as dramatic artist, creates his mimic world of humanity, and as thinker, analyzes it. We need not try to assign too precise chronological order to the two acts. Nor need we care to distinguish too rigidly between his art and his thought.

And what then does Browning say to us about, not Guido's *deeds*, but Guido's *self*,—that self which underlies the life? He first gives us the various superficial judgments of the character which the different speakers in the poem have from their respective stand-points formed. "Half Rome" pronounces one of these surface judgments; the "other half Rome" another. "Tertium quid" doesn't get any deeper down. The two lawyers are little concerned with the inner soul of the prisoner for and against whom they are to plead. Caponsacchi sees in Franceschini only the murderer of Pompilia. Pompilia herself, so near to death that she almost counts as one of those who (in Tennyson's phrase) can

> " Look us through and through,
> With larger other eyes than ours,
> To make allowance for us all,"

she sees in her hateful husband one whom his mother had loved even as *she* loves *her* babe. She looks forward to the possibility of good for him through the touch of "God's shadow," wherein there "is healing." It is the old Pope alone who (as vicegerent of the Searcher of hearts) is represented as penetrating into the dark mine of this human soul, flashing into its recesses the lamp of his own living conscience.

Pope Innocent's utterances are of course dramatic in the first instance. Being the speech of a very old man, they are characterized by that leisurely long-windedness of discourse, that meditative slowness in the wielding of weighty arguments, which (by the way) is the mark of senility by which Browning also characterizes the utterances of the aged St. John in the *Death in the Desert*. But though thus dramatic, we may take it that Pope Innocent's estimate of the matter represents, on the whole, that view which Browning himself, as a philosophic thinker, accepts, about this Guido Franceschini, whose position in Nature is one of the problems which his "art" has proposed to his "mind" to solve.

There seems substantial agreement between the Pope's impression of Guido's character and the impression which that character, when judged out of the sinner's own lying mouth, is skilfully so contrived as to make upon us. Guido the Pope views as a being morally responsible, who might have been unlike what he now is *if* he had chosen. His life is termed

> " a man's immense mistake,
> Who, fashioned to use feet and walk, deigns crawl."

He is found "reprobate," inasmuch as there had been in his outward condition so much to make goodness easy to him that the feebleness of the moral sense in him when

> " furnished forth for his career
> When starting for his life-chance in our world,"

was only adjusted fairly, so as to afford him that requisite amount of difficulty in right doing which could constitute it *virtue*.

The Pope notes how Guido's probation had been life-long, how opportunities had been open to him of retrieving that *immense mistake;* how, even after attempted crime, he might have been "saved so as by fire," could he have known the "mercy of a minute's fiery purge, by the furnace-coals of public scorn and private remorse refining away from his soul its baser part, the alloy of force and guile." Saved *thus*, or saved not by fire, but by the recognition of Divine Love—at the birth of his infant, Pompilia's son—had he only so chosen.

To another of these unaccepted opportunities of deliverance from the evil in him, Guido himself adverts (in a very remarkable passage occurring in the first of his own monologues). He tells how there swept over him a strange wave of good impulse when he—after his journey of murderous intent—arrived at Rome during the festival of the birth of Christ :

> "Festive bells. Everywhere the Feast o' the Babe,
> Joy upon earth, peace and good will to man!
> I am baptized. I started and let drop
> The dagger. "Where is it, His promised peace?"
> Nine days o' the Birth-Feast did I pause and pray
> To enter into no temptation more.
> I bore the hateful house, my brother's once,
> Deserted,—let the ghost of social joy
> Mock and make mouths at me from empty room
> And idle door that missed the master's step—
> Bore the frank wonder of incredulous eyes,
> As my own people watched without a word,
> Waited, from where they huddled round the hearth
> Black like all else, that nod so slow to come—
> I stopped my ears even to the inner call
> Of the dread duty, heard only the song
> "Peace upon earth," saw nothing but the face
> O' the Holy Infant and the halo there
> Able to cover yet another face
> Behind it, Satan's which I else should see."

In this account of the strange, and to him unwonted, experience that thus visited him, Guido seems to be, for once, speaking direct truth, though so large a proportion of his copious utterances are only the sophistries by which he essays to defend his wretched cause. The tissue of curiously interwoven cowardice and audacious cunning of which the monologue consists is here crossed by a thread of plain truth. His statement here may count as simply historical.

[This is an instance of the gain which in artistic respects results to Browning's poetical conception of such a character as Guido's, from his acceptance of the necessity to let it rank under a general "working together for good;" for hereby we find produced by him a character, not a mere piece of mechanism calculated to produce certain evil results in the dramatic story, but an entity whose spiritual incongruities and unexpected turns of disposition make it seem more alive.

Browning's villains being under the operation of two natures, we cannot calculate beforehand what they will do any more than we can calculate on the course of action of the human beings in real life.]

For that brief nine days' space only was this evil soul covered by the overwhelming wave of good ; but the fact of its baptism therein remains uneffaceable. There was thereby established as true that there was in the man susceptibility to righteousness, that he was not mere devil or conscienceless brute.

Let us note here how Browning places this transient manifestation
of Guido's better self just in the period of time immediately following
that at which he had left behind his ordinary mental condition of dull,
passionless cruelty, and the sluggishness that sought pleasurable excite-
ment in devising ingenious daily tortures for his wife's heart, and had
broken out into a mood of violent and murderous anger. The man had
"risen up like fire, and fire-like roared," and then in the flame and
smoke of this great cloud of wrath and jealousy had journeyed, rushing
blindly, Rome-wards. In Browning's view of human nature vehement
passion of any sort tends to rouse, in the general whirl and tumult caused
by it in a man's consciousness, the dormant forces of good that may be
in him, bringing him thus nearer to better possibilities. You remember the passage in the *Two Poets of Croisic*, where he says his "hope"
is "in the *vivid horse*" rather than "*the steer sluggish and safe*"?

That there *were* forces in Guido's nature originally not evil is not
belied by the general impression left by the second of his monologues.
Notwithstanding all the arrant cowardice and miserable clinging to life
shown by a bold sinner at the last extremity, which the Count utters in
words ranging through all varieties of violence and guile till they reach
the final shriek of

> "Abate, Cardinal, Christ, Maria, God, . . .
> Pompilia, will you let them murder me?"

there is yet throughout the earlier portions of his speech evidence discernible of qualities which make it conceivable that this soul, if "remade"
by God hereafter, might yet retain its personal identity; that a residuum
of it might, after æons of purgatorial influences should have refined
away its mass of base material, become the centre of a new and yet continuous self. In the fact that Guido's original vitality and strength
have, by the combined action of forces without and within him, sunk
under the power of evil so vile, lies the tragic interest of his character.
By Browning the tragedy of a human history is viewed as lying in the
soul's waste or misuse of opportunities in its probation, long or short
earthly life meaning only longer or shorter probation; all the accidents
of the outer condition are only accessory to the interests of moral and
spiritual life in each man.

Guido's earthly life was a total failure. But the Pope, in finally
pronouncing on him the doom of death, speaks, not in the spirit of a
judge who would banish a felon from the world of the living lest he
should do more harm to folks there, but rather in that of a physician,
who, seeing that the man's ill is past *this* world's cure, relegates him to
the chances of another condition.

For him, he says—

> " I have no hope,
> Except in such a suddenness of fate."

He speaks here of the moment of his execution :--

> "I stood at Naples once—a night so dark
> I could have scarce conjectured there was earth
> Anywhere ; sky or sea or world at all.
> But the night's black was burst through by a blaze ;
> Thunder struck blow on blow ; earth groaned and bore
> Through her whole length of mountain visible.
> There lay the city, thick and white with spires,
> And like a ghost disshrouded, white the sea.
> So may the truth be flashed out by one blow,
> And Guido see one instant and be saved.
> Else I avert my face, nor follow him
> Into that sad, obscure, sequestered state
> Where God unmakes but to remake the soul
> He else had made in vain—*which must not be.*"

There is in this passage so much that hardly is needed for the dramatic exigencies of a seventeenth-century Pope, that one cannot but feel that it is the later thinker who approaches the question himself, about one of his representative villains.

In the hateful " elder man " of the *Inn Album* there are indications (in some ways more tangible than in Count Guido) of the unused better self.　This man has keen intellectual perceptions of moral distinctions ; he nowhere calls evil good.　He has subtle discernment of the quality of the earthly blessings he has forfeited.　Just herein does the tragedy of his life lie ; in his clear vision of the heaven of noble human love, between which and himself a great gulf has, by his own act, been set. His heart has become bound in coils and coils of guileful motives, yet it asserts itself in a direct sincerity for once, when he says, in reverting to that moment of his past experience, when a flash of human passion revealed truth to him,—when,

> " Either I *lost*—or, if it please you, *found*
> My senses— .　.　.　.　.　.　.
> .　.　.　.　I see.　Slowly, surely creeps,
> Day by day, o'er me the conviction—here
> Was life's prize grasped at, gained, and then let go.
> That with her, maybe for her, I had felt
> Ice in me melt, grow stream, drive to effect
> Any or all of the fancies sluggish here
> I' the head that needs the hand she would not take,
> And I shall never lift now."

He sees

> " Her visionary presence on each goal
> I *might* have gained had we kept side by side."

And later on, the passionate appeal to the woman from whose love he had shut himself out by his grievous wronging of her, has a strange sort of pathos by reason of its being prompted by complicated impulses of a twofold nature, only one part base. We, the readers, are given insight into the half-genuineness of his transient feeling; while *she*, his former victim, is seen by us as discerning in his entreaty only the latest device of his guile. *She* does not perceive that this appeal made thus to her by the world-hardened man is not wholly the utterance of a mere lustful desire to lure her to a life of sin with him, but is in some measure also the last despairing gasp after a heaven of good made by a soul as it sinks down into an earthly hell of vileness. She is, in his eyes, symbol of the better life that he might have attained to, and has missed.

That he is still capable of thus feeling,—that, even perverted, the desire of self-surrender to a nature which has seemed to him to represent what is " highest and best and most real," finds even a temporary place in his heart, is an evidence of his being not wholly dead in sin.

There is true tragedy here in the antithesis of the man's passionate mood (a mood in him so rare, so transient), over against the steady uniform cynicism and malice that have grown to be habitual with him.

Perhaps nothing elsewhere in Browning's poetry surpasses in artistic effect his representation here of rapid transition from one mood to its opposite. We feel as if we had witnessed a burst of sun-warmth find its way for an instant through enveloping clouds, only to be caught back into them again.

One aspect of Browning's villains is all that we are now considering. I need hardly say that though classed together under this aspect, the two *dramatis personæ* of which we have just spoken have little in their whole complexion in common. One broad distinction between them is this, that while Count Guido is represented as singularly devoid of wit or humour of any sort (the solemn seriousness of his cunning being never relieved by any play of double consciousness), the acute old rascal of the *Inn Albım*, on the other hand, is thoroughly alive to a sense of the ludicrous. The devil that inspires *him* is " der Schalk," Mephistopheles. We see him finding a source of exquisite amusement in the wielding of his power over his simple-minded comrade, and amusement too in his cynical self-analysis.

Let me note here the fact that the *Ring and the Book* contains two other wretches, yea three, besides Count Guido (his brothers Paolo and Girolamo, and the Archbishop), of whose individual souls Browning takes no account. I do not, however, think that by this fact anything we have said here is at all invalidated. These other villains are not brought amongst the actors in the drama, they never speak *in propriâ personâ.* We are not supposed to come directly into contact with them in imagination. They are, as it were, "out of focus" in the group; and it would distort the proportion of the picture, and be incorrect as art, to in any way engage too definitely the attention of the reader on *their* personality and the problems relating thereto. Browning is thoroughly a painter, and never for ethical purposes breaks through the rules of his art. To remember this explains a good many apparent inconsistencies in his poetry.

Using the word "villains" to mean the human evil agents in a story, two noticeably come before our view in the diorama of *Pippa Passes.*

The ceaseless antagonism going on between forces of good and evil in Nature, is in none of Browning's poems more strongly set forth than in this: the girl Pippa being for the time the unconscious, or only very dimly conscious, medium through which the good force in the world— the "not-ourselves-that makes-for-Righteousness" — acts, and the antitheses to her, being the human agents who energize on the side of "*der Kraft die stets das Böse will,*" in tempting their fellow-men to evil. These latter are prominently here, "Ottima" and the "Intendant" of the Bishop, Uguccio Stefano.

It is noteworthy concerning one of these, how Mr. Browning achieves by one line of verse—some five or six words in it—the investing with a spiritual interest for us a dramatic figure which otherwise would stand only as a type of morally loathsome corporeal beauty— Ottima, the "great white queen : magnificent in sin," in whose "great round full-orbed face not an angle broke the delicious indolence." In *her*, even, we are bidden to discern a significance of character beyond what belongs to her actual deeds. Browning indicates in her the unlimitedness of a human personality. Temptress of her weaker paramour, whom her hot sensuality has dragged with herself into foul murder, made still fouler by ingratitude, she has, nevertheless, potentialities not included in this sequence of criminal acts. We are shown a germ of good in her, which might conceivably grow to cast out the mass of cruel-heartedness and impurity. We see how in her, just at the moment of death, passion liberates itself from its baser elements of selfishness. Though she has become instinctively aware that she herself has nothing more to gain from Sebald, whom the sounds of Pippa's pure voice (singing as she passes of "God in His heaven") have suddenly filled with loathing for his sin, and for her who sinned with him, yet in this supreme crisis of her life's probation Ottima's feeling leaps for *one* moment to the height of a self-abnegating love. The egoistic and sensual elements in her passion are left behind; it attains the womanliness that "means only motherhood." She utters the "*Not me—to him, O God, be merciful!*" She desires to shield his life with hers. She would take upon herself *alone* God's punishment of their joint guilt, if only so Sebald might escape it. This is one of the most striking passages where Browning's ethics and art join. For his pictorial effects he depends very much on his arrangements of contrasts of light and shade; and here the moral darkness of the rest of the picture is deepened to us by the introduction of this single streak of moral light across one part of the canvas. It is as a bit of Rembrandt. How characteristic, too, of Browning is his thus making passion seem to purify itself by its very intensity!

An exception to the rule that Browning finds a soul of good in things evil, apparently presents itself in the *Intendant* with whom we find the Bishop in discourse in Scene iv. of *Pippa Passes*.

In all that we are shown of *him*, there seems no redeeming trait of humanity. When he himself suggests to "Monsignor" the two possible reasons, either of which may have induced him to spare the life of the infant whom he had been engaged to murder by the brother of the prelate,—the "either the child smiles in his face, or most likely he is not fool enough to put himself in the employer's power so thoroughly. The child is always ready to produce, as you say, howsoever, whensoever,"—we feel perfectly in agreement with him as to the second reason being the *more likely* one (even though the villain's immediate motive for saying so is his desire to frighten the Bishop out of any disposition to bring his evil deeds to justice). "I always intended to make your life a plague to you with her,"—so he says, and so the truth of the matter lay. And now that he sees that it is all up with the game he had been playing, there is not a particle of human mercy in his mood, when, as his last chance of getting out of the business with his life whole, and some of his ill-gotten gains into the bargain, he makes his vile proposal to the Bishop, of "making away" with the girl for him by a method which is "not the stupid, obvious kind of killing."

Must we say that Browning's representation of this character is out of keeping with the general scope of his teaching? I do not think it appears so, when we accept this scene in the poem, not as a dramatic portraiture of two *characters*, but as a "study" of a *phase of temptation* presented to a soul, and its deliverance therefrom. The emphasized point in the story is not, who and what the tempter was, but what sort of offer did he make to the person who underwent the probation; and how did that person fare under the trial?

To the temptation to a dastardly acquiescence in the villainy of the Intendant Maffeo, the Bishop is just on the point of yielding, when he is suddenly caught back by a force of good that acts upon him through the clear, fresh sounds of Pippa's singing as she goes by; and this gives him courage to bring the villain to justice, regardless of consequences to himself. It is on the personality of the Bishop that attention is directed in this group. As to what a more direct view of the odious Intendant's individual character might reveal to us, remains an open question, which Browning chooses to leave so.

The vagabond Bluphocks is shown to us rather as a tool in the hands of a wicked man, than as a villain prompted by any evil motives of his own. No moral sense in him appears to be awake. The broad fact of this world being patent before him, that the sun does " rise on the evil and the good, and the rain fall on the just and the unjust," he feels no need to concern himself with any differences between them. Knocking about in the world, he *must* make a livelihood somehow; he is as *unmoral* as a professional London thief might be. His pocket-full of zwanzigers, the payment given by the Intendant of the Bishop for the innocent Pippa's intended ruin, are to Bluphocks not the price of blood, but simply zwanzigers,—coins which will keep him afloat and in the ease of carelessness as long as they last; and then some other like bit of lucky chance may come to him.

There are some of Mr. Browning's pictures of evil that explain themselves to us better if accepted as mere studies of this or that attitude of feeling rather than as portraits of character. To seek in these for any traces of good in evil would be not to the point.

An instance of this is the highly-finished study of one phase of human hatred—the hatred felt not for any definite injury done, but on account of the groundless antipathy (of which probably most people have had some slight experience), intensified by the compulsory comradeship in the oppressive monotony of the conventual life. I refer of course to the soliloquy of that Spanish monk who is shown to us as looking on with a hideous snarl of " g-r-r-r !" at the inoffensive gardening operations of the obnoxious " Brother Lawrence," whose melon-flowers of the " fruit-sort " he had been at the trouble to " keep close nipped on the sly."

Here we have simply a study of a morbid mental condition, resulting from the unhealthy inactivity of the cloister routine; and as to what the real nature of this very unamiable monk would have been had his energies found legitimate scope in the outer world, Browning does not, of course, undertake to say. Probably, since his cloistered feelings were anything but languid, even in the midst of the sluggishly-peaceful influences surrounding him, there may have been in him a good deal of force of character, which he might have turned to better account under luckier circumstances.

Let us accept the picture as we find it.

Of other studies of evil attitudes of feeling which Browning has given us, we may say the like—that as they are not representations of a character, but of one mental attitude of human feeling, they are not contradictory (though of course not directly confirmatory) of his faith in human possibilities. But of these time does not now allow examination. As studies of criminal act not prompted by criminal motive, but by some curious twist in the conscience and instincts, we might select the pictures of two murderers, *Porphyria's lover*, and the husband in *A Forgiveness;* the first of these pictures containing only the single feeling in which the deed originated ; the other tracing, through a complex history of mental condition, the conscience's reasons for the act of bloodshed.

One character we *do* find in his books which cannot be made to fit in with his creed of universal hope—the mother in *Ivan Ivanovitch*. She is perhaps Browning's solitary *unredeemable* human being. There is discernible in her no soul which could be cleansed from guilt by any purgatorial process—no passion which might be transmuted from force of evil to force of good. To such a creature Ivan's axe brings simple annihilation ; nothing of her survives to be consigned to future reclaiming discipline. Her fault had not been *moral*, had not been sin, to be punished by pain inflicted on the soul ; it was merely the uncounteracted primary instinct of self-preservation, and as such it is fitliest dealt with by the simple depriving her, without further penalty, of the very life which she had secured for herself at so horrible a cost. It is not as if any mother-instinct in her had striven with the self-preserving instinct, and had been overborne by it in a moment of frenzied fear. No ; no revulsion of impulse occurs when she arrives alone at the village ; no wish that *she* had been sacrificed for her children, or that she had shared their fate. In the complacent sense of peace and satisfaction with which she views her own sole and single safety, what hope is there of any regeneration for her, by any conceivable process? The impression left with us at the last is, that this thing in the semblance of woman is a bit of creation lower in the scale of existence than the brutes, and has no lot or part in the destiny of humanity. We are satisfied to think that the headless body and severed head are all that remain of "Louscha" when the strong-armed carpenter has dealt his righteous blow. And we feel that the dramatist is content thus to leave her.

I reserve for the last of Browning's dramatic figures at which time now allows us to look, the "Chiappino" (unstable, rather than actively bad man), of whose life the poetry and prose is set forth in *A Soul's*

Tragedy; because that poem contains one passage which seems to strike the keynote of all Browning's thought about, and artistic dealings with, his sinful characters.

"*I judge people by what they might be, not by what they are, nor will be,*" the Papal legate says in a speech in which his tone, playfully ironical on the surface, is grave with meaning underneath. What he there says is directly regarding the individual character of Chiappino. (You remember, of course, how there is one noble moment in his life, when he constrains his friend Luitolfo to escape in the disguise of his garments, and remains in his stead to meet well-nigh certain death, rewarded by Eulalia's approval; and how there comes afterwards a falling away from this altitude into a range of base motives and acts.)

"Judge of men by their profession, for though the bright moment of promising is but a moment, and cannot be prolonged, yet if sincere in its moment's extravagant goodness, why, trust and know the man by it, I say, *not by his performance, which is half the world's work,* interfere as the world needs must with its accidents and circumstances. The profession was purely the man's own. *I judge people by what they might be, not are, nor will be.*"

Judgment, the same in *kind,* extends to other characters (in Browning's view) in whom evil is more pronounced than it is in poor Chiappino. Even with regard to the worst, he holds that

> "Not on the vulgar mass
> Called 'work' must sentence pass,"

but on

> "All instincts immature,
> All purposes unsure,
> That weighed not as his 'work,' yet swelled the man s account.
>
> . . . .
> *All* [they] *could never be,*
> *This they were worth to God.*"[1]

C. EPILOGUE.

Objection may very possibly be felt to the attempt made in thi Paper to make certain things in Browning's poetry square with each other. It may be asked, Why need we try to reconcile the philosophic and moral doctrines of the one part of his work with the purely artistic part, the portraits of human character, which we meet with elsewhere in it? Why cannot we leave him a poet's privilege of inconsistency? If each of his utterances seem to us to manifest some quality of beauty or interest, may we not be content to accept *each* as the natural outgoing of one mood or another, and to find its justification in its truthful expression of that particular mood?

[1] *Rabbi Ben Ezra.*

To this one can only reply, that this privilege of inconsistency in their writings seems to be only the right of the lesser order of poets, those in whom their receptivity (being greater than their original force) brings them by turns under the various surrounding influences. For such it *is* allowable to record accurately, with whatever beauty of expression may be, the variations of their mental conditions. Let, to-day, optimistic views of life, individual and collective, prevail with them over other theories ; let pessimistic be uppermost to-morrow (the all-important change of philosophic creed being possibly due to some change in the weather, or to some small occurrence in their private mental history). The more of these inconsistencies there are to be found in their work, the better ; for on this variegatedness does the charm of their poetry depend. That there *is*, in the poetry of moods unfettered by any consistency of purpose, a peculiar charm, is undoubted ; but it is a grace of art which no real student of Browning's poetry would desire to claim for it. Mr. R. H. Hutton says, "Browning has no moods." If I recollect rightly what he says in an essay of his, which I have not read for many years, he speaks of this as if it were a *defect*. The statement itself I accept as quite true ; but I cannot find therein any indication of inferiority to the mood-poets, but rather an indication of attainment in a branch of art distinct from theirs, and, shall we not say, *higher?* I prefer looking upon Robert Browning not as the maker of a number of poems which we may criticize separately, taking for our approval whatever suits our fancy ; but rather as the maker of a poem (extending from *Pauline* to the *Jocoseria* volume) in which the component parts all *must* bear relation to each other ; any want of agreement between the parts being destructive of the significance of the whole. I look upon him as an architect, designer of a building which in its purpose is an ideal philosophy of the Good and Beautiful : in which " *evil is null, is nought, is silence implying sound ;* " and it seems to me that if we are to approve the plan of the architect, we must, in our mind's eye, bring together all the parts of the building, comparing one with another, in order to find that they do really support each other. In Browning's architecture the first patent fact is, that it follows the law of variety. A longer acquaintance with it shows us that it is also obedient to the law of unity ; just as at first sight the law of variety seems to prevail in a Gothic cathedral, in which all the while the law of unity is really operant, all the parts of the building having reference to and converging towards the altar, and so forming a whole. And the unity of the structure is not at all destroyed by the fact that in the different parts of the whole, which are the accretions of centuries, there are manifold varieties of material and of workmanship.

In that queer jingle of rhyme with which Browning concludes his latest volume, he insists on the unity of his life-work. He says that "*darkling I keep my sunrise aim ;*" and implies, moreover, in the "*I look to my ways,*" that there is a dominant purpose extending through the whole course of his art.

Because of this unity of Browning's ethical purpose throughout his score (and more!) of volumes (whose extent has become so inconveniently long on one's book-shelves), I have not thought that there would be any gain in arranging in chronological order his portraits of character which we have glanced at this evening,—though in some aspects of his poetry one *must* pay attention to the dates of the writings.

With regard to his thought and theories of life, it is true, indeed, that the supernatural optimism which his earlier books affirmed with the ease of confident assurance, is maintained in some of the later, e. g. *La Saisiaz,* with the effort of militant faith ; nevertheless, it is on that theory that the poetry of his poems rests. With Mr. Browning's personal beliefs let no critic meddle, of course : but the working-hypothesis of his art seems to be certain notions of good and evil,—the same through the five decades of his literary work.

If I have suggested to any Browning-student a further examination than I have been here able to attempt of those apparent anomalies in his writings, which to my mind *do* seem to resolve themselves into law, I shall have done what I aimed at doing in this Paper. In all literary criticism, even true views of one aspect of a writer's work require the corrective of counterpart views of truth.

E. D. W.

April 17th.

JAMES LEE'S WIFE.

By Rev. J. H. BULKELEY.

(Read at the 16th Meeting of the Browning Society, Friday, May 25, 1883.)

LET me be a little personal in my preface. I remember well one bright Sunday morning, in Cambridge, in 1864, which I and a friend spent in reading *Dramatis Personœ* under an old mulberry-tree in Queen's College garden, and from that time until last year I had supposed that *James Lee* was still in existence, and was surprised to find, when the printed list of lecture subjects was issued, that I had unconsciously undertaken to write a paper on a poem called *James Lee's Wife*. As a Browningite conservative, I protest against the change of title and the addition to the poem. As Shakspere's *Julius Cæsar* does not go by the name of those who conspired against him, but the central personage, though we see very little of him, is allowed rightly to give his name to the drama, because the characteristic action of others centres in him ; as *Maud* is not called 'Maud's Lover' ; or, to bring an illustration from still nearer home, as *Pauline* is not called ' Pauline's Lover,' so, it seems to me, there was no sufficient reason for changing the title of this poem. The former title was as good, perhaps better.

There are some alterations in punctuation in the edition of 1872, but with, perhaps, the exception of the pronoun adjective relating to God, in the line

" God does, endure his act,"

having a small instead of a capital initial letter, and of the word ' Love,' in the line.

" Oh Love, Love, no, Love ! not so indeed ! "

being spelt with a capital instead of a small *l*, the only alteration of real importance is the long addition to the sixth poem, by which, according to a recent critic,[1] " its difficulty is complicated." At any rate, this addition,

---

[1] The Rev. H. C. Beeching, in *Modern Thought*, Nov. 1882.

made, or certainly published, eight years after the original publication, seems to me, in its abruptness, its argumentativeness, and its comparative roughness of versification, to be out of keeping with the rest of the special poem. It was written in another mood, and probably was occasioned not by the flow of the thought, but by the supposed duty of making things clearer to the British public.

No doubt it is right that badly-turned verses should sometimes be rehammered on the anvil, that obscure poems should be made clearer, if this can be done without sacrifice of their first tone, of their original thought. But here the case is different. Here hammer and anvil have been used not to alter what was there at first, but to weld on to it something of different metal, of almost incongruous workmanship. However, we must with all loyalty, but a little grumbling, take the poem as it is.

James Lee's Wife describes, not in detail, but by lyrical flashes, an unhappy married life, as far as it has its effect on the mood, and at last on the critical conduct, of the wife. The husband we are meant to know very little about, and we do not wish to know any more. He was not a saint, and Miss West would not have included him among her villains. He was no Tito, not even a drunkard, as far as we are told, like poor Agnes Brontë's copy of her brother; and, on the other hand, he was no selfish pedant like Dorothea's infatuated choice, no absorbed genius like —the popular idea of Thomas Carlyle. What, then, made their married life so out of joint, that 'On Deck' came to be the end of it? For one thing, lack or decay of beauty in the wife, but, for the most part, just incompatibility of temperament, of character, of aim—what in John Milton's divorce court would have given "ample room and verge enough" for an absolute divorce or a prudent separation.

She was a poet, an artist, fond of reveries, fancies, feelings; liking the idea of love in a cottage; wishing to give and to receive endearments of devotion. Now he would have told you that he was not " one of that sort." So far from the wind or Leonardo da Vinci having said what some poet or his wife made them say, he did not believe one word of it, indeed he was quite sure that the wind never spoke at all. As Lady Scott is once said to have remarked to Sir Walter, when he was expressing his admiration of a flock of sheep in a picturesque position, that she always liked them best at dinner, so James Lee had no sympathy with his wife's poetic tendencies, and, no doubt, showed his growing dislike of being cooped up with her, in cold weather, in a foreign country, in a house of four rooms. She took her pleasure in copying casts and writing verses on the sea-shore. He took his in some other way. And to a great extent, in consequence of this, and because it was not in him, he could not lavish endearments on her, and her watching and waiting, and beseeching piteous looks, very naturally "turns now to a fault." And so the little domestic tragedy drew to its fated close, more real and pathetic than if it had been terminated by the dagger or the poisoned cup.

Lessons of endurance, of resignation and hope, from art, nature, philosophy, and religion, if received into the soil of her thought, were either not assimilated, or took their bent of sudden growth from her characteristic tendencies. She found the situation impossible. She knew, or fancied, that he no longer loved her at all, if indeed he had ever loved her, had ever gone beyond wishing her to love him.

Without abandoning the broad shadow of a hope that somehow, somewhere, Love might make him hers, as she was still wholly his, she leaves him, and finds her life's work in some other sphere. She had painfully felt and experienced what the old rabbi in *Jocoseria* had discovered from his three months' dream of amatory experiment.

> "Before me stood the phantasy ye style
>   Youth's love, the joy that shall not come to grief,
>   Borne to endure, eternal, unimpaired
>   By custom the accloyer, time the thief.
>
> .   .   .
>
>   But now the dream
>   Fresh as from Paradise, alighting fared
>   As fares the pigeon, finding what may seem
>   Her nest's safe hollow holds a snake inside
>   Coiled to enclasp her."

Let us now go through the series of poems somewhat in detail, noticing their general connection, their special meaning, and, should it be needed, their special difficulties.

AT THE WINDOW.

The wife, like Sisera's mother, is anxiously looking out of the window for her husband, though James Lee was no Sisera. One day's absence from him has caused the world to change. Will he change too? So the note of coming disaster is sharply struck, but is lost at once in the rapture of approaching joy.

BY THE FIRESIDE.

The reunion has not realized her hopes, and as they sit together by the fireside near some "bitter coast of France," she notes how the fire is of "shipwreck wood," and this is to her an omen of the possible shipwreck of their married life. The sailors on the stormy sea may envy the light and comfort of their home fire, but hearts at home may be gnawed by worms and run to dust. She shudders as she imagines

some wife who once watched her husband in that very house, and found
—oh, hell of ruin—that his love had gone.

The difference between the tone of these poems is very great indeed.
What time—probably not long—has elapsed we do not know, or what
special incidents.   Much is left to the individual imagination.   Personal
absence, even very temporary, with the consequent sharply-cut presence,
is often of great advantage in searching out the hearts.   But the impression on the wife, thus expressed, is unmistakable.   The bright allegro,
with scarce a note of doubt, has passed into this slow broken movement
of "doubt, hesitation, and pain."[1]   The tragic mask is on.   She may
struggle as she will.   *Facilis descensus Averni.*   We know that the worst
must come.

IN THE DOORWAY.

She had looked for him from the window of their home.   They had
sat by the fireside together.   Now she stands in the doorway and looks
back on him.   Once more, in reality or fancy, he will be by her side, no
more at home, but on the wild sea-shore; and thence we are never to
think of them as again together in heart or thought, except perhaps in
the future of a quenchless hope.   Now we find her in no brighter mood.
The swallows will soon be flown.   The sea, the fig-tree, the vine, everything is stricken with the coming winter.   She feels a more chilling
winter in her own heart, turns her back on the too sympathetic landscape, and mentally expostulates with her husband.   Is there no room for
love in their little house, their little barren field?   Must they allow the
weather to dominate their hearts?   Nay, God's spirit is in them, which
can make a happy world for itself.

> " Then live and love worthily, bear and be bold."

ALONG THE BEACH.

It is of no use.   "There is a rapture on the lonely shore," but not
for her.   Her thought is entirely introspective.   Perhaps her husband
is smoking by her side, inwardly or outwardly cursing her sullen mood;
perhaps he has just left her, having " been lectured and blubbered over,"
as he would describe it.   At any rate this is not spoken to him face to
face ; all these poems are soliloquies.   Now she had loved him, and loves
him still, not because he was great, or greatly good, though there was
a "little good grain too," but because she—loved him.[2]

[1] *The Lost Leader.*

[2] " Do I wrong your weakness and call it worth ?
  Oh, Love, Love, Love, not so indeed."

The appeal, the small 'l' being changed to a capital, is to the principle of
love personified, not to James Lee himself, as might have been meant in the poem
as first published.

How did such a woman come to love such a man? It is the old question.

> " Tell me, where is Fancy bred,
>   In the heart or in the head,
>   Where begot, where nourished ? "

No, we cannot give a round answer, motives and characters are so varied ; but that women of poetry and sentiment have lavished and do lavish their effluence of affection and passion on men with spiritual qualities very inferior to theirs, this no one will deny. She had devoted herself to him, very naturally to his weaknesses as well as to his good points,

> " His flowers to praise, or his weeds to blame,
>   But, either or both, to love."

But he had resented her watching, her educating, her critical expectations of the good that she hoped would come at last, when

> " rivers of oil and wine
>   Would flow, as the Book assures."

He did not like this spying sort of love, as Byron did not like Lady Byron setting herself the task of making him better. In spite of her disappointment, she cannot help recognizing this working out of events as " an old story," and bitterly she thinks how the world may turn such an experience into a song about love, such as her husband's, flying away because the suspicion of his being bound to her by marriage, or her watching, cuts across his pride or liberty. Let him and the world with him find their pleasure in one mere laughing eye after another. Why should *they* look beyond, into the heart ?

ON THE CLIFF.

It is a relief to find her again gazing on the outside world. She has thrown herself down on the turf, all the greenness of it dried up by the summer sun, and, as she looks towards the sea, her eyes rest on a barren rock. In her pessimist mood she relishes the dreariness of the barren turf and still more barren rock,

> " Death's altar by the lone shore,"

for they speak to her of herself, and of her husband's want of love. But a bright, living grasshopper springs up from the dead grass, a butterfly settles on the rock.

> "No turf, no rock, in their ugly stead,
>   See, wonderful blue and red."

Her soul receives a momentary ray of brightness. The minds of men, such as her husband, may be "level and low, burnt and bare," but love such as hers can surely beautify even them!

READING A BOOK, UNDER THE CLIFF.

We know that the "some young man" of verse seven is Browning himself, that he published the first six verses when he was twenty-six years of age. They seem to me very beautiful. It is true that their flow and pathos is not in close keeping with the rest of this section, but they are read from a book, and the feeling of discrepancy is thus obviated.

James Lee's wife has taken to reading to help her in her trouble, and she comes across this passage in which the young poet apostrophizes the wind,—in his next poem it may be the sea or the moon,—asking whether it were expressing deep feeling, such as

> "Love at last aware
> Of scorn, hopes early blighted,"

or just mocking human sighs, or suggesting a wishfulness to help humanity, centred in him, the poet.

She shuts the book in disgust. Here is this imaginative, conceited young man amusing himself by fancying what the wind says to *him* —to him so certain of all he is, and is to be. He can well afford to make the wind say what he likes. But let him wait until he has grown older and looked the facts of life in the face—

> "And some midsummer morning, at the lull
> Just about daybreak, as he looks across
> A sparkling foreign country, wonderful
> To the sea's edge for gloom and gloss,
> Next minute must annul."

(It is in the morning as it is in the evening,

> "For note, when evening shuts,
> A certain moment cuts
> The dead off, calls the glory from the grey." [1])

> "Then, when the wind begins among the vines,
> So low, so low, what shall it mean but this?
> Here is the change beginning, here the lines
> Circumscribe beauty, set to bliss
> The limit time assigns."

Change, change, that is what the wind says. We cannot

> "draw one beauty into our heart's core
> And keep it changeless."

---

[1] *Rabbi Ben Ezra.*

Then rejoice in change, rise in it. Perhaps it is God's way of educating us. That is all very well for God. He does not grow old or ugly,
He can afford to wait. "Only for man," only for James Lee's wife,
idealizing the last of "that little good grain too,"

> "Only for man, how bitter not to grave
>   On his soul's hands' palms[1] one fair good wise thing
>   Just as he grasped it."

AMONG THE ROCKS.

Again she turns to the shore, whence she had got more comfort, if
less teaching, than books had given her, and it does not fail her. What
great artist of, if harmonized, pagan and Christian sentiment will make this
poem into a picture for us? But he will make us laugh if he does not
do it very well. The old giant Earth lies on the sea-shore, and thrusts
out his rocky knees and feet. Mere brown old earth he may be, but he
smiles, for he knows that he is made beautiful by the rippling of the
tide on his feet, and at his ear the sea-lark twittering as she rests on one
of his own heaps of rough stones. Life is such, and always has been.
An easy love for an easy love gives and gets a satisfaction, but not the
eternal life. By self-denial, by reverent service for what is earth, you
give and also gain heaven.

> "He who loseth his life shall gain it."

BESIDE THE DRAWING BOARD.

The first four poems are, to some extent, mentally addressed to her
husband. In the next four she does not speak to him, not directly of
him. She argues more abstractedly. The agony is not less deep, but
the personal thought is more restful, more reserved, steadying itself for
the great leap. It is not until she has left him that she returns to the
direct address. The weather is getting colder, her husband is off for the
day, and perhaps longer, to the nearest watering-place. We find her
alone at her drawing, her and a peasant girl, who has come to sit as a
model. But she has a cast of a hand by Leonardo da Vinci, and so turns
from the coarse hand of flesh and blood, and instead copies the cast, in
her passionate longing for perfection,

> "Laying the red chalk twixt my lips,"

and so,

> "With soul to help, if the mere lips failed,
>   Kissing out the lines of perfect beauty."
> "As like as a Hand to another Hand."

---

[1] Here, of course, there is an allusion to palmistry.

How foolish to say so when one has such hands as these before one for comparison and contrast.   The cast tells its own tale to the imaginative sympathizer.   As I, the mere "worm," have tried passionately to draw the cast, so He, the Divine master, the "god," tried to draw the real dead hand from which the cast was taken—

> "Looked and loved, learned and drew,
> Drew and learned and loved again.'

It was in vain ; even his "pencil could not emulate" the beauty of it. . But the

> "beauty mounted into his brain,"

and produced the conceit which lives in the cast.   See, on the wedding-finger there is a ring, that, to fancy's eye—I repeat, to fancy's eye—was placed there by Da Vinci on the finger which "outvied his art,"

> "In token of a marriage rare :
> For him on earth, his art's despair,
> For him in heaven, his soul's fit bride."

This last line, in connection with the fact of Leonardo da Vinci having lived and died unmarried, cannot fail to remind many of us of the leaf put inside the dead hand of Evelyn Hope by her living lover, and the belief that she would, some day,

> "wake, and remember, and understand."

The third section of this poem is written in a changed mood.   Perhaps the acute work of drawing and kissing out the delicate lines of the hand, of imagining this origin of the ring on the finger, had exhausted her.   She feels less of the artist and more of the woman, and so looks with pity on the poor peasant girl, whom she had turned from in disgust, and who has been waiting all this time, wondering what the English lady had meant by her antics, and looking disappointed at *her* hand not being properly admired and copied.   Then the artist too wakes up to the real beauty, the use and beauty, of that "poor coarse hand," from which she had turned to what now seems, in its way too, but a "*poor*, clay cast."   Would Da Vinci himself have turned in disgust from such a hand,

> "Because he could not change the hue,
> Mend the lines and make them true"?

Not so have we read how he spent years in studying anatomy, not so have we seen, from his wonderful drawings, anatomical and artistic, how he made minute studies of parts before he painted a whole.   Surely he would have turned on her with a flash of indignation from under his bushy eyebrows, with an unrestrained and unrestrainable 'fool,' for despising this rough peasant hand, because some merely ideal or perhaps once realized conception of beauty in shape is not found here. Compare this dull, lifeless clay cast with these

> " Lines and hue of the outer sheath,"

and, intimately connected with it,

> "The flesh, and bone, and nerve beneath " !

> " Is not the poorest, coarsest human hand
> An object worthy to be scanned
> A whole life long,"

because it was made, not to be loved and admired by æsthetic persons, judging according to some fancy of what a hand should be, but to do? The hand, the owner of a hand and brain, must look onwards, must not long too much for love and admiration and personal satisfaction. Art is long, life is short, and the art of life is not less long than the art of drawing.

> " Shall earth and the cramped moment's space
> Yield the heavenly crowning grace ?
> Now the parts, and then the whole ! "

> " On the earth the broken arc, in the heaven the perfect round ! "[1]

And thus she brings the lesson very home to herself. She, of "stinted soul and stunted body," she who had characteristically failed in sympathy with her husband, in spite of all her art and intellect, and whom this ineffectual life may narrow still more ; she who is not personally beautiful, " faded " (as she calls herself in the next poem), " the harsh, ill-favoured one," with her " coarse hanks of hair," and " skin like the bark of a gnarled tree," why should she go on with her querulous plaint, " I love," and therefore, insisting on the due reward,

> " I must be beloved, or die " ?

What, is there, then, nothing to be done by a living hand, a living woman ?

> "Go, little girl, with the poor coarse hand !
> I have my lesson, can understand."

The lesson was, that she must leave this life of artistic idling, of want of sympathy, of incongruity, of selfish, infatuated longing to grasp what was fading from her eyes, of hopeless, impatient craving for her husband's love. Perhaps her absence might work better than her presence on his heart. At any rate, for her, her course had become clear, —to go and do what she had to do in the world.

[1] *Abt Vogler.*

The die is cast, and in the next poem we find her—

ON DECK.

There is no more abstract reasoning, no more getting lessons from books, or rocks, or casts. She does not waver in her set purpose, her clear duty; not for an instant. But it is just because there is no more hesitation, and she has set her face as a rock, that the "you," "you," "you" returns to her lips; that in impassioned, regretful, hopeful, heavenly words she must pour her heart out at her absent husband's feet. His love for her, if it ever existed, if it was ever more than a wish to be loved by her, is now quite dead and gone. She knows it too well, but, with a touch of irony, she asks him to "concede in turn," that

> "Such things have been as a mutual flame."

Love is not always so entirely on one side. Her husband has a soul; love may let it loose some day, and he may come to look on her, as she looks on him, as a second, a very self. Such assimilation may—oh, sweet thought to dwell on!—become possible for him.

He must have seen *how* she had loved him.

> "You may, or you must, set down to me
>   Love that was life, life that was love;
> A tenure of breath at your lips' decree,
>   A passion to stand as your thoughts approve,
>   A rapture to fall where your foot might be."

And if such an intense feeling for her should arise and conquer his whole being at last, what to her would be the consequence? The answer is given with sweet subtlety and sublime devotion in the last two verses of the poem.

> "But did one touch of such love for me
>   Come in a word or look of yours,
> Whose words and looks will, circling, flee
>   Round me and round while life endures,—
>   Could I fancy 'As I feel, thus feels He';
>
> Why, fade you might to a thing like me,
>   And your hair grow these coarse hanks of hair,
> And your skin, this bark of a gnarled tree,—
>   You might turn myself! Should I know or care,
>   When I should be dead of joy, James Lee."

This last poem may be compared with the last verse of *Mary Wollstonecraft* in *Jocoseria*, but compared for contrast as well as similarity.

> " Strong and fierce in the heart, Dear,
>   With—more than a will—what seems a power
> To pounce on my prey, love outbroke here
>   In flame devouring and to devour.
> Such love has laboured its best and worst
> To win me a lover ; yet, last as first,
>   I have not quickened his pulse one beat,
> Fixed a moment's fancy, bitter or sweet,
>   Yet the strong fierce heart's love's labour's due,
> Utterly lost, was—you ! "

But James Lee, in his wife's thought, was not utterly lost to himself, or to her.

Also it might be compared with *Any Wife to any Husband*, where, in spite of married life having continued unbroken to death, and the character of the husband being much higher than that of James Lee, there is, partly because the wife is dying, not so much hopefulness as in the concluding verses of this poem.

Did she do right? No doubt this question will be asked and discussed, though, in a delicate work of art like this, published in a volume that has the distinct title of *Dramatis Personæ*, it might well be left alone. At any rate she did what she thought was right, and she knew a good deal more about her husband than Mr. Browning has chosen to tell us. She left him from no base motive, with increased rather than abated affection, not without a high hope of his coming to love her at last.

But if she was right, being what and where she very specially was, it does not at all follow that ordinary women under ordinary circumstances should follow her example. Neither do I understand the poet as suggesting any set philosophy of domestic life, certainly not as teaching that married life cannot be happy unless the individual characteristics of husband and wife are emotionally fused into one another, and He and She become an hermaphroditic It.

James Lee's Wife is a case by itself, in its various circumstances artistically and vividly harmonious, but not a universal case by any means.

A few notes in conclusion about the style of the poem.

Such a vulgar simile as

> " We both should be like as pea and pea,"

coming where it does, almost makes one's blood run cold ; and " real fairy, *with wings all right*," of poem five, sounds rather out of place. At least to a novice the sudden irruption of such exclamations as,

" Now, gnash your teeth," " Ah, the sting," " Fool !" must be rather startling. In the new part the leaving of the line,

> " One motive of the mechanism,"

without a corresponding rhyme may have been intentional, and may well escape observation where the argument is of more importance than the verse.

There are some remarkable lines, in their rhythm musically full of special meaning. Here are instances.

> "On the weather-side black, spotted white with the wind."

The little gusts of wind are there.

And note the intense statement, followed by the rapid question.

> "And so I did, love, so I do !
> What has come of it all along ?"

And in these well-known four lines contrast the rocky, letter-sounding jaggedness of the first three with the flow of the fourth.

> "Oh, good gigantic smile o' the brown old earth
> This Autumn morning ! How he sets his bones
> To bask i' the sun ; and thrusts out knees and feet,
> For the ripple to run over in its mirth."

And mark again, in the concluding verse of the sixth poem, how the longing is expressed by the necessitated dwelling on the strong monosyllabic words, and their passing into a rush of three short sounds with the clenching " grasp " at the end.

> " Only for man, how bitter not to grave
> On his soul's hands' palms one fair, good, wise thing,
> Just as he grasped it."

I have already quoted two very similar lines from *Mary Wollstonecraft.*

> "Yet the strong, fierce, heart's love's labour's due,
> Utterly lost, was—you."

And the different poems are as wholes well suited to the different moods they express. I would not, however, thus speak of poem six, where the metre, though appropriate for the flow of the early reverie, is not in such accordance with the more abrupt style of some of the consequent argument, and I have already said something about poem eight. But some of the poems are exquisite in their rhythmical fitness.

For instance, compare the first and second poems. How, in the first, the almost regular swing of anapæst and iambics carries us along with it as the eagerly expectant wife rushes with open heart towards her returning husband! How, in the second, the strong, broken beat of the metre, with its dead stop at the end of each verse, lends its aid to the expression of painful hesitating thought! And, in the last poem, how the metrical arrangement of dactyl, anapæst, iambic, spondee, trochee is admirably adapted for the impassioned composite flow of strong regret and perhaps stronger hope; and yet, how the fixedness of purpose comes out in the pause of the fifth line! And mark how this rule of pause is only once broken through, at the end of the last verse but one, when even this barrier gives way, because the heart is so overflowing with emotional thought that it must find the promptest utterance.

James Lee's Wife is noteworthy as containing specimens of the author's work of three different kinds and times—of 1836, 1864, and 1872. Also it is noteworthy as being the only poem of the kind that he has written, and it might profitably be compared with *Maud*, *The Angel in the House*, and other modern poems of the same kind, where the events, in their series, are lyrically expressed as they impressed themselves on the mind and moods of the chief agent or patient.

Without going into details, we may briefly observe that *Maud* and *The Angel in the House* are much longer poems than this; that while *The Angel in the House* is a story of quiet domestic life, and in *Maud* the leading incidents are sketched with sufficient allusion for us to follow them in their sequence, of *James Lee's Wife* it might truly be said,

"Story, God bless you, I have none to tell, sir."

Sometimes we hear a friend saying in a picture-gallery, that though this or that picture be preferred by the newspaper critics or by the public, yet that he would prefer his own special favourites for the walls of his own study or drawing-room. So, if to a true lover of the suggestively beautiful, some imperious deity were to say—"Now you must read through one of these three poems every month. Take your choice," he might answer, "Not *The Angel in the House*, it is too quiet, it would not sufficiently raise me out of my humdrum life; not *Maud*, for, with all its enthusiasm and occasional beauty, it is much too tempestuous; I will take *James Lee's Wife*, not merely because it is the shortest, not because I consider it a perfect poem, but because in it I recognize the beloved master's hand, because it has in it much that is so true and elevating, both of art and of heart."

ABT VOGLER.

BY MRS. TURNBULL.

(Read at the 17th Meeting of the Browning Society, Friday, June 22, 1883.)

It would be an interesting, if a somewhat futile question, to ask what are the causes which determine genius in its choice of a fitting mode of expression—of the special art whereby to reveal its ideas to the world. What inherent faculties, or what particular influences, operate to guide it in its choice? Is it an affair of what we call chance, the circumstances which happen to surround the man of genius in early life, or is it the predominance of certain inborn faculties, which determines him without hesitation or doubt to use poetry, music, painting, or sculpture as the one natural, adequate vehicle of expression?

When we read how those great minds Michel Angelo and Leonardo da Vinci turned restlessly from one to the other, as if unable to find the art which could all express the thoughts which burned within them; or when in later times we regard the efforts of men such as Blake and Shelley, we are led to put these questions; nay, to go further and ask, "Does genius always find its right mode of expression? May not occasionally a gigantic mistake be made?" Perhaps Blake made one when he recorded his tremendous visions in wild drawings and incoherent verse, instead of putting them into music—the exponent of that dim borderland where thought and feeling, ideas and emotion meet and mingle into one—the special province of Blake.

As it is, we feel that his imagination bursts the bounds of form, and struggles in vain with the necessary limitations of realistic art. We know he had also the gift of music, for he sang those other-world songs of his to melodies of his own equally quaint and beautiful—surely comparable only to nursery rhymes of child angels. If this gift had been cultivated and the technical training acquired, we might have had lyrics like those of Schubert, and symphonies grand as those of Beethoven.

Much the same might be said of Shelley. We cannot read his verse, so exquisite and rhythmical in its music, and try to grasp its meanings, so super-subtle and evanescent that they seem to elude us and refuse to be translated into tangible language, without feeling that music would have more fitly expressed them.

England could afford to spare one name from her muster-roll of poets, to place it instead side by side with those of Mendelssohn and Beethoven. But the determining cause was wanting, or the early musical training and surroundings, or, what is more probable, the want of a great national musical life as background. A Shakspere is the outcome of a vigorous national intellectual life; a Beethoven is the outcome of a great musical one.

This co-operation of the time and the man has never yet been possible in this country, therefore we still look for our great composer. We have been led into this train of thought by reading that Browning, in his early life, hesitated into which of the three channels—poetry, painting, or music—he should direct his genius.

"What arrogance!" some one who has a superficial acquaintance with our poet may exclaim; but to those who have studied his work it only appears natural.

When we read his poems on art—or indeed in every chance reference to art scattered through his volumes—we are so much struck by the truth and unerring rightness of both instinct and judgment, that we are tempted to wish that this artist had painted us pictures; or, again, when we turn to his poems dealing specially with music, like this of *Abt Vogler*— "Would that this man, with the ear and soul of a musician, had made music for us," rises involuntarily to our lips; but when the vast company of men and women which he has created pass before us, each one revealing to us the secrets and lessons of his existence—*St. John* his firm, simple faith in Love,—*Luria* his grand, unconquerable faith in Humanity,—and *Rabbi Ben Ezra* chanting his triumphant song of faith in Life and Death (three out of the host)—we can only say in humility and gratitude, "Let us thank God for our great poet and teacher!"

The Abbé Vogler, thanks to Miss Marx, is no stranger to us, but it may be interesting to note why Browning chose to depict his feelings instead of those of a more famous musician.

He is seldom heard of now except as being the master of Weber and Meyerbeer, his compositions are neglected and forgotten, and his wonderful improvisings on his beloved instrument have faded away for ever into silence.

This is just what Browning wanted. He wished to fix our minds specially on the fleeting nature of music,—its evanescence as compared with the other arts,—heard once, and then gone past recall; so it suited his purpose better to choose the grave and thoughtful priest, the now almost forgotten Vogler, than a famous composer like Beethoven and Mendelssohn, whose thoughts can never die, but live on in those immortal tones

> "Whose echoes roll
> From soul to soul
> And grow for ever and for ever."

Abt Vogler has been extemporizing on his instrument, pouring out through it all his feelings of yearning and aspiration; and now, waking from his state of absorption, excited, and trembling with excess of emotion, he breaks out into the wish, "Would it might tarry!" In verses one and two he compares the music he has made to a palace,[1] which Solomon (as legends of the Koran relate) summoned all creatures, by the magic name on his ring, to raise for the princess he loved; so all the keys, joyfully submitting to the magic power of the master, combine to aid him, the low notes rushing in like demons to give him the base on which to build his airy structure, the high notes like angels throwing decoration of carving and tracery on pinnacle and flying buttress, till in verse three its outline, rising ever higher and higher, shows in the clouds like St. Peter's dome, illuminated and towering into the vasty sky; and it seems as if his soul, upborne on the surging waves of music, had reached its highest elevation. But no. Influences from without, inexplicable, unexpected, join to enhance his own attempts; the heavens themselves seem to bow down and to flash forth inconceivable splendours on his amazed spirit, till the limitations of time and space are gone— "there is no more near nor far."

Music, Hegel says, frees us from the phenomena of time and space, alone of all the arts shows us how these are not essentials, but mere accidents of our present condition. Space has no existence in music, and a harmonic chord as such is absolutely immeasurable by time.[2] Thus music overcomes for us what no other art can, and herein lies its transcendental and supernatural quality.

In this strange fusion of near and far, of heaven and earth, presences hover, spirits of those long dead or of those yet to be, lured by the power of music to return to life, or to begin it. Figures are dimly descried in the fervour and passion of music, even as of old in the glare and glow of the fiery furnace.

---

[1] Is there an affinity between music and architecture in so far as harmony and proportion are essential elements of both? Goethe called architecture "petrified music," and adds, "the tone of mind produced by architecture approaches the effect of music."—*Conversations*, p. 378.

[2] F. Hueffer.

Verses four and five are a bold attempt to describe the indescribable, to shadow forth that strange state of clairvoyance when the soul shakes itself free from all external impressions, which Vogel tells us was the case with Schubert, and which is true of all great composers—"whether in the body or out of the body I cannot say."

In the sixth verse we come to a comparison of music with the other arts. Poetry, painting, and sculpture deal with actual form, and the tangible realities of life. They are subject to laws, and we know how they are produced; can watch the painting grow beneath the artist's touches, or the poem take shape line by line.

True, it needs the soul of the artist to combine and interfuse the elements with which he works to create any true work of art, but music is almost entirely independent of earthly element in which to clothe and embody itself. It does not allow of a realistic conception, but without intermediate means is in a direct line from God, and enables us to comprehend that Power which created all things out of nothing, with whom *to will* and *to do* are one and the same.

Schopenhauer says, "There is no sound in Nature fit to serve the musician as a model, or to supply him with more than an occasional suggestion for his sublime purpose. He approaches the original sources of existence more closely than all other artists, nay, even than Nature herself."

Heine has also noticed this element of miracle, which coincides exactly with Browning's view expressed in the lines :

> " Here is the finger of God, a flash of the will that can,
>   Existent behind all laws, that made them, and, lo, they are ! "

Now, these seven verses contain the music of the poem; in the remaining ones we pass on to Browning's platonic philosophy.

In the eighth verse a sad thought of the vanished music obtrudes— "never to be again." So wrapt was he in the emotions evoked, he had no time to think of what tones called them up, and now all is past and gone. His magic palace, unlike that of Solomon, has "melted into air, into thin air," and, "like the baseless fabric of a vision," only the memory of it is left.

> " Nothing can be as it has been before ;
>   Better, so call it, only not the same."[1]

And, depressed by this saddest of human experiences, the same "Divine despair" which oppresses us

> " While looking on the happy autumn fields,
>   And thinking of the days that are no more,"

James Lee's Wife, vi. 13.

he turns away impatient from the promise of more and better, to demand from God the same—the very same. Browning with magnificent assurance answers, "Yes, you shall have the same."

> "Fool! All that is at all,
> Lasts ever, past recall."

> "Ay, what was, shall be."

Swinburne has dared to arraign God for giving us the thirst for love, which yet He never satisfies, but Browning believes that the ineffable Name which built the palace of King Solomon, which builds houses not made with hands—houses of flesh which souls inhabit, craving for a heart and a love to fill them, can and will satisfy their longings;

> "For God above
> Is great to grant, as mighty to make,
> And creates the love to reward the love."

Altogether, I know no other words in the English language which compress into small compass such a body of high and inclusive thought as verse nine. (1) God the sole changeless, to whom we turn with passionate desire as the one Abiding-place, as we find how all things suffer loss and change, ourselves, alas! the greatest; (2) His power and love able and willing to satisfy the hearts of His creatures—the thought expatiated on by St. Augustine and George Herbert here crystallized in one line:

> "Doubt that Thy power can fill the heart that Thy power expands?"

(3) Then the magnificent declaration,

> "There shall never be one lost good—"

the eternal nature of goodness, while its opposite, evil (by which alone goodness could be known), exists only as an accident, is merely the reverse side of good, is a non-essential which shall one day pass away entirely, and be swallowed up of good. Here we have the philosophical truths regarding the nature and mystery of evil enunciated by Maimonides, Spinoza, and Hegel—thoughts to engage one for a lifetime.

Now follows an announcement, as by tongue of prophet or seer, that we shall at last find all our ideals complete in the mind of God, not put forth timorously, but with triumphant knowledge—knowledge gained by music whose creative power has for the moment revealed to us the permanent existence of these ideals.

The sorrow, and pain, and failure which we are all called upon to suffer here, and which to many are such stumbling-blocks, are seen to be proofs and evidences of this great belief. Without the discords, how should we learn to prize the harmony?

Carried on the wings of music and high thought, we have ascended one of those Delectable mountains—Pisgah-peaks from which

> " Our souls have sight of that immortal sea
>   Which brought us hither ; "

and whence we can descry, however faintly, the land that is very far off
to which we travel, and we would fain linger, nay, abide, on the mount,
building there our tabernacles.

But it cannot be. That fine air is difficult to breathe long, and
life, with its rounds of custom and duty, recalls us. So we descend
with the musician, through varying harmonies and sliding modulations
akin to those of Bach's first prelude, deadening the poignancy of the
minor third in the more satisfying, reassuring chord of the dominant
ninth, which again finds its rest on the key-note—C major—the common
chord, so sober and uninteresting that it well symbolizes the common
level of life, the prosaic key-note to which unfortunately most of our
lives are set.

We return, however, strengthened and refreshed, braced to endure
the wrongs which we know shall be one day righted, to acquiesce in the
limited and imperfect conditions of earth, which we know shall be
merged at last in heaven's perfect round, and to accept with patience
the renunciation demanded of us here, knowing

> "All we have willed, or hoped, or dreamed of good shall exist."

Thus we close this remarkable poem—one unique in the English
language.

The only one I can compare it with is Wordsworth's ' Ode on Intimations of Immortality.' However dissimilar in some respects, both are
co-related by the "faith that looks through death" and change—the
strong grasp of spiritual realities which they both show.

In an age like the present, when the faith of many is drifting,
anchorless, when dull grey clouds of doubt have settled down on most
of our noblest intellects, have we not indeed cause for thankfulness that
Browning is among "the last who believe"? He does not shrink from
plunging into the thickest, blackest clouds, his faith being fixed stead-
fastly on the Sun of Love beyond, which pierces through and suffuses
even the horror of darkness.

How bracing, invigorating, and full of hope is the philosophy of life
that he gives us! Surely his scheme of the weal and woe is the best
antidote to that dreary fatal pessimism which threatens to sap alike the
faith, and virtue, and courage of this century.

As Browning's view of music may appear exaggerated and over-
drawn to some people, it may be well to examine a little more closely
into it. To do this we must cast a glance back on the treatment of music
in English literature, and we shall at once notice the marked importance

which it assumes in the works of one school of writers, viz. the Neo-platonists.[1]

Take Milton, who was a musician, and whose verse charms us as it moves along grave and stately as his own organ tones, and who has written beautifully on music in his 'Hymn on the Nativity,' and in his 'Lines at Solemn Music' has sung of

> "That undisturbed song of pure consent
> Aye sung before the sapphire-coloured throne."

Though he proves to us that he feels and has mastered the sensuous beauty of music, yet he has not left a single line to show that he apprehended its spiritual significance, that by it he had transcended time and space, or that to him it was the evidence of things unseen.

Neither has he given us one subtle touch like that of Shakespeare's "I am never merry when I hear sweet music"; indeed those few lines in the 'Merchant of Venice' are worth all that Milton has written on music put together.

> "Look how the floor of heaven
> Is thick inlaid with patines of bright gold.
> There's not the smallest orb which thou behold'st
> But in his motion like an angel sings,
> Still quiring to the young-eyed cherubins :
> Such harmony is in immortal souls."

Or again :

> "The man that hath not music in his *soul.*"

Mark you, not in his ear, nor in his head, but in his soul. And this because Shakespeare was a platonist and Milton was not.

To give the idea of music common to all the Neo-platonic school, and which meets one constantly in the works of More, Norris, &c., I cannot do better than quote the quaint prose of Sir Thomas Browne, which, besides having a touch of sublimity of its own, remarkably indicates the views since adopted by Schopenhauer and Wagner, and which Browning exemplifies in his poem.

"There is a music wherever there is a harmony and order or proportion ; and thus far we may maintain the music of the spheres, for those well-ordered motions and regular paces, though they give no sound to the ear, yet to the understanding they strike a note most full of harmony. Whatsoever is harmonically composed delights in harmony, which makes me much distrust those heads which declaim against all church music. For myself, not only from my obedience, but my particular genius, I do embrace it ; for even that vulgar and tavern-music which makes one man merry and another mad, strikes in me a deep fit of devotion, and a profound contemplation of the first composer. There

[1] When we read in the 'Timæus' such words as these we do not wonder at it: "He whose care it is to form his body rightly should exercise his soul in music." "The soul reacts on the body, and by nothing so powerfully as by music."

is something in it of divinity more than the ear discovers; it is an hieroglyphical and shadowed lesson of the whole world and creatures of God—such a melody to the ear as the whole world, well understood, would afford the understanding. In brief, it is a sensible fit of that harmony which intellectually sounds in the ears of God."[1]

Here we have the truest and most adequate word on the philosophy of music, and the right theory of its effect. Those who with Milton consider it merely as a sensual pleasure, regard music as a sensation of sound, affording gratification to the ear; but Sir T. Browne and Browning along with him go deeper, and find in music an intellectual pleasure, consisting not so much in the sensuous pleasure received through the ears, but in the ideas, the harmony and proportion, which the mind only can apprehend, " the soul itself contemplating the beauty and agreement of it."[2] Thus the harmony that is in immortal souls must co-operate with the external sound to be music in its highest sense. That it should open to us the unseen and spiritual, more than an ear for music, or a merely voluptuous enjoyment of melting sound, surely is necessary.

Music, like all the other arts, is a revelation to us of truth, of the eternal ideas which abide in the mind of God, and more than any other art reveals these directly to us, without the aid of form and substantial embodiment. It is the most super-sensuous and incorporeal of all the arts, and therefore it requires a clear intelligence and an open soul ready to receive and vibrate to its pure and subtle influence.

Now, we are not all gifted with ears, but we can all, if we like, gain this receptive attitude of spirit, open and willing to hear what the music may speak to us—whether simple dreams of childhood and youth, or foretastes of the beatific vision.

But we need not expect to attain this if we regard music as an agreeable noise, a pleasant accompaniment to talk, or the idle employment of an idle hour. We must remember that as the eye only sees what it has the power to see, so the ear and the mind only hear and apprehend what they bring with them the power to hear and apprehend, and that " all high things are difficult of attainment as they are rare."[3]

---

[1] 'Religio Medici.'
[2] 'A Letter concerning Love and Musick,' by John Norris. Most interesting.
[3] Spinoza's 'Ethics.'

ANDREA DEL SARTO AND ABT VOGLER.

By HELEN J. ORMEROD.

*Read at the Sixty-second Meeting of the Browning Society,
Friday, November 30, 1888.*

FROM amongst Browning's poems on painters and musicians, the two poems *Andrea del Sarto* and *Abt Vogler* stand out unrivalled—both as literary works of art—abounding as they do in those " purple patches " of beauty, which in these instances clothe most luxuriantly the sometimes rugged forms of the poet's genius—and as studies of character, revealing to us on the one hand the lover and the man, as well as the artist ; whilst, on the other hand, the musician alone is considered. Should the story of Andrea's life, his outward success, and deep inner sense of failure seem unduly lingered over in this paper, it is only because the story of Abt Vogler's life, and his apparent failure but hidden sense of artistic success have been already dwelt upon in a recent paper. I would take this opportunity to remark that the two characters are looked upon from Browning's standpoint, and that in speaking of them I look on them as the artist and musician whose characters are revealed to us in the poems.

Before proceeding to study Andrea's character it may be advisable to recall the Florence of the early part of the sixteenth century, noting, the while, the historical accuracy of the poet, and also the effective dramatic background of the poem.

The opening years of the sixteenth century found Michael Angelo chiselling his immortal David, the spirit of God breathing through him on the unshapely mass of marble, and bringing beauty out of it ; they found Raphael visiting Florence, and painting there some of his loveliest pictures ; they found Leonardo himself in the beautiful city, the very walls of which still echoed with the inspired utterances of the prophet-monk, who had but just put off his old San Marco dress for the new red garb of martyrdom. And looking back into the years of previous centuries, we see Dante and Beatrice amidst the haze of the past, and Giotto planning out his Campanile, and Fra Angelico with his angel companionship; but time would fail to tell of all the great and noble men whose names are associated with Florence.

We find mention made, in the course of the poem, of George Vasari; painter, and author of *The Lives of the Most Excellent Italian Painters, Sculptors and Architects;* and here there is too remarkable an instance of Browning's accuracy in matters of history to be overlooked. Andrea del Sarto died in 1530, and Vasari was born in 1512. The poem was supposed to be spoken in 1525—five years after the death of "that famous youth the Urbinate"; this would make Vasari only thirteen years old, and yet Andrea in speaking of a painting is made to say, "'Tis copied. George Vasari brought it me." These dates would startle us, but for the reassuring teachings of history. Vasari, from his earliest years, showed unmistakable signs of artistic talent, and at the age of *twelve*, in the year 1524, his father brought him to Florence, and Andrea himself gave him lessons.

The scene of the poem—(the poem itself being suggested, we are told by Mr. Fotheringham, by "a picture in the Pitti Palace . . . . the painter and his wife are in talk over a letter which she holds . . . . she is cold and masterful, he loving and submissive,")—is laid in Andrea's studio in his house at Florence. The hour is that of twilight, and the shades of evening are falling on the sunny slopes of Fiesole. The sweet twilight hour throws its spell over Andrea, and with true artistic observation he notes "yonder sober pleasant Fiesole." Then he observes how

> " A common greyness silvers everything,—
> All in a twilight, you and I alike."

And suddenly he draws attention to how

> " That length of convent wall across the way
> Holds the trees safer, huddled more inside ;
> The last monk leaves the garden ; days decrease,
> And autumn grows, autumn in everything."

And later in the poem, in the midst of his love and reminiscences, he exclaims

> " See, it is settled dusk now ; there's a star ;
> Morello's gone, the watch lights show the wall,
> The cue-owls speak the name we call them by."

Browning invariably presupposes considerable knowledge, both artistic and historic on the part of his readers, and it is often necessary to refer to biography or history for the better understanding of his poems. It may now be advisable to sketch in the rough outlines of Andrea's life, as they would be found in any encyclopædia. Andrea Vannuchi (called *del Sarto* from the occupation of his father, a tailor) was born at Florence, 1488, became a painter of considerable note, visited the French court, executed commissions for Francis I., but on being recalled to Florence by his improvident wife, he misappropriated a large sum of money entrusted to him by the French King for the purchase of works of art for a museum. After this he never returned to France, and was afterwards deserted by his profligate wife (whom he had married with a knowledge of her character, and in spite of the remonstrances of friends); he died of the plague in 1530.

Such are the bare facts of the man's life. Birth, life and death—these are common to all; but when once an individual rises to eminence, how eagerly is his history scrutinized; and it frequently happens that the more we know of the personal and inner life of an artist, the more readily can we understand his work. For instance, in Andrea's paintings, why does the same type of female beauty constantly recur? and why are his paintings, though faultless, soul-less? In answer, however, to these, and other queries, we must let Browning's wonderful poem speak for itself, coming, as it seems, with terrible reality from the depths of the artist's unrequited love, and moral degradation.

The problem of useless suffering, such as is described in this poem; the agony of spirit which came to no great end, is an almost hopeless one to solve; and for months remained obscure to me. Then, as a revelation, came Mazzini's glorious thought "Remorse or Martyrdom." There, for me at all events, was the solution, and I should like to quote the sentences bearing on the subject—"All the sophisms of the wretched philosophy that seeks to substitute the doctrine of I-know-not-what fatalism to the cry of our human conscience, avail not to silence the two inevitable witnesses in favour of human liberty—*Remorse and Martyrdom* . . . all the martyrs of Faith protest against the servile doctrine, and cry aloud unto you: ' We also loved life, we also loved the beings who made that life dear, and who implored us to yield. Every impulse of our hearts cried *Live !* But, for the salvation of the generations to come, we *chose* to die.

"From Cain down to the vulgar spy of the present day, all the betrayers of their fellows, all the men who have chosen the path of

evil, have heard, and hear in the depths of their secret soul a voice of
blame, disgust, and reproof which says unto them : ' *Wherefore did
you forsake the right path ?* ' "

Thus it is that remorse makes a hell of the soul ; while one touch
of the divine self-forgetfulness which culminates in martyrdom, can
draw a soul within the glory of heaven.

Andrea's first deviation from the right path was his marriage with
Lucrezia (known to be a woman of ill-fame) ; and it was followed by
dishonesty to the French King, and unfilial neglect of his parents in
their old-age and poverty.

Judging from the following quotation one may infer that the
misappropriated gold was hateful to Andrea, just as certain silver
was to Judas Iscariot :

> "When I look up from painting, eyes tired out,
> The walls become illumined, brick from brick
> Distinct, instead of mortar, fierce, bright gold,
> That gold of his I did cement them with !
> Let us but love each other."

In that last line we find the clue to the whole, for money was
chiefly valuable to Andrea, inasmuch as it pleased Lucrezia.

> "That cousin here again ? . . .
> More gaming debts to pay ?   You smiled for this ?
> Well, let smiles buy me ! have you more to spend ?"

Towards the close of the poem Andrea thus reviews and sums up
his life's history :

> "I took his[1] coin, was tempted and complied,
> And built this house, and sinned, and all is said."

Referring to his parents, he thus speaks :

> "My father and my mother died of want.
> Well, had I riches of my own ? you see
> How one gets rich ! Let each one bear his lot.
> They were born poor, lived poor, and poor they died ;
> And I have laboured somewhat in my time
> And not been paid profusely.   Some good son
> Paint my two hundred pictures—let him try !
> No doubt there's something strikes a balance."

And thus the gold of ill-gotten gains is weighed in the balance
against the glory of heaven, and found wanting.   Let us for a
moment turn to Abt Vogler's balance.

[1] Francis.

> " All we have willed, or hoped, or dreamed of good shall exist ;
> Not its semblance, but itself ; no beauty, nor good, nor power
> Whose voice has gone forth, but each survives for the melodist,
> When eternity affirms the conception of an hour.
> The high that proved too high, the heroic for earth too hard,
> The passion that left the ground to lose itself in the sky,
> Are music sent up to God by the lover and the bard ;
> Enough that he heard it once : we shall hear it by and by."

A strangely distorted idea of compensation floats at times in Andrea's brain ; thus he refers to his disgrace at the French court :

> " At the end, God, I conclude, compensates, punishes.
> 'Tis safer for me if the award be just
> That I am somewhat under-rated here.
> Poor this long while, despised ; to speak the truth,
> I dare not, do you know, leave home all day
>
> For fear of chancing on those Paris lords ;
> The best is when they turn and look aside,
> But they speak sometimes—I must bear it all."

It is evident that the extreme sensitiveness peculiar to the artistic temperament was not lacking in Andrea, yet a strange apathy—or, as he thinks, *peace*—comes on him at times.

> " Love—we are in God's hands.
> How strange now seems the life He makes us lead,
> So free we seem, so fettered fast we are,
> I feel He laid the fetter—let it lie ! "

Thus does Andrea set up his will in opposition to the will of God, and then accepts the fetter, as one laid on him by God Himself !

Mention is made at times of physical fatigue, fostered no doubt by the constant remorse which preyed on him ; and the woman who ought to have tended him in his weakness, deserted him ; leaving him a prey, first to remorse, and then to the plague which raged in Florence shortly afterwards.

Regarding Andrea as an artist, it must be understood that I try to view him, not only as he was, but also as what he felt he might have been. The theme sounding throughout this twilight reverie is, what he might have been without Lucrezia—Raphael, Leonardo, Angelo, they "live for fame," they achieve the highest, but these three are without a wife, so :

> " still they overcome,
> Because there's still Lucrezia, as I choose."

Had Andrea taken advantage of the new start afforded him in France (probably the flood in the tide of his affairs) he might have left behind him an honoured name, and glorious fame, but the baneful influence of Lucrezia was paramount.

> " A good time was it not, my kingly days !
> And had you not grown restless . . .
> Too live the life grew, golden and not grey . . .
> You called me, and I came home to your heart."

He looked back with longing and regret to that

> " long festal year at Fontainebleau,
> I surely then could sometimes leave the ground,
> Put on the glory, Rafael's daily wear."

But even then Lucrezia's face was seen in the background,

> " To crown the issue with a last reward"

—and her reward was dishonour and ignominy from without, infidelity and desertion in his home. One's heart goes out in pity to Andrea— richly gifted, perfect in his craft, yet ever feeling that his work was nearer heaven than himself. It is strange that his thoughts so frequently turned heavenwards, feeling as he did his unfitness for it, yet making no effort after a higher life. In another of Browning's poems on art, *Pictor Ignotus*, the painter shrinks from the thought of heaven, and longs for a continuance of earth and earth's plaudits.

> "Oh, thus to live ! I and my picture linked
> With love about, and praise till life should end,
> And then, not go to heaven, but linger here,
> Here on my earth—earth's every man my friend—
> The thought grew frightful, 'twas so wildly dear."

In Andrea's mind there was the ever-present desire to compare himself with Raphael. It is said that on visiting Rome, he was at first much depressed by the sight of Raphael's cartoons, realizing, as he did, the inspiration of the young Urbinate, and almost resenting the difference between it and his own more earthly art. The pictures painted on canvas are poor indeed compared to those conceived in the mind of an artist ; but Andrea could only conceive that which he could perfectly execute. His delight is almost childish, when he detects a fault in Raphael's drawing, which he can rectify.

> " And indeed the arm is wrong !
> I hardly dare . . . yet only you to see,
> Give the chalk here—quick, thus the line should go !
> Ay, but the soul ! he's Rafael's ! rub it out ! "

A field for conjecture opens before us, as the workings of the artist's mind are unfolded. Had Andrea in him the genius of those great ones, for equal companionship with whom he yearned, and was it crushed by his heartless wife? or must heaven have remained for ever closed to him? that heaven into which men who were his inferiors in their craft could enter.

> " Their works drop groundwards, but themselves I know
> Reach many a time a heaven that's shut to me,
> Enter and take their place there, sure enough,
> Though they come back and cannot tell the world.
> My works are nearer heaven, but I sit here."

Like Adam, he laid the blame on the woman, and like Adam he too was shut out of Paradise. It may be that had Andrea given up his unworthy love, that deep saying of James Hinton's might have been verified in his case—"Never be afraid of giving up your best, because then God will give you His Better." The entry to that heaven of the soul might have been God's "Better." There is a touching anecdote told of Blake, when in his days of old age and poverty, a little girl was taken to see him in his garret. He took the child in his arms, and blessing her, prayed that she might find life as beautiful as he had found it. Truly he had entered and taken his "place there, sure enough"!

Andrea now comes before us in his character of lover-husband. The poem opens with a pathetic appeal to his wife "not to quarrel any more"; promising even to paint a picture for one of her lovers, if she will but let him sit.

> "Here by the window with your hand in mine,
> And look a half hour forth on Fiesole,
> Both of one mind, as married people use,
> Quietly, quietly the evening through,
> I might get up to-morrow to my work
> Cheerful and fresh as ever. Let us try."

The picture brings tears to the eyes of those who realize what the life-long strain of unrequited love meant to the artist.

> " You turn your face, but does it bring your heart?"

To make up for the waste of time and smiles involved by the wife giving the husband her company in this sweet twilight hour, Andrea adds:

> "Don't count the time lost neither, you must serve
> For each of the five pictures we require;
> It saves a model. So! keep looking so!"

That Andrea's was a finer nature than Lucrezia's may be gathered from his consciousness of wrong-doing, which at once raises him to a higher level than his wife, of whom history fails to record a single redeeming trait, except that of her beauty. If Andrea's paintings did not testify to that we should be reminded of it in the poem, by his expressions of lover-life admiration :

> " Your soft hand is a woman of itself "

—and again :

> " Let my hands frame your face in your hair's gold,
> You beautiful Lucrezia that are mine ! "

and then :

> " My serpentining beauty, rounds on rounds,
> How could you ever prick those perfect ears
> Even to put the pearl there ? "

(Was a thought of Lilith in Browning's mind when the adjective *serpentining* suggested itself to him ?)

> " My face, my moon, my everybody's moon,
> Which everybody looks on, and calls his,
> And, I suppose, is looked on by in turn,
> While she looks—no one's ; very dear, no less."

I cannot leave this passage without contrasting another with it, spoken from the heart of the great poet who writes of Andrea's unhappy love ; in each passage the moon is used as a figure.

> " This to you, yourself my moon of poets !
> Ah but that's the world's side, there's the wonder.
> Thus they see you, praise you, think they know you !
> There, in turn, I stand with them, and praise you.
> Out of my own self, I dare to phrase it,
> But the best is when I glide from out them
> Cross a step or two of dubious twilight,
> Come out on the other side, the novel
> Silent, silver lights and darks undreamed of,
> Where I hush and bless myself with silence.'

It would seem, from the following remark of Andrea's,

> " You at the point of your first pride in me,
> (That's gone you know !) "

that Lucrezia, when she became his wife, had a certain pride in, though not love for him ; but even this had vanished.

> " You don't understand
> Nor care to understand about my art."

And again :

> " You don't know how the others strive
> To paint a little thing like that you smeared
> Carelessly passing with your robes afloat."

But nothing rouses her to interest; and surely, of human experiences it is amongst the saddest, when the being most beloved is indifferent to the work and fame of the lover. Nothing chills like indifference; sarcasm and censure may sting, even crush for a time, but above the dead level of indifference only a heaven-taught spirit can rise.

Most pathetic is the scene, when Andrea quotes words spoken by Michael Angelo about himself, and burned into his very soul; only to find that Lucrezia had even forgotten who was the speaker.

> " Do you forget already words like these ? "

Yet after all—

> " You smile indeed !
> This hour has been an hour ! another smile ?
> If you would thus sit by me every night
> I should work better—do you comprehend ?
> I mean that I should earn more, give you more. "

The poem ends as follows, the last line bringing before us with sharp distinctness the profligacy of the wife and the infatuation of the husband :

> " You loved me quite enough it seems to-night,
> This must suffice me here.   What would I have ?
> In heaven perhaps new chances—one more chance.
> Four great walls in the New Jerusalem
> Meted on each side by the angel's reed
> For Leonard, Rafael, Agnolo, and me
> To cover ; the first three without a wife,
> While I have mine ! So, still they overcome
> Because there's still Lucrezia, as I choose. ·
> Again the Cousin's whistle. Go, my Love ! "

We turn from this picture of artist life, half reluctant to put down the poem, because of its dramatic strength and because of its deep undercurrent of remorse which gives it so intense a human interest ; and yet glad to exchange the depths for the heights occupied by Abt Vogler.   But we will first leave the musician for a few words about music.

To those who are not themselves musicians, it may be suggested that in music, as in painting and poetry, there may be an art, inferior possibly in execution, but distinguished by a touch of genius, a mysterious something which no technical training can impart. This extemporization by Abt Vogler on his own instrument was a moment when inspiration was breathed upon him ; and it seems almost like sacrilege to descend from the heights of art, to the dissection of the poem into musical parlance;—however the attempt must be made.   Perhaps such an attempt cannot be better prefaced than by giving a fragmentary conversation as it occurred ; the speakers numbered three besides myself, a lady of Scotch extraction, troubled in spirit because of her non-comprehension of the " star " simile in the line—

"That out of three sounds he frame, not a fourth sound but a star"

—an artist, and a musician.

"But why did he say a *star ?*" persisted the lady, turning to me.

" Why shouldn't he ? a star is perfect and beautiful, and rays of light come from it, and a poet must say something. Besides, he wanted a rhyme to 'are '."

"It seems to me he might as well have said a *spade* but for the rhyme."

" But because he was a poet he didn't.   What do you think of the line ?" I asked the artist.

"I have a glimmering of the sense, but I wouldn't undertake to put it into words," he answered.

I then handed the book to the musician, who, after reading the verse exclaimed, "But what does she want to know ? Why ! it's all there, and there's nothing to explain !"

This is very much my own feeling, but having been asked to explain a few musical phrases, I must endeavour to comply.

It may be remembered that the musical instrument of Abt Vogler's invention was probably his orchestrion,[1] in which he embodied all the results of his simplification of organ systems, and by which he attained superior effects of tone and power, with fewer and shorter pipes.   All this was founded on the theory of harmonics. The great advantage of his orchestrion lay in the fact of it being movable, and thus he could take his own instrument about with him on his concert tours.

Having fixed his once imaginary instrument in a material form, we find him in the poem, longing next to put his extemporization into shape and form, but as ever before " the gone thing was to go."

I remember when a child hearing a lady ask an old, self-taught Yorkshire organist, "What was that piece you played after service yesterday morning ?" and the old man replied, " Eh, mistress ! if you was to ax me from mornin' till neet, I couldn't play t'same piece over again, for it came straight out o' my 'ed !"

[1] Patti is reported to have one, which cost her £4,000.

So it is; an extemporization is a passing thing; perhaps with some composers an occasional melody may come unsought, which lingers in the memory and may be reproduced at leisure; but the phantasy as a whole vanishes as a sunrise mist. It is considered dangerous for young musicians to indulge too freely in the delights of extemporization; for in the study of music it may be analogous to day-dreaming in the study of literature, and Schumann warns students not to give themselves up too often to this faculty.

We may suppose that Abt Vogler had carelessly struck a chord on his orchestrion, or possibly, as I before suggested, on his simplified organ at Darmstadt, and then all unexpectedly, as such impressions always come, his soul was flooded with heavenly melodies and harmonies, and for a time he lost himself in the exquisite phantasy. When the ecstasy was passing he remembered the key in which he began to improvise.

"I feel for the common chord again"

—and we may conclude that as he wished to end in C major, it was the key in which he began. But he had wandered far away from the original key. It would be impossible in the limits of this paper to enter upon the subject of modulation as the musician slides by semitones, till he suddenly finds himself on a neighbouring minor, possibly E flat, he "blunts it into a ninth" (a ninth from C would be D, one note above the octave); here he surveys for a moment the flight his fancy had taken, and the musical heights he so lately occupied.

"Which, hark, I have dared and done, for my resting-place is found,
The C major of this life: so now I will try to sleep."

I was asked after my last paper to explain what "C major" meant! I can only suggest that "C major" is what may be called the natural scale, having no sharps or flats in its signature. "A minor," with A (a third below C) for its keynote, has the same signature, but sharps are introduced for the formation of correct intervals. Pauer says that minor keys are chosen for expressing "intense seriousness, soft melancholy, longing, sadness, and passionate grief"; whilst major keys with sharps and flats in their signatures are said to have distinctive qualities—perhaps Browning chose "C major" for the key, as the one most allied to matters of everyday life, including rest and sleep.

Vogler's musical system was, as has been already remarked, based on the teachings of the harmonic scale. Hence the accusation of writing

M

books on arithmetic, rather than music ! If you strike a note sharply on the piano, and hold it down, a series of scarcely audible sounds will be distinguished as arising from it. Speaking generally, first the octave is distinguished, then the fifth, then the keynote another octave higher, then the third, &c. Here then is the foundation on which all chords are built. The fifth and the third are the intervals of which the common chord is formed.

There must be some present who have heard in Handel's *Messiah* the fine bass solos, "Why do the nations so furiously rage together ? and "The trumpet shall sound," or in *Judas Maccabeus*, "Arm, arm, ye brave !" The opening notes of each of these solos are the notes of the common chord, the keynote with its major third, fifth, and octave treated as a melody : that is to say, as a sequence of sounds, following each other. Treated harmonically, (that is to say, written above each other, and sounded simultaneously either by separate voices, or on an instrument)—there is the common chord ! Therefore the common chord, as it is called, the keynote with its third and fifth, contains the rudiments of all music.

> " And I know not if, save in this, such gift be allowed to man,
> That out of three sounds he frame, not a fourth sound, but a star.
> Consider it well ; each tone of our scale in itself is naught ;
> It is everywhere in the world—loud, soft, and all is said ;
> Give it to me to use ! I mix it with two in my thought,
> And, there ! ye have heard and seen, consider and bow the head !"

It has been suggested that a comparison between the arts of music and painting might now be made ; but to look upon them as sister arts, between whom comparison would be invidious, seems the more congenial way. This much may be said, that painting has perhaps a more calming influence than music, which is sometimes painfully exciting ; I now speak more of executants, than spectators or listeners. I was amongst the last pupils to whom Mr. Gastineau, the water-colour painter, gave lessons ; we were speaking one day of music and painting. "There will probably come a time," said the old artist, "when music will be too painful for you, and then you will find painting will soothe you." And I remember answering with a school-girl's wisdom of inexperience, "Painting could never comfort me, if music failed," and he simply replied, "You are very young now !"

One of the joys of the musical in the future state may be the hearing of music without the almost unbearable longing for the sound of a silenced voice, or the painful yearning for a lost joy ; for the voice will be heard again, and the joy fulfilled, or not desired. I believe that it is given to music to create feelings of more intense joy, and more acute pain, than to any other art, but Abt Vogler reminds us of the recompense for the pain.

> " Sorrow is hard to bear, and doubt is slow to clear,
> Each sufferer says his say, his scheme of weal and woe ;
> But God has a few of us whom He whispers in the ear ;
> The rest may reason and welcome ; 'tis we musicians know."

The calm born of contemplating nature is very great ; and yet remorse in the heart would be sufficient to give a feeling of autumnal depression to everything, such as we notice in Andrea's mood. I heard the Rev. Hay Aitken say in the course of an impressive sermon, "You must be at feud with nature, if you are out of peace with God."

Abt Vogler is often quoted as confirming (were confirmation needed) Browning's belief in the immortality of the soul ; and certainly in the poem there is no uncertain sound ; in reading it through again I was reminded of a beautiful remark of Mrs. Owen's that our " life is but an interruption of eternal life." And it would seem that the Musician's music, including all that is highest, most heroic, and divinely self-forgetting, goes to be part of the music of heaven.

I should like to draw attention to the different views of past, present, and future presented to us by the two characters in the poems.

> "All we have willed, or hoped or dreamed of good shall exist."

At first, as we saw, Abt Vogler's frame of mind was one of grief that his beautiful thought was gone. "Never to be again" ; this thought grows until it yields to the nobler one, "There shall never be one lost good" ; and this in turn to the belief that all will be perfected hereafter.

> "On the earth, the broken arcs ; in the heaven, a perfect round."

The contrast with Andrea is indeed sharp and distinct. Andrea, turning to his unworthy earthly love, only finds disappointment.

> "Come from the window, love,—come in, at last
> Inside the melancholy little house
> We built to be so gay with."

In thinking of the future he says, "In heaven perhaps new chances "—but even there he realizes that Lucrezia will prevent him from standing with "Leonard, Rafael, Agnolo." Abt Vogler, as he surveys his life-way from the heights, recognizes a purpose in everything.

> "Why else was the pause prolonged, but that singing might issue thence ?
> Why rushed the discords in, but that harmony should be prized ? "

Andrea's retrospect view is full of what might have been ; realizing his opportunity at the court of Francis when he " surely then

could sometimes leave the ground"; but again his course was spoiled by
Lucrezia, who called to him to come back to her.

Thus gradually we are led to the subject of apparent failure; and
I heard some disappointment was expressed after the reading of my
last paper on Abt Vogler, that I had not then dwelt on the subject.
It seems to me to rest entirely on the individual idea of success and
failure. Blake, in his garret, would have seemed a doubtful object
for congratulation to the fashionable world, but would he have spoken
of failure?

I was reading Sir Julius Benedict's short life of Weber the other
day, and will give a passing illustration from it. When Weber was
alone in London—suffering, nay, dying—he, the gifted composer of *Der
Freischutz, Oberon,* and *Euryanthe,* gave a concert with a view to
providing for his family after his death. The result makes one blush
for the leaders of the fashion of the day. A fashionable singing master
gave a concert on the same day in a nobleman's mansion. The
Signor's profits amounted to upwards of £400, whilst Weber's were
less than £100. But viewed from this distance, who succeeded, and
who failed? And would Weber in his supreme hour of pain and
weakness ever believe otherwise, than that he was taught of heaven?

In reading Dr. George MacDonald's story, *Home Again,* I was
struck with a remark of his bearing on the "apparent failure"
question. "A man may fail to effect, or be unable to set hand to work
he would fain do, and judged as Browning says in his *Saul,* by what
he would have done if he could. Only the *would* must be as true as
a deed; then it is a deed. The kingdom of heaven is for the dreamers
of true dreams only!"

Let us for a moment look at the lines about the will in *Andrea,
Abt Vogler,* and *Saul.* Andrea says:

> " In this world, who can do a thing, will not,
> And who would do it, cannot, I perceive;
> Yet the will's somewhat—somewhat, too, the power—
> And thus we half-men struggle."

Abt Vogler speaks as we have already heard:

> " All we have willed, or hoped, or dreamed of good shall exist."

And in *Saul* the lines run thus:

> " What stops my despair?
> This:—'tis not what man Does which exalts him, but what man Would do.
> See the king—I would help him but cannot, the wishes fall through,
> Could I wrestle to raise him from sorrow, grow poor to enrich,
> To fill up his life, starve my own out, I would: knowing which,
> I know that my service is perfect."

The world in general seems too ready to praise men who are rich in rank and this world's goods, and yet who in their secret hearts must be ashamed of their Mammon-worship, and failure to attain to the highest. Some of these would confess to success with a sigh, knowing as they spoke that the spiritual life is the higher life, and the material, the lower life.

Mr. Harry Quilter, in his admirable *In Memoriam* article on Frank Holl in the *Universal Review*, spoke strongly on this subject; and I should like to quote one sentence: "Is there no help for it? Must all our great artists nowadays succumb to this devil in disguise who whispers to them of social advancement, and an income of ten thousand a year? Believe me, such things are inimical to art, if not inconsistent with it. The artist has one great advantage over all the rest of mankind; it is this, that his best pleasures cost—nothing! Think what that means. It means that his ten thousand a year, his social position are in *himself*; they can never be taken from him save by his own act. But to preserve them he must live that straightforward, honest life in which alone they can flourish," &c.

What is the value of success, when it depends on the verdict of the voice of the multitude? What matters failure, as viewed by the outside world, when the soul has entered the Holiest of Holies?

I noticed in a painting of mountain glory how the central and loftiest peaks are most golden in the after sunset glow; the successive heights more or less in the glory, while the lower ranges fade from view, or are hidden by sunset clouds and mists. Surely this is typical of those who have truly succeeded. The nearer heaven, the greater the glory—this glory being reserved alike for the conclusion of day and life. What seems great to us in the mid-day glare may be hidden from sight in sunset clouds; while the highest mountains are often hidden from view at noontide in a haze of white heat.

Looking backwards in history, how the glory centres on one pure lofty peak! And as we look again, we know that on that height a thick darkness once rested 1800 years ago, as though to blot out that scene of apparent failure, and the death on the Cross. But the darkness passed away, and the light shone, and has glowed yet brighter with every century, for the peak now so exalted was the once despised hill of Calvary.

We are too ready to pass judgment on who succeed, and who fails. Oh, if one could but remember that the ground whereon we tread may be holy ground, that heaven may be about us; and we too blind to see, too ignorant to know.

LA SAISIAZ.

By the REV. W. ROBERTSON, Sprouston, Roxburghshire.

Read at the Sixty-third Meeting of the Browning Society, Friday, January 25, 1889.

It is not surprising that Mr. Browning—the note of whose poetry is the interest displayed in all that helps or hinders, stimulates or depresses the individual soul in its moral development—should have very frequently touched upon the question of immortality and defined the influence which the acceptance or rejection of this doctrine has on human life. Not merely has he directly discussed certain bearings of the question in such poems as *Easter Day, A Death in the Desert, Rabbi Ben Ezra, Cleon,* and *Karshish ;* in numberless others, of which *In a Year, The Patriot,* and *The Grammarian's Funeral,* may be named as examples of varying importance, he has—as if in an incidental manner—adverted to it as an ultimate conviction lying ready for use, so to speak, in the background of consciousness. But in taking up *La Saisiaz* as an expression of Mr. Browning's opinions we find certain features which distinguish it from the poems I have named. In the first place, it is the production of a considerably later period of his life ; and the years which have intervened between the publication of this poem and of those I have just referred to, have been years in which all convictions have been shaken to their foundations. No man is so great as to be completely above and beyond the influences of the spirit of his time, and we shall not be surprised if we find that Mr. Browning's attitude in *La Saisiaz* towards the problem of the Future Life bears the marks of this world-conflict. A second distinguishing feature of *La Saisiaz* is that here we have, for once at least, a poem by Mr. Browning which is, in no sense of the word, dramatic. Mr. Browning, we all know only too well, has been true

to the determination which he must have early formed, not to "unlock
his heart with a sonnet-key." He has been exclusive : he has kept
the world at arm's-length : he has not worn his heart upon his sleeve.
We cannot, of course, for a moment admit that the reverent student
of Browning is to be for ever excluded from a knowledge of his mind ;
but as little can it be denied that the veil is not uplifted to the careless eye : the secret is not yielded up to the hasty glance. He who
runs may *not* read. Mr. Browning has spoken words which the
children of wisdom justify ; but if it was his intention, as it would
appear to have been, to speak to the unthinking crowd in such
manner that, hearing, they might hear and *not* understand, we must
give him credit for having carried out his intention with singular
success. *La Saisiaz*, however, we are permitted to believe, is not
a dramatic poem. The writer speaks in his own person, and the
opinions expressed are Mr. Browning's opinions.

1. The introduction to *La Saisiaz* bulks somewhat largely when
compared with the main body of the poem, occupying twenty-two—
or, by another computation, thirty-two—pages out of eighty, and
ought not therefore to be passed by without reference. The fulness
of detail in these introductory pages would seem intended to prepare
our minds for the impartiality and unflinching severity with which
popular beliefs in the succeeding pages are to be treated, and the
baldness of the question which is immediately to be asked and
answered—

> "How much, how little, do I inwardly believe
> True, that controverted doctrine ?"

It is in no ordinary mood that he approaches the discussion. However coolly men may often take up the problem, for him it has become
a matter of intense personal interest. He means on this occasion to
grope his way back to the ultimate facts on which the conviction is
based, and he seeks to prepare our minds for the earnestness of the
discussion that is to follow by detailing the tragic circumstances
which have forced the question upon him. With an artist's instinct,
therefore, he opens his poem by picturing himself as standing on the
height alone—

> "Singly dared and done the climbing both of us were bound to do—"

with the added hint that in the ascent every sweet was touched with
bitter. He then works his way backward, not telling us the tale
with the directness of a mere reporter, but in the form of such a
soliloquy on recent events as might naturally occur to him at the

moment.   His mind wanders back over these events, the prevailing
thought being his recollection how completely absent was all forebod-
ing of coming ill, and his sense of the profound gulf that now divides
him from his friend.   Five days before he and she had determined to
ascend the mountain.   He recalls the light and careless talk of the
evening preceding the day which had been fixed for their ascent—
every word so significant now from its very triviality, so oppressive
in its suggestion of human blindness and ignorance.   Not thus would
friends converse if they foresaw with what appalling suddenness the
thick curtains of night were to fall and hide them from each other for
ever.   He recalls the commonplace close of that day, the injunction
to remember to-morrow's engagement, the nothings of French politics
hardly worth repeating, the last dying sparks of adieus on the stair
landing—then all was dark.   Next morning even there was still no
premonitory hint of the coming cloud as he went for his early plunge
in the pool.   He returned, expecting everywhere to meet and greet
the tall white figure, and entered the house just in time to find that
death had, at that instant, "captured her in cold forever—" her, the
full beauty of whose nature he alone had known,

> "an Alpine-rose which all beside named Edelweiss."

The friends bury her body in the quiet little churchyard, and, now
ill at ease in such a scene, they resolve to leave it ; but before depart-
ing, the poet performs one loving duty in making the ascent " which
both of them were bound to do."   We are thus brought naturally
round to the point from which we started—on the summit where the
poet stands alone with the question forced upon him in a manner that
cannot be evaded " Here I stand : but you—where ? "

It would have been my wish, had I been able to accomplish it, to
have discoursed upon La Saisiaz as a work of art, and not merely
as a contribution to the study of a problem of philosophy.   To neglect
the thought of Mr. Browning's poems, however, in order to devote our
attention to the form, is not always an easy task, and less easy with
regard to La Saisiaz than with most of his works : but before leaving
these introductory pages we may look back for a moment and note
some of their poetic features.   Briefly then, it may be said, we observe many of the characteristic marks of Mr. Browning's style—
simplicity and directness of narration befitting the sad story ; sustained vigour of thought, and picturesque force of language ; the
keenest observation of nature, and what we might call an almost
ruthless accuracy of description.   As regards the much-talked-of

obscurity of Mr. Browning's writings—though its occurrence can only be denied by the blind worshipper of his genius—it must be concluded that he has been often charged with obscurity in passages which are only marked by conciseness, or are found on examination to be as simple and direct as the abstruse nature of his subject will admit.   No one, certainly, can bring against the introduction to *La Saisiaz* the charge of needless obscurity.

Coleridge, you recollect, in speaking of some verses of Wordsworth's declares that if he had met them howling in the desert he would have recognised their authorship.   Similarly we might quote many verses from this introduction which bear every mark of Mr. Browning's peculiar genius.   When we meet such lines as these

> " Five short days, sufficient hardly to entice, from out its den
>   Splintered in the slab, this pink perfection of the cyclamen ;
>   Scarce enough to heal and coat with amber gum the sloe tree's gash,
>   Bronze the clustered wilding apple, redden ripe the mountain-ash " :

we feel how keen is the insight here, how vivid is the picture which is called up before us, and what a world of observation is condensed into the words, each of which is as a scintillating point of light. Such lines, in which he seems to take the first words that occur to him without regard to their lack of poetic association if only they are accurate, vivid, and forcible enough, could not be met with in any desert without proclaiming their author.   And again, in lines such as these

> " Blanc, supreme above his earth-brood, needles red and white and green,
>   Horns of silver, fangs of crystal set on edge in his demesne " ;

or this, in which he describes how the rising sun transmutes to glory the dark mass of Jura—

> " Gay he hails her, and magnific, thrilled her black length burns to gold " ;

we have instances of Mr. Browning's characteristic power of passing at one instant, in the midst of an ordinary narrative, to the heights of imaginative expression.

2. At the close of these twenty-two pages of introduction we are brought round once more, as I said, to the point from which we started, but ten pages still intervene between us and the real commencement of the argument of the poem.   The question to be answered—now so pressingly personal—is, " Does the soul survive the body ?" and he asks himself if he can bear to know the truth, should the truth happen not to coincide with his wishes.   He believes

he can.   He is weak ; he can but weakly question, he can but weakly
answer ; but

> " Weakness never needs be falseness, truth is truth in each degree
>   Thunder-pealed by God in Nature, whispered by my soul to me."

He cannot pretend to reproduce in *his* words the thunder of God's
reply.   Still, weak human answers are sufficient for weak human
questions, and by questioning himself he can discover what the human
heart has to say in reply—remembering also that the thunder-peal
may be—" Mine is but man's truest answer—how were it did God
respond ?"   If then he could talk calmly with his friend on the
question of a future life when she was alive, he will not falter now
when the question to decide is, " Was ending ending once and always
when you died ?"   What remains of his friend, dear and true ?   He
casts his eye on the peaceful earth-bed where she was laid, and
asks was it only " a tribute to yon flowers and moss ?"

He then bethinks himself that many have an answer ready for
him.   " Not wholly a tribute to the earth," say they ; " there remains
a memory and an influence."   Some, it appears, desire only, in George
Eliot's words, to

> " . . . join the choir invisible
> Of those immortal dead who live again
> In minds made better by their presence."

He takes up this answer of modern scepticism and weighs it in the
balance.   Certainly a memory of her remains with me, he says, but
how inadequate a memory !   Had but fortune favoured, what beauty of
soul might have been developed from such promise !   Besides, what
heart knows another ?   His memory of her is only of what of her he
knew.   Then he, treasuring this meagre recollection of her beauty,
lives his week or year and dies at last leaving an equally inadequate
memorial of himself in the heart of some friend, and finally both
memories perish and the only husk of comfort left is

> "This—that somewhere new existence led by men and women new
> Possibly attains perfection coveted by me and you."

They, owning life a burden and unhappy, fought and struggled : some
late generation may possibly enjoy what they so earnestly desired.

The bare statement of this creed seems sufficient at once to weigh
it in the balance and to declare its vanity, for he immediately leaves
the subject.   That we may not lightly pass over important words,
however, let us take up the crucial thought of the passage—which is
not that of the unfulfilled life and the undeveloped soul, nor of the
inadequacy of the memory, nor even that both memories fade and

vanish for ever from human knowledge—not these, significant though
they be—but this, that in some new existence a new generation of
men and women "possibly attains perfection coveted by me and
you." *Possibly*—this is the fatal word which pricks that hollow
bubble-substitute for immortality.   Where is the certainty of this
perfection that some sanguine eyes foresee?   Who can tell whether
the human race is even on the road towards painlessness and happiness?   Can any one declare that he has grounds for the conviction
that such a destiny awaits the race of men?   Granted that the
English race, the Teutonic race, the Western races if you will, have
progressed during the last thousand years, there is absolutely no
foundation for the belief that this progress will continue.   Former
civilisations have vanished from the earth.   "Assyria, Greece, Rome,
Carthage where are they?"   One after another they caught up the
flaming torch of civilisation, bore it for a brief space, then allowed it
to drop from their weary hands, and finally retired from the contest.
What assurance have we that the same fate may not be in store for
us?   And further, we can form no conception of this distant and
perfected future, for history and science alike fail to forecast it.
Even if physical science had free scope and could work out its best,
if the time should ever come when there shall be no more hunger and
no more pain (and science would seem rather to predict the reverse,
that—in the increasing intensity of the struggle for existence—
these will augment rather than decrease) there can notwithstanding
be no future however distant in which the ugly facts of decay,
separation, and death, shall not dominate human life, and these are
ills before which hunger and pain dwindle into insignificance.   Then
" *coveted by me and you.*"   The happiness of some remote, much less
only possible future, cannot satisfy the longings of the present.   An
ideal "for me and you"—the perfection, not of the race, but of
individual men and women, would be something worth living for : but
who can find satisfaction or stimulus in striving to produce a problematical generation of Shakespeares in some remote æon?   Would
such a product, even if it could be brought to birth, atone for the
sufferings and the pain with which each tedious inch was won by those
who went before?   As well imagine that the misery and want of the
East End of London are satisfactorily balanced by the happiness and
luxury of the West.   It is small comfort, to use a phrase of Professor
Huxley's somewhere—it is small comfort to the three-toed horse of
the *Eocene* period to know that his fortunate descendant, a million of
years after, is to be the winner of the Derby.

I. I pass now to the first of the two main divisions of the poem,
and, with Mrs. Sutherland Orr's invaluable volume in our hands, it is
unnecessary that I should follow, too closely, the course of the
argument. The poet starts by assuming the fact of his own individual
personality, and external to him of a power, not himself, that makes for
—he knows not what, any more than the rush knows whence the
stream comes that carries it, or whither it is carried. These two
facts he calls the Soul and God, both so certain as to be beyond
proof: he knows of nothing equally certain.[1] He is now, that is
incontrovertible : will he also be ? He touches upon some of the
arguments usually given in answer to this question only to dismiss
them—God's goodness, God's power, man's desires. On these matters
he cannot speak : he will keep to the sure ground of personal experience. He knows "what to me is pain and pleasure." Beyond
this all is surmise. He will state then the results of his own experience, and his first judgment on life is that he cannot regard it as
the outcome of wisdom if he is debarred from assuming that this
world is a place of probation for man's soul. He must believe that
life is a training-school where men are educated. But he has no
sooner given expression to this judgment than he sees its inadequacy.
He is met by the inevitable question *Cui bono ?* What is the use of
training and perfecting a human soul ? Does the end justify the
means ? Can we accept it as a satisfactory explanation of all the
sorrows and trials of this world that they are imposed for the mere
purpose of teaching us half a dozen virtues ?

> " Needs there groan a world in anguish just to teach us sympathy " ?

Must friends die only that we may fully know their love, and
flowers fade that we may merely learn to prize their beauty ? Was
there no way but this to teach man how precious are love and beauty ?
In a word, can we accept it as a satisfactory explanation of this
world that it is

> "Only a machine for teaching love and hate and hope and fear " ?

No, he replies, it is not satisfactory, and though he will bear it if
it is of necessity, he cannot regard it as the creation of a God "allgood,
allwise, allpotent." What then ? The "traversed heart" must tell
its story uncommented on. Grant a second life, he says, assume that
our present state is one of preparation for a life to follow, and that

---

[1] *Cf.* Newman's conviction of the existence of "two, and two only, supreme
and luminously self-evident beings, myself and my Creator."

instant our earthly experience becomes intelligible. In failure, misfortune, defeat, he will now "acquiesce." Over all these things he will be more than conqueror, for they will be seen to be essential elements in the divine plan of education. Loss brings true gain, knowledge rises from recognised ignorance, the preciousness of beauty is discovered amid surrounding ugliness, truth amid falsehood, and love through loss.

> "Only grant my soul may carry high through death her cup unspilled,
> Brimming though it be with knowledge. . . . .
> "Grant me (once again) assurance we shall each meet each some day,
> Walk—but with how bold a footstep ! on a way—but what a way !
> —Worst were best, defeat were triumph, utter loss were utmost gain.
> Can it be, and must, and will it ?"

Yes, can it be ? He has stated his case, the grounds of his "surmise." He presents us with *a working hypothesis* of life.

In attempting an amplification of this working hypothesis, I must first of all point out that Mr. Browning is not (as has been sometimes stated) postulating immortality, in this poem at least, on the ground that a future life is required to atone for the ills of the present. This is to attribute to him a style of argumentation which, in the poem, he explicitly rejects. It is not the injustice of life that afflicts him, it is its unintelligibility. He is led to hope for immortality because without it he can find no rationality in life, no explanation of its evils, and no motive for effort. He has found in his experience that this world is a scene of education : grant that such a fact was designed, and that some use is to be elsewhere made of the developed soul, and immediately life becomes intelligible. Refuse to grant it, and all the suffering and sacrifice of man, his struggles after distant ideals, his crushing sense of failure, his anguish and remorse, become unmeaning.

Mr. Browning designates his inference a "surmise"; nevertheless it is the real ground of his belief. It suggests an answer to the question : What is the end or purpose of man's life ? Why am I here ? Human life is to be judged by the standard either of its utility for the world or for the individual soul. The former alternative is, we have already seen, rejected by Mr. Browning in the passage where he employs the phrase, "Possibly attains perfection coveted by me and you." We may further add that by the hypothesis of mortality, the value of the world (in serving which the soul finds its utility) is deteriorated. If men are but temporary and transient beings, their sufferings, when past, are as unimportant and need concern us as lightly as the fate of

last year's leaves.   If we are told to look to the future of the race
and find, in utility for that, an adequate explanation of the " problem
of our being here," and a sufficient motive for sacrifice, we must
reply that we cannot work for a future which we do not know.   We
can understand sacrifice for those we love, we can understand sacrifice
for those we do not love in obedience to the will of God, but we cannot understand sacrifice for a generation of whose needs we can form
no conjecture, and whose very existence is to some extent contingent.[1]
Are we told that we shall become nobler through this pursuit, and
attain a higher degree of intellectual, moral, and spiritual development ?   True, we shall; and just at the moment when we " know
most " we shall " least enjoy "; at the moment when we have
attained the noblest height we shall be snuffed out of existence.

Life judged by such standards Mr. Browning affirms to be
incomplete and unintelligible.   He adopts the Christian theory
which declares the final cause of life to lie in a good for the individual.   The highest altruism is enjoined in the Christian system no
less imperatively than in some anti-Christian systems; but in the
Christian, altruism is never set up as the end of human life.   The
end of my existence must be an end for me : my ideal of life an ideal
for me.   Christianity declares sacrifice to be only a means, and the
end, the result, or, as it is sometimes called, the reward (though
Christian rewards, properly understood, do not minister to selfishness)
is *perfection of character*.   In and through self-sacrifice (though not
through self-sacrifice alone) is perfection attained, and only so conceived, as it appears to me, does conscious and voluntary self-sacrifice
become rational.   Altruism, pure and simple, and apart from any
personal ideal, is suicide pure and simple.   Life, not death—self-
realization, not self-annihilation, is the goal proposed by Christianity.
If we are asked to keep the Commandments it is that we may enter
into life ; if to sacrifice ourselves, it is that we may realize ourselves.
The Christian maxim is not " die," but " die to live."   Now, if I rightly
interpret Mr. Browning, his contention is that this educative purpose in life is irrational if men are mortal—that if we find life to
be so regulated as to bring forth a moral result, character namely,
if the individual soul becomes nobler and purer, this end cannot be
designed in order merely to present a finer tribute to the flowers
and moss.

It may here be allowable to remark that the Christian theory,
which Mr. Browning accepts and expounds, has at least one merit—

[1] R. H. Hutton.

it attempts to read a meaning in human existence, and to present a solution of the problems of life. The Christian believes that a purpose is expressed in human life. He does *not* believe that he fully understands this purpose. The existence of evil, moral and physical, is, in its more terrible forms at least, in his creed as in every other, the crowning difficulty, the ever-present fact which has to be accounted for. He sees in instances here and there that pain and suffering—in a word, evil—fills a useful function. God, he affirms, has not chosen to make a perfect and completed world—such a world would have been, to say the least, uninteresting. But He has chosen to make a progressive world, and evil is one of the necessary factors of progress. Hunger is a stimulus ; pain, a guide ; sorrow, a purifier ; loss reveals the true value of precious things ; effort strengthens man's character ; and peace is only won through war. But these simple explanations are not universally applicable. "Lo, these are parts of His ways : but how little a portion is heard of Him" (R.V.—"Lo, these are but the outskirts of His ways : And how small a whisper do we hear of Him"). They are but keys to the mysterious and changing cipher in which the world is written ; and when, by these keys, we have, as we think, successfully interpreted a line of this world-hieroglyphic, we find at the next line that our key has failed us. Much pain, and sorrow, and suffering seem utterly disproportionate to the resulting good—sometimes no result of good is perceptible at all. But the Christian holds firmly to so much as he can understand, and so far as he does understand it, the meaning seems to be that man is here to be educated. Man is not here to work, but to be worked upon. The production of character is, after all, the one result which never fails. Whether you are ruling a kingdom, or sweeping a crossing, or lying on a sick bed, character is ever being formed and built up. Every act, whether it be a success or a failure, is a stone added to the edifice of character which is being reared. If naked, man comes into this world, not naked he goes hence, but loaded with this heavy burden of character he departs elsewhere—if there be an elsewhere.

Such is the estimate of life, as it appears to me, on which Mr. Browning bases his "surmise" that it will continue.

From the foregoing argument it is patent that we are far astray if we imagine that Mr. Browning means to adduce "evidences" of immortality. To have presented, as "proofs" of a future life, the ordinary stock-in-trade of the apologetic theologian, would have been wide of his purpose. His purpose is of quite another nature. As in

Cleon he reproduces the feelings of one who looks with horror on the blank darkness of annihilation, and clings to this present life because there is "no work, nor device, nor knowledge, nor wisdom, in the grave whither thou goest"; so in *La Saisiaz* he adopts another and more important Biblical precedent, and seeks to bring immortality to light by first bringing "life" to light. He bases his belief in immortality on his sense of the value of man's present existence. The soul is worth training. Man's perfected soul is too fair a product to be lost. Heaven and earth, pain and pleasure, love and hate, light and darkness, promise and disappointment, success and failure, are all at work, like a potter's wheel, moulding into finer shape this soul of man. It is an agonizing process. But only grant that all this agony is not meaningless and purposeless, that it has a significance for the individual—only grant a second life, he says, and I acquiesce in every hour of disciplinary pain, I rejoice in it, I triumph in it.

This is the argument of the poem so far as we have gone, and in no sense of the word can it be called "proof." You can prove that the world is round on evidence which compels conviction in every sane mind, but Mr. Browning pauses in his discussion of immortality at a point where belief in it is manifestly compatible with doubt. In what remains of the poem he proceeds to account for this uncertainty in which he finds the question involved.

II. The second main division of the poem is the lengthy dialogue between FANCY and REASON which it is unnecessary I should analyse in detail. I may summarise his argument briefly thus. He has found, as I said, that the course of his argument has landed him only in "surmise." This, at first sight, seems unsatisfactory, and he proceeds to ask himself the question, What would be the effect on human life if immortality were no surmise, but a conviction so certain that a man could not, in any mood, question it? He finds that such a hypothesis would be fatal to his foregoing argument—that the effect of such a conviction would be to destroy that probationary element in life which he has declared to be the very basis of the belief. If the next world were always and clearly known as the scene of certain reward for obedience here, earth could no longer be "man's probation place." The immediate effect of certainty would be to destroy man's freedom of choice. If evil could be seen to be inevitably followed by punishment, and good as inevitably followed by reward, no man could disobey laws so patent and importunate, there could be no merit in obeying them, and obedience to them could not constitute a moral discipline. The moral law is not so certain and palpable as to compel

obedience.   " To know the good and yet the wrong pursue " is the
commonest of adages.   There *are* laws so patent and palpable as to
necessitate immediate obedience; but for such obedience man gets no
credit.   The moral law man may evade, many laws he must obey :
" therefore," says Mr. Browning,

> " . . . not without a purpose these man must, while those man may
>   Keep and, for the keeping, haply gain approval and reward."

The moral law is not subject to evasion through Divine impotence,
but of purpose that obedience may be disciplinary.   Similarly, if the
fact of immortality, as a scene of rewards and punishments, lay in
the region of scientific and demonstrated truth, obedience to the
moral law would no longer be an affair of effort and struggle, and
the discipline of the soul would no longer be possible.   Only from
the hypothesis that this life is a scene of probation can immortality
be inferred (such is the argument in the earlier portion of the poem) :
only by not holding this inference as a matter of demonstrated certainty can our present existence remain a scene of probation (such is
the argument in the later portion).

   I need not do more at this point than remind you that in *Karshish*
Mr. Browning has expressed the same opinion in a manner more
indirect, but on that very account perhaps more convincing.   The
certain and immediate conception of the unseen world, possessed by
Lazarus, paralyses him, it injures his sense of the true proportion of
earthly things, and lifts him out the region of conflict and struggle
and therefore of probation.   *La Saisiaz* closes with the judgment that
future life is, and can only fulfil its disciplinary function by remaining,
a hope—"a hope; no less, no more ".

   I may be allowed here, as previously, to pause, and attempt a
re-statement of the argument which I have thus briefly summarised.
And I purpose making use of the terminology of theological science,
because by so doing I may be able, perhaps, more accurately to define
the place in modern thought which Mr. Browning has here taken up.

   By certain writers surprise has been expressed that Mr. Browning
should have declared the question of immortality to lie in the uncertain region of " hope " ; and some have even attempted to infer that
his deliverance on the subject in 1877, when *La Saisiaz* was published,
expresses a less assured conviction than what was his when he wrote
A Death in the Desert or *Rabbi Ben Ezra.*   Now, on the contrary, Mr.
Browning has taken up in this division of the subject no less than
in the others, as it appears to me, the purely Christian position.

   In the earlier portion of the poem he affirms that life has no

N

meaning for him unless he is allowed to regard it as a scene of
probation or education. That this is the Christian position will be
granted. Is it also in harmony with Christianity to maintain that
future existence must present itself to us as a great "hope," and that
if it were a certainty it would interfere with our moral progress here?
That it is so can, I think, be easily demonstrated.

The Christian position is that spiritual progress is gained through
walking by faith and not by sight. What do these two words mean?
Sight means certain knowledge—knowledge based on scientific demonstration. (I cannot pause here to discuss the prior philosophical
question whether so-called scientific knowledge may not be based on
unproved assumptions. The phrase, of course, can only be employed
by those who imagine themselves possessed of some valid criterion of
knowledge.) We know by sight that fire burns, that water will
drown, that the world is round, that $2 + 2 = 4$. For knowledge of
these facts we require only observation and a sane mind. Once proved
they are proved for ever: we do not require a second time to assure
ourselves of them. The knowledge of them depends, in no sense, on
our moral nature—only on the sanity of our intellect. We reach
these truths without moral struggle, and we hold them without
inward effort. We speak of our *knowledge* of these matters—not of
our *belief* in them. No man, who rightly employs the Queen's
English, ever says that he *believes* $2 + 2 = 4$. He *knows* it.

Now what is faith? When the Christian says that he walks by
faith and not by sight or knowledge, he means that his life as a moral
being rests on certain convictions whose truth he may not at every
moment be able to demonstrate, but to whose intrinsic worth he pays
a homage which the things of sight are quite incapable of eliciting.
An act of faith is an act of surrender to the claims of quality rather
than of quantity. Faith is not, as is often popularly supposed, belief
on insufficient evidence. It is trust in a particular kind of evidence.
It is loyalty to certain instincts and intuitions of our nature—a
loyalty which could no doubt be defended on scientific grounds—but no
arguments which might be adduced in support of these instincts and
intuitions would account for the authority which they claim and the
homage which we yield them. The obligation of duty, or the voice of
conscience, is not so palpable and coercive as at all times to compel
obedience, but it never fails to draw from us a conviction of its
supremacy. To surrender ourselves to the unexplained command of
conscience is an act of faith. That part of our nature which accepts
the conclusions of proof we name sight; that which perceives the

intrinsic worth, and acknowledges the authoritative supremacy of conscience or the moral law we name faith.   Our adherence to the objects of faith—unlike our conviction of scientific truth—varies with our spiritual state.   It demands an inward conflict.   Faith is thus an act of surrender in the dark to conscience.   It is thus also nearly synonymous with *trust*—whose beauty as a human trait may be more generally acknowledged.   Now there is no room for trust except in darkness.

According to the Christian system all religious convictions belong to this order of beliefs.   They rest not on the evidence of sight but on instincts of loyalty and reverence.   It is thus that the exercise of faith, but not of sight, is disciplinary.

Now in thus explaining what is meant by faith and distinguishing it from sight, I have explained what Mr. Browning means by "hope." For faith and hope, as here employed, are identical in meaning, but the latter word is used with reference to those objects of faith which lie in the future time.   The obligation of duty is a present object of faith : the future life is an object of Christian hope.   It follows that the exercise of hope, in this sense, is disciplinary.   Belief in immortality, then, rests on certain moral adhesions which we require a constant moral effort to maintain.   It is this moral effort which confers on hope its probationary value.

We err then, it appears to me, if we imagine that when Mr. Browning says "hope" he means hope in its ordinary and familiar sense.   I may "hope" that to-morrow may be a fine day ; but this is a vain hope.   It is hope based on insufficient evidence.   I have no ground for *expecting* a fine day.   But when Mr. Browning "hopes" for a second life, it is no groundless hope, it is an expectation based on his working hypothesis, on his conception of the value of this earthly life as he has known and experienced it.   This life bears marks of a meaning and a purpose ; Mr. Browning reads it as the scene of probation and education : and from this again, judging by the same standard, he infers a second life for which the present is a preparation.

But it may be objected that Mr. Browning has made many of his characters (who may be believed to speak, more or less directly, his own thoughts) express the profoundest confidence in a life beyond the grave.   Let me very briefly point out what relation this position of confidence holds to that of "hope" in *La Saisiaz.*

From the religious point of view, as we have seen, it is regarded as fatal to that conception of moral progress which alone sheds any

intelligibility or rationality on life, that immortality should be a
matter of certainty and not of hope.   Life would in its every
action become a sordid calculation of chances.   It makes for
righteousness if truth is sought for its own sake, and right is followed
in scorn of consequence : it would not make for righteousness if at
every call to sacrifice we whispered to ourselves that present loss
would be future gain.   Yet when the uttermost call is made—when
all, or all that makes life worth having, has to be renounced—when the
soul is *in extremis*, then on no rational principle can the surrender be
made if there be not the inward conviction that all is not lost, that
one day it will turn to us for a testimony.   For this last supreme
surrender we require a justification, a sanction, and we find an
adequate one in our belief in immortality which we are allowed to
summon forth from the recesses of consciousness and implicitly to
trust.

Now every student of Mr. Browning knows that with him the
only thing worth study is a soul, and the study is significant in proportion to the gravity of the crisis in which the soul is placed.   His
subjects are being constantly presented to us in such critical hours
—hence the frequent reference to immortality in his works.   Thus it
is at his last hour—his ultimate surrender—that "The Patriot"
exclaims :

> "'Tis God shall repay—I am safer so."

The Grammarian " threw himself on God, and, unperplexed, seeking
shall find Him."   Abt Vogler rises from despair through the consolation of the thought " there shall never be one lost good—what
was shall live as before."   The young wife of *In a Year* falls back
for ultimate help on the yearning, " What comes next ?   Is it God ?"
David, in the agony of his need for some conception adequate to lift
off the morbid depression from the gloomy spirit of Saul, catches at
the same thought.

> " O Saul, it shall be
> A Face like my face that receives thee—a Man like to me
> Thou shalt love and be loved by for ever."

Yet what does all this amount to but just this, that belief in
immortality is not to be held mechanically or as a mere matter of
course.   It ought not to be allowed to enter among the motives of
our ordinary life.   It is for use only in supreme moments.   It should
be employed as a justification of sacrifice, not as a motive for it ; as
a sanction for giving up what is precious to us here, not as a reward
for our self-denial.   This, we believe, is Mr. Browning's position, and
it is surely in harmony with Christianity.

In *Natural Religion* Professor Seeley takes up precisely the same position as has been here expounded, on the use and abuse of belief in a future life. One might almost say that the purpose of that book is to enforce the maxim regarding immortality, " Believe it, and then think as little about it as possible."

You will not desire, I fancy, that I should proceed to show how much all that has been said is in harmony with the teaching of the Gospels. I may only point out the striking fact that on not more than perhaps three reported occasions did Christ ever speak of the life after death, and on these occasions the reference was forced on Him by interrogation from bystanders. He concerned Himself with the present ; if a future is referred to, as it often is, it is not the future after death, but a future on earth. Almost every phrase He uses—when stripped of the wrappings in which the ages have encased it—is found to refer to this present world. He spoke of no events that were not to take place before His own generation had passed away. Those standing by were not to see death till all these things were accomplished.

It does not follow from the views here expounded that to regard this life as a preparation for another world will in any degree interfere with the devotion and attention justly due to our present existence. To look on this life as a dream and the future life alone worthy of consideration is directly contrary to the spirit of Christianity. Man's sole concern is with the present. But, as Professor Seeley says, " To hope even with enthusiastic conviction for a future life is one thing ; to be always brooding over it so as to despise the present life in comparison with it is another—" a sentence which is, I believe, in closest accordance with Mr. Browning's view, and strictly illustrates the spirit in which this lecture has been written.

To sum up. It is an error to say, as regards *La Saisiaz*, at least, that Mr. Browning bases his belief in immortality on the conviction that a second life is needed to atone for the ills of the present. He does not judge the present world to be a scene of probation because he believes in immortality ; on the contrary, he believes in immortality because, in his experience, he has found this present state to be one of probation. It is neither the miseries nor the failures of this present life that oppress him—it is its meaninglessness, and he believes in immortality because in it alone does he find that which confers rationality and intelligibility on life.

Again, if he rests content with finding immortality a hope, we must remember that with him belief in a future life is expressed in

forms of hope, precisely as belief in the existence of God is expressed
in the language of faith.   In both cases the conviction rests, not on
exact or mechanical proof, but on the intimations and intuitions of
reverence, loyalty, and love.

Human life, it may be said, is like the child's toy, a heap of
letters, from which you may pick out what letters you like and frame
what words you choose, and with your words you may form some
ghastly tale of cruel oppression and blind and meaningless injustice
(like *The Story of an African Farm*) under which no mortal could
live, and yet learn that a Higher Power was leading him, firmly, yet
with pity and love, to finer issues.   It cannot be said that Mr.
Browning picks out the letters that suit him.   He takes this world
precisely as he finds it, and to him it presents itself as " probation-
place for man."   Much is inexplicable, much problematical.   In two
facts only does he find a firm basis : " He at least believed in soul—
was very sure of God."

The instincts and intuitions of the race are strong, and, for the
most part, seek for no justification of themselves.   As a rule they
fulfil their function without challenge, and ask no troublesome or
perplexing questions.   Many are the deeds of heroism and sacrifice
" done at an instinct of the natural man."   But man is self-conscious,
and he will sometimes pause and turn in upon himself, and ask if
this marvellous existence of his has no meaning and no end.   Is life
merely a fruitless round, a barren rise and fall, where you sacrifice
yourself for me and I for you, and is the long-drawn ebb and flow of
human existence to end at last in blank extinction ?   Such is man's
prospect if there be no second life.   The race itself—man, Nature's
last work—

> " Who seemed so fair,
> Such splendid purpose in his eyes,
> Who rolled the psalm to wintry skies,
> And built him fanes of fruitless prayer,"

will go down into the pit, and all his thoughts will perish.   The
energies of our system " will decay, the glory of the sun will be
dimmed, and the earth, tideless and inert, will no longer tolerate the
race which has for a moment disturbed its solitude.   The uneasy
consciousness, which in this obscure corner has for a brief space
broken the contented silence of the universe, will be at rest.   Matter
will know itself no longer.   Imperishable monuments and immortal
deeds, death itself and love stronger than death, will be as though
they had never been.   Nor will anything that is be better or be

worse for all that the labour, genius, devotion, and suffering of man
have striven through countless generations to effect." [1]

Meanwhile there is no evidence that the modern world is willing
to resign itself with a good grace to such a prospect.   Year by year
and century by century the race grows older, and no help comes when
it seems to want it most.   The griefs of the earlier world, like those
of childhood, might find sudden and passionate expression, but they
were short-lived.   Soon their tears were dried and their wounds
healed, for Nature, " the homely nurse," could quiet their hearts and
put them to sleep with the toys and sweets of the present and the
tangible.   But the human race seems to grow more sensitive and
more self-conscious as it grows older—more thoughtful and more
perplexed.   Pain smites it with a keener pang, love grows more intense
and more enduring, death now casts a deeper shadow.   Like Cleon,
the age knows most when it can least enjoy ; it bears the burden of
the mystery more sadly as one after another of those simple explanations of life which satisfied the past, fails it ; it feels most
acutely just when the last anodyne is losing its soothing influence.
If one poet of past time foresaw that a man must leave his lands, his
home, and his dear wife, he was yet ever ready to advise his friend
to brush the unwelcome, intruding thought aside, and relieve the
present pain with huger logs and deeper draughts of the red
Falernian wine.   Another of a different age and race was not
displeased to think that

> " We are no other than a moving row
>   Of magic shadow-shapes that come and go,
>   Round with the sun-illumined lantern held
>   In midnight by the Master of the show."

But it is a sadder note that sounds through modern literature.
When Rousseau gives casual expression to his expectation of meeting
again, in the other life, the woman who had loved him, and whom he
had wronged, you remember how Mr. John Morley thus comments
upon his words, the usual reserve and self-control of the philosophic
historian breaking down under the stress of his passionate revolt
against the bitterness of death—"To pluck so gracious a flower of
hope on the edge of the sombre echoless gulf of nothingness into which
our friend has slid silently down, is a natural impulse of the sensitive
soul, numbing remorse and giving a moment's relief to the hunger and
thirst of a tenderness that has been robbed of its object ; " we should
realise "that we have none of this perfect companionable bliss to

[1] *The Religion of Humanity*, by the Right Hon. A. J. Balfour.

promise ourselves in other worlds, that the black and horrible grave is indeed the end of our communion, and that we know one another no more."

The Story of an African Farm is a book not undeserving of the epithet which Matthew Arnold applied to Emily Brontë's *Last Lines*, it is "too bold"; yet its author appears to me to merit some of the descriptive expressions that are applied in Arnold's poem to the author of *Wuthering Heights*, inasmuch as among her contemporaries she

> " Knows no fellow for might,
> Passion, vehemence, grief,
> Daring."

If, in this book, she flings from her, somewhat scornfully, the "dreams" of men regarding immortality, she yet, as it is curious to note, seems to seek and find a stony peace in what is not less an empty dream, the thought of rest in the Universal Unity—forgetful that this Unity is the creation of, and exists only for, the conscious mind.

Mr. Browning, on the other hand, finds in life a ground of hope, and his attitude in *La Saisiaz* towards the question of immortality, as one of faith, trust and hope, is precisely the same as that expressed in the more famous poem :

> " Behold, we know not anything,
>   I can but trust that good shall fall
>   At last—far off—at last, to all,
> And every winter change to spring."
>   .   .   .   .
> " I stretch lame hands of faith, and grope,
>   And gather dust and chaff, and call
>   To what I feel is Lord of all,
> And faintly trust the larger hope."

I wish to add a few words on *La Saisiaz* considered as a work of art.

1. Much of what I said about the introduction is applicable to the poem as a whole—notably the reference to the sustained energy of the writer's style and the ease with which, in the midst of a philosophic argument, he can take instant flight on the wings of his imagination, to the heights of poetic expression. Such a phrase as "Hope the arrowy" in the connection in which it occurs illustrates this, and many others could be quoted.

Then that "indescribable gusto" which Keats distinguished in the elocution of Edmund Kean, appears to me a not improper phrase to apply to some of Mr. Browning's verses, of which this line may stand as an example

"Bronze the clustered wilding apple, redden ripe the mountain-ash."

The following remarks, however, I offer with much more diffidence.

2. When I turn to ask—In what does the argument of this poem differ from that which might be met with in the work of a prose writer? What has Mr. Browning as poet contributed to the discussion of the question? I find some difficulty in answering. The same writer, it appears to me, could have stated his case with equal power, effectiveness and attraction, in prose. Indeed there are large portions of the poem which do not differ in any real manner from brilliant prose. The leading thoughts could find full and adequate expression in a philosophical treatise : they do not appear to me to gain much by being expressed in the poetic form. Perhaps it might be said that the poem suffers from its simple directness of purpose, from its almost didactic aim. It suffers from the fact that Mr. Browning is throughout speaking in his own person, and thus affords a justification, if that were needed, of his resolution not to unlock his heart with a sonnet-key. Other poems could be named, such as *Bishop Blougram's Apology*, or *Caliban upon Setebos*, equally argumentative ; but the reasoning in these is subservient to the revelation of character which constitutes their main significance as poems. In *La Saisiaz* Mr. Browning appears to me to subordinate, if not indeed to sacrifice, the poetic and prophetic elements to the ratiocinative.

3. Again, *La Saisiaz* illustrates Mr. Browning's characteristic lack, or at least neglect of, musical expression. We have only to remember that this poem is written in the same measure as *Locksley Hall* to recognise to the full in what respects it differs from the work of a master-artist in melodious forms. Such lines as that which I quoted

"Scarce enough to heal and coat with amber gum the sloe-tree's gash " ;

or these—

"Gay earth drop her garlands shrivelled at the first infecting breath
Of the serpent pains which herald, swarming in, the dragon death " ;

or these—

" Barked the bole, and broke the bough, and bruised the berry, left all grace
Ashes in death's stern alembic, loosed elixir in its place ! "

are quite in Mr. Browning's manner, and typical examples of the poem, and while we cannot fail to recognise their marvellous force, brilliance and keenness of observation, we cannot call them musical.

He seldom employs phrases that have a poetic flavour, that carry with them any poetic associations. I do not of course deny that musical lines are to be met with here, as in all Mr. Browning's poems, but they occur only frequently enough to remind us " with a shock of mild surprise " how seldom they occur.

4. Once more may I venture to remark that the poem appears to me to illustrate Mr. Browning's characteristic lack of pathos. Whether the absence of the pathetic element from his works is owing to his determination to keep the world at a distance and allow no eye to behold the heart in its weaker and tenderer moods, I cannot say. Its absence from *La Saisiaz* is certainly not owing to the lack of opportunities of introducing it. The unfulfilled life, the appallingly sudden death, the piteous work of interment, the lonely grave among the mountains in the land of strangers, would have been, we may be sure, in the hands of some other poets, more fully described and more pathetically treated. Again I do not deny that pathetic lines might be quoted from Mr. Browning's works, e.g. Mildred's words in *A Blot on the 'Scutcheon*—

> . . . . . . " I was so young—
> I had no mother, and I loved him so " ;

but in this matter, as in others, we must judge a poet's power—not by a line here and there—but by the wealth and weight of his utterance—by noting whether the mood descends frequently, readily, and spontaneously upon him, and whether in the present instance it comes naturally to him to touch the tender chords. Judging by this standard we cannot say that the pathetic mood is characteristic of Mr. Browning. It occurs so very seldom in the mass of his work. We have only to note how characteristic, how spontaneous, how constant is his flow of humour, to know what we might expect if pathos had been equally ready to come at call. This is the more surprising as humour and pathos are so frequently found combined in the same writer. On this evening of the 25th of January many—not Scotsmen merely—will meet over two hemispheres in order to give expression to their love and admiration of one who was not inferior to Mr. Browning in humour, in strength, in keen-eyed observation, in sarcastic force, but with Robert Burns the pathetic mood was as familiar and recurrent as the humorous or the witty.

These remarks may be mistaken, but the Browning Society seems to me the proper place in which to vent them. Limitation of power is a note of all human effort : to say that Mr. Browning has limitations is only to say that he has what no man has ever been without.

ON "A TOCCATA OF GALUPPI'S."

By Mrs. ALEXANDER IRELAND.

Read at the Sixty-sixth Meeting of the Browning Society,
Friday, April 26, 1889.

To analyze the subtle, nameless charm of this poem would seem
as thankless a task as to resolve a woman's tear into its component
chemical elements—a task as barren of adequate result. Rejecting
the word *analysis*, to which *A Toccata of Galuppi's* scarcely lends
itself, which, indeed, it almost sets at *defiance*, let me try to express
something of what the poem suggests to me.

And, first, let me read it.

*   *   *   *   *   *   *   *

The haunting sweetness of these verses, with their deep under-
current of aching dissatisfaction, have led irresistibly to these
thoughts, born of a loving, if ineffectual study.

What may be called the "musical triptych" among Browning's
poems seems to consist of, first, *Master Hugues of Saxe-Gotha*,
which turns on the fugue, the eminently Protestant form of music
—it is intricate, theological, and hair-splitting; second, *Abt Vogler*,
surely well-named the symphony, with all the world, with all the
human heart in it, truly Catholic in character; and third, *A Toccata
of Galuppi's*, music of the worldly type, slight, delicate, fascinating,
with echoes of the sigh and the sneer, a light ripple on the shore of
human life-passion, bearing, here and there, some deeper note of life's
pathos, its incompleteness, its hopeless longing, blent with monotony of
gay, light repetition. For the *Toccata* or "*Touch*-piece," by its very
signification, does but *touch* its theme rapidly, even superficially, for
the most part; so that the interpolation of solemn chords and emotional

phrases, inconsistent with its traditional character, may naturally, by force of contrast, lead to some suggestion or recognition of the jarring inequalities of life.

A Toccata of Galuppi's touches on deep subjects with a mere feather-touch of light and capricious suggestiveness, interwoven with the graver mood, with the heart-searching questionings of man's deep nature and mysterious spirit.

The *Toccata* as a form of composition is not the measured, deliberate working-out of some central musical thought, as is the *Sonata* or *sound-piece*, where the trained ear can follow out the whole process to its delightful and orderly consummation, where the student marks the introduction and development of the subject, its extension, through various forms, and its whole sequence of movement and meaning, to its glorious rounding-off and culmination, spiritually noting each stage of the climbing structure and acknowledging its perfection with the inward silent verdict, "It is well."

The *Toccata*, in its early and pure form, possessed no decided subject, made such by repetition, but bore rather the form of a capricious Improvisation or "Impromptu." It was a very flowing movement, in notes of equal length, and a homophonous character, the earliest examples of any importance being those by Gabrieli (1557— 1613), and those by Merulo (1533—1604); while Galuppi, who was born in 1706 and died in 1785, produced a further advanced development of this particular form of musical composition, with chords freely introduced and other important innovations. We feel assured that the *Toccata* treated of in Browning's poem must have possessed considerable light and shade, for while its joyous lightness conjured up before the listener's mind the bewildering vision of festal scenes in ancient Venice, while it drew around him the balmy night of May, the intoxicating fragrance of roses and love and youth, the atmosphere surcharged with fulness of sensuous life, there were yet thrilling and tender cadences, surely some strains that had a "dying fall," dissonances even, powerful enough to interpose, with obtrusiveness, grim doubts in the very heart and core of the charmed moment— doubts transient, quickly put aside or stifled, but ghastly in their suggestion of impending change, doom, and death.

We learn that Baldassare Galuppi was born October 18, 1706, on the island of Burano, near Venice, whence he was known as "Il Buranello," and that he first learned music from his father, a barber, who played the violin at the theatre. At sixteen, Baldassare came to Venice and earned his bread by organ-playing. At this time, doubtless, he took irrevocably into his being the solemn harmonies of Church music, which so twined themselves about his inmost spirit as occasionally to startle us by their solemn presence in his lighter, and more showy compositions. Whilst thus struggling to earn a living Galuppi came to know Marcello, then a student of music in the Conservatorio degli Incurabile, of which the eminent musician Lotti was Director. Lotti was a remarkable man, and composed some immortal music, notably a magnificent *Miserere*, still annually performed in Venice on Maunday Thursday, and strangely enough there is among his works a madrigal, *Spiritode Dio*, which he composed for that very ceremony alluded to in *A Toccata of Galuppi's*, —namely, the espousal of the Adriatic by the Doges. Through the intervention of Marcello, Galuppi obtained admission into that musical school of which Lotti was the Director, that school which produced so many eminent musicians. Lotti, besides his post as Director of the Incurabile was also *Maestro di Capella* of San Marco, and in both these appointments he was succeeded at his death by his pupil Galuppi, who rapidly developed his remarkable powers. I may just mention that in Hullah's " Part-Music," first edition, there is a charming motet and madrigal by Lotti ; also, in Hullah's " Vocal Scores and Part Music," second edition, a fine *Credo* by him. And we remember with pleasure that this same Lotti, the instructor of Galuppi, wrote that dainty little song, revived in modern days, of which the ear never tires—

" Pur dicesti, O, bocca, bocca, bella !"

Lotti died in 1740.

Like his great master, Galuppi composed many operas which were performed with varying success throughout Italy. But though rich in melody, always written with taste, and never overloaded, none of them survived the revolution of Rossini, fatal to so many of Galuppi's contemporaries."

Soon after 1762, he being then first organist at San Marco, and also Director of the " Conservatorio degli Incurabile," Galuppi gave up both posts in order to go to St. Petersburg, invited by the Empress Catherine II. Having first improved and remodelled the orchestra, no easy task in those days, he produced his *Didone Abbandonata*, with extraordinary success. In 1768, Galuppi returned to Venice, were Dr. Burney found him in 1770, prosperous and respected, still *maestro* of the Incurabile. Burney speaks of the fire and imagination manifest in his compositions, and of the novelty, spirit, and delicacy of his music. The autograph of his opera, *Il Vilano Geloso*, which he composed conjointly with Garsmann, Marcello, Scarlatti, Sacchini, and others, is now in Vienna ; also a grand *Credo, Gloria*, and other Church music still occasionally performed there. Galuppi also wrote for the harpsichord, and a sonata of his, of rare beauty, is printed in the *Alte-Clavier-Musik* of Pauer. He was most prolific in composition, since Fétis gives a list of fifty-four operas of his, five of which were written in one year.

But the noble music of his which has survived outweighs much of this youthful gush. And Galuppi must have possessed very remarkable versatility. We can well believe that, as Browning tells us, he was "good alike at grave and gay." We figure to ourselves that very *Toccata*, with its traditional gaiety, broken now and again by solemn passages and pathetic touches. According to Browning's masterly description, we listen "with *heart*, not *ear*," to "those lesser thirds so plaintive—sixths diminished—sigh on sigh !" We detect the human longing after a larger life and fuller happiness, the thrilling note of life's incompleteness, its deep restless doubt, its obscure, haunting recognition of death ! Then, "those suspensions, those solutions," those relentless unfoldings of the inexorable, unlovable law of change, hint ominously at the impending shadow, and wring from the hearts of the careless listeners the question "*Must we die ?*" But again, "the commiserating sevenths" give a hope. "Surely some pitying power will interpose on our behalf, give us still the cup of living joy, still the unending round of ball and masque, still the moonlit waters, the scent of many roses, the rhythmic movement of fair women, the very delirium of sensuous ecstasy."

> "Life might last—we can but try ?"

Breathless with the dance, they have lingered a while, idly listening to Galuppi's wondrous melodies, and lo ! the vibrations of that music have touched and shaken within them those mystic fibres that bind men and women to life ; there is a stirring in the deep spiritual nature—questionings, unwelcome and obstinate, press on their consciousness. But they soon repel the chilling touch, and cling closer to the life of their passionate love, to each other, and we hear, athwart Galuppi's solemn strains, the kiss, the whispers, the tender caressing breath of that perfect love-duet,—"Were you happy ?" "Yes !" "And are you still as happy ?" "Yes ! And you ?" So far the music has been in the region of the incomplete, the minor key, with the yearning thrill of the half-satisfied soul. Now it changes to the *major* key, the tone of decision, of imperative demand ; and the question " Must we die ?" strongly borne in on the consciousness, clamours for an answer. So the " dominant's persistence," its exacting craving, repeated in each harmonic combination, receives its reply—in the octave of the tonic—the inevitable close, the foregone conclusion, which lifts the dominant into fulness ! This certainty without appeal was no fitting theme for an accompaniment of light, loving repartee, the note struck was too jarring, and with careless words of praise, the youthful pair stroll away from the too eloquent music, and are again lost in the whirling dance.

As to the structure, the machinery of the poem, granting that any such be cunningly concealed within its graceful lines, one can enjoy the verses without any desire to disintegrate or individualize its diverse voices, so sweetly discoursing ; but, once having essayed to formulate its meanings, to assign to the supposed speaker each phrase of its dialogue, once having sought the " *raison d'être* " of *A Toccata of Galuppi's*, one finds considerable difficulty. The remark has been made, I believe, that some Browning students are prone to attribute to their author much that he never meant, that they evolve whole schemes of thought and motive utterly foreign to the poet's intention, that they read subtle and complicated design where the poet has " sung but as the linnet sings." Granted that in some cases it is so—notably in these imperfect words of my own. Then let me suggest how interesting it would be to know what Shakespeare might feel in conversation with—Dr. Edward Dowden ! An extreme case, I admit.

There is, of course, much verse extant which causes no controversy, such as that well-known poem where the lines occur :—

> " I take my little porringer
> And eat my supper there."

Here we note a delightful absence of all ambiguity. Again, in a widely differing sphere, such a poem as *Paradise Lost*, grand and mighty as it is, yet by its very title, gives the reader the master key to its drift. Not so with the works of Browning.

But which is the most wonderful power—to present in finished poetical form ideas more or less noble, with unmistakable clearness, thus finite to a certain extent ; or to produce that which shall strike out and compel, from other minds, such varied and strongly-conceived plans of opposed motive and meaning, created in them by the living force of a human spirit, and, right or wrong in their interpretations, coming nevertheless straight from the region of intellect and imagina-

tion ? Not to us, perhaps, is it often given to guess aright at mysteries
behind the veil—still less, clearly to behold them ! We wander vaguely
through the palace of the Master's thought, and we lose our way.
But some of us have caught a strain of distant music, a glimpse of a
flying figure, we seem to hear a dim echo as of multitudinous foot-
falls, we have seen a wondrous light stealing below massive portals.
Eagerly, blindly, we press on and on ! Differing minds see differing
aspects of the great design : in short, when the Master's hand
touches the strings there will come forth diverse melodies, according
to the nature and scope of the instrument.

The poem we are considering I find extremely difficult as to the
cohesion of ideas and thoughts. Stanza xiii. I take to be ironical.
The voice suggests that, as the glow of life in the vitality of old
Venice is now dead, there may not be very much more life or hope
for a future to the student's joy in his scientific researches, though
these do appear of more serious concern than the old frivolities. There
is nothing in mere delight, whether of sex or science, that shall
guarantee its own permanence ; and the fateful cold hand may erase
the one as easily as the other, in the absence of some more solid claim
in the personality for a future !   And the poem closes with a
momentary admission that the warm brief beauty of gay Venice represents at least one element in the complete life which is denied to
scientific research—namely, the human element. The life of mere
knowledge *is* partial and cold and chilly. It is no more immortal
by its severity than the other by its frivolity. There is still much
that remains enigmatical in the poem, but in its mere breadth of
suggestiveness it renders a noble service.

Let me conclude with the dream-picture given to my thought by
A Toccata of Galuppi's. Imagine a modern scientist—I will not
invidiously specify his field of research ; one, however, unlikely to
expand the ideal side of human nature. He has overlaid the dreams
of youth with ponderous, impassable strata of exact knowledge—
statistics and the like. In him the subjective has long yielded its
place to the abstract, and impersonal. Let us call this man " Doctor
H." ; suppose him to have passed " a stormy youth," to have been
ardent and imaginative, to have drunk deep of the cup of human
passion, to have been chilled by disillusion, to have had his bound-
ing life-pulses suddenly, permanently checked by some staggering
shock of Fate, to have fossilized gradually but almost totally !
Circumstances have forced him into a path widely at variance with
his original bent—" *Kein Tempel, ohne Gottheit.*" His had been

love and beauty, reading the eyes of fair women in the moonlight—
now it is dry and dusty learning. He has become an advanced scientist,
with a following of admiring worshippers; himself worshipping at no
shrine—merely possessed by a dogged desire for unearthing hidden
mysteries of science. Take our imaginary Dr. H. as the first
speaker in the poem, the man whose thoughts are revealed to
us, and suppose we can also hear the voices which speak to him—
to which his own spirit replies again. We cannot see these visions
with the outward eye, but "we see a cherub that sees them."
Doctor H., then, has retained in his half-congealed nature a true
artist's love of music. It was stifled, but not dead, for that loves
dies hard. He has been, we will say, at one of the Monday Popular
Concerts, and has heard a *Toccata* of Galuppi's. It wakes the
slumbering echoes, penetrates the dense layers of insensibility, dis-
solves a spell, and charms him back to a tender enthusiasm. Floating
before him, comes a vision of old Venetian life—deeply interwoven
with that latent passion for beauty, once his breath of being.
Though he says he was "never out of England," he must have been
an art-student, cultivated and advanced in music and painting alike.
For the lines "was a lady such a lady, &c.," clearly embody, in a
few telling phrases, the very marked type of beauty portrayed by
Giovanni Bellini, a Venetian painter who died in 1516, the most
eminent of a family of artists of that name, the teacher of
Giorgione and Titian. No one who has been privileged to look on
his heavenly conceptions of female beauty can fail to recognize the
type. Dr. H., then, despite his modest disclaimers, seems gifted with
the glorious dower of Mr. Browning's own rare artistic culture,
and speaks accordingly.

So he sits, dreaming to the music, rapt in spirit, calling up to
fancy the pageant of the festival—the whirling dance, the venerated
figure of the *maestro*, "stately at the clavichord." It does not seem
to me that Galuppi played the music for the dances, but that, in
some solemn lofty chamber apart, he gave his grand masterpices; for
the lover is made to say as he listens, "I can always leave off talking
when I hear a master play," and I gather that the music thus
attracting him was obviously not the music of the whirling dance without. The reflection comes to Dr. H., "How is it now with those poor
butterflies? where now are the lovers? in what vast unknown are
these vibrations of music spreading and losing themselves?" He is
forced to the bitter conclusion that these lives are wasted and
unfruitful, if not positively harmful, and the thoughtless, happy,

frivolous creatures annihilated and ended! "O, the pity of it." So the man of science goes home to spend an hour in his laboratory before retiring. He sits down to reason, to think himself back to the mental stand-point of some thirty years ago. He takes up the learned treatise on which he is engaged—a paper dealing with his latest discovery, that in which truly he "triumphs o'er a secret wrung from Nature's cold reserve"! But his nerves are still thrilled by the weird music—still the fatal refrain haunts him—the sum of it all, "Dust and ashes—dead and done with."

We see the solemn shade of Galuppi in the dusk of the dimly-lighted room, we hear his mocking gibe. His music has lived indeed, lived to breathe its message afresh to human ears and human hearts, but not so with the gay pageants of Venice. We hear the hollow taunting tone of the *maestro* as he accuses the hapless scholar of taking "mathematics as a pastime,"—a withering accusation, this. Nor does the prospect of an eternity of "physics and geology," and even *that* held out as a very doubtful matter, succeed in cheering the man of science. The gray shadow clings to him—the chill of his loveless age makes his nerves creep. He dimly suspects that it had perhaps been better and lovelier to "bloom and drop;" he doubts whether, after all, his ideal of later life, his scientific research, be actually more worthy, more noble, more fitted to enjoy immortal existence, than the life of the senses, the warm night of May, the perfumed breeze, the kiss, the whisper, the thrill of music and the mazy dance! Ah! those faces of heavenly fairness peering out of the gloom, those rose-lips, those shining eyes of fire, those thickly meshed braids of gold hair, those soft caressing tones—all lost—all fled—all gone! "Qui sait où s'en vont les roses?

NUMPHOLEPTOS AND BROWNING'S WOMEN.

By Mrs. GLAZEBROOK.

Read at the Sixty-seventh Meeting of the Browning Society,
Friday, May 31, 1889.

It is a strange, weird allegory—not so noble as that very fine one in *Paracelsus,* beginning "Over the seas our galleys went," nor so vivid as *Childe Roland,* nor so graceful as the story of the cricket which forms the epilogue to the *Two Poets of Croisic.* I would, indeed, say at once that I have not chosen this poem for special study because I consider it very beautiful. On the contrary, I venture to think that in point of form and style Mr. Browning has not done his best for us in it. It is obscure, occasionally grotesque. Even when we know it well, it is very difficult to form a clear mental picture of the poet's conception. If we give it to a friend to read for the first time we shall hardly fail in the result of our experiment—he begins cheerfully, but after a few lines we see that he is already groping in a *Selva oscura* and his expression becomes more and more bewildered, until at the end—if he does persevere to the end—he tells us that he has not the remotest idea what it is all about. But, of course, this very difficulty has a certain fascination for us, who have given our friend the poem, and feel bound to find a meaning for it. It belongs, also, to a very interesting volume—the volume containing *Pacchiarotto*—which was written at a period when, although the visitations of the "spirit of delight" may seem to have been rare, Mr. Browning was in an unusually communicative and self-revealing mood, and more willing to take the public into his confidence about his methods and principles than at any other time. *Numpholeptos* seems to me to resemble the majority of its companions in the volume in its general characteristics—in its lack of beauty and finish, in a certain aggressiveness, a certain tendency to paradox, combined with real, fundamental interest and importance of subject-matter. I may add that I was tempted to offer this short paper to the Society by a remark of our Hon. Secretary at a recent meeting. His words were to the effect that he wished members would more frequently make short studies of single poems than discuss Browning at large. I had puzzled over *Numpholeptos* a good deal, and had at last made out an interpretation, which not only made the poem itself clear to me but also threw light on that extremely interesting subject which is generally spoken of comprehensively as "Browning's Women." And so, with apologies to Mr. Slater, I must confess that I shall wander a little into "Browning at large." But how can we help this? Surely no other poet puts so much of himself into each one of his poems. Each is characteristic, and yet impossible to be thoroughly understood by itself. The more we study a single poem, the more we find how much it, at once, needs explaining by, and helps in return to explain, all the rest of the poet's work.

It will be well to begin our study of *Numpholeptos* by recalling the outlines of the allegory.

In the centre of a magic wheel of light stands a transcendently fair and virtuous "nymph." She is a perfect being, and her purity is typified by the absolute whiteness of the light in which she dwells. Beyond the limits of the circle immediately surrounding her, the light is broken up into its component rays—red, blue, yellow, "every dye o' the bow born of the storm-cloud,"—they stretch from centre to circumference, and form the spokes of the luminous wheel. At the feet of the nymph kneels her lover, the son of earth, who has ventured to set his heart on this supernatural being. She has imposed on him various quests ; he has fulfilled her commands, and now comes to implore her love in recompense of his obedience. One coloured ray after the other he has, at her bidding, explored to the end, and has returned with full experience of the path he has pursued. But each time he is received, not with the golden glow of love, but with "the sad, slow, silver smile" of "pity, pardon," which even changes, as he persists in his prayer, until

> "its sweet and soft grow harsh and hard—
> Forbearance, then repulsion, then disdain."

For she will only grant her love on condition that he comes back unstained with the colour of the ray he has traversed. This he cannot do. In the very ardour of his obedience he knows "no stay nor stint," and becomes suffused in turn with yellow, or scarlet, or purple. To her only the whiteness of perfect light is tolerable : she beholds with aversion the deeply-dyed figure, "absurd as frightful," who claims his reward. For a moment he revolts :

> "No, I say,
> No fresh adventure ! No more seeking love
> At the end of toil, and finding, calm above
> My passion, the old statuesque regard,
> The sad petrific smile ! "

Who is she to demand impossibilities of him ? She attempts nothing, achieves nothing ; she remains motionless while he spends his strength in endeavours to do her bidding. Why does she presume to dictate to him ?

But the rebellious outburst is soon over. He submits again, and starts on a new journey—

> " All the rest
> Be resignation ! Forth at your behest
> I fare. Who knows but this—the crimson-quest—
> May deepen to a sunrise, not decay
> To that cold sad sweet smile ?—which I obey."

It is obvious that the meaning of the allegory depends on the interpretation we assign to the nymph. Who, or what, is she ? If we know this the rest is plain enough.

Three alternatives suggest themselves.

She may be just some one individual woman, and the whole poem a simple love story told in allegorical form. I reject this theory with some diffidence because it has (so it seems) the sanction of so high an authority as Mrs. Sutherland Orr. But the whole tone, style, and effect of the poem, all its individuality and character, seem to me to forbid this narrow interpretation. The story—a man striving in vain to attain the high standard of service demanded by the woman he adores—might very well have been chosen as a subject by Mr. Browning, but he would not, I think, have told it in this way. He tells stories of that kind simply, dramatically, circumstantially. Here we have a mystic scene ; a picture, as it were, half concealed by a veil, with one corner only lifted, suggesting far-reaching vistas beyond. Or, to change the metaphor, we hear in the poet's voice a deeper tone than that of mere narration ; in the very difficulty and irregularity of utterance there seems to be evidence of some important, universal truth which he is endeavouring to express. This is, of course, only the personal impression made by the poem ; it can hardly be explained or justified, and must be taken for what it is worth. But it is in the sureness of such impressions that the master of style reveals his mastery; and we lose half the meaning of poetry if we refuse to be susceptible to them.

Then, secondly, the nymph may be the personification of Philosophy. And this I believe her to be, in part. But I think she is more. There must be some good reason for that outburst at the end, which makes so much of her being a woman—of her "she-intelligence," her "pretence to match the male achievement!" her "thrice-superfine Feminity of sense"—all this would be irrelevant, and rather absurd, if applied to Philosophy or Knowledge, who might very well resent the attribution of a sex which it never claimed, and which entailed quite gratuitous abuse.

And so I am brought to the third alternative, which is the one I hold. The nymph is the ideal woman—a modern Beatrice or Laura—a being endowed with all beauty, all knowledge, all purity and virtue, who was born centuries ago, in the days of mediæval chivalry, in whose honour many songs have been sung, and many lances have been broken. Dante describes her beautifully for us in the *Vita Nuova*, the book which tells the story of his early love. She is "that most gentle lady, the destroyer of all vices and the queen of all virtues," in whose presence evil is abashed and all gracious sentiments are aroused; who made her poor lover so unhappy by denying him her salutation one day when she met him in the streets of Florence. She does not seem to have done much—the woman the great seer "loved so well, who married the other"; her short life was quiet, uneventful, untempted; we may sometimes wonder a little that Dante should have accepted so meekly her somewhat shrewish rebukes in the Earthly Paradise. He might so well have replied that it was easy for her, who had spent her days in the peaceful seclusion of her father's or her husband's home, to find fault with him, who had borne the heavy burden of government in the unruly city, and had endured the pangs and weariness of exile. For him, indeed, it was necessary to wash away his stains in the waters of Lethe, but still he could show a nobler record of accomplished deeds than she, who had kept her garments spotless.

She dwells—this nymph, this ideal woman—in a carefully-guarded abode of peace and virtue, and the man goes forth to make his way in some one of life's careers which she has chosen for him. Of course she insists that he shall be pre-eminent in his profession. He must be the bravest of soldiers, the most eloquent and devoted of clergymen, the wisest of lawyers, the most imaginative, the most skilful of artists. But she does not perceive that with the achievement must be the inevitable shortcomings. There is not time in life for one man to accomplish everything; while he is doing one thing thoroughly he must leave others undone. And even his character may be impaired. For one good quality may be developed to excess, so that it passes the mean of virtue, or it may be developed at the expense of others equally good. With vigour and courage may be some failure in patience and forbearance; with subtlety, some lack of decision; with eloquence, some want of sincerity and reserve. It is one of the elements of tragedy in life. Attainment is inseparable from renunciation.

> "Entbehren [1] sollst du! sollst entbehren!"

This is the cry of a "Welt-schmerz" which seems to have had its tides in the world's history. It flowed in Virgil's time, it ebbed in the days of the serener Shakspere; it was rising when Goethe wrote; and now its flood beats hard against our nineteenth-century shores.

The nymph in the allegory reproaches her lover with these "defects of his qualities." The contemplation of her own well-balanced character —no one virtue obtrusively large, nor another inconveniently deficient —has made her fastidious; her smoothness cannot endure his roughness; she desires victory, but not the stains and the scars of the victor; and so she refuses him her love. The poor man fails to attain the prize for which he laboured.

Now we know how all Mr. Browning's sympathies are with that struggling lover. He tells us, again and again, that man must not expect to be perfect in this life, but that he must set his heart on doing some one thing, and must be content not to do others.

> "Let a man contend to the uttermost
> For his life's set prize, be it what it will!"

And the nymph is just what, according to him, a human being should not be. She is "a perfect round," a "finished little piece," possessing capabilities neither of growth nor attainment, and, as she stands there in her self-complacency and conscious superiority, we can scarcely wonder at the rebellious irritation which possesses her lover for a time; rather, indeed, does it surprise us that he returns to his allegiance.

But then, Beatrice was dead and buried long ago. She did good in her generation. She was the embodiment of beauty and order in a rough and violent age. She was an element of gentleness, of ideality, of striving after perfection in the life of men who sorely needed purity

---

[1] Miss, feel the want of.

and stimulus. As she was a mediæval creation, so she satisfied a craving of the mediæval soul. She led Dante into Paradise. Is it not somewhat ungracious of a modern poet to dig her up from her grave, and throw the bright light of the present day on her pale features? Why should Mr. Browning spend his strength on this old-fashioned nymph?

For women, now, would surely repudiate that ideal, which represents them as so stationary, so untempted, so elevated above the trials and vicissitudes of life. They cannot realize it, nor do they desire to do so. Many have to go out into the world and get their own living, and work as hard as men do. And others who stay at home do not find life all repose and seclusion by any means. It is often difficult for them to develop their own individuality and to live the " higher life " in the midst of household anxieties and interruptions; and not seldom are they tempted to envy men who have regular hours for work and regular hours for relaxation. And, as a matter of fact, women hardly ever do complain of men's little roughnesses and sharp corners. They are very tolerant towards the defects for the sake of the qualities. Indeed, Mr. Browning himself repeatedly insists on that faculty of women for taking men as they are, for loving in spite of faults—on their constancy, in fine.

> " The man was my whole world, all the same,
> With his flowers to praise or his weeds to blame,"

says James Lee's clear-sighted, intellectual wife. The whole theme of that very pathetic poem, *Any Wife to any Husband*, is the superior constancy of the woman.

Thus it would seem that there is a certain anachronism in this protest of Mr. Browning's—that he is fighting an enemy who no longer exists. But it is not like him to make a mistake of this kind. He maintains intimate communications with the " spirit of the age," and seldom fails to discern its tendencies. That nymph of his must be alive somewhere.

And in some pages of Mr. Ruskin's we find her in all her vigour. It would be presumptuous indeed to say that Mr. Browning had any particular book in his mind when he wrote *Numpholeptos*, but it is curious how completely we have in *Sesame and Lilies* a description of that ideal against which he is protesting. " She enters into no contest, but infallibly adjudges the crown of contest. . . . The man, in his rough work in open world, must encounter all peril and trial . . . often he must be wounded, or subdued; often misled; and *always* hardened. But he guards the woman from all this; within his house, as ruled by her, unless she herself has sought it, need enter no danger, no temptation, no cause of error or offence." She is to be taught—we must all know the beautiful, eloquent periods almost by heart—to speak foreign languages, and to understand history when she reads it, and to take interest in the newspapers, and above all things not to presume to study theology, and then man is to be "entirely subject" to her, receiving from her "not only . . . the reward of all toil, but . . . the direction of all toil."

There she is, painted by a master-hand, tinted with all the delicate colours of an artist's imagination, dangerously alluring in her beauty; but false to her age, stationary in the midst of progress, complete while all the rest of the world is developing. She is an idol whom Mr. Browning may well wish to destroy.

But at the end of *Numpholeptos*, we remember, the lover repents of his short revolt, becomes obedient again, and starts on another hopeless quest. This is probably one of those quick transitions, one of those sudden returns upon himself, to which readers of Browning have to become accustomed, and in which indeed much of his characteristic humour and power of seeing two sides of a question are to be found. He seems to say, "After all, I have not the heart to destroy her. She is so beautiful, and has lived in the world so long that we cannot do without her. I know that she demands impossibilities, and that she does not understand life and its limitations; and I am a much more practical and useful person than she is with all her claims to superiority; but, still, I will be her slave as the rest of the world has been for so long, for I have no wish to be different from my fellow-creatures."

We, however, in this protestation of allegiance, may hear the proverbial true word spoken in jest. For Mr. Browning is indeed not guiltless of idolizing that nymph. He is quite right in believing her not to be dead. She is a very conspicuous personage in modern literature, and he helps to prolong her life. His own heroines are some of her representatives. For what is the fatal defect with which he reproaches the nymph? Is it not her ineffectiveness, her impotence, her inability to achieve, develop, attain? And then consider the heroines of his poems. Beautiful as they are—pathetic, intellectual, sensitive—are they not, nearly all, ineffective? The majority are either victims or failures. Pompilia is a gentle, innocent creature. But what does she do? Her only effect upon her husband is to provoke him to increased cruelty, and finally to crime. It may be urged with justice that she developed much that was noble in the character of the priest, Caponsacchi. But that was a side issue. It can hardly be called a sufficient purpose for her life. Then there is James Lee's wife. She is a most interesting person, with deep affections and a powerful, highly-trained mind. Yet she fails entirely. She makes "the great refusal," gives up all hope of winning her husband's love and leaves him. Several of the heroines fail in clearness of insight; they make fatal mistakes or they are dupes—Anael, for instance, in the *Return of the Druses*, the heroine of *An Inn Album*, Constance in *In a Balcony*. And Mildred in *A Blot on the 'Scutcheon*—whether we call her a victim or by a severer name, certainly her life is a failure. We may feel pity for her, but not admiration. Guendolen has been compared to Beatrice, but surely there is an immense difference, from an artistic point of view, between one generous woman who succeeds in saving an innocent friend, and another who fails to save a guilty friend. Now, of course no one would be so optimistic as to require all heroines to succeed. That would be untrue to the facts of life. There must be Cordelias, Desdemonas, Ophelias in the world. But there are also the Portias, the Isabellas, the Hermiones—women who, in the strength of their purity and their courage and their intelligence, bring saving help to mankind; and I think we have a just cause of complaint against our greatest living poet that he has given us no heroines of this type. He will bequeath to posterity no woman's character "cast in the heroic mould." Two of his women indeed do exercise redeeming power. One is little Pippa, who does good all unconsciously, and is more like a fairy or an angel than a human being; the other is Balaustion, whose power is not in her womanliness, but in the poet-nature which (to use a phrase often, to me quite incomprehensibly, applied to Mr. Browning) "knows no sex in souls."

How glad we should be if the poet, who has done so much for us in the way of inspiration and enlightenment, would "add but another grace," and setting aside for a time his subtleties and casuistries and intellectual enigmas, would create for us some one fine womanly character, a real human being, not perfect, but able to achieve her purpose in life, and worthy to be a sister of the noble heroines of Chaucer, Shakspere, and Scott.

But, indeed, it is no new creation that we are asking of Mr. Browning. She is there already—that noble ideal woman—haunting all his poetry. We feel her presence, though her form we only see in glimpses now and then. Will he not show her to us once in the fulness of her stature? Hers are the "great brow And the spirit-small hand propping it"; she is "the dearest poet he ever knew, Dearest and greatest and best to him" (*Paul.* 223); she is his star that has opened its soul to him, his "lyric Love, half-angel and half-bird And all a wonder and a wild desire" to whom his work is dedicated; the "One word more" is for her; in the supreme moment of the vision of "Prospice" she stands ready to receive him. She is like some beautiful, half-finished statue, still imprisoned and partly concealed in the marble block; and we are reminded of stories of sculptors who feared to complete their work lest it should fall short of the ideal they had imagined.

> "Who that one, you ask? your heart instructs you."

Do we hear Mr. Browning replying thus to us with reproachful sadness? Does he tell us that the marble is monumental, and the silence is the silence of the grave? Ah! yes. We know who that "lyric Love" is; but the knowledge makes us more importunate. For it is the noble daughters and wives and mothers of real life who inspire the "fair women" of literature, and thus become

> "the sweet presence of a good diffused,
> And in diffusion ever more intense."

THE WIFE-LOVE AND FRIEND-LOVE OF ROBERT BROWNING.

By the Rev. J. J. G. GRAHAM, M.A. Oxon.

*Read at the Sixty-eighth Meeting of the Browning Society,
Friday, June 28th, 1889.*

Our Poet's Wife-love and Friend-love, only so far as depicted by himself, are the subject of my paper to-night ; and I fear it will afford little scope for discussion, though much for your kind patience and indulgence, but at any rate it will possess the merit of excluding the *odium theologicum*—a bold assertion when a paper on *Saul* last session provoked a discussion on the Athanasian Creed.

I. Robert Browning at the age of thirty-four was married, September 12th, 1846, to Elizabeth Barrett. "That woman was for him *the choice of God*," as he for her, a "perfect pair ! each born for the other," proved by fifteen years of as perfect wedded happiness as falls to the lot of few literary characters, who for the most part contract unfortunate marriages. To this trite remark our poet presents a noble and memorable exception. What *he* thought of her, we shall see from the passages hereafter cited ; what *she* thought of him, may be seen from her so-called *Sonnets from the Portuguese*, addressed to her husband before her marriage, from which she forthwith gained fresh life and health.

> "'Guess now who holds thee ?'—'Death,' I said. But, there,
> The silver answer rang,—'Not Death, but Love.'"

The beautiful opening verses of *Jocoseria* are said, and I think, correctly, to contain an allusion to his wife—

> "Come then, complete incompletion, O comer,
> Pant through the blueness, perfect the summer !"

At her advent the blank world is changed to both of them, and, in
her case,

> " All that *was* death
> Grows life, grows love,
> Grows love ! "

Though no poet is less autobiographical than Browning, he pays
her again and again a tribute of affection in the following passages
which have been culled from his various and voluminous works :—
They are eight in all, at least so far as I have discovered—the first
three, extracted from *By the Fireside*, *The Guardian Angel*, and *One
Word More*, published, *during the lifetime of his wife*, in *Men and
Women*, in 1855 ; and the other five, *after her death*, between the dates
of 1864 and 1876. These are taken from *Prospice*, published in 1864 ;
The Ring and the Book, its invocation at the end of Part I., 1868, its
dedication at the end of Part XII., 1869 ; *Balaustion's Adventure*,
1871 ; and from the epilogue to *Pacchiarotto, with other Poems*, 1876.
I will cite them in their chronological sequence.

1. The first allusion is found in the poem entitled, *By the Fireside*.
This poem tells us more than any other of the happy married life of
Browning, though we are bound to consider all but the personality in it
fictitious. It is now placed among the *Dramatic Lyrics* in the third of
the six volumes of his Poetical Works, published in 1867. In a note at
their commencement he expressly tells us, that these pieces are "always
dramatic in principle, and so many utterances of so many imaginary
persons not his ; " therefore we feel bound, as I have said, to consider
the circumstances of this poem merely imaginary, while we are justified
in regarding the portraiture as that of Elizabeth Barrett Browning ;
and as such, a personal reminiscence and utterance if any poet ever
made one. Not only is she described, " those dark grey eyes, that
hair so dark and dear," " that great brow, and the spirit-small hand
propping it ; " this he mentions twice ; and who that looks on her
portrait prefixed to the first volume of her poetical works can fail to
see the likeness ? Not only this, but as we read we cannot but feel
that she, the friend, the lover, and the wife, must have been present
to his mind's eye as he wrote ; nay, perhaps, sitting by his very side,
as he describes so minutely the scene and story of what might have
been their courtship—his avowal of his love—her prompt acceptance
—" leaning " on each other " and loving it over again "—all just as
it happened, or might have happened, by that ruined chapel, half-way
up in the Alpine gorge. As he sits, presumably in Florence, by the

fireside, in 1855, nine years after his marriage, his wife too sitting mutely musing or haply reading by his side, he recalls the happy past, and thinks of the dark autumn evenings in life's November, and what he means to do then.   Only prose, not verse, will then engage his attention; Greek literature, the *Alcestis* (1871), the *Hercules Furens* (1875), the *Agamemnon* (1877), will still have their charm, though his own muse may be silent, and his soul now all glowing with love and happiness may have lost its "pleasant hue."   These were his thoughts then, but time has shown that he thought wrong ; for in 1876, in life's November, he writes in the poem, *At the Mermaid*, speaking for Shakespeare and surely for himself too—

> " Have you found your life distasteful ?
>   My life did and does smack sweet.
> Was your youth of pleasure wasteful ?
>   Mine I saved and hold complete.
> Do your joys with age diminish ?
>   When mine fail me, I'll complain.
> Must in death your daylight finish ?
>   My sun sets to rise again."

The hue of his life is still as pleasant as ever.   Neither in 1887, in life's December, are the voices of the music of his soul dumb, as witness his last published volume, *Parleyings with Certain People*.   It is at the twenty-first stanza the allusion to his own wife under the fictitious name of " Leonor " begins, and continues to the end of the poem.

> " My perfect wife, my Leonor,
>   Oh heart, my own, oh eyes, mine too,
> Whom else could I dare look backward for,
>   With whom beside should I dare pursue
> The path grey heads abhor ?"

With whom beside indeed ?   Browning never had a second love ; he is still a widower, though his wife died in 1861, twenty-eight years ago.   He seems to have said with Leontes in *The Winter's Tale*, " No more such wives ; therefore no wife.   I'll have no wife, Paulina."   He then goes on to say, *surely in his own person*,

> " With me youth led . . . I will speak now,
>   No longer watch you as you sit
> Reading by fire-light, that great brow
>   And the spirit-small hand propping it,
> Mutely, my heart knows how.

My own, confirm me !   If I tread
   This path back, is it not in pride
To think how little I dreamed it led
   To an age so blest that, by its side,
Youth seems the waste instead ! "

Alas, how little he knew of the future ! how little he then thought that
in six short years he would have to tread the long remaining path of
life "alone, aloof ! "   This path of which he here speaks led only to
fifteen years of wedded bliss, in his "happy Tuscan home," not to a
blest old age, as he fondly thought.   Forty-two years plight ! and may
many more be added thereto !

" My own, see where the years conduct !
   At first, 'twas something our two souls
Should mix as mists do ; each is sucked
   In each now : on, the new stream rolls,
Whatever rocks obstruct.

Think, when our one soul understands
   The great Word which makes all things new,
When earth breaks up and heaven expands,
   How will the change strike me and you
In the house not made with hands ?

Oh I must feel your brain prompt mine,
   Your heart anticipate my heart,
You must be just before, in fine,
   See and make me see, for your part,
New depths of the divine !

Come back with me to the first of all,
   Let us lean and love it over again,
Let us now forget and now recall,
   Break the rosary in a pearly rain,
And gather what we let fall !

Hither we walked then, side by side,
   Arm in arm and cheek to cheek,
And still I questioned or replied,
   While my heart, convulsed to really speak,
Lay choking in its pride. "

Much of this, of course, is part of the imaginary framework of the
poem, but all would have actually occurred had he met Miss Barrett
in some romantic Alpine gorge.   He then goes on to describe what
would inevitably have taken place, and what did take place somewhere else.

" We two stood there with never a third,
   But each by each, as each knew well :
Had she willed it, still had stood the screen
   So slight, so sure, 'twixt my love and her.

Worth how well those dark grey eyes,
   That hair so dark and dear . . .
You might have turned and tried a man,
   Set him a space to weary and wear.
But you spared me this, like the heart you are,
   And filled my empty heart at a word.

I am named and known by that moment's feat ;
   There took my station and degree ;
So grew my own small life complete,
   As nature obtained her best of me—
One born to love you, sweet !

And to watch you sink by the fireside now
   Back again, as you mutely sit
Musing by fire-light, that great brow
   And the spirit-small hand propping it,
Yonder, my heart knows how ! "

When Mrs. Browning wrote *Lady Geraldine's Courtship*, she was unknown to her husband, and thus alludes to him—

" Or from Browning some 'Pomegranate' which, if cut down the middle,
Shows a heart within blood-tinctured, of a veined humanity."

A correspondence soon followed, then love, health, marriage.

2. The next allusion to his wife occurs in *The Guardian Angel.* Originally published in *Men and Women*, but now placed among *Dramatic Lyrics* (Poetical Works, vol. iii. p. 214). This picture was painted by Guercino, and is now in St. Augustine's Church in Fano. Browning relates to his friend, Mr. Alfred Domett ("Alfred, dear friend ! "), formerly Prime Minister of New Zealand, how he visited this Church accompanied by his own Guardian Angel, his wife.

" We were at Fano, and three times we went
   To sit and see him in his chapel there,
And drink his beauty to our soul's content
   —My angel with me too.

*   *   *   *   *

My love is here. Where are you, dear old friend ?
How rolls the Wairoa at your world's far end ?
   This is Ancona, yonder is the sea."

3. The third allusion, in the poems he wrote during his wife's lifetime, is indeed the whole, we may say, of that touching and exquisite poem entitled, *One Word More.* To E. B. B., London, September, 1855. We will extract such portions as sufficiently tell the

story of his deep and lasting love. It is the dedication to his wife
of the collection of poems called *Men and Women.*

> " There they are, my fifty men and women
> Naming me the fifty poems finished !
> Take them, love, the book and me together :
> Where the heart lies, let the brain lie also.
>
> Rafael made a century of sonnets,
> Else he only used to draw Madonnas :
> These the world might view—but one, the volume.
> Who that one, you ask ? Your heart instructs you."

This was Rafael's mistress, La Fornarina. Love had turned him
into a poet.

> " You and I would rather read that volume,
> Would we not ? than wonder at the Madonnas
> Seen by us and all the world in circle.
> You and I will never read that volume.
> Suddenly, as rare things will, it vanished.
>
> Dante once prepared to paint an angel :
> Whom to please ? You whisper ' Beatrice.'
> While he mused and traced it and retraced it,
> Says he, ' Certain people of importance
> Entered and would seize, forsooth, the poet.'
> Says the poet, ' Then I stopped my painting.'
>
> You and I would rather see that angel,
> Painted by the tenderness of Dante,
> Would we not ? than read a fresh Inferno.
> You and I will never see that picture.
> We and Bice bear the loss for ever."

Unlike Rafael and Dante, Browning has only verse and nothing
else to offer his wife.

> " I shall never, in the years remaining,"

—alas, he knew not how few they were to be, only six—

> " Paint you pictures, no, nor carve your statues,
> Make you music that should all-express me ;
> So it seems : I stand on my attainment.
> This of verse alone, one life allows me ;
> Verse and nothing else have I to give you.
> Other heights in other lives, God willing :
> All the gifts from all the heights, your own, love !

P

Which shall we admire most, Browning's religion or his wife-love? Both how deep-seated!

> " Yet a semblance of resource avails us—
> Shade so finely touched, love's sense must seize it.
> Take these lines, look lovingly and nearly,
> Lines I write the first time and the last time.
> He who writes, may write for once as I do.
> Love, you saw me gather men and women.
> Hardly shall I tell my joys and sorrows,
> Hopes and fears, belief and disbelieving:
> I am mine and yours—the rest be all men's,
> Karshish, Cleon, Norbert and the fifty.
> Let me speak this once in my true person.
> Pray you, look on these my men and women,
> Take and keep my fifty poems finished;
> Where my heart lies, let my brain lie also!
> Poor the speech; be *how* I speak, for all things.
> Not but that you know me! Lo, the moon's self,
> Here in London, yonder late in Florence "

still presents always the same face to the world; but a different one to " the moon-struck mortal." " If that moon could love a mortal ('tis the old sweet mythos) she would turn a new side to her mortal "

> " Side unseen of herdsman, huntsman, steersman.
> God be thanked, the meanest of his creatures
> Boasts two soul-sides, one to face the world with,
> One to show a woman when he loves her!
>
> This I say of me, but think of you, Love!
> This to you—yourself my moon of poets!
> Ah, but that's the world's side, there's the wonder,
> Thus they see you, praise you, think they know you!
> There, in turn I stand with them and praise you—
> Out of my own self, I dare to phrase it.
> But the best is when I glide from out them,
> Cross a step or two of dubious twilight,
> Come out on the other side, the novel
> Silent silver lights and darks undreamed of,
> Where I hush and bless myself with silence.
>
> Oh, their Rafael of the dear Madonnas,
> Oh, their Dante, of the dread Inferno,
> Wrote one song—and in my brain I sing it,
> Drew one angel—borne, see, on my bosom! "

4. I now come to the allusions found in his poems written after the death of his wife. The first is from that entitled *Prospice* (Poetical Works, vol. vi. p. 152, 1864). He had written in one of his

earliest poems, *Paracelsus*, eleven years before he found his own
" ministering life-angel "—

> " 'Tis only when they spring to heaven that angels
> Reveal themselves to you ; they sit all day
> Beside you, and lie down at night by you,
> Who care not for their presence, muse or sleep ;
> And all at once they leave you, and you know them ! "

He took good care that these words, too true of almost all of us,
should not be true of him. If any man ever loved his wife, and
knew her while living here to be an earthly angel, soon to be changed
into a heavenly one, that man was Robert Browning. No need for
him to wait till death revealed the angel he had lost, from that
moment he looked forward to re-union. And why should he fear his
own death ? " Fear death " ? Not he. Three years after the sad blow,
as we call it, he writes thus cheerfully and manfully, *Prospice*, Look
forward. There is but " one fight more, the best and the last." Then
re-union for ever.

> " For sudden the worst turns the best to the brave,
>   The black minute's at end,
> And the elements' rage, the fiend-voices that rave,
>   Shall dwindle, shall blend,
> Shall change, shall become first a peace out of pain,
>   Then a light, *then thy breast*,
> *O thou soul of my soul! I shall clasp thee again*,
>   And with God be the rest."

Again I say, we must admire our poet's firm faith and piety, no
less than his strong deep wife-love.

5. The next tribute of affection, the gem of the whole collection,
is what he calls a " Posy " to the Ring with which he encircles his
wife's finger in the wonderful and beautiful dedication of his masterpiece, *The Ring and the Book* (Part I. l. 1390—1446). A " Posy "
was a motto inscribed on a ring, and sometimes on a knife, in olden
times. Thus in *Hamlet*, Act iii. sc. 2—

> " Is this a prologue or the posy of a ring ? "

and in the *Merchant of Venice* :—

> " A paltry ring
> That she did give me ; whose *posy* was
> For all the world like cutler's poetry
> Upon a knife—Love me and leave me not."

And what a cluster of flowers too have we here !

> " A ring without a posy, and that ring mine ?
> O Lyric Love, half angel and half bird,
> And all a wonder and a wild desire,—
> Boldest of hearts that ever braved the sun,
> Took sanctuary within the holier blue,
> And sang a kindred soul out to his face,—
> Yet human at the red-ripe of the heart—
> When the first summons from the darkling earth
> Reached thee amid thy chambers, blanched their blue,
> And bared them of the glory—to drop down,
> To toil for man, to suffer or to die,—
> This is the same voice : can thy soul know change ?
> Hail then, and hearken from the realms of help !
> Never may I commence my song, my due
> To God who best taught song by gift of thee,
> Except with bent head and beseeching hand—
> That still, despite the distance and the dark,
> What was, again may be ; some interchange
> Of grace, some splendour once thy very thought,
> Some benediction anciently thy smile :
> —Never conclude, but raising hand and head
> Thither where eyes, that cannot reach, yet yearn
> For all hope, all sustainment, all reward,
> Their utmost up and on—so blessing back
> In those thy realms of help, that heaven thy home,
> Some whiteness which, I judge, thy face makes proud,
> Some wanness where, I think, thy foot may fall ! "

This, written probably some years before, was published seven years after the death of his wife, called the Poet of Suffering, from the weak state of her health. In 1839 she broke a blood-vessel, and before her marriage only anticipated an early death. Then all her thought was,

> "if God choose,
> I shall but love thee better *after* death."

But brighter days were now in store for her, and she exchanged her " near sweet view of Heaven for earth with him."

> " My own, my own,
> Who camest to me when the world was gone,
> And I who looked for only God, found *thee* ! "

Well may he call her " half-angel and half-bird and all a wonder and a wild desire." She was the lark singing in the morning and soaring to heaven ; she was the eagle, strong of wing, braving the sun ; best of all she was " yet human at the red-ripe of the heart," and was summoned by sickness "to drop down," like the lark from the sky, like the eagle from its aerie, " to toil for man, to suffer," and soon to die. Sickness and sorrow for the loss of her brother darkened the chambers of her soul, "blanched their blue, and bared them of the glory "—the glory of her verse: she was too ill and too sad even to write her poetry. This was her lot on this " darkling earth "; still, it was amidst her sufferings, and in spite of her sufferings, that her bold heart at times " braved the sun "—"took sanctuary " for a brief moment " within the holier blue "; ever and anon taking up her poet's pen, and singing her sunlike soul out at heaven's very gate. The same voice, so loved on earth, now greets her in heaven; neither soul knows any change. The divine gift of song, best taught by the divine gift of her, is all due, the poet feels, to God: and he can never commence nor conclude his song without thinking of all he owes to her and God; without praying her to " hearken from the realms of help "; without beseeching God, with bent head and imploring hand, "that still, despite the distance and the dark, what was once, again may be "—some sweet interchange of thought, if not of speech, on her part full of grace and splendour, on his of benediction anciently her well-known smile. So causing her to bless back to him on earth, some of her own whiteness, the idea of which makes her face, he judges, even in heaven to shine with a brighter and prouder joy; some of her own wanness, which is excess of whiteness,[1] reflected on him from her realms of help, where on the golden floor, he thinks, her foot may fall.

" *Whiteness*" is goodness, purity, innocence, guileless truth, unselfish love—perfect in heaven, marred and stained on earth; also it denotes heavenly joy, delight, and gladness. " *Wanness*," the exaggeration of whiteness, the excess of all this, angelic goodness, childlike, lamblike innocence, perfect peerless truth and Godlike love. Wanness is " a whiter hue than white"; "quintessential whiteness." The sun has a wannish glare; the lightning flash is wan rather than white; white-heat has a wan tinge; so we may correctly describe the white-heat of intensity as wan, whether of intense love or intense goodness, or intense feeling, as the player in *Hamlet*, "from the working of his soul, all his visage wann'd." We can but attain to *some* whiteness, *some* wanness here; but she is *all* whiteness, *all* wanness there. Our better thoughts, our holier aspirations, our longings to be pure and wise and good and gentle all too soon pass away; but still again and again recur,

---

[1] " Whiten to wanness." *Parleyings*, p. 209.

flashes of heaven's own light, transient and intermittent, lighting up the chambers of the soul, as the lightning fills the room with wanness though but for a moment's space.

Dr. Furnivall interprets the "whiteness" to mean "the glorified person of the Poetess," and "wanness," "Heaven's lucent floor." It may be so. The colour of a star is yellowish-white, or wan, and Keble has "Heaven's *star*-sprinkled floor."

Whether, however, the Poet meant all this or not, I believe neither he nor I nor any one can say, but only that the words are capable of bearing some such meaning. Not even the Poet himself? No—he speaks by a divine afflatus, by a true and real inspiration, though not by such a direct revelation from heaven as inspired the sacred writers ; but in both cases, I believe, they themselves did not and do not understand the full meaning of all they write. More is meant than meets the eye and ear. Even poets by the mere act of writing, and perhaps by Heaven's decree,

> " do attain
> To something like prophetic strain."
> " As little children lisp, and tell of heaven,
> So *thoughts beyond their thought* to those high bards were given."

And so it comes to pass that great bards are unable, even if we could ask them, to interpret all the mystic words they have sung in "their sage and solemn tunes" ; and we may lawfully find in their creative work meanings which even they themselves never meant nor intended.

6. I now pass on to the concluding lines of this wonderful performance, at the end of the Twelfth Part of *The Ring and the Book:—*

> " If the rough ore be rounded to a ring,
> Render all duty which good ring should do,
> And failing grace, succeed in guardianship,—
> Might mine but lay outside thine, Lyric Love,
> Thy rare gold ring of verse (the poet praised)
> Linking our England to his Italy !"

In these words the Poet dedicates to his wife, whose blessing he had invoked at the commencement, the whole work, and "rounds the rough ore" which his poetic fancy supplied to a perfect ring of pure gold. He begins and concludes this, his longest poem, with thoughts of her whom he had loved and lost. Keeping up the simile which gave its name to the whole poem, he compares his work to the artistic work of

the Etruscan jeweller, who mixes an alloy with the pure gold that it
may bear the file and hammer, which alloy is dissolved by acids, and
the perfect ring "the shape remains." And now he desires to lay
his finished work by the side of his wife's ; and if it fail in " grace "
and favour, so that " the British public like it not," and few read it,
still it can serve the purpose of guarding and recommending hers,
fabricated in the same artistic way as his own—

> " Might mine but lie outside thine, Lyric Love,
>   Thy rare gold ring of verse (the poet praised)
>   Linking our England to his Italy ! "

Linking her English stories, *Aurora Leigh* and the rest, with the
Italian one here completed.

7. We are not surprised to find Browning, ten years after he had
lost

> "the best of wives
> That ever was toward husband in this world,"

acceding at once to Lady Cowper's suggestion and request, that he
should make the *Alcestis* of Euripides the subject of a poem—" that
strangest, saddest, sweetest song " ; we can understand why he so
readily complied, being touched with " its beauty, and the way it
makes you weep." He " embalms in the amber " of *Balaustion's
Adventure* the story, and his translation of, in the main, the whole
play, which contains our next allusion. In this, Euripides, Mrs.
Browning's favourite Greek poet, presents us with the beautiful
picture of a devoted woman saving the life of her husband by sacri-
ficing her own. Balaustion means in Greek " wild-pomegranate-
flower," who is a Rhodian girl that saves her own life by reciting
this play to the Euripides-loving Syracusans, B.C. 413. This is her
adventure which she tells to her four girl-friends. The motto prefixed
to the poem is four lines taken from the twelfth stanza of Mrs.
Browning's *Wine of Cyprus*—

> " Our Euripides, the human,
>   With his droppings of warm tears,
>   And his touches of things common
>   Till they rose to touch the spheres."

And the first two lines are twice quoted at the close of *Balaustion's
Adventure*, as if their melody had some peculiar charm for our Poet.

The second time he thus touchingly alludes to his own best of wives,
his own Alcestis—

> " I know the Poetess who graved in gold,
>   Among her glories that shall never fade,
>   This style and title of Euripides,
>   *The human with his droppings of warm tears.*"

We must not omit the further allusion at the end of the poem to the
thrice-repeated stanza, and the picture of Sir Frederick Leighton on
the subject of Alcestis—

> " And all came—*glory of the golden verse,*
>   And passion of the picture * * *
>   * * * of the play which gained no prize !
>   Why crown whom Zeus has crowned in soul before ?"

8. The only other allusion to his wife which, after a careful and
loving perusal of the whole of his works, I have been able to detect,
occurs in the epilogue to *Pacchiarotto, with other Poems,* published in
1876, fifteen years after her death.   This "one woman in the world,"
"the best—oh best by far of womankind," seems never to have been
forgotten, or a successor thought of.   Like Admetus in the foregoing
poem, Browning says—

> " Gone is she : no wife for Admetus more !
>   And I shall bear for thee no year-long grief,
>   But grief that lasts while my own days last, love! "

> " 'The Poets pour us wine '—
>   Said the dearest poet I ever knew,
>   Dearest and greatest and best to me."

The reference is again to Mrs. Browning's poem, *Wine of Cyprus,*
given to her by her blind old friend, H. S. Boyd, to whom the stanzas
are addressed—

> " Is it not right to remember
>   All your kindness, friend of mine,
>   When we two sat in the chamber,
>   And the poets poured us wine."

They are the Greek poets, Æschylus, Sophocles, Euripides, Theocritus,
and Pindar, whom they studied together.   " In grateful affection,"
she inscribes this, and three sonnets at the end of vol. ii. of her
Poetical Works, to Hugh Stuart Boyd on his Blindness, his Death in
1848, and his three legacies to herself, an Æschylus, a Gregory
Nazianzen, and a clock.

These, then, are the several allusions to his wife scattered throughout his voluminous works; and I am thankful to find so many, and
to be able to quote his own words, without unjustifiably prying into
his private life.   Browning was the last man to "sonnet-sing" about
himself.   He protests against this very strongly in the volume containing our last allusion.   He entirely dissents from Wordsworth's
dictum that—

> "Shakespeare unlocked his heart with this same key."
> "Did Shakespeare! If so, the less Shakespeare he!"

Of course, every one would like to see the inside of our great Poet's
house—house of life and house in Kensington, but he says—

> "No: thanking the public, I must decline.
> A peep through the window, if folks prefer;
> But please you, no foot over threshold of mine!"
> . . . . . "Whoso desires to penetrate
> Deeper, must dive by the spirit-sense."

This I am attempting to do in this paper, and again thank him for
leaving his window so far open, and his "bosom's gate ever so little
ajar."

> "Ready to hear the rest! How good you are!"

II. Well, then, having enjoyed this brief delightful glimpse of
Browning's wife-love through this partially open gate and window, I
will now a little prolong my gaze to notice the allusions to some of
his friends sparsely scattered through his works.

This strong love of one man for another, sometimes seen even
"passing the love of women"—friend-love, "wonderful, even passing" wife-love, as in the instance we read of in our Bibles—has again
and again been exemplified in the world's history.   The soul of one
man knit with the soul of another man, so that they love each other
as their own souls was the love of Jonathan and David; and how
touching the story: "They kissed one another, and wept one with
another, until David exceeded."   Dear as a brother, dearer than a
wife, I can hardly say this of any of our poet's friends, after having
dwelt so long on his wife-love, almost amounting to wife-worship;
but this warm heart finds its fellow-heart in one woman, while it
beats in unison with many friends.

> "I love, am loved by
> Some few honest to the core,"

are his own words. He seems to have been, again to quote his own words,

> "the proper
> Friend-making, everywhere friend-finding soul."

And I doubt not there are some amongst ourselves who know him personally who can say, as Ben Jonson did of Shakespeare, "I loved the man, and," what I hope they may be unable to add for many a year to come, "do honour his memory, on this side idolatry, as much as any."

And first I will take a peep through the window he has himself left open by his own act and deed in his several dedications.

Here we meet with some great and well-known names in the literary world—John Forster, William Macready, Sergeant Talfourd, Bryan Waller Procter, Walter Savage Landor, Thomas Carlyle, and Alfred Lord Tennyson. These, except the last one mentioned, are all now dead. So truer are his words at this late period, than even at the commencement of *Sordello*, where the poet himself addresses his imaginary yet real audience—"few living, many dead," "friends summoned together from the world's four ends," "there's a realm wherein I have many lovers," this old word meaning, as in Shakespeare, endeared friends of either sex. Amongst those whom he regards with "affectionate friendship," "in all affectionate admiration," "in grateful admiration," are Amédée de Ripert-Monclar, to whom he dedicates *Paracelsus*, in 1837 ; William C. Macready, *Strafford*, in 1837 ; the author of *Ion*, *Pippa Passes*, in 1841 ; and John Kenyon, *Dramatic Lyrics*, in 1842, 1845, and 1855.

Still stronger language is found in the dedication prefixed to the six volumes of *Poetical Works* published in 1863.

"I dedicate these volumes to my old friend, John Forster (elsewhere he speaks of him as 'the writer whom I am proud to call my friend '), glad and grateful that he who, from the first publication of the various poems they include, has been their promptest and staunchest helper, should seem even nearer to me now than almost thirty years ago."

Perhaps a still warmer strain is used in that to *Colombe's Birthday*, in 1841.

> "No one loves and honours Barry Cornwall more than
> Does Robert Browning ;
> Who, having nothing better than this play to
> Give him in proof of it,
> Must say so."

How reciprocal was their affection may be read in that poet's *Familiar Epistle to Robert Browning*, dated 1839 and 1846, in his *English Songs*, p. xxv., where he so truly foretells that he will " win a name of might."

But the warmest of all, inasmuch as the affection survives death, is seen through the open window of the dedication to *Sordello*, 1863, to M. Joseph Milsand, of Dijon.

" DEAR FRIEND,—Let the next poem be introduced by your name, therefore remembered along with one of the deepest of my affections, and so repay all trouble it ever cost me. . . . I trust to continue ever yours, R. B."

He is " the man of men " alluded to in *Red Cotton Night-Cap Country*, vol. xii. p. 122, appropriately in that poem, as Browning passed the summer of 1872 with his friend at St. Aubin, in Normandy, and his full " heart relieves itself,"

> " Milsand, who makest warm my wintry world,
>   And wise my heaven, if there we consort too."

Nor is he forgotten in his latest work in 1887, *Parleyings with Certain People,*

> " In Memoriam
>   J. Milsand
>   Obiit iv. Sept. MDCCCXXXVI
> *Absens absentem auditque videtque.*"

The absent both hears and sees the absent. Their friendship is un-impaired by death—though gone to " the realms of help," the absent is present in spirit, and still sees and hears the absent in body. Even had Milsand not been named, after reading that part of this dedication which we have omitted, " the historical decoration was purposely of no more importance than a background requires ; and my stress lay on the incidents in the development of a soul : little else is worthy study. I, at least, always thought so—*you*, with many known and unknown to me, think so," we should have been at no loss to know whom he referred to when he wrote

> " That man will read you rightly head to foot, *see into your soul.*
>   He knows more, and loves better, than the world
>   That never heard his name, and never may."

And surely *a fortiori* we may apply this " *auditque videtque* " to our poet's absent deceased wife ; and if so there is a plain allusion to her which we have omitted to notice in the Prologue to *Fifine*, written in 1872. She is the

> "Certain soul
> Which early slipped its sheath,
> And has for its home the whole of heaven,
> What if it thus look beneath,
> Thus watch one who in the world,
> Both lives and likes life's way,"

floating in his poetic sea of passion and thought, like the butterfly in the air watching the swimmer in the sea.

> "Does she look, pity, wonder
> At one who mimics flight,
> Swims—heaven above, sea under,
> Yet always earth in sight."

And now passing by the lady alluded to in *Sordello*, iii. p. 109, "My English Eyebright," in Greek, Εὐφρασία, Miss Haworth, which Mrs. Orr tells us refers to one of Browning's oldest friends, the next on our list is Walter Savage Landor ; and it was largely owing to Browning's considerate kindness and pecuniary assistance that Landor was enabled to pass the last few years of his life in comparative ease and comfort. The open window and door ajar are in *Sordello* and the dedication to *Luria*, which show the strong friendship which existed between these two poets, or rather poet and prose-poet, for when Browning styles him "a great tragic poet," he is referring to his *Imaginary Conversations*, which are in prose.

Landor thus writes of his friend,

> "Since Chaucer was alive and hale,
> No man hath walked along our roads with steps
> So active, so inquiring eye, or tongue
> So varied in discourse."

Our poet in the latter part of the third book of *Sordello*, where he is so delightfully personal, calls Landor

> his "patron-friend,
> Whose great verse blares unintermittent on
> Like your own trumpeter at Marathon.
> . . . . . .   Friend, wear
> A crest proud as desert while I declare
> Had I a flawless ruby . . . . . .
> . . . . . . I would, for that smile which went
> To my heart, fling it in the sea, content,
> Wearing your verse in place, an amulet
> Sovereign against all passion, wear, and fret."

Such being his estimation of his friend we are not surprised at this dedication to *Luria*.

> " I dedicate
> This last attempt for the present at dramatic poetry
> To a great dramatic poet ;
> ' Wishing what I write may be read by his light : '
> If a phrase originally addressed, by not the least
> Worthy of his contemporaries,
> To Shakespeare,
> May be applied here, by one whose sole privilege is in
> A grateful admiration,
> To Walter Savage Landor."

This is somewhat misleading as to the estimation in which Shakespeare was held by his contemporaries.   On referring to the preface of *Vittoria Corombona*, by John Webster, where the phrase in question occurs, we find that Shakespeare is classed with six other dramatists with equal praise, Chapman, Jonson, Beaumont, Fletcher, Dekker, and Heywood, and the words of Webster are—

> "Wishing what I write may be read by *their* light,"

not singling out Shakespeare as eclipsing all others, as we all should do now.

Browning seems to have been attracted to John Webster by his laborious and obscure style, so like to his own, but his own is so incomparably superior.   J. A. Symonds, in his edition in the Mermaid Series, says what he might with truth have said of Browning's poetry, "owing to condensation of thought and compression of language Webster's plays offer considerable difficulties to readers who approach them for the first time."

Another friend was Miss Thackeray, now Mrs. Richmond Ritchie, to whom he dedicates *Red Cotton Night-Cap Country*, and with whom, together with Joseph Milsand already mentioned, he spent the summer of 1872 at St. Aubin, called in the poem, St. Rambert.

> " Best loved of sea-coast-nook-ful Normandy ! "

To her he says,

> "what eye like yours—
> The learned eye is still the loving one ! "

Milsand appears to have lodged with him, but Miss Thackeray lived "some five miles farther down." She named the place and people too,

" White Cotton Night-Cap Country," and promised a novel under this nomenclature,

> " Normandy shown minute yet magnified
> In one of those small books, the truly great
> We never know enough, yet know so well."

The book promised on the beach has never, I fear, been forthcoming. How truly was she, "sweet mocking friend."

The dedication of selections, first series, in 1887, must not be omitted, which for terseness and strength of friend-love has seldom been surpassed.

> " Dedicated to
> Alfred Tennyson.
> In poetry—illustrious and consummate.
> In friendship—noble and sincere."

In the forewords to some earlier selections published 1865, in the series of Moxon's Miniature Poets, Browning says of Tennyson :— "This little gathering of the lightest of my poems contentedly looks pale beside the wonderful flower-show of my illustrious predecessor— dare I say ? my dear friend ; who will take it, all except the love in the gift, as a mere nosegay's worth."

Perhaps for equal terseness and neatness of expression we may here quote the dedication to *Pippa Passes*.

> " I dedicate my best intentions, in this poem,
> Admiringly to the author of ' Ion,'
> Affectionately to Mr. Sergeant Talfourd."

Ten years before he penned the dedication to Tennyson he thus writes of his friend Carlyle, in the preface to his transcription of *Agamemnon*.

Having called his own work an ἀκέλευστος ἄμισθος ἀοιδά, he adds, " No, neither ' uncommanded ' nor ' unrewarded ' : since it was commanded of me by my venerated friend, Thomas Carlyle, and rewarded will it indeed become if I am permitted to dignify it by the prefatory insertion of his dear and noble name." In an earlier part of this preface he makes a quotation from Matthew Arnold, and terms him his " eloquent friend."

And now, passing by in sacred silence the name of another friend, Anne Egerton Smith, with whom and his sister Browning was staying at La Saisiaz, and whose sudden death there gave rise to the poem thus entitled, we take our final peep through the open window of the dedications in that very graceful and unique one to *Balaustion's*

Adventure, to the Countess Cowper, and in doing so we pronounce our poet the very prince of dedicators.   It is as follows :

" If I mention the simple truth : that this poem absolutely owes its existence to you—who not only suggested, but imposed on me as a task, what has proved the most delightful of May-month amusements—I shall seem honest, indeed, but hardly prudent, for how good and beautiful ought such a poem to be !

" Euripides might fear little ; but I, also, have an interest in the performance ; and what wonder if I beg you to suffer that it make, in another and far easier sense, its nearest possible approach to those Greek qualities of goodness and beauty, by laying itself gratefully at your feet ? "

Thus in spite of his own protest disclaiming all self-revelation, he has by his own act and deed enabled us, as it were, to see inside his house of life without any earthquake laying the frontage bare—to slip as it were inside his breast, there to catalogue and label those whom we may fairly suppose he loves best.

Other people have left their windows open for the unscrupulous British public to peer through, and give us a glimpse of the friend-love which *they* bear towards our poet.

1. Archdeacon Farrar's *Early Days of Christianity,* 1884.

" To
Robert Browning, Esq.,
Author of *A Death in the Desert,*
And of many other poems of the deepest interest to all students of Scripture,
I dedicate
This volume
With sincere admiration and esteem."

2. Alfred Tennyson's *Tiresias and Other Poems,* 1885.

"To my good friend
Robert Browning,
Whose genius and geniality
Will best appreciate what is best,
And make allowance for what may be worst,
This volume
Is
Affectionately inscribed."

3. W. G. Kingsland's *Essay on Robert Browning,* December 1886.

" O strong-soul'd singer of high themes and wide—
Thrice noble in thy work and life alike—
Thy genius glides upon a sea, whose tide
Heaves with a pain and passion infinite !

> Men's hearts laid bare beneath thy pitying touch ;
> Strong words that comfort all o'erwearied much ;
> Thoughts whose calm cadence moulds our spirit-life,
> Gives strength to bravely bear amid world-strife ;
> And one large hope, full orb'd as summer sun,
> That souls shall surely meet when LIFE is won !
>
> So round thy heart our grateful thanks entwine ;
> Men are the better for these songs of thine !
> At eve thy muse doth o'er us mellower swell,
> Strong with the strength of life lived long and well."

Will our President allow me to add his *multum in parvo* prefixed to his Bibliography ?

> " To Robert Browning.
> ' A man '
> True as steel,
> A poet
> Searcher of men's minds and souls."—F. J. F.

And now, leaving these open windows, there seems to have been only one other friend, Alfred Domett, who could tempt Browning to leave his " bosom gate " ever so little ajar. Through this the peering eye sees nearly as far as through the window. The poem entitled *The Guardian Angel* is addressed to him. " Alfred, dear friend !" and again,

> " Where are you, dear old friend ?
> How rolls the Wairoa at your world's far end ? "

A longer poem speaks of him under the name of Waring.

> " Meantime, how much I loved him,
> I find out now I've lost him ;
> I who cared not if I moved him,
> Who could so carelessly accost him,
> Henceforth never shall get free
> Of his ghostly company.
> Oh, could I have him back once more,
> This Waring, but one half-day more !
> Back, with the quiet face of yore,
> So hungry for acknowledgment
> Like mine ! I'd fool him to his bent ! "

No more ! Alas, the window is shut, the blind drawn down, the bosom's portal barred and bolted.

"A DEATH IN THE DESERT."

BY MRS. M. G. GLAZEBROOK.

Read at the 48th Meeting of the Browning Society, February 25th, 1887.

AMONG the *dramatis personae*, associated with characters so diverse as James Lee's wife and Mr. Sludge, Rabbi Ben Ezra and Caliban, is St. John. The substance of "A Death in the Desert" is the dying speech of the most loved and the last surviving of Christ's disciples. The poem is extremely characteristic of its author. The choice of subject, the manner of presentation, the form of the intricate argument, are all illustrative of Mr. Browning's peculiar genius. In one respect it is exceptional, for it is his only poem which is concerned with Christian faith, as a product of history. "Christmas Eve" and "Easter Day" are Christian in sentiment and tendency; several others—notably "La Saisiaz"—are inspired by Christian hopes and enthusiasms; one—the strangely interesting "Epistle"—has for its subject an incident of the Gospel narrative; but no other goes back to the origins of Christianity and traces from them a systematic development. Like most of Mr. Browning's poems, "A Death in the Desert" can be only partly understood by itself. It must be studied with its whole environment. The circumstances of its production must be considered; knowledge of the poet's principles and methods, acquired by study of his other works, must be brought to bear on it. It needs that freedom of interpretation which he always seems to demand. For while he is lavish in suggestion, he is very chary of information. Very rarely does he give his readers ready-made opinions. His teaching stimulates, it does not forestall, thought. He thinks it best, he expressly tells us so himself, to present his arguments in dramatic form,

> "By making speak, myself kept out of view,
> The very man as he was wont to do,
> And leaving you to say the rest of him:"

Q

and by this method he evades the burden of proof.   A psychologist, not a logician, he shows how men do, not how men ought to, believe and think ; a poet not a moralist, he represents religion as a striving after a beautiful ideal, rather than as obedience to the dictates of duty.

The form of " A Death in the Desert " was determined by that attack upon the historical bases of Christianity which was so vigorously maintained in Germany in the beginning and middle of the present century.   We know from the unattractive description he gives of the professor in " Christmas Eve," that Mr. Browning had little sympathy with the German theologians.   Their destructiveness, their scepticism, their disregard of the emotional and personal elements in religion, their finality, were not indeed likely to make them acceptable to poets.   To what was " simple, sensuous, passionate," they seemed in direct opposition.   In the too few recorded words of another English poet, whose devout, earnest soul reflected much of the religious disturbance of his time, we can note traces of the distress they occasioned.   Though Clough could not help admitting the truth of their general conclusions, he did so with obvious repugnance to the methods by which these were obtained, and with a strong conviction that they were not final.   The clouds and darkness which were enveloping the new Sinai—the mount of law and knowledge—were, he felt, to be dispelled in time by a new revelation : some prophet will arise

> "To dare, sublimely meek,
>   Within the shroud, of blackest cloud,
>   The Deity to seek."

The discredit cast upon the authority of the evangelists filled him with a sense almost of bereavement,

> "lost, invisible and gone,
> Are, say you, Matthew, Mark and Luke and Holy John ?
> Lost, is it, lost, to be recovered never ?"

And something of this feeling, with less despondency, less painfulness, seems to have been with Browning when he wrote the poem we are considering.

In the critical examination of the evangelical records, the fourth gospel suffered most.   Strauss—in this instance following his early master and later antagonist, Baur—denied that St. John had anything to do with its composition.   The author, he held, was neither St. John nor any one else who had personally known Christ : nor, in accordance with a widely-accepted theory, did he believe it to be the work of a pupil of St. John, who, after the death of his master, related, from memory or from fragmentary notes, traditions and sayings which had been taught him, and made out of them a continuous history. Strauss pronounced it to be a controversial work, written late in the second century after Christ, by a profound theologian of the Greek Gnostic and anti-Jewish school, whose design was not to add another to the existing biographies of Christ, not to represent him as a real man, nor to give an account of any human life, but to produce an elaborate theological work in which, under the veil of allegory, the Neo-platonic conception of Christ as the Logos, the realised Word of God, the divine principle of light and life, should be developed. With this purpose, the writer made a free selection from the sayings and doings of Christ as recorded in the three Gospels already written, and as freely invented others. All the events, all the words, of the Gospel thus composed, are subordinate to the main design, which was worked out by the author with an artistic completeness most ingeniously traced by his German interpreters. Each miracle symbolises some important dogma, and its narration must be understood to mean that it embodies some deep spiritual truth, not, necessarily, that it ever actually took place. The author manifests, throughout, his ignorance of Jewish customs, and his antagonism to Jewish sentiments.

The whole subject is full of interest, but it forms a chapter in Biblical criticism, and a detailed discussion of it would be out of place here. The bases on which this elaborate theory is founded consist in the whole character of the fourth gospel, and with this we are all familiar. We recall at once its spirituality, its philosophy, its subjectiveness ; and throughout, from the opening words, which contain the essence of Neo-platonism, to the last long discourses to the disciples, we are conscious of the revelation of a dogmatic and mystic religion ; we recognise a faith of which the realities are not material miracles, acts of healing, violations of natural law, but the changes worked in the soul by divine love, the regeneration effected by new and higher desires, new and higher motives.

But, in his poem, Mr. Browning restores the St. John of orthodox belief. We have again the loved and loving disciple who leant on his Master's breast at supper, and in his old age continually bade his " little children, love one another." He is learned in Greek philosophy and speculative, as the author of the Gospel called by his name must have been ; mystical and visionary as became him who had received the revelation of Patmos. He is full of the responsibility which rests upon him as the last survivor of those who had seen and known

Christ ; fearful, also, of the heresies and "anti-Christs" already
beginning to disturb the Church, of whom the Ebionites, or followers
of Cerinthus, who denied his Lord's divinity, give him cause for most
anxiety.

He is dying in a cave in the desert, whither he has fled for refuge
from his persecutors : his only attendants are four faithful disciples.
The situation is, presumably, of the poet's own creating, for tradition
is very vague as to the date and circumstances of St. John's death.
It is conceived with all Mr. Browning's dramatic vigour and ready
comprehension of appropriate detail.   The introduction, with its
strange exactness, is meant to certify the authenticity of the manu-
script whence the record is taken.   It is supposed to be a parchment,
written in Greek by Pamphylax, one of the four attendants, which
has come into the possession of a later disciple through Xanthus,
another of the witnesses.   The narration is, therefore, that of
Pamphylax, and was written, as his concluding words tell us, on
the eve of his martyrdom.

Forced to fly, St. John, old and dying, has been concealed by his
followers in a cave.   For some time they had kept him in a dark and
secret recess, but now, aware that the end is near, they bring him to
an outer chamber of the grotto, into which the sun's rays can just penetrate, and there, in the dim light, they watch his lips and the fleeting
smiles which promise some parting words before the silence of death
overtakes him.   Outside the cave, a Bactrian, an ignorant, half-
savage convert, guards them from surprise, ready, if need be, to
sacrifice his own life for the protection of the few remaining moments
of his master's.   In vain, for some time, the four watchers within
try to rouse the dying man from his trance : they touch his lips with
wine, they bathe his forehead with cold water, they fill the cave with
strong, pungent perfume, and still he only turns and smiles in his
sleep, and does not wake.   At last, one of them, " the Boy,"

"Stung by the splendour of a sudden thought,"

fetches one of the leaden plates on which his master's gospel is
engraved, and, passing his fingers over the letters, reads aloud, " I am
the Resurrection and the Life."   The words, which are the key-note
of his faith and teaching, restore St. John to consciousness : he opens
his eyes, he sits up and looks around, and in the stillness of the desert
noon-tide and the rapt attention of his listeners, he delivers his last
charge.

The clue to the discourse which follows is given in a parenthetical
note of the supposed narrator's, explaining one of St. John's special

doctrines. He distinguished the soul of man, we are there told, into three component souls. The first, and lowest, is that which has to do with earth and corporeal things, the animal soul, which receives primary sensations and is the immediate cause of action—"*what Does.*" The second is the intellect, and has its seat in the brain: it is superior to the first, but dependent on it, since it receives as material the actual experience which the animal soul supplies; it is the feeling, thinking, willing soul—"*what Knows.*" The third, and highest, is the spirit of man, the very principle of life, the divine element in man linking him to God, which is self-subsistent and therefore independent of sensation and knowledge, but nevertheless makes use of them, and gives to them existence and energy—"*what Is,*"

> "What Does, what Knows, what Is; three souls, one man."

This doctrine supplies an explanation of the spiritual and subjective character of St. John's faith. His personal intercourse with Christ, his acquaintance with the human life of his Master on earth, was actual experience acquired by the lowest soul—"*what Does.*" To him, now, this actual experience seems only the "very superficial truth," and much inferior to the true, spiritual, informing knowledge which succeeded it. At the time, it had so little affected his whole nature, he had so little comprehended its full significance, that when it was all accomplished, and he knew the entire life of Christ, with its marvels of healing, and its command of supernatural powers, when he knew all that had been done by Him,

> "Who trod the sea and brought the dead to life,"

he could, nevertheless, with the other disciples, forsake Him in the hour of danger. But, in time, actual experience completed its work, and became material for the soul above—"*what Knows*"—by which it was developed into knowledge,

> "Ay, but my soul had gained its truth, could grow:"

and the fruit of that growth—ripened knowledge—he imparted to others. On them, thus presented, it had a powerfully transforming influence. Those who had never known Christ on earth believed in Him, through the disciple's teaching, with a real, devoted faith.

> "Another year or two,—what little child,
> What tender woman that had seen no least
> Of all my sights, but barely heard them told,
> Who did not clasp the cross with a light laugh,
> Or wrap the burning robe round, thanking God !"

But man's knowledge cannot be absolute : it is subject to change and development. The knowledge imparted by St. John underwent change in the minds of those whom he taught: it was questioned, doubted, it lost much of its power. More evidences were demanded, more facts ; and patiently, again and again, St. John re-stated what he knew. Already his own knowledge was becoming transformed.

> " Of new significance and fresh result ;
>   What first were guessed as points, I now knew stars,
>   And named them in the Gospel I have writ.
>   For men said, ' It is getting long ago :
>   Where is the promise of his coming ?'—asked
>   These young ones in their strength (as loth to wait)
>   Of me who, when their sires were born, was old."

He wrote his gospel for them, and told them all he had heard and seen of the life of Christ, and he thought that, in the main, they believed ; and so, satisfied that he had fulfilled his mission, and that

> "Though the whole earth should lie in wickedness
>   We had the truth, might leave the rest to God,"

St. John fell sick, and was ready to die.

He sank peacefully into the sleep of death ; but, roused by his attendants, he awakes with the startled, fearful anxiety of sudden waking :

> " Yet now I wake in such decrepitude
>   As I had slidden down and fallen afar,
>   Past even the presence of my former self,
>   Grasping the while for stay at facts which snap,
>   Till I am found away from my own world,
>   Feeling for foot-hold through a blank profound,
>   Along with unborn people in strange lands,
>   Who say—I hear said or conceive they say—
>   ' Was John at all, and did he say he saw ?
>   Assure us, ere we ask what he might see ! '"

It is at this point of the argument that the modern application— the reference to present forms of belief, the development suggested by Strauss, yet here represented in opposition to Strauss—is introduced. The transition is very ingeniously emphasized by the supposed re-awakening of St. John. Our own times seem to be invoked with those "unborn people in strange lands." With prophetic foresight St. John imagines how future generations, when new lands are discovered and old cities are laid waste, shall ask of his doctrine :

> " I see you stand conversing, each new face,
>   Either in fields, of yellow summer eves,
>   On islets yet unnamed amid the sea ;

> Or pace for shelter 'neath a portico,
> Out of the crowd in some enormous town,
> Where now the larks sing in a solitude ;
> Or muse upon blank heaps of stone and sand
> Idly conjectured to be Ephesus."

He wants to make sure that the knowledge he imparted in his gospel shall become in others the abiding faith it has become in him. In his heart, Christ still lived, still died to sin, and rose again to righteousness. He had fulfilled already the promise of His coming again. But how was the spiritual resurrection to be accomplished in less spiritual hearts ?

> "Can they share,
> They, who have flesh, a veil of youth and strength
> About each spirit, that needs must bide its time,
> Living and learning still as years assist
> Which wear the thickness thin, and let men see—
> With me, who hardly am withheld at all,
> But shudderingly, scarce a shred between,
> Lie bare to the universal prick of light."

To him, that life of Christ has become the one ever-present reality, the principle of life, the power which raises man to communion with God, which gives energy to experience and knowledge—in the only true sense, "*what Is*"—

> To me, that story,—ay, that Life and Death
> Of which I wrote 'it was'—to me, it *is* ;
> —Is, here and now ; I apprehend nought else."

He sees the life of Christ, the manifestation of God's love on earth, still being enacted wherever men are rescued from sin, and relieved from pain :

> "Is not God now i' the world His power first made !
> Is not His love at issue still with sin,
> Visibly when a wrong is done on earth ?
> Love, wrong, and pain, what see I else around ?"

And in these ever-repeated acts of redemption the resurrection seems continually to take place again. Love is re-united to Power, salvation springs triumphantly from the graves of sin and death :

> "Yea, and the Resurrection and Uprise
> To the right hand of the throne,—what is it beside,
> When such truth, breaking bounds, o'erfloods my soul,
> And, as I saw the sin and death, even so
> See I the need yet transiency of both,
> The good and glory consummated thence !
> I saw the power ; I see the Love, once weak,

> Resume the power : and in this word ' I see '
> Lo, there is recognised the Spirit of both
> That moving o'er the spirit of man, unblinds
> His eye and bids him look."

So strong, indeed, was this faith, that it became the absolute proof of the reality of Christ's human life ; because he believed so firmly, he was convinced of the truth of that actual experience, of which the recollection was beginning to fade in the brighter lights of knowledge of faith.   Thus " *what Is* " became the real evidence of " *what Does.*"

This argument he applies to the Pagan fable of Prometheus's gift of fire to mortals.   The fire was stolen from Jove and given to mankind by Prometheus—that was the original fact.   The story of this theft and gift was the historical knowledge gained.   The existence of fire is the abiding reality, and it is this which gave credibility to the fable.   Thus again " *what Is* " becomes the evidence of " *what Does.*"

But we know now that the story of Prometheus is an invention. Can it be that the story of Christ is an invention too ?   Did He exist at all ?   Is He not the ideal Man created out of man's own conceptions of goodness and love ?

> " One listens quietly nor scoffs, but pleads
> ' Here is a tale of things done ages since ;
> ' What truth was ever told the second day ?
> ' Wonders, that would prove doctrine, go for nought.
> ' Remains the doctrine, love ; well, we must love,
> ' And what we love most, power and love in one,
> ' Let us acknowledge on the record here,
> ' Accepting these in Christ : must Christ then be ?
> ' Has He been ?   Did not we ourselves make Him ?
> ' Our mind receives but what it holds, no more ! "

In the course of this argument, which St. John puts into the mouth of an imaginary objector, the idea of God as the union of perfect love and perfect knowledge—or power—prevails.   This conception is most fully illustrated in *Paracelsus*.   In that poem, Mr. Browning, according to his custom, works out a highly metaphysical notion by " draping it in sights and sounds."   Paracelsus fails, because, in striving after the attainment of knowledge, he neglects love : Aprile fails because love engrosses him entirely, to the exclusion of the desire for knowledge.   They meet, and each sees his error ; but Aprile dies at the moment of recognition, and Paracelsus lives only to acknowledge on his death-bed that his aim has been beyond human possibility : God alone combines, in perfection, love and knowledge.

St. John sees the manifestation of divine love in Christ's life on earth:

> "Such ever was love's way: to rise, it stoops;"

but he foretells that in later times it will be questioned whether Christ be not rather the subjective personification of human love:

> "We acknowledge Christ—
> A proof we comprehend His love, a proof
> We had such love already in ourselves,
> Knew first what else we should not recognize
> 'Tis mere projection from man's inmost mind,
> And, what he loves, thus falls reflected back.
> Becomes accounted somewhat out of him;
> He throws it up in air, it drops down earth's,
> With shape, name, story added, man's old way
> How prove you Christ came otherwise, at least?"

The manifestation of divine power or knowledge—for perfect knowledge is absolute power—is the visible world. But how do we know this? All we know is, that there is a world governed by certain laws. To the power which made and rules this world we ascribe our own attributes, will and love; and history says that in past times these attributes were attested by evident tokens—miracles, interruptions of the ordinary course of nature—of wrath and pleasure. No miracles, however, take place now, though reward and punishment are as urgently required:

> "Therefore it was mere passion and mistake,
> Or erring zeal for right, which changed the truth,
> Go back, far, farther to the birth of things:
> Ever the will, the intelligence, the love,
> Man's!—which he gives, supposing he but finds."

So the ancients used to ascribe to their gods human bodies and human passions. First the bodies, then the passions, were discarded; and in time the equally human attributes of will, power, and love, will be discarded likewise. Only law will remain.

In reply, St. John shows how the soul of man is trained by degrees, and how this process of gradual training is the whole purpose of life. Help is given to man for each step in his ascent; but, that step reached, the help is withdrawn; as new heights come in view, he has "new needs and new helps." Through progressive truths he approaches the knowledge of God. In the early stages of his education he needed sensible proofs of God's existence, and these were granted to him by miracles; but his belief in God once established, such outward signs became superfluous and ceased. He advanced to a

higher faith, to the spiritual recognition of a divine power of purifi-
cation and wisdom within him, to the conviction of the existence of
an all-controlling providence which depended, for authority, on no
extraordinary manifestations.   The enduring evidences of Christ's
divinity are the love and knowledge He left to mankind: His
miracles were but first appeals to hardened hearts.

And now, when man has gained such love and knowledge, will he
doubt their very source?

> " Wouldst thou unprove this to re-prove the proved?
> In life's mere minute, with power to use that proof,
> Leave knowledge, and revert to how it sprung?
> Thou hast it ; use it, and forthwith, or die ! "

For this looking back and this doubt endanger his very existence.   If
he can recognise in the ruler of the universe a being without will or
love, a power to whom only law can with certainty be attributed,
then man, in whom will and love as well as power—in however
small degrees—are known to be combined, must be acknowledged
to be greater than his creator :

> " He is as surely higher in the scale
> Than any might with neither love nor will,
> As life, apparent in the poorest midge,
> (When the faint dust-speck flits, ye guess its wing)
> Is marvellous beyond dead Atlas' self.
> Given to the nobler midge for resting-place ! "

Thus, through his knowledge, he loses God, in seeking whom he
gained knowledge ; his progress is stopped, for he has found—and,
finding, has lost—the object of his progress :

> " His life becomes impossible, which is death."

St. John's discourse concludes with words which are an epitome
of Mr. Browning's religious faith as we recognise it in many of his
other writings.   Man's life consists in never-ceasing progress.   The
god-like power is imparted to him gradually, and step by step he
approaches nearer to absolute truth—to divine perfection.   But in
this mortal life the goal can never be attained : the ideal, which he
strives to realise here, exists only in heaven, and awaits him as a
reward of all his faithful efforts.   For, should he cease to strive, and
renounce the divine ideals, he forfeits his right to life, and brings
upon himself the condemnation of death :

> " If ye demur, this judgment on your head,
> Never to reach the ultimate, angels' law,
> Indulging every instinct of the soul,
> There where law, life, joy, impulse, are one thing ! "

Thus St. John's last message of enlightenment and warning is delivered : with words of self-devotion yet lingering on his lips, he dies. His disciples bury him at evening, and disperse their several ways.

The general purport of the poem can scarcely be doubted, as we look back upon it as a whole and consider its main conclusions. The tendency of the argument is to diminish the importance of the original events—historical or traditional—on which the Christian religion is based. "It is not worth while," the writer seems to say to Strauss and his followers, " to occupy ourselves with discussions about miracles and events, which are said to have taken place a long time ago, and can now neither be denied nor proved. What we are concerned with, is, Christianity as it is now : as a religion which the human mind has, through many generations, developed, purified, spiritualised; and which has re-acted upon human nature and made it wiser and nobler. Shall we give up this faith which has been so great a power for good in the world, and which, its whole past history justifies us in concluding, will continue its work of improvement, because our belief in certain events is shaken or destroyed? It would be vain, indeed, thus to build our religion on a foundation so unstable as material evidence. For human sensations are not infallible ; they very often deceive us ; we think we see objects, which are really the illusions of our own brain, others we see in part only, or distorted; others we fail to perceive at all. Our faith, essential as it is to the well-being of the deepest parts of our nature, must not be dependent on such controlling powers as these."

This last argument, it should be noticed, is suggested in the beginning of the poem, where St. John, when he first wakes, says how easily he could believe that he is living again his past life, how easily he could even doubt his own identity :

> "If a friend declared to me,
> This my son Valens, this my other son,
> Were James and Peter—nay, declared as well
> This lad was very John,—I could believe !
> Could, for a moment, doubtlessly believe."

And, again, in a later passage, he suggests that the very objects surrounding them may not appear the same to him and his attendants :

> "What do I
> See now, suppose you, there where you see rock
> Round us !"

but it may, in return, very justly be asked if Mr. Browning can really intend to advocate that something less than perfect truthfulness, which would be implied in the continued unquestioning acceptance of a dogmatic religion in its entirety, after the bases of many of its doctrines have been impugned. Does he wish to condemn honest research, and to put a check upon free enquiry? Can he be so at variance with the spirit of the age, as not to sympathise with that desire to investigate the origin and growth of knowledge which gives so high a scientific value to the best of contemporary work? A hostile interpretation of the advice not to look back to the sources whence our knowledge springs might represent it as a strong encouragement to insincerity and wilful self-delusion.

All that we know of Mr. Browning's candour and keenness of perception forbids us to accept such a conclusion. But it is quite consistent with his customary method to have put the case against Strauss in this forcible, dramatic form. He was, we may suppose, offended by Strauss's ruthless attack on much that mankind has held sacred for ages. His religious sense was revolted by the assumption that there was nothing in Christianity which could survive the destruction of the miraculous and supernatural elements in its history. He desired to represent Christianity as an entirely spiritual religion, independent of external, material agencies. In order to make his argument as powerful as possible, he chose for his mouth-piece one of the personal followers of Christ, on whom, it might be supposed, the actual human life of his master had made a permanent and lively impression. With the details of Biblical criticism he had nothing to do, his principles were unaffected by discussions about the authenticity of the various parts of gospels; so, in defiance of Strauss, the disciple he chose was that very John, whose personality, as recognised by long tradition, had been so much discredited. He showed how even in one of the disciples the recollection of wonders and signs could be transcended, and at last obliterated, by a spiritual faith which was sustained by the needs and faculties of the soul. The poem is, in effect, an eloquent protest in defence of "the breath and finer spirit of all knowledge."

There is no need to claim originality for the metaphysical conceptions which the poem illustrates: nor, on the other hand, would we endeavour to show how full of learning it is, by tracing its ideas to the books of many philosophical writers. The true artistic value of the poem consists in the lucidity with which a difficult argument is developed, and the dramatic unity of purpose and vividness with which it is invested.

SOME NOTES ON
BROWNING'S POEMS REFERRING TO MUSIC.

By HELEN J. ORMEROD.

Read at the Fifty-first Meeting of the Browning Society, May 27, 1887.

THESE slight notes on a subject of considerable interest, seem still more inadequate, as in writing them, the many-sidedness of the poet becomes more apparent. He is able, as we know, at will, (and this regardless of century or country) to create the artist, the lover, the monk, the bishop, the courtier, the physician, the theologian, and indeed who not ? But now, for the moment, regarding Browning's poems on music only, I am again impressed by the variety of character, and diversity of knowledge found in them. Four poems claim our special attention, as they teach us much of certain musicians and their music , these, as will readily be guessed are *A Toccata of Galuppi's ; Master Hugues of Saxe-Gotha ; Charles Avison ;* and last, but being most beloved, certainly not least, *Abt Vogler.* These then, are the four poems of which I purpose to speak a little in detail.

Saul, with its grand prophetic utterances, is less strictly a poem on music and of musicians, than a wonderful account of the conflict for ever being waged in the heart of man between good and evil ; in this instance the evil spirit being exorcised by the holy spirit of song setting forth great religious truths. In many of Browning's poems music is introduced as an accessory to general effect, as in *The Grammarian's Funeral, Serenade at a Villa, Up at a Villa—Down in the City.* In the *Heretic's Tragedy,* the organ solemnly sounds the Plagal

Cadence, one of the most impressive of ecclesiastic cadences, in which the chord of the subdominant[1] precedes that of the tonic.

In *Balaustion's Adventure* we have a fine descriptive bit of musical writing, alluding to an effect allowed in modern music—

> " And, as some long last moan
> Of a minor, suddenly is propped beneath
> By note which, new-struck, turns the wail, that was,
> Into a wonder and a triumph, so
> Began Alkestis. ' Nay, thou art to live ! ' " &c.

A fine example of this sudden change from a minor moan to major rejoicing may be found in Beethoven's Mass in D ; when at the close of the Andante in $\frac{3}{4}$ time in the opening chorus, the soft minor chorus " Christie Eleison " is broken in upon by the major chord of D, thus turning " the wail that was, Into a wonder and a triumph."

In *Fifine at the Fair*, we find allusions to Schumann's charming *Carnival*. The hero of the poem lazily shifted the burthen of his thoughts, "to the back of some musician dead and gone," and found Schumann's bright music " chiming in exactly with the sounds and sights of yestereve." He described how he " somehow-nohow played the whole of the pretty piece," compared food for the body to food for the soul, and remarked on

> " Our Schumann's victories
> Over the commonplace, how faded phrase grew finer
> And palled perfection piqued, up-startled by the brine,
> His pickle, bit the mouth and burnt the tongue aright."

A comparison worthy of the Don Juan who made it ! He next comments on the sweet monotony of the successive flat keys, and on the difficulties of such " unconscionable stretches " as " tenths and twelfths," and finally dreams " gone off in company with music," and, let us hope, profiting hereafter by the example of devotion and constancy set him in this instance by the musician.

Youth and Art would claim more than a passing notice, were it not that no poem could bear less directly on the subject of music itself ; for here we find the singer deliberately leaving her art for a title and an income ; she marries the " rich old lord," and becomes herself " queen at *bals-paré*,"

> " Life's unfulfilled, you see ;
> It hangs still, patchy and scrappy :
> We have not sighed deep, laughed free,
> Starved, feasted, despaired,—been happy.'

---

[1] The subdominant is the fourth note of the scale, and as its name signifies is the note below the dominant. The tonic is the key-note.

Happiness in this case could have been but once—

"And we missed it, lost it for ever."

Let us close the page on this sad story of a spoiled life, spoiled by the singer herself, because she chose to listen to the voice of the world and fashion, rather than to God's whisper in her ear, and turn to the contemplation of musical life in other phases, reaching complete-ness as told in *Abt Vogler*. Life, as regards worldly affairs, well described in the line just quoted—"Starved, feasted, despaired, BEEN HAPPY,"—suffering keenly from rebuffs, censures and misunder-standings from without; and yet, happy beyond measure in that sense of nearness to the Divine, and in the possession of that hidden well-spring of life, inspired only by Love and Art, perhaps known only in all its fulness when Love and Music are at once the inspiration.

I shall first take *A Toccata of Galuppi's* for a few minutes' consideration. What a scene rises before us as Baldassaro Galuppi plays his Toccata on the tinkling clavichord of the day, and with what a master hand the poet sketches in for us, so to speak, the dramatic background! The beautiful Italian spring-weather, the sea warm in the May sunshine, but then, as now, balls and masks proving more attractive to the fashionable throng than the sweet spring-tide of nature; suddenly a couple of dancers are singled out from the crowd, and we have a glimpse of a Venetian beauty—

"Cheeks so round and lips so red,—
On her neck the small face buoyant, like a bell-flower on its bed
O'er the breast's superb abundance, where a man might base his head,"

and her cavalier,—

"He, to finger on his sword,
While you sat and played Toccatas, stately at the clavichord.
       *   *   *   *
'Brave Galuppi! that was music! good alike at grave and gay!
I can always leave off talking when I hear a master play!'"

I cannot help wondering if manners were more highly cultivated amongst the Venetians last century than they are now amongst the English; or if the old Italian favourite awed his listeners into silence by the magic of his touch; but some mighty reason must have existed to command silence in that gay throng, for the hearing of a Toccata! That minor predominated in this quaint old piece (Toccata by the way, means a *Touch* piece, and probably was written to display the delicacy of the composer's touch) is evident from the mention of—

> " Those lesser thirds so plaintive, sixths diminished, sigh on sigh,
> Told them something! Those suspensions, those solutions,—'Must we die!'
> Those commiserating sevenths,—'Life might last! we can but try!'"

The interval of the third is one of the most important; the signature of a piece may mislead one, the same signature standing for a major key and its relative minor; but the third of the opening chord decides the question, a lesser "plaintive" third (composed of a tone and a semitone), showing the key to be *minor;* the greater third (composed of two whole tones) showing the key to be *major.* Pauer tells that "the minor third gives the idea of tenderness, grief and romantic feeling." Next come the "diminished sixths," these are sixths possessing a semitone less than a minor sixth; for instance from C sharp to A flat: this interval in a different key would stand as a perfect fifth. "These suspensions, these solutions"—a suspension is the stoppage of one or more parts for a moment, while the others move on; this produces a dissonance, which is only resolved by the parts which produced it, moving on to the position which would have been theirs, had the parts moved simultaneously. We can understand that "these suspensions, these solutions," might teach the Venetians, as they teach us, lessons of experience and hope; light after darkness, joy after sorrow, smiles after tears. "These commiserating sevenths," of all dissonances, none is so pleasing to the ear, or so attractive to musicians, as that of minor and diminished sevenths, that of the major seventh being crude and harsh; in fact the minor seventh is so charming in its discord as to suggest concord; again to quote from Pauer—"It is the antithesis of discord and concord which fascinates and charms the ear, it is the necessary solution and return to unity which delights us."

After all this, the love-making begins again, but kisses are interrupted by the "Dominant's[1] persistence till it must be answered to;" this seems to indicate the close of the piece, the dominant being answered by an octave which suggests the perfect authentic cadence, in which the chord of the dominant is followed by that of the tonic.

The Toccata is ended, and the gay gathering dispersed; I cannot help the thought that this old music of Galuppi's was more of the head than the heart, more formal than fiery, suggestive rather of the chill of death than the heat of passion. The temporary silence into

---

[1] The dominant is the fifth, and most characteristic note of the scale, called by the Germans *der herrschende Ton.*

which the dancers were surprised by the playing of the Maestro is over, and the impressions caused by it are passed away, just as the silence of death was to follow the warmth and brightness of the glad Venetian life—

> " Then they left you for their pleasure, till in due time, one by one,
> Some with lives that came to nothing, some with deeds as well undone,
> Death stepped tacitly and took them, where they never see the sun."

Vanitas vanitatum seems to me the moral of this poem—

> " ' Dust and ashes ! ' so you creak it, and I want the heart to scold.
> Dear dead women, with such hair too—what's become of all the gold
> Used to hang and brush their bosoms ! I feel chilly and grown old."

Let us leave Galuppi's old Toccata with its varied associations, and hear what Master Hugues of Saxe-Gotha has to say to us through the intricacies of his fugue, vainly summoned from the Silent Land as he is by the organist. After looking through all obtainable works on German musicians, I have come to the conclusion that *Master Hugues* is a fictitious name, though I cannot believe him to be an entirely fictitious character ; for I feel sure the poet must have had some well-loved fugue sounding in his ears as he wrote, and if the fugue was real, why not the composer ?

> " Forth and be judged, Master Hugues !
> Answer the question I've put you so oft :
>   What do you mean by your mountainous fugues ?
> See, we're alone in the loft."

What a world of memories, Master Hugues, are called up by this description of your F minor fugue ! And although it may sound involved, being written in five parts, yet it is in strict accordance with musical law, for the greater the composer, the more he shows his greatness by accepting and glorifying the fetters worn by his lesser brethren. As I write, in fancy I hear one of Bach's majestic fugues, thundered out from the fine organ of Upton Church, Torquay, as one seldom hears them nowadays. There, in that cool, quiet church near that southern sunny sea, I learned to know and love those organ fugues as personal friends, each with its own identity.

To return to the poem before us ; let me ask you to notice the descriptive word *mountainous*—" What do you mean by your mountainous fugues ? " The word *fugue* itself is from the Latin *fugare*, to put to flight ; I suppose with the idea that one part chases another throughout the piece ; but how much more is involved in this

R

descriptive term of Browning's? It was once my privilege to assist at
a rehearsal of Bach's Cantata, *My spirit was in heaviness* (a work
abounding in fugal choruses), under the leadership of the late Mr.
Edward Hecht, of Manchester; in his desire to make each part introduce the subject with due effect, he exclaimed: "Remember, ladies
and gentlemen, it is as though you were builders, adding stone after
stone, pinnacle after pinnacle, to an architectural pile, until you reach
the topmost stone of some grand cathedral!" So here, the term *mountainous*, as applied to this fugue, may have the same meaning; range
after range, peak after peak rising in mountain glory, bringing before
my mind's eye those scenes of Himalayan grandeur, culminating in the
snowy crests of Everest and Kinchinjunga, so ably depicted by Alex.
Scott, of Darjeeling—as many visitors to "The Colonies" will
remember. To return to the fugue: "First you deliver your phrase;"
the phrase is the subject, and "subject" is the accepted name of the
theme or phrase on which the whole fugue is based. To give a
familiar instance of a fugue, within the reach of all, I would refer you
to Handel's "Amen" chorus in the *Messiah*. We now hear that
Master Hugues's subject is "answered no less, where no answer
needs be." The answer, or response, is the correlative of the
subject, and the subject and answer determine the character of the
fugue; speaking in general terms, the *answer* is (as nearly as
possible) the *subject* transposed from the tonic to the dominant.
"Off start the two on their ways," "the Two" signifying subject and
answer:—

> "Straight must a Third interpose,
>   Volunteer needlessly help;
> In strikes a Fourth, a Fifth thrusts in his nose,
>   So the cry's open, the kennel's a-yelp,
> Argument's hot to the close."

It is so difficult to describe the fascination of a fugue to any one who
does not love to hear, play, sing, or write them, as the case may be,
and my feeling about this poem is, that the writer of it knows
enough about the construction of a fugue to rejoice in it, and that he
(using the composer, Master Hugues, as his mouthpiece) is laughing
the while at the organist who, so far, has only mastered the mechanical
difficulties of the piece, and at that part of the world at large who
think it all "wrangle, abuse and vociferance." As the organist goes
on trying to disentangle the knotted skein, the truth enforces itself
on his mind that there's more in this confusion of sound than at first he
imagined—

> "Something is gained, if one caught but the import—
> Show it us, Hugues of Saxe Gotha!"

It seems to me that Browning must have meant, through the teachings of Master Hugues, to show that out of chaos springs order; out of doubt comes belief; out of great tribulation the kingdom of Heaven. The organist, struggling to understand the difficult fugue long since shelved by the younger folk, appealing to the composer himself for elucidation of the mystery, is, to my thinking, no inapt illustration of an upright, hard-thinking man, striving vainly to solve the difficult problems of life around him, turning at last to God Himself for help with the old cry, "Why—wherefore?" Then, again :—

> "Friend, your fugue taxes the finger ;
> Learning it once, who would lose it ?"

Who would lose the teachings and experience of life, past bearing though they seemed to us at times, taxing alike physical and mental powers of endurance; yet, who would lose them?

> "Truth's golden o'er us, although we refuse it—
> Nature, thro' cobwebs we string her."

These two lines are in allusion to the organist's sudden thought of how the gilt mouldings of the roof, almost blotted out by spiders' webs, may be like the hidden beauty of the fugue :—

> "All's like . . . it's like . . . for an instance I'm trying . . .
> There ! See our roof, its gilt moulding and groining
> Under those spider-webs lying !
> *　　　*　　　*　　　*　　　*
> So your fugue broadens and thickens,
> Greatens and deepens and lengthens,
> Till we exclaim—'But where's music, the dickens ?
> Blot ye the gold, while your spider-web strengthens
> Blacked to the stoutest of tickens ?'"

Verse xxviii seemed to me a little difficult at first :—

> "Hugues ! I advise *med pœnd*
> (Counterpoint glares like a Gorgon)
> Bid One, Two, Three, Four, Five clear the arena !
> Say the word, straight I unstop the full-organ,
> Blare out the *mode Palestrina*."

The *mode Palestrina* seems to be an expression coined for the moment by the poet (I suppose in reference to the Dorian, Phrygian, and Lydian modes, &c.). Palestrina was the great master of the Polyphonic school. In true polyphony each voice sings an interesting part of its own, at the same time not forgetting its fellow voices, but answering and supplementing what they say, yet all in strict obedience to the laws of harmony. Hence the future development of fugue, although I believe the first formal fugue was not written by Benevoli until about fifty years after Palestrina's death. Our organist in the poem seems for a moment to be baffled by the five contending parts, and, "at his own risk," bids them "clear the arena," probably intending to compare one of Palestrina's stately and masterly compositions with the fugue ; his last word however as an organist is lost, for the wick burns down in the socket, and not wishing to come to an untimely end on the dark "rat-riddled stairs," and not carrying "the moon in his pocket," he calls for a light, and the thread of his discourse is abruptly snapt.

It is Mr. Ruskin, I think, who makes the delightful assertion that laughter is often a proof of love : we never laugh at those we dislike, but we often laugh—lovingly and tenderly—at those we love ; and I am reminded of this throughout the account of this fugue, and this is the reason why Browning holds up to friendly ridicule the Subject and Answer, and One, Two, Three, Four and Five generally, and gives to each part its separate identity. In *Charles Avison* we find him turning with loving memory to fugues :—

> " Give me some great glad subject, glorious Bach,
>   Where cannon-roar, not organ-peal, we lack ! "

And again—

> "Such a Fugue would catch
> Soul heavenwards up."

This reminds me that it is time to modulate to the next poem, *Charles Avison ;* so making "fugue" the leading note to the next key, we find ourselves introduced to the almost forgotten organist of St. Nicholas Church, Newcastle ; probably (until brought to light in the *Parleyings*) only known to some as the composer of the once popular air "Sound the loud Timbrel," now for ever to be associated with his "bold-stepping" C major March. There is something delightfully quaint and unexpected about this poem ; the black-cap tugging at his prized cloth-shred in the driving snow shower of "uncomfortable March," the on-looker, watching the struggle to its victorious close ; and then, thinking of the cold *March* weather, suddenly this lusty old March of Avison, by a strange freak of memory, rings in his head. As the black-cap discovered the "brown-frayed flannel bit" far afield from his usual haunts, so the poet describes his soul travelling back through the years and pouncing on this "relic of a brain long still." It is interesting to find Browning apostrophising "great John Relfe" (who published a work with a view to the simplification of thorough-bass and composition) as " Master of Mine," for it seems very natural that the poet should have studied with some enthusiastic theorist (whether John Relfe or another), as I have always been impressed by the amount of musical knowledge possessed by him ; and so far as my memory serves me he is the only poet who is able to avail himself of this added facility of illustration or explanation. I have been referred to Rossetti's *Monochord*, but richly gifted as he was both as painter and poet, and fully capable of true artistic elevation as he heard music, it is evident that it was more or less of a mystery to him, and the " flame turned cloud, and cloud returned to flame." A mono-chord was an ancient instrument, not of ten strings, but only one. I should imagine Rossetti meant by his " monochord " one range of emotions, whether of " Life or Death," " regenerate rapture," or " coverts of dismay." Dryden in his *Ode on St. Cecilia's Day* in-dulges in a little musical phraseology, but he is superficial in comparison to Browning. A severe contrapuntist friend, also an organist, took up a volume of Browning's poems from our table and exclaimed in unfeigned surprise : " Why, *this fellow* understands music ! "

This lively, self-satisfied March of Avison's is in the key of C, with "the Greater Third " signifying the major key; and with no modulation except the almost necessary one from tonic to dominant. We next leave modern days and music—Brahms, Dvorak, Wagner, and Liszt being mentioned as representative names of the modern school—and travel back with the poet—to whom ? Handel only?—not so—Buononcini, Geminiani, Pepusch, and Avison were there to dispute his priority—the said dispute being promptly decided by posterity. The discussion as to the relative merits of Buononcini and Handel waxed warm enough, and many will recall Dean Swift's celebrated epigram on the subject :—

> " Some say that Signor Bononcini
> Compared to Handel is a ninny ;
> While others vow that to him Handel
> Is hardly fit to hold a candle.
> Strange that such difference should be
> 'Twixt tweedle-dum and tweedle-dee."

Geminiani (Avison's master) was a famed violoncellist, who lived for some time in England ; and in a treatise published by Avison we find him preferring both Buononcini and Geminiani to Handel. That Geminiani believed in Handel to some extent, but perhaps only as an executant, is evident from the fact that he always stipulated, when he played solos at concerts, that Handel should be asked to accompany him. The *Alexis* referred to is one of six cantatas written by Pepusch, and received with considerable favour in their day—forgotten now—(while *The Messiah*, *Judas Maccabeus*, *Israel in Egypt* and others gain added glory from year to year):—

> "Such were feats
> Of music in thy day,—dispute who list—
> Avison of Newcastle, organist!"

We are told next, how in those days musicians were absorbed heart and soul in the new music of the time, just as now in Wagner's music. (I wonder if Browning has a lurking suspicion that Wagner may be almost forgotten a hundred years hence, as some of the last century musicians are by us now?) The beautiful passage about the Tannhäuser song, and the parenthesis on "Soul" follow quickly, both most ably touched on in Mr. Arthur Symons's paper; after which comes a powerful description of the working of Mind, yet with the "Soul's sea" always beneath. And then we come to an interesting inquiry into the relative capabilities of the arts; but I will leave this fascinating subject for a few minutes until we hear what the poet has to say in *Abt Vogler*. A second address to the departed "John Relfe" follows: this time he is likened to a master chemist, from whose laboratory his pupil (the poet) ventures to abstract a bottle containing "reactives," by the help of which he sprinkles "discords and resolutions" broadcast over the page.

> "He (Avison) lacked
> Modern appliance, spread out phrase unracked
> By modulation, fit to make each hair
> Stiffen upon his wig—see there—and there!
> I sprinkle my reactives, pitch broad-cast
> Discords and resolutions."

In this I am reminded of the remark of an old, self-taught Yorkshire organist, to whom I showed a modern cantata, every page of which bristled with accidentals. The old man said, as he handed the book back to me: "It's same as if he'd takken a sieve, and riddled sharps and flats all over t'page!"

The poet amuses himself by imagining the change which would be wrought in Avison's March by "such irreverent innovation;" then, still indulging in musical metaphor, he modulates through the key of "A minor with the Lesser Third" (the relative minor of *C* major with its *Greater* Third) back to the original key; the minor moan of section twelve being well suited to A minor, to be followed by the March blared forth "in bold C major." In section fourteen the wish to embellish the simple March with musical innovations is again upper-most, and by judicious treatment fit it for "March music of the Future"; when suddenly, by a strange freak of fancy, the poet goes to the past instead of the future, and now imagines a "sable-stoled procession to Tyburn," moving to "droning plain song," and wreaking "a classic vengeance on the March;" it moans—

> " Larges and Longs and Breves displacing quite
> Crotchet-and-quaver pertness."

The Larges, Longs, and Breves were the long-drawn notes, which were used in the early days of music. Not satisfied even yet with the varied forms, past and future, assigned to the March, it is suddenly rearranged by the poet to express the patriotic jubilations of the people, exulting in the escape of the celebrated Five from the arrest of the King :—

> " Hark the hymn !
> Rough, rude, robustious, homely heart a-throb
> Harsh voice a-hallo, as' beseems the mob !
> How good is noise !   What's silence but despair
> Of making sound match gladness never there ?"

Leaving the March as a fit outlet for patriotic demonstration, we will turn to *Abt Vogler*, only however to return to *Charles Avison* for the discussion of the interesting question of the relative merits of the sister arts of Music, Painting and Poetry.

Of all Browning's poems on Art, *Abt Vogler* seems to me to shine out a star of the first magnitude amongst others, less con-spicuous for their brilliancy, though scarcely less beautiful. Before holding intercourse with the old musician-priest, bathed as he still is in the golden glory which was about him like an halo in his ecstacy of extemporization, it may be helpful to us if we know something of the life and surroundings of the Abbé, who was an organist and theorist of considerable note in the closing years of the last, and the opening ones of this century. His great delight was to visit all European cities in which were to be found organs of any note, the simplification of organs and the introduction of new reeds, amounting almost to a mania with him. We are told that he was beloved by all who knew him, and that he was unsurpassed in reading at sight and accompanying, but especially was he celebrated as an extemporist. We have a charming glimpse of the Abbé in his later years in the church at Darmstadt; after Mass was concluded (one of his Tonschule pupils having acted as organist) and the church was left by all, excepting the Abbé, and one or two favourite pupils; he would propound a theme for improvisation, generally ending by playing himself—playing as he never did, except when alone with "his three dear boys" in the otherwise empty church. From the mind of at least one of these boys, the impression left by these performances was never effaced, for Weber always described them as something never to be forgotten. It is not drawing too much on the imagination to picture this scene as similar to the one on which the poem is founded.

The poem opens with the regret that "this beautiful building," the improvisation, has vanished seemingly for ever; and the musician longs that, like Solomon's enchanted palace for the delight of his Princess, it might rush into sight at will; but regret soon loses itself in artistic exultation over the "gone thing." Likening his extemporization to the palace, the Abbé compares the organ keys to a crowd of builders uniting to raise the building with rampired walls of gold, until by a great effort the "pinnacled glory reached and the pride of my soul was in sight. In sight? not half!" For the higher the inspiration, the nearer it is to heaven; and the nearer it is to heaven, the more intense is the light which reveals the imperfections of the best human endeavour; but then follows the perfect moment of artist life.

> " What never had been, was now; what was, as it shall be anon ;
>   And what is—shall I say, matched both ? For I was made perfect too."

To experience a moment such as this—one of actual participation in heaven's glory—a lifetime of toil, or even apparent failure, were well worth the living. And now the divine origin of music is claimed, and thus its unquestionable superiority over the other arts :—

> " We see that the forms are fair, we hear how the tale is told ;
> It is all triumphant art, but art in obedience to laws,
>   Painter and poet are proud, in the artist list enrolled."

> "But *here* is the finger of God, a flash of the will that can,
>   Existent behind all laws : that made them, and lo, they are !
> And I know not if, save in this, such gift be allowed to man,
>   That out of three sounds he frame, not a fourth sound, but a star."

These are wonderful words, but difficult of explanation, as I know from experience. Let us, just for a moment, consider the matter from a somewhat material point of view. Imagine, for instance, our greatest painter or poet, shipwrecked let us say, on a strange coast, and amongst people speaking an unknown tongue; what would the painter be without his colours and canvas, or the poet without the gift of tongues? But the musician—not merely a *singer*, who makes a careful study of every ballad, or fashionable song of the day, before singing it in public, but a musician—one who could sing such songs of love and longing, of home and country, of joy and sorrow that their meaning would be clear enough—this musician would be joined by others, the music of the country would be his before many days were over; given two other voices, and there would be a trio: the same with instruments. This is but a rude illustration of a great truth, but it may help to show, how three sounds, treated harmonically, form, *not a melody*, but the triad—a perfect chord. With this as with many other mysteries—" Ye have heard and seen, consider, and bow the head." Before proceeding with this interesting subject, I should like to give a quotation bearing on it from *Balaustion's Adventure*, when the reproach is brought against her that she sees too much through masks and veils, etc.

> " What's poetry except a power that makes?
> And speaking to one sense, inspires the rest,
> Pressing them all into its service; so
> That who sees painting, seems to hear as well
> The speech that's proper for the painted mouth;
> And who hears music feels his solitude
> Peopled at once—for how count heart-beats plain
> Unless a company, with hearts which beat,
> Come close to the musician, seen or no?"

Let us next observe how the composer of a great work is at once *en rapport* with musicians throughout the world; not only do they appreciate his work, but they actually take part in it. Think for an instant of Mendelssohn's *Elijah*. As soon as he had finished the score of the oratorio in the month of August, 1846, he held a rehearsal performance in Leipzig, at which the leading performers there assisted, and at once took the work into their affections. Mendelssohn then came to London, where he conducted three rehearsals; then the full rehearsal at Birmingham, followed by the eventful day itself, the 25th of August 1846, when *Elijah* was given at the Festival—a performance, which to have assisted at, would have been well worth the living for. Thus writes the composer the day following to his brother: " Had you only been there! During the whole of the two hours and a half that it lasted, the two thousand people in the large hall, and the large orchestra, were all so fully intent on the object in question, that not the slightest sound was heard amongst the whole audience, *so that I could sway at pleasure the enormous orchestra and choir.*" Thus in the space of about three weeks, thousands of musicians, or musical kindred spirits both in England and Germany, came under the almost magical personal influence of the composer ; and this is but one case out of many, for the purpose of illustration, that great musical works come within the reach and participation of all lovers of art. Not only, as is the case with painting, can they look at and rejoice in the beautiful work of the artist ; or, as with poetry, read the poem in the quiet of their homes with infinite pleasure and profit to themselves ; but in music, the performers lend themselves to the will of the composer, and borrowing a thought from *Abt Vogler*, as builders they unite to raise the glorious palace of sound—

> "Ah ! one and all, how they helped, would dispart now, and now combine,
> Zealous to hasten the work, heighten their master his praise ! "

until :—

> " The emulous heaven yearned down, made effort to reach the earth,
> As the earth had done her best, in my passion, to scale the sky."

And again—still following the train of thought suggested in *Abt Vogler* —it seems to me that in music the Spirit of God works more directly in man than in the sister arts, because more is left to actual inspiration ; of course, now I speak of composers only, as distinguished from mere performers.

In painting the artist has at first the picture before him, and what is required of him are the materials wherewith to reproduce it. *All painting begins by imitation,* the desire to reproduce ; in other words to imitate, such a landscape, such a favourite animal, such a dearly-loved face.

In poetry the language has first to be fashioned, and then the poetry at first consists in telling of what has happened in our midst ; tales of life and death, of love and heroism.

But with music it is very different. We are told, on the highest musical authority, that the most strictly correct musical intervals in nature are the most unpleasing to the ear and the least desirable to perpetuate—such as the caterwauling of cats, and even the monotonous cry of the cuckoo and coo of the wood-pigeon. Therefore man has had to stretch out his hand to attain to music, and music being of heavenly origin he has reached something from heaven

itself ; and thus it is in the intensest glow of musical ecstacy and
inspiration that heaven is opened to man.   In *Charles Avison* the
want complained of in music is, that it cannot "run mercury into a
mould like lead," "shoot liquidity into a mould," or in some way
"arrest Soul's evanescent moods."   Here speaks the cool, dis-
passionate by-stander, seeing—or at least so he thinks—wherein
music fails, and wishing for some means of arresting the "hates,
loves, joys, woes, hopes, fears of earth."   It has just occurred to me
that somewhat the same expression is used by the "Don Juan" of
Fifine at the Fair when he is comparing music to cookery, and old
tunes with modern effects to standard dishes with new
condiments :—

> "As with hates
> And loves and fears and hopes, so with what emulates
> The same, expresses hates, loves, fears and hopes in Art ;
> The forms, the themes—no one without its counterpart
> Ages ago ; no one but mumbled the due time
> I' the mouth of the eater, needs be cooked again in rhyme,
> Dished up anew in paint, sauce-smothered fresh in sound,
> To suit the wisdom-tooth, just cut, of the age."

Abt Vogler at once takes a higher stand, and would not admit
the fixing fast of evanescent moods to be the highest aim of music ;
he thinks music is imperfect until perfected by re-admission to
heaven :—

> "There shall never be one lost good ! what was, shall live as before,
> The evil is null, is nought, is silence implying sound ;
> What was good, shall be good, with, for evil, so much good more ;
> On the earth the broken arcs ; in the heaven, a perfect round."

Again to quote from *Charles Avison*—

> "To strike all this life dead,
> Run mercury into a mould like lead,
> And henceforth have the plain result to show—
> How we Feel, hard and fast as what we Know—
> This were the prize and puzzle ! which
> Music essays to solve ; and here's the hitch
> That baulks her of full triumph else to boast."

Thus speaks the critic—now for the musician, who knows :—

> "All we have willed or hoped or dreamed of good, shall exist ;
> Not its semblance, but itself ; no beauty, nor good, nor power
> Whose voice has gone forth, but each survives for the melodist,
> When eternity confirms the conception of an hour.
> The high that proved too high, the heroic for earth too hard,
> The passion that left the ground, to lose itself in the sky,
> Are music sent up to God by the lover and the bard ;
> Enough that he heard it once ; we shall hear it by-and-by."

The grandeur of this thought is almost too much for us to take in. But what an infinitely nobler inspiration, to know that our best will be taken by God Himself, and kept by Him until such time as we come for it—that the highest moment of life will be chronicled in heaven, than to hanker after saving the "hates, loves, joys, woes, hopes, fears of earth," "from chance and change we most abhor."

Looking back generally on these two poems *Charles Avison* appears to me suggestive of the man who "on glass may stay his eye," while *Abt Vogler* pleases to

> "Thro' it pass
> And then the heavens espy."

Or turning from George Herbert to Browning himself for help in explanation of this, *Charles Avison* reminds me of "the heaven that's shut" to Andrea, while *Abt Vogler* can "enter and take his place there," sure enough.

Charles Avison is speculative, almost analytical, of the earth earthy; while in *Abt Vogler* we gain admission to the Holiest of Holies. In *Charles Avison* we have the reasonings of an outsider, in *Abt Vogler* the white-heat enthusiasm of one of those favoured few "whom God whispers in the ear."

We leave *Abt Vogler*—our last glimpse of him is as he surveys the heights he recently occupied, (his Mount of Transfiguration) with the glory of heaven still about him. He feels for the common chord, slides down by semitones until he reaches the original key—

> "The C Major of this life ; so now I will try to sleep."

BROWNING'S JEWS AND SHAKESPEARE'S JEW.

By Professor BARNETT.

Read at the Fifty-fourth Meeting of the Browning Society, November 25th, 1887.

WHEN we count up the things which we expect a great poet to do, not least of them is the rendering of truths that are universal,—world-truths and not partisan-truths. Robert Browning has been praised for representing a noble Christianity which cannot be ticketed and pigeon-holed, but which is nevertheless so really catholic; the accidents of the historical faith are with him so subordinated, that many people—as for instance, I think, the distinguished founder of your society—do not like to call the religious spirit of the poet Christianity at all. But this is a small matter, after all, to quarrel about. All that would not have been without Christ, some of us will persist in calling Christian.

A great poet generalises the spirit of his time. As men read Virgil now to know the highest capabilities of the age of Augustus, its real spirit, what it hands on to posterity as its contribution to progressing civilisation ; as they read Homer to catch something of the spirit of his age of fighting heroes ; as we go to Shakespeare and the greatest of his contemporaries for knowledge of the reflection and romance of their age of restless giants ; so, I think, people will turn to Browning hereafter to find the best that could be thought in the great age in which we live. It *is* so great, surely, that we, who live in it, never perceive its greatness till we mark its high achievements in such thinkers as Browning.

It is not easy to settle to what extent a great dramatist or dramatic poet does really and truly transfer the personalities of the

age he is representing into his work. Certainly the mere use of
"properties" will not do it. An exact reproduction, in staging, of what
antiquarian investigation tells us about the age of the historical
Cæsar or the historical Macbeth helps us less to understand a bygone
race than even the fatally faultless archæology of a common "school"
of painting. Indeed, we may perhaps see reason to go further, and
say that a dramatic poet is great *in spite of* his antiquarian knowledge. It would be hard to imagine in what particular, for instance,
Shakespeare would gain by being more accurate about Macbeth and
Hamlet and the barbarous age they lived in. All, perhaps, that we
can say is that he would have moved easily in his shackles. At all
events, we have in Browning, the Shakespeare in whose time we are
lucky enough to live, a thinker hardly less in magnificent range
and depth of thought than he of the sixteenth century; and that in
spite of encyclopædic learning.

The reason sounds commonplace enough. The human soul is the
same in every age. Its passions are expended over the same objects,
—the difference lying in the varying proportions in which it applies
its strength to each severally—and, perhaps, in the reasons it gives
therefor.

It does not, after all, matter to us whether Shakespeare got his
Lear, his Macbeth, his Othello from Holinshed, Giraldo Cinthio, or
any one else. They are certainly not recognisable as archæologically
perfect reproductions, but they are as certainly human beings, and
therefore their tears are for all time. This is true, too, for much of
Browning's work. The tragedy of an Andrea del Sarto must surely
be re-enacted over and over again so long as there are souls to ruin
and such warnings are unheeded; nor is it to Abt Vogler only that
the divinest comfort is given. But then it must be confessed that
Browning has, besides these everlasting truths of human nature, fixed
and painted for us more successfully than any poet or maker
has ever done the very people as they lived and moved, not dressed
up lay-figures, but themselves. Browning has lived after and in an
age of (to use a cant term) criticism. But that has only failed to limit
his scope. Better; he has lived the lives of these people, and he can
think as they thought; not as they only, but (and here is the point)
as all the del Sartos and Abt Voglers of all time.

It is not without significance that these two greatest dramatic
poets, Shakespeare and Browning, should have applied themselves to
the peculiarly interesting problem of the Jewish consciousness, the
Jew himself, so to speak. The problem, to begin with, has a special
attractiveness. Here you have a national or at least tribal feeling

maintained in the midst of very hostile surroundings, with merely a *nominal* local centre; resting entirely on the strength of isolated tradition; a people of peculiarly clean and healthy life, yet living, as it seems, *on* and not *in* its environing society.

If we consider shortly the differing ways in which the problem presents itself to Shakespeare and Browning respectively, we shall have a very instructive and notable contrast between not only them, but also the spirits of their respective ages.

We have for comparison Shakespeare's *Merchant of Venice* and Browning's *Filippo Baldinucci* and *Holy Cross Day. Jochanan Hakkadosh, Rabbi Ben Ezra,* and *Saul* do not enter into the field of observation. These last deal with a consciousness far transcending the mere national and personal feeling of *Filippo Baldinucci* and *Holy Cross Day;* there is nothing, I mean, peculiarly Jewish in them, although, to be sure, the high compliment paid to the Jewish race and history by Mr. Browning's so entitling his noble poems could not have been quite fortuitous. But *Filippo Baldinucci* and *Holy Cross Day* are meant to deal with real persons, at definite times, in definite places. They have a story, a whole and complete πρᾶξις, just as Shylock has. The works of art to which Browning has given their names are histories not merely concerning souls, but concerning the Jewish soul at particular crises.

In this respect, again, Shylock stands very much apart from other creations of Shakespeare, except those, of course, that come from his hand in his treatment of national history. There is nothing particularly British about Lear or Scotch about Macbeth or Danish about Hamlet. Theirs, again, are histories concerning the human soul, quite apart from racial or national qualifications; more particular, to be sure, less transcendent, than *Rabbi Ben Ezra* and *Saul* and *Rabbi Jochanan,* but clearly of the same description, general.

Both Shakespeare and Browning apply themselves to the Jewish problem as it presents itself at a special period, not the "Middle Ages" as they are called, but (the difference is important) when Christianity was becoming more self-conscious, less brutal, more Christian; and when, therefore, Christians may be supposed to have been becoming uneasy, and, reforming themselves, to have been, naturally perhaps, a little anxious to find excuses for a few of the pleasant sins they had a mind to. The persecution of heretics is a very fascinating exercise, for the reason that we are less hard on our own offences if we persist in contemplating and exaggerating, and can punish, the sins of others.

The historical synchronism is, then, the first point common to the two poets; and of course there are subordinate details of correspondence arising from this primary point. The fact of persecution is put by both poets with perfect honesty. Filippo Baldinucci is, of course, entirely frank about it; he is nothing if not frank:

> " We Christians never dreamed of scathe
> Because we cursed or kicked the crew."

Antonio in the *Merchant of Venice* was, according to Bassanio,

> " The kindest man,
> The best-conditioned and unwearied spirit
> In doing courtesies."

Yet, he did not merely laugh at Shylock's losses and mock at his gains—which was pardonable, I daresay—but, he scorned his nation, thwarted his bargains, cooled his friends, heated his enemies; to him Shylock is no better than the devil quoting Scripture:

> " An evil soul producing holy witness
> Is like a villain with a smiling cheek,
> A goodly apple rotten at the core."

Antonio is told, and he makes no denial (and Shylock is at least no liar),

> "Signior Antonio, many a time and oft
> In the Rialto you have rated me
> About my moneys and my usancies; . . .
> You call me misbeliever, cut-throat dog,
> And spit upon my Jewish gaberdine. . . ."

A " well-conditioned " gentleman could not do this; it would be impossible to associate such gross discourtesies with (say) Sir Thomas More or Lord Chancellor Bacon. But an ill-conditioned, splenetic, dyspeptic, and melancholy person might well be so guilty; in which light there is very little that is inexplicable in Antonio's melancholy. Still, the fact remains, a man who passed for a gentleman with his contemporaries behaved to a Jew in a way that would be nowadays considered ill-bred in Whitechapel or the Seven Dials; and his contemporaries thought him " well-conditioned." Clearly then public opinion was at the back of such insults. Buti or his farmer could be

> " Firm with *Florence at his back.*"

The testimony of Holy Cross Day is quite as strong.

> " It got to a pitch, when the hand indeed
> Which gutted my purse, would throttle my creed."

In both poets the persecutors show a strong desire to "convert." First, observe, it is necessary to "gut" the purse and then—"convert." So Antonio—

> " I am content so he will let me have
> The other half in use, to render it
> Upon his death unto the gentleman
> That lately *stole his daughter ;*
> Two things provided more, that, for this favour,
> He *presently become a Christian. . . .*"

Of course the "conversion" must mean very little. Filippo Baldinucci, Buti, and his farmer, Antonio and the Bishop himself, had small acquaintance with Christ, whatever they had with " Christianity."

I should like to extract a quotation made by Mr. Beeching in his admirable edition of the *Merchant of Venice* on this point. [I think by the way that Mr. Beeching has quite misread Antonio and Shylock too; and he certainly does not make out his case for the one or against the other.] He quotes from Corcoryat's *Crudities*—

" Pitiful it is to see that few of them (the Jews) living in Italy are converted to the Christian religion. For this I understand is the maine impediment to their conversion. All their goodes are confiscated as soon as they embrace Christianity ; and this I heard is the reason, because whereas many of them doe raise their fortunes by usury, in so much that they doe sometimes not only sheare but also flea many a poore Christian's estate by their griping extortion ; it is therefore decreed by the Pope and other free Princes in whose territories they live, that they shall make a restitution of all their ill-gotten goods, and so disclogge their soules and consciences when they are admitted by holy baptism into the bosom of Christ's Church."

The methods were severe indeed.   The holy work

> " Began, when a herd of us, picked and placed,
> Were spurred through the Corso, stripped to the waist ;
> Jew brutes, with sweat and blood well spent
> To usher in worthily Christian Lent.

> " It grew when the hangman entered our bounds,
> Yelled, pricked us out to his church like hounds ;
> It got to a pitch, when the hand indeed
> Which gutted my purse, would throttle my creed ;
> And it overflows when, to even the odd,
> Men I helped to their sins, help me to their God."

The farmer's method was more roguish than cruel, but the lives led by Jews in Florence must have been hard :

> " How Hebrews toil
> Through life in Florence, why relate
> To those who lay the burden, spoil
> Our paths of peace ? We bear our fate.
> But when with life the long toil ends,
> Why must you—the expression craves
> Pardon, but truth compels me, friends !—
> Why must you plague us in our graves ?"

At least, these were " harsh deed," " unkindly word," " frowning brow," and " scornful lip."   And Venice was not far from Florence.

Both poets agree in making their Jews usurers.   That is accurate enough, no doubt.   Venice and Florence had the Jews they deserved. The Rabbi's son in *Filippo Baldinucci* says,

> " For, don't I see,—let's issue join !
> Whenever I'm allowed pollute
> (I—and *my little bag of coin*)
> Some Christian palace of repute. . . ."

And in *Holy Cross Day*—

> " *Whom now is the bishop a-leering at ?*
> I know a point where his text falls pat.
> I'll tell him to-morrow, a word just now
> Went to my heart and made me vow
> To meddle no more with the worst of trades ;
> Let somebody else pay his serenades."

And Browning, at least, as we read, pours scorn on the vileness of those who used their Jews for vile purposes, and then—affect to pay them with—God.   The persecutors are pagans of the least pleasant type.

> " ' Jew, since it must be, take in pledge
> Of payment '—so a cardinal
> Has sighed to me as if a wedge
> Entered his heart—' this best of all
> My treasures ! ' Leda, Ganymede,
> Or Antiope : swan, eagle, ape,
> (Or what's the beast of what's the breed ?)
> And Jupiter in every shape."

Shakespeare and Browning both, Browning not more frankly than Shakespeare, admit the strength of kin-affection of their Jews. Shylock's turquoise, we remember, was very dear to Shylock ; and his daughter, graceless, and light of character and finger as she was, was his daughter, and at least as dear to him as his ducats ; and according to Shakespeare that was very much.

It is very remarkable that both poets allow the high general morality of the Jews.   Shakespeare's Shylock is no such monster as Marlowe's Jew of Malta.   And Filippo Baldinucci reports without any denial of the statements made, the plea of the Jew that the " sacred " picture overlooking the burial ground should be turned to the Christian high-way, if only in that highway's behoof :

> " Removal, not destruction, sirs !
>   Just turn your picture ! Let it front
> The public path ! Or memory errs,
>   Or that same public path is wont
> To witness many a chance befall
>   Of lust, theft, bloodshed—sins enough
> *Wherein our Hebrew part is small—*
>   Convert yourselves ! . . ."

It is possible, I suppose, to refer this notable purity of morals in large measure to the isolation in which the Jews lived. To be sure isolation does not always produce such results ; but the isolation in this case is peculiar. It is not local isolation ; the people lived in the midst of an actively criticising society—and sometimes more than criticising ;— a high standard of tribal respectability had to be kept up ; and always has been. Such isolation certainly strengthened all natural domestic affection. Shylock himself is eloquent on this ; the incident of the Jewish son's mission in *Filippo Baldinucci* is only one instance of Browning's sense of it. Shakespeare has a very significant indication of the nature of current Christian morality. When Jessica breaks at least two commandments in her effected plan :

> " I will make fast the doors, and gild myself
> With some more ducats, and be with you straight,—"

Gratiano, (a kind of chorus, be it observed) exclaims,

> " Now, by my hood, *a Gentile and no Jew !* "

Both poets recognize the complexity of Christian motive. It would be ridiculous to deny that the desire to uproot heresy is often based on a real zeal for truth. Shakespeare, although the " conversion " of Shylock is only another part of his punishment, is really angered at the misuse of money of which Shylock is supposed to have been guilty, and his main sympathies are quite certainly *not* with the professional money-lender, though he could lend money himself, and was clearly a good man of business. But Shakespeare did not trouble himself about what we call " faith," and very probably thought with the old Baldinucci that faith meant liberty to " curse and kick the crew," and with the younger, that the same faith was made manifest by pelting them with stones. It was chiefly the irony of the social situation that struck Shakespeare ; naturally. His Christians are

s 2

mostly, in this play, contemptible enough, the best of them Bassanio, with his adventuring, and Antonio with his recklessness and dyspepsia.

The Jews are made patient and courteous in both Shakespeare and Browning. Shakespeare records his impressions; Browning has gone further. He gives us a reason. He has penetrated the national consciousness in a way that could, of course, be no part of Shakespeare's purpose. For this point, the chief poem is *Holy Cross Day*. The difference between Browning and Shakespeare in this respect is really one of the main differences between them; and it is the difference of their times. Browning is a religious and Christian poet rather than a romantic one; a preacher, not a playwright. A great majority of his greatest studies deal with Christianity, either directly, or, as in the poems under special consideration now, indirectly, through some story, "telling a truth obliquely." He has set himself to examine the "Christian" spirit at various times, and a great deal of his work in casuistry, so to speak, is bent on stating the complicated problems of life as they appear to the Blougrams from within or the Cleons from without. Certainly Christianity means something more to him than it does to those who can view it only in relation to the circumstances of their little day. It is clearly to him a Spirit and not a System. It is because of this, in virtue of it, that he has gone so far to divest Judaism also, as it is called, of its accidental characteristics.

Browning, like Shakespeare, is often commended for his accuracy in small matters. There is however no very strong evidence in his work that he has in matters Jewish anything like his knowledge in other matters. I must confess his Jewish "antiquities" sometimes seem to me peculiar. I should, for instance, like to know his authority for making a cemetery-chapel, or mortuary, into a synagogue. As a matter of fact, such a thing is nearly impossible. Where the dead lie is unclean; and the burial places of all orientals are away from the buildings they hold sacred. The same consideration makes the pound of flesh story ten times improbable. The touch of a dead body was in the highest degree unclean. And again, Browning makes his Jews in *Filippo Baldinucci* go on a *Sabbath* morning to bury their dead—again a thing quite impossible. That would have been a gross and unheard-of pollution of the most sacred of days. Such criticism, it may be said, is absurdly small. But I mention it really to prove Browning's claim to a much higher gift than exact antiquarian knowledge. With slips like these, quite patent and simple, he has still penetrated the national consciousness; so little do

externals matter.   There is hardly any parallel between Browning
and Shakespeare in this respect; Shakespeare never addressed
himself, as I have said, to a precisely similar task.

Holy Cross Day professes to give some explanation of the self-
respecting pride of the Jews in the face of all they were suffering, and
had suffered, and were still to suffer.   Whatever their active faith
may be now, there is no doubt that they were, in the days of Filippo
and Buti, Barnabas, Job, and Solomon, raised far and away above
their vulgar semi-pagan persecutors by the consciousness of being
reserved for greater things.   We are too much inclined to judge the
Jew of those days by the poor creatures who take refuge in the
purlieus of London from the barbarous miseries of Russia and Poland
and Germany.   In the sixteenth and seventeenth centuries European
Jews seem to have been generally well-bred and prosperous.   Shakespeare and Browning do not contradict tradition.   Nothing could be
finer in its loftiness and patient dignity than the first address of the
"posse" of Florentine Jews to Buti and the farmer—

XIII.

"Friends, grant a grace!   How Hebrews toil
    Through life in Florence—why relate
To those who lay the burden, spoil
    Our paths of peace !   We bear our fate.
But when with life the long toil ends,
    Why must you—the expression craves
Pardon, but truth compels me, friends !—
    Why must you plague us in our graves ?

XIV.

"Thoughtlessly plague, I would believe !
    For how can you—the lords of ease
By nurture, birthright,—e'en conceive
    Our luxury to lie with trees
And turf,—the cricket and the bird
    Left for our last companionship :
No harsh deed, no unkindly word,
    No frowning brow, nor scornful lip !

XV.

"Death's luxury we now rehearse
    While, living, through your streets we fare
And take your hatred : nothing worse
    Have we, once dead and safe, to bear !
So we refresh our souls, fulfil
    Our works, our daily tasks ; and thus
Gather you grain—earth's harvest ;—still
    The wheat for you, the straw for us.

XVI.

"'What flouting in a face, what harm
  In just a lady borne from bier
By boy's heads, wings for leg and arm?'
  You question.   Friends, the harm is here—
That just when our last sigh is heard,
  And we would fain thank God and you
For labour done and peace achieved,
  Back comes the Past in full review!

XVII.

"At sight of just that simple flag,
  Starts the foe-feeling serpent-like
From slumber.   Leave it lulled, nor drag—
  Though fangless—forth, what needs must strike
When stricken sore, though stroke be vain
  Against the mailed oppressor!   Give
Play to our fancy that we gain
  Life's rights when once we cease to live!"

So much the speaker addresses to the gentle feelings of his
Christian oppressors.   Then he caps it with a bribe, which very
naturally brings to utterance his hate and contempt for Christian
hypocrisy.   "Convert yourselves"—and no doubt, "he cut up
rough."

The conversation after the second insult is remarkable.   Five
lines are enough :

" The Farmer has the best ; he rates
  The rascal, as the old High Priest
Takes on himself to sermonize—
  Nay, sneer, 'We Jews supposed, at least,
Theft was a crime in Christian eyes!'"

The   Farmer   is   discourteous   all   through,   the   High   Priest
"sermonizes" at first ; no doubt, gently and loftily asserts bare
demands with appeal to courtesy and honour.   This is just what
the Farmer would call sermonizing.   But, again, the hardness and
hypocrisy of his Christians goad him to a passionate taunt—

" We Jews supposed, at least,
  Theft was a crime in Christian eyes."

The bearing of the High Priest's son in his mission to Buti is
perfect.   It is worth while noting that for this incident Mr. Browning.
is indebted to his own invention, and shows thereby, if any showing

were needed, whom he thought nobly of. Certainly not the shallow, cowardly Gentile, from whom the apparition of

> " A six-feet-high herculean-built
> Young he-Jew with a beard, that baulks
> Description,"

wrings a sudden cry for help, and makes him try " to smuggle out of sight the picture's self." He begins calmly, with great bitterness, but with much self-control, when suddenly he becomes furious and murderous. Why? Because the Farmer suggested that he had risen to—the height—of conversion to Christianity. To the Jew this must have been, as Browning feels, a real insult. He felt himself already leagues above a "Christianity," as it called itself, to which so plain a matter as theft was no crime.

The old Rabbi had begged, at the first, that there should be peace for the highest conceivable reason. He would, he and his people would, fain thank God for labour and peace; but just when God's peace seems to be theirs,—back comes the Past. The feeling of hatred, impossible to real Christianity, is quickened again—

> " Starts the foe-feeling serpent-like
> From slumber."

It was not with Christ or Mary that the Jews had a quarrel. Baldinucci speaks from his own imbecile little soul when he supposes that even Jews contemporary with him would reserve a place in their hierarchy of saints for Pilate.

The sense of watching and waiting for a Messiah lent to the Jews a dignity which such sorry fellows as the Farmer and Buti and the bishop in *Holy Cross Day* could not possibly understand. They could declare with R. ben Ezra that they were

> " At watch and ward,
> Till *Christ* in the end relieves our guard.
> By His servant Moses the watch was set :
> Though near upon cock-crow, we keep it yet."

How much the bishop and his fellows " believed " in the coming of Christ the poem I quote from shows. The Jews felt truly.

> " In one point only we sinned, at worst."

They look around them and see a degraded society :

> " Dogs and swine
> Whose life laughs through and spits at their creed,
> Who maintain thee in word, and defy thee in deed."

What could they possibly think? It may have been, they thought, that they had given the Cross to Him to whom the Throne was due. But they appeal to divine justice :

> "Thou art the Judge. We are bruised thus.
> But, the judgment over, join sides with us !
> Thine too is the cause !   .   .   .   .
>
> We withstood Christ then? Be mindful how
> At least we withstand Barabbas now !
> Was our outrage sore ? But the worst we spared,
> To have called these——Christians, had we dared !
> Let defiance to them pay mistrust of thee
> And Rome make amends for Calvary."

Of all the gross insults and cruelties the worst was what ?

> "The summons to Christian fellowship !   .   .   .   ."
>
> " We boast our proof that at least the Jew
> Would wrest Christ's name from the Devil's crew,
> Thy face look never so deep a shade,
> But we fought them in it, God our aid ! "

The current morality of Christianity—at least in high places—is never spared Browning's scathing condemnation. What the thick-headed Baldinucci says in stanza xxvii is significant enough of current sacerdotal morality amongst Christians :

> " They'd say their prayers and sing their hymns
> As if her husband were the Pope."

And the leering bishop in *Holy Cross Day* is unpleasant enough to think of.

To the Jews of Baldinucci's youth what else could the " religion " called " Christianity " appear but an only half-systematized hypoc-risy ? In both the poems I have quoted this feeling is very prominent. The quarrel of the Jews was not with Christ or Mary ; they quarrelled with the whole spirit of papal religion. It must never be forgotten that the very " faith " was only half held by its professors. At the best, these people worshipped, if anything, a meretricious art, or at all events, an art that lent itself with astounding readiness to mere-tricious uses. The Rabbi's son finds " sacred " pictures cheek by jowl with pictures of beast-gods—

> " How comes it these false godships frisk
> In presence of—what yonder frame
> Pretends to image ? Surely, odd
> It seems, you let confront The Name
> Each beast the heathen called his god ! "

And now note the Cardinal's reply. "You and I have different opinions of what is 'Truth.' Certainly it is no particular view of past events. To us"—this is what the assertion comes to—"all the canvases convey some truth. Anyhow, now that Christ is undoubtedly born, why should we fear to parade these things that can do us no harm?" Yet they were pictures of the very grossest incidents of heathen mythology.

> " 'Tis truth, we prize!
> Art's the sole question in debate!
> These subjects are so many lies.
> We treat them with a proper scorn
> When we turn lies—called gods forsooth—
> To lies' fit use, now Christ is born.
> Drawing and colouring are Truth.
>
> Think you I honour lies so much
> As scruple to parade the charms
> Of Leda—Titian every touch—
> Because the thing within her arms
> Means Jupiter, who had the praise
> And prayer of a benighted world!
> Benighted I, too, if, in days
> Of light, I kept the canvas furled! "

We cannot affect to think ill of Greeks and Romans because the incidents of their mythologies were sometimes repulsive. But the case is different with the self-conscious and reflective sensuality of the sixteenth and seventeenth centuries. The inventions and imaginations of early civilization are the faults, sometimes, of reckless and mischievous children who cannot keep their hands off things or keep things out of their heads, for very marvelling. But the profligate Bishop or Pope was one of those who were curious and filthy in spite of shame and knowledge. So Art, through which God uses us to help each other, was cursed and perverted to the destruction of church and churchmen by the churchmen themselves.

There is, of course, another side to this, besides the sinister one suggested by the Cardinal, and that is, that to the greatest spirits of the Renaissance the traditions of Greek and Roman and Hebrew were *all* true in a peculiar sense and *all at the same time*. They half believed in their Ledas and Ganymedes and Jupiters; the lives lived around them, if not their own, showed it. But they *also* believed in Christ and Calvary, and therefore they were not averse to painting themselves and their contemporaries at the foot of the Cross.

Now the Jews could never see things in this light. They were obstinate, undoubtedly, and they had never allowed their definite convictions and traditions to be sapped by imaginative art. Their interpretation of tradition, therefore, was not artistic; it was literal. So, although they saw, perhaps, only one side of the universe, they saw *it* persistently and really believed in what they saw. Moses and Aaron and David and the rest of them were all the more real because the Jews had never seen differing representations of them in art. They had all the realness of abstraction. There is nothing like Art for destroying religions that depend on this or that attitude towards historical facts. Hell cannot be believed in after it has been painted. It is outside the regions of "fact" that religions are strong; and rightly. And that is why the Jews never could understand the impartiality of people like the Cardinal of *Filippo Baldinucci* and the Bishop of *Holy Cross Day*, whose practices and lives seemed so much at variance with the purity of which they were the official representatives. Of course the impartiality seemed to them to be hypocrisy.

Once more and lastly. In the incompleteness and perpetual hope of the Jews, Mr. Browning sees some feeling akin to that which inspires so much of his own philosophy,—the brokenness of good here, and the promise of the perfection and completion of it in some future, whether Messianic or not. The Jews lived in Life and not Art. They could find no such complete satisfaction in Art as their Gentile contemporaries. So they declared themselves

> "At watch and ward
> Till Christ at the end relieve our guard."

That was Life.

ABT VOGLER, THE MAN.

By HELEN J. ORMEROD.

Read at the Fifty-fifth Meeting of the Browning Society, January 27th, 1888.

IT is impossible to attempt, in this paper, to do more than give a sketch of the career of Abt Vogler, this sketch being taken from the more finished work by Dr. Karl Emil von Schafhäutl: *Abt Georg Joseph Vogler : Sein Leben, Charakter, und Musikalisher System,* &c., with occasional assistance from the masterly article on Vogler which appears in Sir G. Grove's *Dictionary of Music and Musicians,* by the Rev. J. H. Mee, Mus. Bac., with regard to which Dr. von Schafhäutl thus comments—"It is worthy of notice that the most reliable biography of Vogler is from the pen of an Englishman." I must also gratefully tender my thanks to Mr. T. Craddock, Mus. Bac., for much kind explanatory help in technical mysteries, which have been rendered clearer to me by his practical demonstrations on the fine organ in Upton Church, Torquay ; also to Dr. Furnivall, for his loan of valuable and interesting editions and MSS. of Abt Vogler's music and theoretical writings.

That Abt Vogler wrote sundry operas, masses, and other musical works, which one hears spoken of but never performed ; that he died at Darmstadt beloved by his pupils, and honourably and lovingly mentioned by his two famous pupils, Carl Maria von Weber and Meyerbeer ; and that he is immortalised by Browning as having extemporised on an instrument of his own invention—this is known to most of us ; and these facts as to the career of the remarkable man seem to have sufficed for most people and many musicians, though our "Papers" have already given us somewhat more.

In thinking of Abt Vogler however in connection with the Browning Society, it is difficult to imagine any form more definite than that of the somewhat idealised figure of the musician priest seen through the softening haze of years, as he is represented to us in Browning's magnificent poem. And at first it seems to border almost on the profane to bring the dream of heaven down to the level of every-day existence. Yet sudden as the change is, from wandering in the heavenly realms of music to the "C major of this life," this view of the poem and life is not without its charm also. In spite of the countless anxieties and disappointments which beset the artistic career, moments of rapture and inspiration such as those described in the poem, are vouchsafed to those favoured few whom "God whispers in the ear." It is my wish now to bring before you a sketch of the enthusiastic musician, the earnest priest, and (using the expression in a higher sense than that in which it is generally used) the cultivated man of the world.

That a more definite position in musical history has not from the first been accorded to this remarkable man, is due to various reasons —chief among them being the more than ordinary jealousy and suspicion roused amongst contemporary musicians, caused on the one hand by the social and literary advantages which, at that time, resulted from Vogler's superior education as a priest; and on the other hand, by his bold enterprise in attacking existing codes of harmony and methods of organ-building. Another probable cause of his uncertain position until lately is accounted for by his wandering life, as at no time was he settled in one place, or even country, for any considerable length of time. Dr. von Schafhäutl has undertaken the vindication of his hero's fame with all the ardour of an enthusiast, and in his preface he thus expresses himself : " No eye-and ear-witnesses now survive to testify to the efficiency of Vogler's life-work and teaching : and in our histories of music he is represented to the public almost as a caricature, growing ever more and more indistinct through the veil of tradition. Therefore I, born in 1803, have taken up the study of Vogler's teachings and work with all the ardour of youth. I have studied and analysed his writings, both practical and theoretical, in order that in this book I may preserve the fame of this highly gifted man, that he may occupy in history the place due to him."

That Dr. von Schafhäutl speaks with authority as a biographer, may be gathered from his opening sentences : " I have accompanied Abt Vogler, who has been so misrepresented by biographers, all my life, and followed the highly gifted man both in his teachings and his work : I have mixed with his best friends and admirers in Munich (where he had only one enemy, and he was an organ-builder), and therefore I believe myself to be more intimately acquainted with the

Abbé than any of my contemporaries, and that I have gained the
right to speak a word with authority, accurately founded on historical
facts, as to the literary but misunderstood genius."

Though it may be impossible to agree with the author in every
point, we cannot but admire the zeal with which he has thrown
himself into the cause. It may be advisable at the outset to refer to
the remark that the title Abbé or Abt was a complimentary one, as
some writers have doubted Vogler's right to assume it. As a complimentary title it does not betoken the head of a monastery, for in
France and Italy all eminent ecclesiastics who held no settled appointment were greeted as Abbé—the word being identical with the
Chaldean Abba, and simply signifying "Father," as in Latin the
word "Pater" is used.

Georg Joseph Vogler, commonly known as Abt Vogler, was born
at Pleicchart, a suburb of Würzburg, on the 15th June, 1749, and
was the youngest of nine children, of whom only three survived.
His father was a court musician, also court violin-maker, at Würzburg. He died at Darmstadt on the 6th of May, 1814, loaded with
honours, both musical and papal, from Rome, Sweden, Bavaria, Paris,
London, &c.

The young Vogler gave early evidence of various characteristics
which distinguished him throughout his life, and are thus described :
"An earnest piety, a wonderful memory, and an equally wonderful
gift for languages." "An untiring energy, and above all an indomit-
able industry and a mighty ambition, which ever urged him on
to be first and best." He passed through the Jesuit Gymnasium
and Lyceum at Würzburg as a matter of convenience, but he was no
Jesuit, neither was he brought up as one. Vogler soon gave promise
of his musical career, thus fulfilling the vocation of his family. He
was a good pianist, and an extraordinary organist, even in his youth.
The Prince Bishop of Würzburg prided himself on his fine choir ;
but the cynosure of all Kapelles in the world was the Mannheim
Court Kapelle. Vogler was fortunate in his testimonials, and the
Elector of the Palatinate gave him a kind reception, and commissioned
him to write a ballet for the Court Theatre. Karl Theodor, then
Elector, was the most cultivated prince of his time, and a man of art
and letters, and he welcomed Vogler even more warmly as a musician
than a theologian. Everything in connection with his court was of the
best, except the opera, and this he determined to remedy by inviting
Vogler to his court. This was an important moment in Vogler's life,
as he was on the point of entering the Franciscan monastery at
Würzburg when he received the appointment of almoner to the Elector.

After a time of doubt and hesitation he accepted the post. Mozart remarks of him that "he came to Mannheim in a miserable state," and "that compassion was shown him;" but this remark is untrue, for his family was anything but poor. His fame as a musician soon spread ; and Bernhard Anselm Weber, at the age of seven, was placed under his tuition. All the time the desire increased within him for a guide to the secrets of harmony, and Italy became the dream of his soul. Thither he was allowed to go by his patron in 1773, first studying under Martini at Bologna, and then under Vallotti at Padua, distracting both teachers by his perplexing questions, leaving Martini when only through the half-course, and causing Vallotti to exclaim in desperation—" He would learn in fifty minutes what it has taken me fifty years to learn !" Vallotti was however delighted with his mathematical exactitude, never having taken a pupil before, because of their deficiency in knowledge of mathematics. When visiting in Venice, Vogler was a welcome guest at the house of the musician Hasse, then seventy-five years old : not only was he a favourite with Hasse himself, but with the great Faustina, a former queen of song.

He was ordained a priest in Rome ; and in 1774 the Elector visited Rome, and was gratified to find that his *protégé* had made a name in the musical world there. Vogler returned to Mannheim towards the close of 1775. There he was appointed Court Chaplain and *vice-Kapellmeister*. Mozart hints that these appointments fell to his lot because of certain ladies at the court; but with his credentials and testimonials from Italy, both as priest and musician, there seemed no need to rely on feminine influence. There was undoubtedly some ill feeling on Mozart's part towards Vogler, and this is rather pointedly touched on (and perhaps only naturally) by Dr. von Schafhäutl. Nevertheless, to Mozart must be accorded the higher place as a musician. Time alone decides as to whether gold, silver, precious stones, wood, hay, or stubble be built on the foundation of music.

At Mannheim, Vogler founded the first of his three schools of music, the second being at Stockholm, and the third at Darmstadt. As a result of this enterprise, he published his first theoretical work in 1776—*Tonwissenschaft und Tonsetzkunst*. He also edited a monthly periodical, which was carried on for three years—*Betrachtungen der Mannheimer Tonschule*. In 1778 the Elector removed his court to Munich, having become Elector of Bavaria. Vogler however remained faithful to his Mannheim school, and probably did not go to Munich till 1780. While at Mannheim, he wrote several important works, including a *Miserere*, about which and its composer, Mozart expresses himself rather strongly in a letter dated November 22nd, 1777, which letter, it must be confessed, is suggestive of spite and personal ill feeling on the part of Mozart, and is incorrect in statement. That these opinions were not shared by other musicians, including even Beethoven himself, we shall presently have occasion to notice.

In December, 1780, Vogler visited Paris, and found there two distinct musical parties, Louis XVI. being the leader of the followers of Piccini, and Marie-Antoinette remaining faithful to Gluck. Vogler was presented to the Queen, who was charmed with his playing, and constituted herself his patroness, frequently sending a carriage to convey him to Versailles, accepting also the dedication of two of his popular compositions. It was at this time that Vogler gave two organ recitals on the then famous organ of St. Sulpice, and as usual excited admiration and wonder at his capacity for arranging the stops. At that time the art of song was scarcely understood by the French (Mozart also having unfavourably commented on the French song-stresses). Vogler despaired of giving an opera, having lost his temper at a rehearsal, and therefore being unpopular with chorus and soloists. The Queen however came to his assistance, and his opera was performed at Versailles with *éclat* under the title of *La Patriotisme*.

From Paris, Vogler proceeded to England, and expounded to the Royal Society his system, with illustrations on his *Tonmaass*. Sir Joseph Banks, President of the Royal Society, expressed to him in appreciative terms the acquiescence of the Society in his system. In 1784, Vogler was appointed chief *Kapellmeister* at Munich by the Elector, and received a commission to write an opera for the carnival in 1786. He chose the subject of *Castor and Pollux*, and, as has been remarked, had full scope for the exercise of creative musical faculty, the scenes being laid " in Sparta, and in the realms of heaven and hell " ! The overture to this opera was one of Vogler's finest compositions. Schumann remarks of it—" It seems to me as if Vogler's contemporaries had not sufficiently appreciated him." After the first production of this opera, however, military rather than musical matters became uppermost in Munich, chiefly through the presence of the famous Benjamin Thompson ; and so Vogler left Munich to travel. In 1784 he went (as we saw) from Paris to London. In May he gave a concert at Lübeck ; on the 30th of May we hear of him at Berlin ; in October, 1785, at Düsseldorf, where we find him placing his pianoforte before the most celebrated pictures in the gallery there, and striving to express in music the emotions caused by the contemplation of them. In November he was in Amsterdam, where he gave an

organ recital, for which 7,000 tickets were sold.   At this time
Gustavus III. of Sweden invited him to his court as *Kapellmeister*,
and music-master for the Crown-Princess.   The Swedish king, himself
a poet, was anxious to advance the cause of art, and especially of
music, in his kingdom.   He received Vogler in 1786 with much
kindness, and told him he considered it an honour to have him in his
service.   Vogler received 2,000 *rix thalers* a year, besides fodder for
two horses, and leave of absence for six out of the twelve months of
each year.   He was pledged to remain for ten years under these
conditions, at the expiration of which time he would be entitled to a
pension of 500 *rix thalers*.   The appointment of the Catholic priest
was looked on with suspicion by the Protestant court, but Vogler
did not care.   He established at Stockholm a music school, and
a school for singing.   He was the first *Kapellmeister* to produce
one of Gluck's operas in its entirety in the Stockholm theatre.   He
utilised every day of his six months' leave.   In 1788 we find him,
accompanied by one of his nephews, journeying to Russia, playing
before the emperor, receiving from him a jewelled golden snuff-box,
and visiting the chief organ-builders, Kirsnik amongst others, who
had already been experimenting on organ-pipes.   Vogler had now
found a kindred spirit; and he engaged the Swedish organ-builder
Racknitz, who had worked under Kirsnik, to carry out his plans for
his portable organ, his "orchestrion."   It had been Vogler's lifelong
endeavour to invent a portable organ on which to perform at his
recitals, and now his efforts were to meet with success.   He had the
instrument for which he had longed, "the instrument of his own
invention" of which Browning speaks, and the plan of it led him to
form schemes for the remodelling and simplification of existing organs.
In the year 1790 Vogler visited England again, and won laurels as
an organist; but an event occurred which called him to Darmstadt.
Louis IX., the Landgrave of Hesse, having died, was about to be
succeeded by his son, and Vogler's patron, Louis X.

Vogler's journey to Darmstadt was a series of triumphs, and in
October we hear of his being present at the coronation of Leopold II.
at Frankfort, and in November giving concerts in Holland on his
orchestrion.   When at Hamburg in 1792 he received the news of the
murder of his royal friend and patron, Gustavus III.   This so em-
bittered his stay there, that at the invitation of the Portuguese Queen
he embarked for Lisbon.   Finding the Queen however too ill to receive
him, he proceeded to Cadiz, and thence to North Africa, India, and
Greece, attracted thither by his desire to study original, national
melodies.   He occupied himself on his return at the end of 1793, in

Stockholm, by weaving these ancient melodies into a work he called *Polymelos*. In 1796 he journeyed to Paris, after following each incident of the French Revolution with the deepest interest and concern, grieving over the degradation and terrible fate of the royal family, and rejoicing over the fall of Robespierre. He made this visit with a view to study the national songs of the Revolution. In 1796 his ten years' engagement at Stockholm came to an end. In 1797 Vogler received a letter inviting him to return to Würzburg, his native place, which was the desire of his heart. His letter, in reply, is too interesting not to be noticed, though too long to quote in full. After dwelling on the advantages of his engagement at the Swedish court, and alluding to the fact that with any superfluous means he possessed and earned he relieved the poor, and helped to support members of his own and his step-father's family, he tells with justifiable pride of his instrument the orchestrion, and thanks God that both bodily and mentally he feels stronger at forty-nine than at twenty-nine years of age. He then relates how, when he came to Sweden, he was not unmindful of his calling as a priest, but said he ventured to speak of himself almost as a missionary in Norway, holding services in out-of-the-way places, and attending to the interests of his church in Sweden. He also visited the persecuted Catholics under the Turks, and adds how he acted as confessor to 1,500 persons in five months, the confessions being made in twelve different languages. This is of special interest, because of the doubts raised as to the genuineness of his priesthood.

Unfortunately his settlement at Würzburg was rendered impossible by pecuniary difficulties resulting from the late war and military preparations for the future. Therefore Vogler acceded to the strongly expressed wishes of the Duke-regent and Crown-prince of Sweden, and did not leave Stockholm until 1798. He altered the cathedral organ at Stockholm; and at this time it is mentioned that he had given upwards of a thousand organ concerts. It seems but natural that at the age of fifty-two he began to think of rest. He journeyed again to his native country and received an invitation to visit Vienna, where a brilliant era in musical history was almost over. Haydn was now seventy-one years old; Salieri, though only fifty-three, was exhausted alike in mind and body; and the musical society invited Vogler to come and personally conduct one of his own works. He arrived at Vienna in 1803, and was received with great enthusiasm. He gave his opera *Castor and Pollux* before a delighted audience, and shortly celebrated the thirtieth anniversary of his priesthood in the church of St. Peter's by a celebration, at which his D Minor Mass was performed.

T

It was during the autumn of 1803 that Carl Maria von Weber, then a youth of seventeen, was placed under Vogler's tuition. In Sir Julius Benedict's *Life of Weber* he thus speaks of the choice of a master : "Instead of trying to repair the mischief done by incompetent teachers, his (Weber's) father selected, in preference to a sound musician like Albrechtsberger, or a master of the art like Haydn, the fashionable composer and organist of the period, Abt Vogler ; a man gifted with the highest social attractions, full of wit and anecdote, *persona grata* at the Imperial Court, and undoubtedly a clever eclectic in his art, adapting himself to all styles, and pilfering right and left with consummate skill. Though much over-rated and extolled as a genius by the musical public of Vienna, he was considered an unprincipled mountebank by the great musical authorities of the period."

Judging from the accounts we read of Vogler, he seems to have encountered the difficulties and met with the discouragements common to all musicians ; while his roving Bohemian proclivities seem to redeem him from the reproach of "*fashionable.*" As regards the charge of "*pilfering,*" both Mr. Mee in his article, and Dr. von Schafhäutl in his *Life,* allude to this groundless accusation. The former thus speaks : "At Berlin he (Vogler) was charged with stealing the pipes removed in 'simplifying' the organ in St. Mary's church. The falsity of the charge was demonstrated, but it shows the feeling against him"—(*feeling* of course against the musical reformer). Dr. von Schafhäutl speaks more in detail : "Much interest was shown in his original system, and the organ in the church of St. Mary's (Berlin) was given over to him for the carrying out of his simplification system. . . . In the remodelling of the St. Mary's organ Vogler removed many pipes that were unnecessary for his simplified organ. These pipes he utilised in the erection of a new organ in the Catholic Hedwigskirche, which he completed at his own expense, and which exists to this day with but slight alterations. Owing to marks of honour bestowed on him by the court, much envious feeling was raised up against him, and he was accused of stealing the pipes he dispensed with from St. Mary's organ. A public testimony from the church officials silenced these truly ridiculous accusations."

As regards the opinions of the "great musical authorities of the period," something may be said on this score also. In the same year (1803) that Weber was placed under his tuition, Vogler's meeting with Beethoven occurred at a musical soirée given by Sonnleithner, when Vogler and Beethoven extemporised alternately, each giving the other a theme. Gänsbacher (also a pupil of Vogler's) thus describes his impressions : "I heard both masters for the first time.

Beethoven's extraordinary powers as a pianist, enriched as his playing was with a wealth of most beautiful ideas, overcame me with astonishment, but could not raise me to the pitch of enthusiasm with which Vogler's masterly playing, unequalled as it was in harmonic and contrapuntal resources, inspired me." In Rinck's autobiography he thus speaks of Vogler: "I rejoiced in his friendship in the highest degree, and I shall never forget the hours I spent in his company. His organ-playing was grand, effective in the utmost degree, and when he played in his best style must have astonished every one. His effective arrangement of stops displayed his real knowledge of organ-building." Haydn bore testimony to Vogler's brilliant powers as an organist, and Schumann remarked, after hearing some of his music, that he had not been sufficiently appreciated by his contemporaries.

After this digression, which seemed almost necessary at this juncture, we will proceed with Vogler's life. In 1804 a change in the musical world of Vienna, occasioned by Sonnleithner's withdrawal from the musical directorship of the opera, coupled also with the appearance of ominous thunder-clouds on the political horizon, induced Vogler to return to Munich. On the first of January, 1806, Bavaria was proclaimed a kingdom. Napoleon reached Munich on the 31st of December, 1805, to assist at the marriage of his adopted son, the Viceroy of Italy. On the 15th of January, 1806, a brilliant performance of Vogler's opera *Castor and Pollux* was given under his direction before the Emperor and many crowned heads, concluding with a "wedding song" composed for the occasion by Vogler. He hoped to have obtained a settled appointment in Munich, but owing to aimless delays on the part of the court, and the failure of his pension from Sweden, Vogler resumed his roving life and went to visit his old friends, travelling through Bavaria and the Rhineland. In June he met his patron the Grand Duke of Darmstadt, and told him of his hopes and fate. His old friend and patron at once offered him a settled appointment in Darmstadt, with ample salary and comfortable, not to say luxurious, domestic arrangements. This was at once accepted by Vogler, and in Darmstadt he found the rest, peace and appreciation for which lately he had longed. Like Ulysses, he returned to his old home after long years of wandering. Here he founded his third school of music, and spent his last years peacefully and usefully. More a favoured friend than a servant of the Grand Duke, he dined every day at the ducal table, and gave lessons to the Grand Duchess. He still went on with his favourite work of simplifying organs; and when his love of change became irresistible he contented himself with visits to Munich, Frankfort, Mainz, &c. In 1810 we find him welcoming

Meyerbeer as his pupil, then a youth of nineteen years of age. In the same month (April) Gänsbacher and Carl Maria von Weber both rejoined Vogler, and thus we find him, happy and honoured in his old age, and surrounded by his favourite and most famous pupils, looked on by them almost as a father, and lovingly called "Papa Vogler." It is at this period that we have a charming glimpse of the old musician, extemporising in the old Darmstadt church. "Never," said Weber, "did Vogler in his extemporisation drink more deeply at the source of all beauty than when, before his three dear boys, as he liked to call us, he drew from the organ angelic voices and words of thunder."

The time however was approaching when it was necessary for teacher and pupils to part. Gänsbacher was the first to leave, and he parted from Vogler and his friends with burning tears. Weber was the next to go, after the lapse of a few months; but Meyerbeer lingered on, having means at his disposal, and Vogler found it necessary at last to urge him to go out into the world. Vogler thought often with longing of his native town of Würzburg, and it was his great desire to leave a memorial of his work there. He was finally commissioned to undertake the simplification of the organ in the Neuminster there. Owing to unfortunate misunderstandings his organ concert at the opening of the organ was a failure, and Vogler was not only sorely wounded, but also sustained a personal pecuniary loss.

In 1812 he visited Munich, where he simplified an organ, and gave a successful organ concert for the benefit of the widows and orphans of the Bavarian soldiers. It was a veritable triumph, and happy indeed was the Abbé, with Meyerbeer on the one side and Caspar Ett on the other, attending to the stops. Shortly after this Meyerbeer left him, and with the departure of this last pupil Vogler's fortune seemed to waver.

Owing to a breach of contract in Munich, he found himself suddenly in considerable financial distress, and pride restrained him from appealing to his patron the Grand Duke, with whom he had had a slight misunderstanding before leaving Darmstadt to visit Munich. With renewed hope he paid a visit to Vienna, but on the way there was robbed of a considerable sum of money. In Vienna everything went wrong, and it was actually necessary for him to place his golden snuff-box, the gift of the Emperor of Russia, in pawn, in order to obtain money for his return journey. In spite of all these misfortunes his musical spirit remained fresh and unimpaired. He composed a new overture to *Samori*, which he laid before the Grand

Duke in 1813, and wrote several hymns and songs during his stay in Munich. On his return to Darmstadt he undertook the building of a new instrument, which he named "Mikropan."

In Vogler's last letter from Munich to the Grand Duke, he said that the air there did not suit his health. Doubtless his recent misfortunes and worries were telling already on his system. He returned to Darmstadt, and was incapable of taking any exercise owing to a sore in his foot. Rinck was one of his last visitors, and found his old friend bright and active-minded as ever. Gottfried Weber spent the day before his death with him, and wondered at the youthful spirit and strength of the gifted old man. He was taken away suddenly in the night of the 6th of May, 1814, with an apoplectic stroke.

Great was the grief of his pupils on hearing the sad news; but as Weber wrote to Gänsbacher, "He will ever live in our hearts." He was buried quietly, but with every token of esteem and honour; and thus passed away this remarkable and gifted man.

It has been a subject of no little consideration to know how far I might enlarge on Vogler's musical and simplification systems before an audience not entirely composed of musicians. As this paper however has been written for the Browning Society, I will confine myself to the consideration of the musical instrument of Vogler's own invention, of which instrument we read at the heading of the well-known poem. I will only ask you to remember that he also invented an instrument for the measuring of musical intervals with mathematical exactitude which he called the "Ton-maass;" that he strongly advocated the tuning of organs at equal temperature; that he devised a method of fingering which was strongly objected to by Mozart, and also by many present authorities, and that his musical compositions were numerous, though in too many instances not calculated to stand the test of time. His organ preludes have much interested me, but having no separate pedal part, it involves more or less difficulty for the organist to arrange the pedal part as he plays; and the characteristics of these preludes are more pleasing than striking or original.

His hymn *Hier liegt im Staub vor Dir* is an interesting composition, well adapted for an anthem. Of his operas, *Castor and Pollux* and *Samori* deserve first mention, while his music to *Hermann von Unna* was an undoubted success—we read of people waiting for upwards of twelve hours at the ticket office before its performance.

It is difficult to know what to say of Vogler's musical system.

The one certainty about it is, that so far it has never been generally adopted; and musicians now are not open to the reproach of being illiterate, as was the case with Kirnberger. Weber, in his enthusiasm for his master thus writes:

> " Before thee never were combined
> Such lore and genius in oue mind."

It is evident that Vogler liked to build up all knowledge from a scientific foundation; and was incapable of accepting facts without proving them. Mozart taunts him with publishing handbooks on arithmetic instead of music; but with Vogler's love of, and skill in mathematics, it was an added pleasure to him to reduce everything to mathematical measurements and exactitude, just as a botanist will dissect a lovely flower and reduce it to a science. His desire was to simplify theory, as well as organs; to introduce new triads, and even chords commonly accepted as discords, without the ceremony of modulation. It was on organ-building that Vogler exercised a real and lasting influence; and I am glad to hear that in some of our leading firms of organ-builders various methods of arranging the pipes and wind are spoken of as "the Abt Vogler plan." In his simplification of organs his one aim was to avoid the use of large and unnecessary pipes; and all his inventions in this direction were based on the theory of harmonics, as elucidated by Tartini—hence the quint on the pedal organ. To Vogler also belongs the credit of the introduction of free reeds; we have been indebted to the Chinese for many inventions, and with them originated this invention, and the first loose *tongue* in the history of music. This primitive instrument of the Chinese was called Tscheng, and was manufactured in great numbers. One of these instruments had found its way to Copenhagen, and was there found by Professor Kratzenstein and Kirsnick. The latter realised the importance of the discovery, and on establishing himself as an organ-builder at St. Petersburg, began to work out the principle. It was to see into this matter that Vogler went to St. Petersburg to see Kirsnick, and finally invited Racknitz to join him in his work. These pipes promised to become the soul of his new instrument, and in 1792 he placed the pipes in his orchestrion, and also introduced them for the first time into a church at Rotterdam. Thus was his unremitting search for the pipes he desired, rewarded.

Another point for which Vogler contended was the order of arrangement of organ pipes—placing the large pipes at the left end of the sound-board, and the smaller ones at the right. The mixtures for which Vogler worked are an undoubted success; and his plan of bringing the wind nearer to the player is an acknowledged benefit.

His difficulties with organ-builders were even greater and more numerous than were his encounters with the theorists and publishers of the period. "Vogler once said to his friends, in a sad hour, full of apprehension, 'It is not only that people will not hear and study my works, but will not even know how and what I thought. Yet it may be that I shall live again, when my enemies think I have passed away for ever.'"

Dr. von Schafhäutl claims for Vogler a place equal to that of the discovers of the steam-engine, and remarks (Vogler having only built *one* organ on his perfected system), "How many thousands of steam-engines were built before they had attained to their present standpoint! It is almost the same in the history of all discoveries before they are admitted to the full rights of citizenship amongst us." Vogler, unfortunately, had no rich Englishman such as Bolton to stand surety for his invention; and his invention, being destined chiefly for use in churches, and not in factories—for the divine art of music, and not for the lower love of greed—did not gain greatly in favour. Strange it is that so many people complain of too much music in the service of God, and would willingly do away with the added expense of a first-rate instrument, organist and choir! content with the idea that anything is good enough for church-music, and with the belief that the musical stands apart from the religious world! Dr. von Schafhäutl speaks as follows, "When I drew attention in a Munich paper to the mangling and neglect of the organ in St. Peter's Church, and complained of the same, I received this answer from an organ-builder, 'Vogler built a concert-organ that no one is able to play.'

"The answer was right after a fashion.

"Churches do not require concert-organs; and likewise it frequently happens that our organists will not play for so scanty a salary!"

In his own instrument, his orchestrion, he combined his inventions and improvements: and had the proud delight of conveying his instrument with him from place to place. It was about three feet square, and higher in the middle than the sides; it contained about 900 pipes, had shutters for crescendos and diminuendos, and naturally the reed stops were free reeds. In his system for simplifying organs, he relied too much, as has been already suggested, on the musical knowledge of the organists, who were at that time rarely men of much education. "The simplified organs," says Dr. von Schafhäutl, "had nearly all the same fate. When Vogler played, every one was charmed, but when an organist followed, who was accustomed to an ordinary organ, it invariably happened, when the first delight was forgotten, that there were the same complaints as to technical difficulties, and the organ's want of power. The only organist who understood the manipulation of these simplified organs was the friend and amanuensis of Vogler at Munich—the organist of St. Michael's Church, Caspar Ett. When the organist of the simplified organ in the Protestant church complained also of his organ's want of power, Ett himself played on it, and the organist exclaimed in astonishment, 'Who could have believed that the organ possessed such power?'

"The power of an organ is usually reckoned by its size and number of pipes and stops. The more stops are pulled out, and therefore added, the stronger of course must be the sound of the organ.

"Vogler drew out stops with reference to their acoustic relationship, and by these means obtained the same power as with twice as many stops."

It was in the church of St. Michael's, Munich, that we hear of him utilising old pipes for a quint, in which he cut an opening to obtain the thirty-two feet sound; it was at once given forth, "and the thunder was heard beyond the church, down the wide Hauptstrasse."

Before leaving the technical side of the question, I have been struck in Dr. von Schafhäutl's work with the constant reference to the triad, or common chord in Vogler's and Vallotti's theory. "Each sound in music," writes Vogler, "is a plurality of three compounded tones—the key-note, the third, and the fifth." This of course refers to harmonics, the principle of which was first explained by Sauveur— but I cannot but recall the lines:

> "But I know not if, save in this, such gift be allowed to man,
> That out of three sounds he frame, not a fourth sound, but a star."

Enough has been said in this outline of Vogler's life to show that he was devoted to his art, and earnest in his religious profession. He was a generous and sincere friend, a kind and thoughtful brother, and as a teacher was almost universally beloved by his pupils. As a reformer, attacking what he considered to be existing abuses, he was absolutely fearless; and this naturally accounts for much ill will. Another ground for hatred was his boldness in declaring Bach's chorals to be unsuited for congregational use, and his subsequent re-arrangement of them.

That organists objected to his "simplification system" was a constant grief to him. His own performances on them delighted his audiences; but the constant complaint was that only Vogler could play on them! This astonished him, as it surprises every one with a gift of his own, to find that what is in his case second nature, may be a serious difficulty in the case of another not equally gifted.

How was it that he failed to attain to that which was greatest and most permanent in music? Dr. von Schafhäutl almost claims for him a place amongst the greatest musicians, but this I can scarcely understand, although if we may trust to Browning's representation of him he

> " Entered and took his place there sure enough—
> Tho' he came back, *and could not tell the world.*"

Vogler himself once admitted that he considered himself deficient in the gift of melody. Possibly, too, his wandering life, with nothing of domestic joy to embellish it, may have tended to the non-fulfilment of his dream of future greatness. There *is* the genius, which like Handel's, soars ever higher and higher, whose craving for the greatest in art seems to extinguish all longings for earthly ties. Others again, have gained an added pathos from life's joys and sorrows. Mendelssohn's exquisite music breathes of refinement and harmonious surroundings, yet he, too, must have had his moments of agonised solitude before " It is enough " could have been written. Chopin's very soul goes forth in his love and longing for the highly-gifted woman who broke his heart, but the world is richer for his suffering.

It is difficult to assign to each his place, when looking on them from our human standpoint. In a mountain-range a world-renowned peak may seem insignificant, because of our inability to gain a desirable point of view; but were it possible to stand on the mountain peak itself, to look down on all the others in no spirit of pride, but of heavenly confidence, this indeed were greatness ! But there would be no confession of weakness, though many of humility: no falling back into the deep. This brings me back to the poem, with which theme I started. Here again we have the instinctive power of the poet thoroughly realising that the Abbé was a born musician, capable of true art, gifted with moments of veritable inspiration when extemporising, yet apparently incapable of sojourning long enough on the heights to render these moments permanent. I have read how, amidst the Himalayan snows, fleecy cloud-banners hang around the highest peaks in the early morning hours; then, as the sun gains in power, they are drawn upwards and disperse themselves in the blue of heaven. Carrying further this mountain simile, it seems as though, in the case of a musician such as Abt Vogler, these cloud-like thoughts of beauty collected about the musician in his inspired moments of extemporisation ; but instead of descending in showers to enrich the world, they were at once drawn heavenwards, and thus, though lost to us, were part of the " music sent up to God."

BROWNING AS A TEACHER OF THE NINETEENTH CENTURY.

By Miss C. M. WHITEHEAD.

Read at the Fifty-eighth Meeting of the Browning Society, April 27th, 1888.

EVERY age has its own characteristics, needs, and faults, which one who aspires to be its poet must in some way or another meet, minister to, or correct.

Past times have not been so complicated as our own. Our progress has its drawbacks. The rush of an overwhelming tide of life has come upon us within the last twenty years. Every year accelerates the whirl with the increased facilities for movement and progress which it brings. The poets of those earlier years had a comparatively easy task. Cowper, Crabbe, and Burns had each his mission, while they left it to Wordsworth to unfold the deep inner life of Nature, and bring home her teaching to the individual heart. Shelley was free to lift his generation into pure ether with his skylark, Coleridge to thrill the same time with his power of visionary insight, Keats to lull it with a charm of verse unknown before, and still fresh fields were left on which Byron and Scott were to gather laurels all their own.

But the poet of the present day has a far harder work. First, he has to make his voice heard clear and distinct from all those who have preceded him, and then if he is to be our teacher and guide he has to touch life at a thousand different points ; nay, more, he has to go down to its depths, and probe its principles and motives at their source. In short, he must be in some sort a "philosopher."

Life has come upon us with a rush that finds us unprepared. We have, those of us who exist to any purpose, to live at the fullest stretch of our powers, at a pressure past ages did not know, and yet we are required to mould this rapid life of ours on the deepest principles of the ages past unless we would wreck it altogether. Like the Jews of old, we have to fight and repair our breaches as we fight.

We are called to take our part in great questions and to decide on them from day to day, and yet we are expected to have formed our decisions and opinions upon firm fundamental principles of reason and thought. We are called many of us into the arena to grapple with problems which tax us to the uttermost, just at the moment when the imperative call to action makes us realise most our lack of intellectual preparation for the work which comes to us, and from which there is no escape because so few are ready to do it. The generation which is rising up now may have its own especial difficulties, but it will realise far better what they are, and enter the conflict more prepared to meet them than this present one has been.

We are called to be actors when we should be students, and the problem presses upon us how can we best live our life, and at the same time learn from our own experience and that of the past. We need the poet, with his gift of "infinite insight," to teach us.

It was said in one of our discussions that we could not expect poems on sanitary matters, or the Channel Tunnel, that we had not got them from Mr. Browning, and could not ask them from any poet. Certainly not, but if the age is commercial, common-place, and unromantic, all the more do we need the poet to put soul into it for us, to sanctify the common-place. As Aurora Leigh says :—

> " Ay, and while your common men
> Lay telegraphs, gauge railroads, reign, reap, dine,
> And dust the flaunty carpets of the world
> For kings to walk on, or our president,
> The poet suddenly will catch them up
> With his voice like a thunder : ' This is soul !
> This is life ! this word is being said in Heaven—
> Here's God down on us ! What are you about ?'
> How all those workers start amid their work,
> Look round, look up, and feel a moment's space,
> That carpet-dusting, though a pretty trade,
> Is not the imperative labour after all."

Yes, can do that, but can also make us feel that even "carpet-dusting" is capable of being a service above its seeming according to the spirit in which it is done.

It is with his gift of "infinite insight" that the poet can look down upon this crowded arena where we have to play our part, and with a loving human sympathy direct us to the deeper principles by which alone we can play it worthily. He is as it were our general, controlling the combat from a height; our critic, watching the rehearsal of our parts; and still more our seer, who from the mountain-tops can read for us the signs of the times, not in detail but in clear strong outlines.

When we are worn out with work, blinded by our individual prejudices, dazzled by the praise of our little circle, or utterly cast down by its blame, we need one by whose side we can throw aside our armour, who will take the part assigned to calm old age in *Rabbi ben Ezra*, and

> "Youth ended, try
> My gain or loss thereby, and weigh the same ;
> Give life its praise or blame."

Work in the world at the present involves entering upon so many problems, and grappling with such stern realities of life, that all deep thinkers who would help humanity are called to hold up a standard of thought and principle which shall not only rest but also invigorate those who turn to them for solace and refreshment. Some minds ask this more than others, especially those forced out into action by the demands of this age, who yet in their inmost souls yearn after the life of quiet thought and study, and vainly strive to unite the two, and welcome therefore any teacher who gives to them what they would seek for themselves, adapted to the needs of the stirring life to which they have felt irresistibly drawn by forces that could not be resisted.

It is my contention that it is such a need which Mr. Browning, more than any one else at the present day, meets and satisfies. He tests our armour for us, and sends us back to our post with the hope that the battle may yet be retrieved, or if it seems lost, that apparent defeat may only mean a surer victory :—

> "But we brought forth and reared in hours
> Of change, alarm, surprise,
> What shelter to grow ripe is ours,
> What leisure to grow wise ?"

To give us that shelter and that leisure, Mr. Browning, I venture to think, contributes more than any other writer of our time.

The points on which Mr. Browning stands as a teacher divide into two very wide classes—

1. Those which touch the more practical questions of the day.

2. Those which concern metaphysical problems. Capable of sub-division again into (1) those which influence life and character in some measure ; (2) those which lie more entirely in the region of abstract thought, which it is impossible to touch in the limits of a short paper, even if I were equal to the task, which I entirely disclaim being.

I would guard myself at the outset from being understood to imply that Mr. Browning authoritatively lays down the law on one side or the other on disputed questions. He rather indicates principles capable of interpretation and application.

For instance, to plunge boldly into one burning question of the day, whole poems on the wrong and cruelty of vivisection would not be so strong as his starting-point with regard to the lower animals :—

> " God made all the creatures, and gave them our love and our fear,
>   To give sign we and they are His children, one family here. "

We hardly need the indignant sarcasm at the expense of those who think the scalpel the appointed means for scientific investigation :—

> " By vivisection at expense
>   Of half an hour and eighteenpence
>   How brain secretes dog's soul we'll see. "

Other later words give a deeper principle by which to test this and kindred subjects—namely, that for a paltry benefit (if benefit it be?) the whole race barters its higher good in gaining any advantage at cost to a living sentient thing :—

> " Never dare alienate God's gift you hold
>   Simply in trust for Him.
>   Love as well you lose
>   Slain by what slays in you the honour.
>   Could you so stumble in your choice. "

We betray our trust to those who are at our mercy, and nothing can compensate for the deterioration of character which follows such a betrayal. It is the world's voice heard in many different strains :—

> " Rightly done,
>   It is the politic, the thrifty way
>   Will clearly make you in the end returns. "

The leading principle over and over again laid down by Mr. Browning is that only self-sacrifice is true worship, and "seals up the perfect man."

"Donald" carries the lesson further, and points a moral to those who instead of welcoming and resting content in the alleviations which science has procured, turn them into a curse by procuring through them the mutilation and prolonged torture of creatures who are in our power.

The story of "Donald" is given as a quick answer to the proposition that in sport "there is little likelihood of a man's displaying meanness." Evidently it does not rank with Mr. Browning as an Englishman's first duty to kill something every day.   The lady of his love lifts

> " The poor snail my chance foot spurned,
>   To feed and forget it the leaves among."

We do not need books like "St. Bernard's" to tell us that the tendency of the present day is to grow callous and careless to individual suffering so long as the race is benefited in the main, forgetful that the race is made up of units which have to suffer for the possible benefit only, of a future generation.   Again and again, to counteract that tendency, is it pressed home upon us that it is

> "Love, not knowledge, that profits,"

and that

> " When we draw a circle premature,
>   Heedless of far gain
>   Greedy for quick returns of profit, sure,
>   Bad is our bargain."

It is the lesson taught by *Paracelsus*.   What avail so-called discoveries, investigations, with possible benefit to future generations, while love, the root of all good, is put aside.

> " I learned my own deep error ; love's undoing
>   Taught me the worth of love in man's estate,
>   Love preceding
>   Power, and with much power always much more love."

It is an age in which the scalpel is applied as ruthlessly to mind, and brain, and soul.   The public demands to know all that ought to be most scrupulously reserved from its gaze, and there are traitors to be found who are willing to show the secrets of the prison-house.   The poet zealously maintains that right of the soul to reserve :—

> " God be thanked the meanest of His creatures
>   Boasts two soul-sides—one to face the world with,
>   One to show a woman that he loves her ! "

In " House " :—

> " The goodman at least
> Kept house to himself till an earthquake came."

Those who clamour to look within forget that it is an earth-quake that must reveal the otherwise well-guarded house ; and in *A Likeness* the poet shows that the effect of irreverent praise or blame is to destroy the value of the thing only fit to be tossed away

> "Half in a rapture, half in a rage."

Every soul has a right to its own reserves, and also to live its own life. Criticism not only fetters but kills out all grace and spon-taneity. In *My Last Duchess* a most pathetic picture is drawn for us of a life simply dying under coldness which forbade it to be its own gracious self, and as one reads it one does so with a thrill of consciousness that to some extent the same snuffing out process is going on in thousands of homes at the present time, and that, in spite of all our boasted freedom and progress, domestic tyranny of mind over mind still too often exists. The early life of John Stuart Mill is one example, where many might be found, of a parent crushing down a child's life in the desire to thwart Nature by moulding it anew on a pattern chosen by an iron will. "The flight of the Duchess " is a pendant to the picture, showing how a stronger soul can find courage to spread its wings and flee in obedience to the call of the gipsy,—type of one or other of the many voices which call on every side, and bid an enthralled soul deliver itself and live its own unfettered life. The old-worldly conventionality would get its death-blow from Mr. Browning if anything could slay it. The whole poem teems with satire on following fashion for fashion's sake, on consciously moulding life on a stated pattern :—

> " So all that the old Dukes had been without knowing it,
> This Duke would fain know he was, without being it.
> 'Twas not for the joy's self, but the joy of his showing it ;
> Not for the pride's sake, but the pride of our seeing it,
> He revived all usages thoroughly worn out,
> The souls of them fumed forth, the hearts of them torn out."

A sly thrust one must feel is given here to mediæval fashions revived only because they were the fashion and not for use or beauty.

In days like these, when, another poet tells us,

> " Every door is barr'd with gold, and opens but to golden keys,"

and services you do not require, and never requested, are thrust upon you only in the hope of extorting some coin of the realm, it

is refreshing to read the protest against even an important service
being paid by silver or gold :—

> " Dropped me—ah, had it been a purse
> Of silver, my friend, or gold, that's worse,
> Why you see as soon as I found myself
> So understood—that a true heart so may gain
> Such a reward—I should have gone home again
> And soberly drowned myself."

The gipsy is the sign of the " great deliverance " which comes to
some in this day from deep convictions, or a call to work—anything
in fact which sets the soul free to choose its own path, whether of
thought or action, unbiased and untrammelled by other minds.

In *Pictor Ignotus*, the painter's art shrinks before the cold,
calculating appraising of the multitude :—

> " Who summoned those cold faces that began
> To press on me, and judge me ?
> And where they live needs must our pictures live,
> And see their faces, listen to their prate,
> Partakers of their daily pettiness ; . . .
> At least no merchant traffics in my heart."

Words fit to be a motto of warning to be inscribed on the walls
of our Royal Academy, from which our noblest painters have been till
late excluded, and only those who could stoop their genius to things
understanded of the multitude could enter.   The right function of
art is given by the mouth of Lippo Lippi :—

> " God's works—paint any one, and count it crime
> To let a truth slip.
> We're made so that we love
> First when we see them painted, things we have passed
> Perhaps a hundred times nor cared to see ;
> And so they are better painted—better to us
> Which is the same thing.   Art was given for that.
> God uses us to help each other, so
> Sending our minds out "

painting so as to give a glimpse of the soul through right and true
delineation of its shrine.

The money-getting spirit of our time is the death of true Art
as well as of other things.

Most true it is of England now—

> " Your shop was all your house."

> " He saw no use of life
> But while he drove a roaring trade
> To chuckle, ' Customers are rife.' "

U

> " Friend, your good angel slept, your star
> Suffered eclipse, fate did you wrong!
> From where these sorts of treasures are,
> There should our hearts be—Christ, how far !"

And far worse than being merely commercial, which might be a glory, our system of trading is rotten to the core—through dishonesty, and still more through our scamping of work, our working for show ; whether it is in a defective bayonet, or in the intellectual world the getting up subjects superficially by the aid of reviews; education meaning passing such and such examinations, not awakening the deep thirst for accurate knowledge which should be the end and object of all study. To all the system of shams Browning calls, " Stand and deliver. How far is your work good ? What is its object, its aim ? Never mind that it fails ; that it should be your best is your sole concern." That is the tone in passages too many to quote that Mr. Browning opposes to the pretence of work mental as well as practical of our day, which is slowly but surely bringing a deep retribution upon us in the pauperism which has its hold on the country.

It is an age also of mediocrity, and of the conceit which accompanies mediocrity, every one thinking his or her experience of vital importance, and as such to be communicated to the world at large by means of a feeble book, or letter to the daily papers. Mr. Browning corrects that mood of mind by showing the littleness of the individual, and that the real ground for a true estimate of yourself and your work is humility.

> " 'Tis looking downward makes one dizzy."
>
> " So you saw yourself as you wished you were,
> As you might have been, as you cannot be,
> Earth here rebuked by Olympus there,
> And grew content in your poor degree."

Old Pictures in Florence gives us our right place in life's history ; we grow patient under our imperfection. " *What's come to perfection perishes*,"—still more that which imagines itself to have reached perfection. It is in humility alone that all progress towards our ideal lies. Our easy self-contentment, our want of aspiration, our dead level of attainment, are the bane of high achievement. Truth and humility, he teaches us, go hand in hand, while one of our chief duties to the age is to be ourselves. It is a true wisdom which speaks from the lips of Bishop Blougram :—

> " The common problem—yours, mine, every one's
> Is—not to fancy what were fair in life,
> Provided it could be ; but finding first
> What may be, then find out how to make it fair
> Up to our means : a very different thing."

To realise our limitation of gifts and graces is the first element of growth.

As a correction to that sense of individual littleness comes the realisation of brotherhood :—

> " A people is but the attempt of many
> To rise to the completer life of one ;
> And those who live as models for the mass
> Are singly of more value than they all."

We get a note of patriotism from Browning which is as a trumpet-call in a time when love of party and power—in short, self-interest—claims the place which love of country once held. *Luria, A Soul's Tragedy, The Patriot*, in different tones speak the same spirit, and give the warning that he who would serve his fellow-men must expect as his reward misunderstanding, ingratitude, and scorn ; and that his sole support must be in the consciousness of his own integrity and God's approval ; nay, even, he must sometimes go on in darkness without that ground of confidence, as when, in *Victor and Charles*, his wife urges Charles to the right course to keep his kingdom, and warns him that not only must the deed " look wrong in the world's eye," but that

> " 'Twill be only in moments that the duty's seen
> As palpably as now—the months, the years, of painful
> Indistinctness are to come."

> " What matters happiness ? Duty—
> There's man's one moment.   This is yours."

But there is one question which cannot be left out in inquiring how much Mr. Browning is in sympathy with the movements of the time, and that is the progress of women ; and here I can only bear witness to the gratitude women must feel with regard to his attitude towards them.

He does not, like our other great poet,

> " set a woman to man
> Like perfect music unto noble words,"

or ask her to " yield herself up,"

> " Seeing either sex alone
> Is half itself."

Mr. Browning does not waste words over defining woman's position, he simply gives it her. I do not think one line can be found implying that she is to gain "mental breadth" by contact with a man's mind, and that her work must fail unless she has

> " A helper *me* that know
> The woman's cause is man's."

He treats men and women on a broad level of equality, judging each individual according to merit, not sex. You can hardly see better the position he accords to woman than by contrasting it with that which Tennyson grants her. She is a being to be lectured, tutored, guided, improved, generally weak until she has been linked long enough to some man to gain strength by contact

> " Yoked in all exercise of noble end."

No man drawn by the latter ever owns " that his own small life grew complete " in a woman's ; that " he must feel her brain prompt his."

There is no shade of patronage in Mr. Browning's tone about women, but a frank acknowledgment of mutual help and assistance between them and men, a recognition of the friendship which is one of the most helpful features of our time. Again and again it is a woman who sees the truth, and impresses it on the men around. Polixena, as we have seen, saw clear and distinct amidst all sophistries the line Charles should take. Guendolen, in the *Blot in the 'Scutcheon*, has the true instinct, and the whole tragedy might have been averted if her voice could have prevailed. Pompilia's trust in Caponsacchi called forth his chivalry, while even Ottima is stronger in her wickedness than her weak partner in sin. Only one of his women fails the man she loves, and in failing wrecks him and herself—Constance in *In a Balcony*. Little as Michal comes prominently before us, we know her chiefly as an inspiration to Paracelsus.

No woman would have dared to claim for herself such superiority in the quality of her love as Mr. Browning unhesitatingly assigns to it in the mouth of the dying wife who says to her husband—

> " Might I go last and show thee ! "

the immortality of love, how the lonely years would be lighted by the
memory of past happiness.

It is perhaps a digression to show here how different is the view
Mr. Browning takes of past happiness from that rendered by
Tennyson—

> " A sorrow's crown of sorrow
> Is remembering happier things."

Happiness he rather thinks the fittest preparation for endurance, and
believes that there *are* minds grateful, humble, and just enough to
realize that joy rightly received gives lasting good.   " Glad for what
was."   He drives home the lesson by the melon-seller in *Ferishtah's
Fancies*, who from his present misery lifts a brow "luminous and
imperial" at the remembrance of the years he basked in royal favour
and enjoyed the good of life.   Healthy souls can stand such teaching.
With all Browning's vast sympathy and penetration into the deeper
woes of the soul, he has no weakening pity for the morbid mind
which hugs its grief.   "Ich habe gelebt und geliebt," he would say,
and rejoice that pain at least had brought experience.

And it is that healthy tone, free from sentimentality, which
makes his view of love so essentially that which suits our day.
Passionate, reverential, as it is, holding in its entirety its rightful
supremacy, it is always manly, never morbid, and always in its
deepest anguish or joy realizes that love is only one of the great
factors in life's experience.   All is not lost because his individual life
is not completed.   Though he knows his fate—

> " My whole heart rises up to bless
> Your name in pride and thankfulness."

And though in that last ride his sense of loss is deepened, yet his
mind is quickened to sympathy with the sum of human pain, and
insufficiency, and failure, and he holds himself in check, remembering
that all lots, however ideal, have some flaw, some goal beyond
unattained.

The sense is never wanting, I think, in his most passionate
utterances, of a firm hand upon himself, as if he never lost sight of
the other side, the possible disenchantment.   Also he recognizes to
the full the right of every individual soul to withhold the gift he
craves, realizes that there may be no responsive thrill, no magnetism
answering to his own ; the humility of true love is never wanting.

No picture of love has been drawn for us, I venture to think,

which combines in itself the perfections of different phases with all
that men and women of the noblest type have grown to demand
now.

It has a touch of old-world chivalry that would stand at nothing—

> " Is she wronged ? To the rescue of her honour,
>   My heart !
> Is she poor ? What costs it to become a donour ?
> There an earth to cleave, a sea to part."

It idealizes the object loved, and sees beauty where none exists, as in
Too Late, and *James Lee's Wife.* It has a tender reverence, as in *The
Lost Mistress ;* a rare pathos, as in *May and Death.* Its foundation
must be truth—

> " Truth is the strong thing.
>   Let man's life be true !
>   And love's the truth of mine."

It includes friendship, which is the heart of true love.

> " Friends—lovers that might have been."

It only fails when honour and trust are dead—

> " Love you lose
> Slain by what slays in you the honour."

And yet it can be very patient. It endures faults, misunderstandings
pleads—

> " Bear with a moment's spite.
>   What of a hasty word ?"

because it lies deeper than outside difference.
    It is undying, for eternity—

> " In the worst of a storm's uproar
>   I shall pull her through the door ;
>   I shall have her for evermore."

Its passion would sweep all before it, but for the under-current of
humility and self-control, as in *The Lost Mistress*—

> " Friends the merest keep much that I resign."

It is a love that asks no reward, that is not self-seeking. Lady
Carlisle says—

> " Ah, have I spared
> Strafford a pang, and shall I seek reward
> Beyond that memory ?"

and still more forcibly Valence—

> " Who thought upon reward ?   And yet how much
> Comes after ! oh what amplest recompense !
> Is the knowledge of her nought ? the memory nought !
> Lady, should such an one have looked on you
> Ne'er wrong yourself so far as quote the world
> And say love can go unrequited here !
> You will have blessed him to his whole life's end—
> Low passions hindered, baser cares kept back :
> Where self-love makes such room for love for you
> He would not serve you now
> The vulgar way."

And enfolding all, like the setting of the jewel, is an element of pure self-sacrifice—mutual, not one-sided—but expressed, if anything, more strongly on the man's side, not expected only from the woman—

> " One to count night day for me
> Patient through the watches long,
> Serving most with none to see."

> " I will speak thy speech, Love,
> Think thy thought.
> Meet, if thou require it,
> Both demands."

Mr. Browning presents us, then, with an ideal picture of love fitted for this age in its manly self-respecting tone, one which really deserves a paper to itself, and not to be glanced at superficially in passing.

It follows as a matter of course that no one lashes as he does the sin of a careless marriage. Whenever I read the *Ring and the Book*, I am surprised that the fashionable and conventional world have not long ago risen to demand that it should be withdrawn from the list of circulating libraries, and I only ascribe its not having done so to the fact that it is unread, and so the story of Pompilia, which in its main detail is being re-enacted every day, does not reach those who should profit by its warning against the mere sordid bargains which pass for marriages only too often—

> " Marriage making for the earth,
> With gold so much, birth, power, repute,
> Or beauty—youth so much in so much lack of these."

Youth and Art shows again what might have been to two souls who missed their life's happiness through worldliness—

> " Each life's unfulfilled you see ;
> We have not sighed deep, laughed free,
> Starved, feasted, despaired—been happy "—

and from the Pope's mouth come the strongest words on the ruin
and havoc the greed for money produces where it enters into the
question of marriage —

> " Not one permissible impulse moves the man,
> From the mere liking of the eye and ear
> To the true longing of the heart that loves.
> All is the lust for money—to get gold—
> Why lie, rob, if it must be murder! Make
> Body and soul bring gold out, lured within
> The clutch of hate by love, the trap's pretence.
> So have success by marriage undertaken in God's face
> With all these lies so opposite God's truth."

One point, the last of the practical questions I may take here, in
conjunction with Guido's crime, and notice how strongly Mr. Browning
puts the argument in favour of capital punishment—

> " For the main criminal I have no hope
> Except in suddenness of fate ;
> So may the truth be flashed out by one blow,
> And Guido see, one instant, and be saved."

Death we see as the great revealer, alike to the sinner and the
saint. For Guido says—

> " You never know what life means till you die.
> Even throughout life 'tis death that makes life live,
> Gives it whatever the significance."

Whilst to Pompilia, death shows

> " how needful now
> Of understanding somewhat of my past,
> Know life a little, I should leave so soon ;
> Nay, got foretaste too
> Of better life beginning where this ends."

Death is ever to Mr. Browning a friend to be met open-eyed—

> " I would hate that death bandaged my eyes—and forbore
> And bade me creep past."

Death is to him the filling up of life—

> " Let age approve of youth, and death complete the same."

Death is the moment of true vision—

> " Wait till life have passed from out the world.

II.

When we turn to the second division, and take the deeper thoughts which influence character and action, first on the threshold stands the question which the deep-seated pessimism of the day is ever asking : " Is life worth living ? "   Mr. Browning's answer is unhesitating : " Thanks that I am a man ; " and yet it is not an answer given in ignorance of the tremendous odds against us at the present time— the aggregate mass of suffering and misery brought home to us as never before, which we are more highly strung ourselves to encounter, the tension of life being greater enhancing our power to suffer.   No one more entirely understands the anguish of living than he does. There is one line which sums it all up and accentuates it as whole poems could never do—

> " Only I discern
> Infinite passion, and the pain of finite hearts that yearn."

" Most progress " means for many at the present day " most failure."   The sense that death may come ere life's task is half done, that those fall from our side who are most needed, most fitted to achieve good for their fellows and to help the race, that evil overmasters good,—all these sources of discouragement Mr. Browning faces, and suggests comfort for.   Death is not the end, he argues, from probability and past experience—

> " Some fitter way express.
> Heart's satisfaction that the Past indeed
> Is past, gives way before Life's best and last,
> The all-including Future.   Soul
> Nothing has been which shall not bettered be hereafter."

The remedy is to

> " Let things be, not seem,
> I counsel rather.   Do and no wise dream.
> Cheer up.   Be death with me of man's calamities the last and worst ;
> What once lives never dies,
> What here attains to a beginning has no end, still gains
> And never loses aught : when, where, and how lies in Law's lap."

But we are in such a hurry to reach perfection, to put an end to our condition of probation, to reach the goal—

> " No as with body so deals law with soul,
> That, stung to strength thro' weakness, strives for good
> Thro' evil, earth its race-ground, Heaven its goal,
> Presumably."

If Cleon felt that there must be a hereafter where fruition and
fulfilment should consummate the attempts and failures of earth—

> " I dare at times imagine to my need
> Some future state unlimited in capability
> For joy as this is in desire for joy.
> To seek which the joy hunger forces us :
> That stung by straitness of our life, made strait
> On purpose to make prized the life at large,
> Freed by the throbbing impulse we call death,
> We burst there as the worm into the fly "—

how much more shall we, with a deeper experience to judge from,
feel that it is

> " God's task to make the heavenly period
> Perfect the earthen ; "

and bear patiently our state of limitation here.

Mr. Browning's warnings against the impatience and hurry of
the age are very strong, at least that I interpret (it may be wrongly)
to be one of the striking lessons Sordello's life is meant to convey.

And curiously, the *Spectator* accuses Mr. Browning himself of the
faults of the time. It says :—"The impatience and excitability proper
to an age of inquisitiveness and of change have had their effect on
our poetry. They have left the mark of hurry on one of our greatest
and most powerful thinkers, Mr. Browning, who ventriloquises for us
under a hundred different masks without perfecting more than a
tenth part of his work." If this is a true charge, it is an interesting
example of what we see every day. A teacher warns people against
a fault which perhaps it needs little insight to recognise as one of his
own ; the greater number cry, "How inconsistent !" Only a few clearer-
eyed, from a sympathy born of self-knowledge, say, "He has learnt
that knowledge through many a wrestling match ; ay, through many
a fall and defeat, in striving for a mastery not yet attained."

Can anyone achieve a perfect limitation in this crowded stage
of the world's history. We are out of breath with the demands upon
us, other times had their own natural limitations, we have to make
our own, a life's study of itself, disturbed by the criticism under which
the most reserved life has to attempt to live. Concentration is a
task seemingly beyond our power, since every work and vocation is
now a tangled thread of many strands.

From Sordello's story we see how a man of less genius than his,
but of more concentrated purpose, fulfils his vocation and serves his

age better than a man of glorious gifts who dissipates his power by scattering it on divided aims. Near the end of his life Sordello saw his mistake—

> " His truth rose again, and naked at his feet
> Lighted his old life's every shift and change,
> Effort with counter-effort ; nor the range
> Of each looked wrong except wherein it checked
> Some other—which of these could he suspect,
> Prying into them by the sudden blaze,
> The real way seemed made up of all the ways.
> Mood after mood of the one mind in him ;
> Tokens of the existence bright or dim
> Of a transcendent all-embracing sense
> Demanding only outward influence.
> A soul, in Palma's phrase, above his soul,
> Power to uplift his power—the moon's control
> Over the sea depths—and their mass had swept
> Onward from the beginning and still kept
> Its course ; but years and years the sky above
> Held none, and so untasked of any love
> His sensitiveness idled and . . . .
>   . . . . disposed itself anew
> At every passing instigation grew and dwindled at caprice,
>   " Not gathered up and hurled
> Right from his heart encompassing the world.
> So had Sordello been without a function by consequence.
>   " Others made pretence
> To strength not half his own, yet had some core
> Within submitted to some moon before
> Them, still superior, still whate'er their force
> Were able therefore to fulfil a course,
> Nor missed life's crown, authentic attribute,
> To each who lives must be a certain fruit
> Of having lived in his degree."

Circumstances and the manifold endowments of his varied genius had mastered Sordello. He had not ruled them by a purpose high above his life to control it " as the moon the tides," consequently some feebler, less gifted man had a power beyond his, because it was " gathered up and hurled right from the heart."

Sordello, arraigning himself at his own tribunal, tells us that " no mere human love or hate " would " equal prove to swaying all Sordello." He needed a power above and beyond himself and his moods. Because he lacked that Divine influence controlling and guiding him, " the Best " eluded him, " might be and was not."

Sordello also failed because he did not balance body and soul. They were at cross purposes, and did not mutually support and aid each other. It is a lesson which a few souls need perhaps in every age, those who are most finely, sensitively strung, who could dream life away in gazing into the vast Beyond till they " touch earth only on tip-toe." Such souls have dangers all their own, they are not understood by those around them for the most part, and their unbalanced natures lay them open to misconception. It is the history of many a wrecked life, the secret of many a mood in our own lives difficult to understand. The spiritual exaltation has been too powerful for the body to sustain, and inconsistencies and eccentricities are its natural revenge. Body and spirit have not been taught and trained so to sustain the force of man's soul, and all crash together because they have not learnt the secret of balance. Many need that lesson because of the tension and pressure of the present time. A warning to ourselves, it furnishes us with an excuse for others with minds of a high order who have made shipwreck on this rock.

> " What made the secret of his past despair ?
> This. Soul on Matter being thrust,
> Joy comes when so much Soul is wreaked in Time
> On Matter. Let the Soul's attempt, sublime
> Matter beyond the scheme, and so prevent
> By more or less that deed's accomplishment,
> And sorrow follows. Sorrow how avoid ?
> Let the employer match the things employed
> Fit to the finite his infinity."

The soul

> " Had fain conveyed her boundless
> To the body's bounded lot,
> And the poor body soon sinks
> Under what was meant a wondrous boon,
> Leaving its bright accomplice all aghast."

It is a marvellous picture the poet has drawn for us of the times all of a higher sensibility must experience when body and soul are at strife, the one overwhelmed with the other; the soul has urged both body and intellect onward beyond their capacity, and the consequence is that the finite is unequal to sustain the Infinite, and an anguish almost incommunicable is the result, which threatens disaster and destruction.

Then the poet, speaking in his own person, gives the assurance that to uphold this wondrous union there needs a third, the Divine, to hold body and soul in a union safe and sure—

> " The Human clear as that Divine concealed
> What utter need ! "

This want of balance is one reason of the inconsistencies of those who aim highest and fail most palpably, but there are other causes, and Mr. Browning gives them most forcibly by the mouth of the old Pope in the *Ring and the Book*. All that they once held firm and strong has become merely a form of words with them—held, but having no influence on their lives, because they pride themselves on having attained ; their creed does all for them, having been once grasped. " Religious parasites," Mr. Browning calls them, theirs is the

> " Vice o' the watcher who bides near the bell,
> Sleeps sound because the clock is vigilant."

They stand on their past achievements, and care comparatively little for the continuing growing life which can alone prevent achievement and creed from becoming dead letters.

In every party in the Church, in every sect, some are to be found who hold a form of sound words, the cardinal article of their faith, from which all life—so far is it from having an influence on their character or work—has fled.

The tale is told of one who visited Huguenot confessors in the galleys, one of their own creed, and he found to his inexpressible grief that the truths for which they had suffered had lost all force and power to them, for the

> " Moral sense grows but by exercise."

Resting on past experience is fatal—

> " Have we not fought, bled, left our martyr mark ? "

The pity of it is, as the Pope goes on to say, summing up the successive disappointments he had experienced from Archbishop, simple monks, nuns,—all having come short of their high professions,—that—

> " It would be sad if in a philosopher ;
> What is it when suspected in that Power
> Who ordained salvation for man, body, and soul ? "

> " Shall he wish back that thrill of dawn
> When the whole truth touched man, burned up one fire."

> " The frail become the perfect rapt
> From glory of pain to glory of joy."

> " Was this too easy for our after stage ? "

Mr. Browning recognizes that those less complicated ages were much easier when martyrdom was the touchstone. Now man has to walk—

> " Bearing to see the light of Heaven still more
> And more encroached on by the light of earth,
> Earthly incitements that mankind serve God
> For man's sole sake, not God's and therefore man's.
> The world smiles. It is the politic, the thrifty way,
> Will clearly make you in the end returns."

What is the remedy for this new Pharisaicism? What will uproot this "ignoble confidence"?

By many different voices Mr. Browning gives the answer: "Test your faith." Doubt that martyrdom to some minds perhaps will

> " shake
> This torpor of assurance from our creed,
> Re-introduce the doubt discarded."

And here comes in one of the chief teachings of Mr. Browning: he does not divide the world off into good and bad; there is no sharp dividing line between the saint and the sinner; both have to stand at the bar of a deeper judgment than that of man.

Hidden motives and springs of thought are dragged out till, testing himself by an entirely new standard,

> " Correcting the portrait by the living face,
> Man's God by God's God,"

each man feels he is one of those

> " Whose very souls even now
> Seem to need re-creating."

Re-creating we do need in this age of unreality, when it is so hard to see ourselves truly.

Mr. Browning teaches us to welcome the day of awakening in whatever form it may come, thankful even for sorest temptation—

> " Was the trial sore? temptation sharp?
> Thank God a second time . . . .
> Learning anew the use of soldiership,
> Self-abnegation, freedom from all fear,
> Loyalty to the life's end! Ruminate,
> Deserve the initiatory spasm once more,
> Work, be unhappy, but bear life, my son."

But if old standards of a flawless exterior are to be distrusted, what is the real test?

It lies deeper than man's judgment can see, in the

> " seed of act,
> God holds appraising in His hollow palm ;
> Not act grown great ; thence on the world below
> Leafage and branchage, vulgar eyes admire ;
> Therefore I stand on my integrity,
> Nor fear at all."

And fearlessly Mr. Browning dares to set before us a pendant to the group we have already seen drawn for us by the Pope, who fell short—were moral cowards—just where their profession should have bid them show courage and disinterestedness, in those who dared to brave the world's opinion, to act in the face of received traditions, in simple faith, firm in the integrity of their true-heartedness.

It seems as if Mr. Browning revelled in the contemplation of simple hearts without one touch of morbidness ; as if—skilful dissector and delineator of the most subtle mysteries of the human heart as he is—he turned, *con amore*, to draw in many a different guise and form those who, free from paralyzing self-questionings, see their duty plain and do it. Pippa, Michal, Polixena, Colombe, Pompilia, Caponsacchi, Norbert, Ivan, with his " How otherwise?" are types of that direct, earnest nature which can say with Pompilia—

> " I know the right place by foot's feel.
> I took it, and tread firm there."

It is the stuff of which fanatics—"earth's fanatics, but heaven's saints" —are made : they hear the one call, and respond to that, and heed not the voices around them which would lure them into other paths ; and their way is easier because of its directness.

This age of ours, with all its subtler temptations, has had a few stars which have shone luminous and

> " Shown sufficient of God's light
> For us i' the dark to rise by."

The directer natures have Mr. Browning's admiration ; the more complex ones his sympathy and help, to guide them to those juster judgments and decisions which have to take the place of fine instinct, by which the happier souls are led.

To that bar of Divine judgment, out of the world's deafening chorus of praise and blame, so ignorant where it thinks itself so wise, he calls us, reminding us how worthless all human judgment is—

> " Our human speech is nought,
>   Our human testimony false, our fame
>   And human estimation words and wind."

" He fears God, why then need he fear the world ? "

Over and over again does Mr. Browning impress this lesson upon us, as if sometimes he had no other that he wished so much to drive home into our hearts, to be our shield against a cruel world—

> " The inward work and worth
>   Of any mind what other mind may judge
>   Save God, who only knows the thing He made,
>   The veritable service He exacts."

Mr. Browning, in the defence which Caponsacchi makes for himself, boldly confronts a point which is a matter of unspeakable surprise and discouragement, more especially in the present time, *i.e.* that great reforms for good, courageous warfare against crying evils, have to be carried on more or less by lonely workers in the teeth of an opposition which does not come only from the avowed enemies of good, but from those bound by every claim to help them. In a recent life written we see how cruel was the disappointment at the desertion of natural friends. The reviling of the world is comparatively easy to endure. It is the unexpected indifference and cowardice of those from whom sympathy would naturally be expected that cuts to the heart.

> " I heard last time I stood here to be judged
>   What is priests' duty—labour to pluck tares
>   And weed the corn of Molinism.—Let me
>   Make you hear this time how in such a case
>   Man, be he in the priesthood or at plough,
>   Mindful of Christ, or marching step by step,
>   How he is bound better or worse to act.
>   For you and others like you sure to come
>   Fresh work is sure to follow—wickedness
>   That wants withstanding."

That is the choice which in various ways comes home to many, between the mere life of thought and culture, and descending to grapple with deadly forms of evil, "withstanding wickedness" perishing, if need be, with the people in doing it.

There is no hesitation in Mr. Browning's tone as to the need of brotherhood to which we are called. Not only in "plucking out tares or weeding out Molinism," and whatever stands for it now, lies duty—

> " Duty to God is duty to her."

Caponsacchi "thought the other way—self-sacrifice"—till he learnt that to save a fellow-creature, even if he undid himself in the doing it,

> " Was the true sealed up the perfect man."

The lesson is repeated in *Ferishtah's Fancies ;* it is unmistakably insisted that these are not the days when a man may wrap himself in selfish isolation of thought and culture—

> " Since they are days when men congregate in towns not woods. "

There lies the part of the thinker.   His thought will be richer because it stimulates thought in those from whose lives it is crowded out.   Life's current will run deeper for the man that holds culture, art, beauty, all that can enrich the charmed circle of his home for others, and not only for himself.

These are the days when in a true socialism the best antidote can be found for much that threatens to wreck society.

> " Let throngs press thee to me
> Up and down amid men, heart by heart fare we.
> Welcome squalid vesture, harsh voice, hateful face ;
> God is soul, souls I and thou, with souls should souls have peace."

It is most interesting to notice in studying Mr. Browning, how, as it were, for fear of exaggerating one side of truth, he turns round and gives you another point, correcting and keeping in check the former view.   Till this manner of his is understood, it seems as if he were contradictory.   You read one poem, and are, after much thought, of one mind with him ; and you take up another, and he turns round and faces you, almost as a perverse mind will sometimes do for the sake of argument when you thought it in agreement with your own.

Thus in the same volume, in the poem called the *Two Camels*, he takes quite the other side, and corrects the morbid scruples of those who now—when theories like those propounded in " England's

Ideal " are rife, and Thoreau's life is held up as the true ideal to which we should one and all return—hardly enjoy anything for themselves, asking how they can in any degree feast whilst others fast.

The same principle, he would say, holds good for enjoyment as for abstinence. To

> " The squeamish scruple,
>   What imports fasting or feasting ?"

The answer comes—

> " Do thy day's work, dare refuse no help thereto,
>   Since help refused is hindrance sought and found."

And again—

> " Desire joy, and thank God for it.
>   Renounce it if needs be for others' sake,
>   That's joy beyond joy."

Not abstinence from and indifference to God's gifts for the mere sake of asceticism, but receiving that we may hand on, knowing the value of the gift we give; tasting that we may sympathise the more—

> " The richness, hearted in such joy
>   Is in the knowing what are gifts we give."

We are nearer to God in giving than in receiving, he says in *Rabbi ben Ezra*—

> " Rejoice we are allied
>   To that which doth provide
> And not partake, effect and not receive.
>   A spark disturbs our clod.
>   Nearer we hold of God
> Who gives than of His Tribes that take I must believe."

And here in *Rabbi ben Ezra* we have a corrective to that spirit of reform which takes possession of a philanthropic age to the exclusion of all care for self-discipline, when there is much hurry to set other people's minds and houses in order, while the reformer's own house and mind are in urgent need of attention.

In a recent short paper the complaint was made that except in the verse I have just quoted there is no touch of Altruism in the poem. But surely it has the highest Altruism in its argument— that our best tribute to the world is to be our highest selves, to learn by our experience a humility which comes from frequent failure of reaching our ideal—and a divine dissatisfaction with our own achievement which is the spur to perpetual progress.

Pippa Passes is the complement of *Rabbi ben Ezra*—being your highest, best self, whether by conscious struggle, or in the unconscious goodness of a child-like nature, you touch and influence more than you know.

> " There was no duty patent in the world
> Like daring try be good and true myself."

Mr. Browning never crowds the whole duty of man into a single poem ; he gives one truth clear and sharp, and enforces it as if there were no other for the time being ; but he will not let those who want the other side of that same truth escape, he pursues and confronts them with their lesson in another poem. It would be an interesting study to see how often this is the case.

To take one example. In *Bifurcation* he gives us, it seems to me, the complement to the story of Caponsacchi in a warning against a false self-sacrifice, very specious and most tempting to some minds. As in the *Two Camels* he blames asceticism for its own sake, so here it is self-sacrifice for the sake of self-sacrifice he counts most dangerous. He fights against the morbid idea that because a path is attractive therefore it must be wrong, and shows we have no right to save our own soul at the expense of another's, wrecking their life that we may feel comfortable, destroying trust and hope in one fell blow, thinking that

> " Heaven will repair what wrong earth's journey did."

To all morbidness Mr. Browning's theories of life are the best tonic ; and his optimism (which has often been dwelt on) is not of that provokingly persistent cheerful nature which refuses to recognise pain and suffering, and denies their very existence. He realises to the full the varied forms of misery and anguish at the present time, and if he cannot give an absolute answer hints at the line whence comfort may spring. To some minds his solutions are fully satisfying, to others they are not. But in the fact of the recognition of trial there is much comfort, especially in questions which involve doubt and bewilderment often shirked and put aside by teachers. Mr. Browning shirks nothing, owns the difficulty, almost the despair. Especially is this so in one of his latest volumes, where he speaks of a trial under which some souls lose faith and heart altogether, *i.e.*, the seeming victory

of evil over good, while God stands as it were aloof and does not
interpose.

The bitterness of such a trial is clearly put forth—

> " No stirring of God's Finger to denote
> He wills that right should have supremacy
> On earth, not wrong.   How helpful could we quote
> But one poor instance when He interposed
> Promptly and surely and beyond mistake
> Between oppression and its victim, closed
> Accounts with sin for once, and bade us wake
> From our long dream that justice bears no sword."

Mr. Browning fully owns that "it is a sore to soothe not chafe," and
suggests comfort after his kind which satisfies some minds for a while
in the reminder that we are asking to understand what is beyond us—

> " Man with the narrow mind must cram inside
> His finite God's infinitude."

He points to the analogy of natural law, how the child grows to be
the man through " infancy's probation "—

> " By foiled darings, fond attempts back driven,
> Fine faults of growth, brave sins which saint when shriven ; "

he does not

> " stand full statured in magnificence.
> No, as with body so deals law with soul,
> That, stung to strength through weakness, strives for good
> Through evil, earth its race-ground, Heaven its goal,
> Presumably."

Failure, Mr. Browning argues, is the natural condition of earth,
failure which God as man deigned to share with men ; it is the old cry
repeated by those who cannot understand " the force of weakness
which shakes the world " ; " Let Him come down from the cross ; "
" Let Him save Himself, and we will believe Him."

In the " Epistle," the poet shows with all his dramatic power
the light in which the Christ appeared to those who could not
pierce the veil of His humanity ; he dares to show that it is only the
Supreme, the Almighty, who could in consciousness of Omnipotence
dare to seem to fail, in knowledge of final victory.

And nearest of all to the Divine, he holds those who, full of a holy
audacity, true to their own unswerving inner truth of motive, move
untouched by blame or praise in a higher atmosphere than their

fellows who can be swayed by the world's voice. Failure to such is a closer co-operation with the Divine, for every demand made upon our faith, our endurance, and generosity, marks our relationship to the Highest, and is an assurance of our own immortality, when the pain of the finite will become the joy of the Infinite, and failure here is a pledge of success there, a very token of sonship—

> " What is a failure here, but a triumph's evidence
> For the fulness of the days ? "

Experience gained below is our best equipment for fuller life above.

To gather up the threads of this desultory paper, I must revert to my original proposition, which was to show from Mr. Browning's own words how fully he is in sympathy with the age, how far he ministers to its varied needs, and how firmly he corrects its faulty tendencies.

How far I have succeeded in my task I leave others to decide.

" SAUL."

By ANNA M. STODDART.

Read at the Fifty-ninth Meeting of the Browning Society, Friday, May 25, 1888.

DAVID tells over to himself, so that no detail shall have time to escape his memory, a wonderful adventure that happened to him the afternoon and evening before, when he was led by a splendid emotional intuition to prophesy as an essential element of the nature of God the saving power of divine love able and willing to suffer for man overwhelmed by the baleful pressure of life, as man may suffer for man. He believes the prediction and proceeds to tell over, " his voice to his heart," the chain of incidents which led to this marvel and through which he was hurried the evening before. He had no time to pause then, to consider whence came the impulse, whither it tended. He knows that every incident was real, has happened, but he knows that when real things are so rare, so exalted as these are, they are elusive too, may " evanish like sleep."

He wakes, as day dawns, in a cool covert of the valley of the Kidron. The brook flows along the deep gorge it has cut in the sun-stricken hills to the west of the Dead Sea and makes its way thither amidst groves of low trees, thickets of oleanders and tamarisks, and a rich luxuriance of irises, scillas and other blossoms of early summer. The sun is fierce by day, but the nights are cool and dewy, the early mornings fresh.

He is alone, as he loves to be, for the keeper who had charge of the flock during his absence at the camp has gone back to Bethlehem.

We can see him, as he sits there, a slender lad quick of movement, his grey eyes humid and dilated, his hair of reddish gold, his face and form instinct with magnetic gentleness and tenderness. He is one with the nature that he loves, the birds flutter near him, the timid creatures of the sand and thickets leap and dart about him, heedless of his presence. Donatello, that sculptor of delicate insight, has moulded for us just such a David. His harp lies near him untouched, and yet he is wont to strike it in praise of God when he awakes at dawn, for to God rise day and night his sweetest songs. He is so near to God in his solitude that he communes with Him all the time, his reveries are all eloquent of God. But this adventure is too strange for praise as yet,—it has to be grasped, realised first, and his heart still throbbing with awe, he calls on his memory to retrace its every circumstance. A messenger from the camp had come to Bethlehem yesterday, desiring him from Abner, the king's cousin, to come at once with his harp, for Saul was ill,—and once before at the king's house at Gibeah he had played and won him back to health. His father had sent a keeper to take his place with the [sheep and bade him follow the messenger to Elah, for there was no time to lose. He plucked a handful of blue irises and twined their broad leaves round the strings of his harp to shield them from the fierce heat of his journey over that desolate region where the sterile hills lie exposed to the glare of noon, and the very stones and sand of the valleys are so scorched that part of it is known as the Valley of Fire. He reached the camp however fresh with the zeal to serve that filled him, and as he stood before Abner, his presence drew from the king's cousin that wonderful welcome in which joy and hope were mingled with love and reverent admiration:

"Yet now my heart leaps, O beloved! God's child with his dew
On thy gracious gold hair, and those lilies still living and blue,
Just broken to twine round thy harp-strings, as if no wild heat
Were now raging to torture the desert!"

The story was soon told. Three days and nights had Saul remained in the royal pavilion, unapproachable, giving no sign, in the agony of that strange illness which overcame him now from time to time, and which seemed to his courtiers like the descent upon him of an evil spirit.

The attacks had come ever since his calamitous estrangement from Samuel. The two strong natures had come into collision and the stern seer had withdrawn the divine guidance of which he was the

channel from the king. Left to himself, Saul, whose headstrong
pride was complicated with an invincible faith in God and sense of
His sovereignty, suffered awful relapses into despair. He endured,
as a fallen angel might have done, the agonies of a helplessness at
which his pride rebelled, but which his faith brought home to him.
The Hebrew mind had evolved no consoling philosophy for humanity
in such straits; it was wanting in the dainty flimsiness which can
seriously find sufficient guidance in modern Epicureanism; its ardent
faith in its own soul made the development of a calm Stoicism
impossible; its capacity to conceive of God barred the way to
Positivism,—all these brave succours to man at war with God were
to come later to faith-atrophied peoples in other lands. The Jews
had no middle course, they were safe in the hands of God or wrecked
in their own. Saul had made his choice and was wrecked. After
a short communing with God, David made his way to the mid-tent, approached through one which formed its antechamber. He had to grope
his way unaided by artificial light and coming from the glare of the
afternoon with eyes too dazzled to profit by the half-light, which
the thick dark hangings of the pavilion permitted to filter through.
When he reached the hangings of the inner tent, he sought courage
again in prayer, "and opened the foldskirts and entered and was not
afraid." At first he could see nothing, and no answer came to his
gentle announcement, "Here is David, thy servant." Gradually
his eyes grew used to the obscurity, he distinguished the great post
which supported the tent from ground to roof, then the beam that
crossing this central support held the folds of the tent-covering
extended on either side, and then slowly it reached his sight that a
figure stood by the main prop with arms stretched along the cross-
beam on either side, as if crucified there, as the king-serpent,
emblem of Christ crucified, hangs on the tree "awaiting his change."
A sunbeam breaking into the inclosure showed him Saul. They stood
face to face, these two whom God had anointed, the one whom He
had forsaken, the other whom He inspired. David untwined the
lilies, which he had gathered beside Kidron, from his harp and began
to play; little preludings of simple tunes at first, the folding tune,
little crooning melodies with which he amused himself in his lonely
shepherd vigils, attracting the shy wild creatures of desert and
cornland about him, the timid jerboa from his burrow in the sand, the
quail from the ripening ears of wheat. Then human associations
began to press in on his memory and his harp swelled to richer strains,
to authentic Hebrew melodies, to the glad song of the reapers in

corn and vineyard to which Isaiah alludes (chap. xvi. v. 10), to the
chants of the singing-men and singing-women who lamented the dead
and whose elegies over great men were preserved and repeated, as we
read in 2 Chronicles xxxv. v. 25 ; to joyous wedding chants; to the
song of the builders as they worked and sped their work with song ;
and lastly to the grand processional chorus of the Levites as they
went up to the altar. This hymn, familiar to Saul's ears, reached
them, and the whole tent shook with his mighty shudder as he woke
to be reminded of the day when he too gladly sought God's altar to
inquire of Him. David ceased, paused in the twilight, to hear if any
sound of life followed that mighty shudder. His scattered fancies
were gradually growing concentrated on his king, as grand even in
his godlessness he towered above the slender young singer. He
caught no further sound and bent once more to his harp, his mind
filled with thoughts of Saul, their utterance shaping itself into his
song. Saul, the ruin, the failure, was before him,—in his thoughts
was another Saul, untried and unfallen, a strong and happy youth
favoured with the gift of life, tingling in every sense with keen
appreciation of its joys, the joys of youthful life, its at-homeness
with nature, its adventurousness for the mere pleasure of using its
strength, its relish of simple meals for healthy hunger, its fresh,
sensuous, irresponsible existence. David's song was of that side of
individual life which is most important to all young natures, which
the young Pagan world distinguished so keenly that it made its creed
of what such life offered, and peopled the world of faith correlative
to it with young and happy gods and joyous, careless fauns and
nymphs. A very real and necessary aspect of life it is, but it is not
all, as the Pagan world illustrates in its later bewilderment and
gloom and the melancholy inadequacy of its gods. So David's
song goes on to tell of growing maturity and of duty gladly undertaken, of trial too and the wisdom it brought, of emulation
with his peers and the skill and polish and development of faculties it
gained him, of the gradual storing up of all his gains, the noble body,
the loving heart, the mental vigour, the high aim, worthy deeds and
spreading fame, till with a nation's glad consent Saul was crowned king.
Yearning to relieve the gloom of his present by a picture of that
radiant past, to remind Saul of his great worth and royalty that he
might arise and shake off despair, David's voice and harp had swelled
and risen to a burst of ardent appeal, and the sound reached the
king. He heard and understood, some vivifying influence stirred all
his frame, and released from the clutch of despair he stood by the
tent-prop pale and worn, but himself again and conscious. The past

has recalled him to life, but the present is inadequate to make life
worth living to him.   Quickly David's thoughts flash forward.
There is the fame of the great which descends to generation after
generation, there is the immortal influence of royal lives, the germs
of ages to come, which are shaped by the illustrious dead of whom the
ages hear and whose memory they record.   The future holds the
recompense for the present and for that Saul must needs thank God
that he exists.   The king is struck by the promise; no longer standing, he reclines on the heap of garments which lie at the base of the
tent-prop.   The blood flows once more freely through his veins, natural
impulses again prompt his movements, he puts out his hand and lays
it on David's brow as he kneels there, his harp on the ground before
him.   The king's tender gaze and caress send a passion of love
through David's heart and he feels that the best he has done falls
utterly short of the best he would do.   What is this to Saul, that his
life is great and has in it royal possibilities for other men and promise
of fame when *he* shall lie low in the grave?   How does it profit Saul's
self whom David loves?   Love would give its gift to the being
beloved that he himself might have it and hold it.   Not the joys of
living, exquisite though they be, not the harvest of an influential life,
the progressive advantages it opens to others, fame now, record after,
undying tribute from posterity : these pass away or they never reach
him and his heart has not a lasting joy the more because of them.
Love would give something immortal, would give what it seems God
himself has never offered.   David would exceed God in the one
particular of loving and in all the rest " show his nothing-perfect
to God's all-complete."   But who but God has created such
love in his heart?   Can God create a faculty He cannot exercise?   No
indeed, *that* answers the question infinitely and yet definitely.   The
heart to love Saul thus is the very gift of God.   Can that heart doubt
then that God's heart loves him too and in proportion as completely
as David loves imperfectly?   There is no boon for Saul which David
can conceive that God will not bestow.   He would give to his king
for the life which has failed, a new life, an eternal life, a dayspring
into which " he will awake from death's minute of night " to find
himself clear and safe in new light and new life.   To give him this,
David would wrestle and anguish, his will to serve Saul for love's sake
is perfect and therefore God's will to serve man whom He loves may
nowise shrink from suffering too.   No, for he stands in spirit at the
very throne of God and " bare to the universal prick of light " learns
there the law of life.

"He who did most shall bear most, the strongest shall stand the most weak.
'Tis the weakness in strength that I cry for! my flesh that I seek.
In the Godhead! I seek and I find it. O Saul, it shall be
A Face like my face that receives thee, a man like to me
Thou shalt love and be loved by for ever: a Hand like this hand
Shall throw open the gates of new life to thee! see the Christ stand!"

Such is the story of the poem. Before passing from it to note in what manner it illustrates Mr. Browning's creed and methods, I should like to say a word about the function of music in working out the story. We know that Browning considers music an important means of rapturous expression, a medium of prophecy in more than the ancient acceptation of the term, and yet here, when the theme is expanded beyond all experience and all imagination, David drops his lyre as useless, his voice alone declares the word that God speaks from his lips. It is as if he were himself the harp of God, vibrating at the touch of the Master's fingers. Up to that point however it is with harp and voice that he reaches the dulled ear of Saul and it is worth while reminding ourselves how the first two kings of Israel had in common this sensitiveness to music. It is a commonplace now of knowledge that from the genius and ardour of the Jews for music the art radiated into other lands, where indeed to this day men of Jewish race are amongst its most gifted exponents. The seer Samuel, who anointed both David and Saul, gave to this art a great impulse during his ascendency. New instruments were invented in his time, notably the psaltery and pipe; his college at Naioth cultivated musicians who were known as prophets and their musical performances as prophecies. Much of his time was spent in training youths for musical service in the worship of God, and it is possible that some of our oldest church-music which is said to have been stolen by friars in disguise from synagogue services may have had its origin in the antiphonal choruses sung and accompanied by the trained choirs and orchestras of Naioth. Both the men whom Samuel anointed to be kings over Israel were trained musicians, one of them more sensitive to the charm of music perhaps than practically musical, although on at least two occasions he was constrained to prophesy, the other a musician of the highest order. It is suggested that David invented the psaltery, and tradition attributes to him a lute on which the wind played as on an Aeolian harp and which hanging near him as he slept awoke him as its strings vibrated the breath of the morning air. In his time the cultivation of music reached its climax amongst the Jews, —in after times when neighbouring empires encroached on Palestine, a chief trophy of their conquests was the carrying into captivity a band of trained Jewish musicians who played at the court festivals of their conquerors. The power of music over the vexed senses and troubled minds of men was thoroughly understood, and the early fame of the young shepherd-singer of Bethlehem brought him into this most dramatic relation with Saul, in which he, destined to supplant him on the throne, knelt before him with tender and healing ministration, soothing his distracted spirit with the sweet songs of Israel. In Browning's first conception of this scene, we find it limited within the bounds of Hebrew possibilities at the time,—in his extended version of 1855, the poem becomes a very noble and exalted lyric bursting all mere realistic boundaries and soaring with the strong pinion of faith into possibilities of which God alone held the impulse and the issue. But it may be urged by those who, admitting the splendour of the lyric, triumphant in thought, imagery and form, still refuse its conclusions and demur to its emotional reasoning, that it is a mere poetical whim to picture David at the moment of sudden spiritual insight which penetrated the very counsels of God and understood His remedy for a world at wreck.

In the life of a very great man now dead, we are told by the man himself that his exclusive devotion to science reduced his mind to the nature of a machine only capable of dealing with certain kinds of facts. In youth, he loved nature, art, poetry; but as he grew more and more absorbed in collecting and marshalling his facts, these tastes languished and died, so that even the sweet influences of the nature which yielded him the facts ceased to reach and refresh him. Charles Darwin was a very great man, and so he knew that each atrophied taste was a loss, that he was poorer without it, that his out-look on humanity was dimmed, his opinion, except on his facts, depreciated by it. He was so great that he could humbly admit his imperfection for want of faculties he had permitted to decay. There are many men and women now-a-days, who suffer defect in the spiritual faculties by which the conclusion of this poem can be reached. They are not all great enough to regret their incompleteness, but vaunt their losses rather, as if Hope and Faith were unsightly growths, deformities that shamed their owner. Those who believe that the Kingdom of God has always been, that His Spirit has in all ages been in touch with the spirit of man, find perfect verisimilitude in the poem.

To understand thoroughly man's need of Christ, we must put ourselves at the standpoint of an age before Christ came. We know how different is the anticipation of an event to its retrospect. We in this generation have never known what it is to be without Christ.

The atheists of to-day are saturated with Christ and strangely enough some of them admit it and think they leave Him behind by doing so. Christ pervades our life in every phase of it, we cannot get rid of Him. In a far more intimate than the general sense, our will is not our own, but is instructed and modified by a thousand influences of which Christ is the main-spring. It is a practical fact to be reckoned with in all estimates of modern life that *Christ is with us.* But Saul's was an age which had no Christ. He was gone wrong and helpless and there was no one with love like man's and power like God's to set him right. He was at war with God and mad with the misery of his unnatural conflict and there was no one to make peace. The noblest spirits of his nation indeed hoped and believed in the coming of an Emmanuel, a Redeemer, a Prince of Peace. What a need they must have felt of Him, what faith and hope theirs must have been, while we who have Him seem wearied of Him. Close to the ruined soul of this man David yearns to bring recreating comfort. He seeks after the right message along the whole scale of human possibilities, pressing every joy of this life into the service,—from the irresponsible delights of youth, when the gradual awakening of his own nature and capacities, the discovery of his circumstances and of all that a world rich in yet untried experiences has to offer him are enough for the eager adventurer, up to the lofty ambitions of a matured and kingly soul which would sway men to great ends while it lasted and leave memories to become law and precedent when it passed away. To the last Saul faintly responds; there is a partial recovery of self-respect; but that is all; the best David has brought brings no joy. Sadder even than the unconscious wreck which he has won back to wan life is this joyless, hopeless suffering of life, this dignity of the king doomed to endure his weird to the end, and David agonises for the further light that shall reveal to him the remedy for a need so great. "Just one lift of God's hand cleared that distance,—God's throne from man's grave." Only God Himself is sufficient for Saul, for humanity at the point of ruin, and the humanising of God in Christ that He may reach down to man and finding him may lift him up into the atmosphere of His own presence which is immortality, is the inevitable assurance which he attains, the supreme conclusion reached by a reason supported by faith and love.

The analogy between the prediction ascribed in the poem to David and those of later prophets who foretold Christ six hundred years before is coming His perfect. It was from the gloom of subjection and captivity that these men broke into their most joyous visions of the coming Redeemer. When the state of the Jewish nation was most hopeless, when its people were sunk in evil and idolatry, when the heel first of the Egyptian and then of the Babylonian was on its neck, when the prophet voices were loud with wrath and tremulous with bitter lamentation, just then from time to time they were exalted "by a lift of God's hand" to "sing aloud and shout, to be glad and rejoice.—The Lord thy God in the midst of thee is mighty; *he will save.*" Mr. Browning follows a method with which he has made us familiar, when he uses Saul's need and David's ministry as the exponents of human helplessness and divine help in an age long anterior to Christ. We know how he prefers the heralds of each new order to its declared representatives,—how obscure men on the verge of a dawn, which they either hailed or longed for, attract him more powerfully than the sons of its morning. Thus Abt Vogler and Galuppi with their blurred memories live in his poems, not Beethoven and Rossini;—thus Fra Lippo Lippi cries aloud for deliverance from the shackles that bound both man and art in the Middle Ages, not Raphael;—thus the nameless Grammarian who toiled his life long for learning's sake to add so little to its sum, is glorified, not the heirs of the Renaissance;—thus Cleon thirsting for God and immort-ality, but with his back turned to the star in the east, proclaims his pensive sense of higher needs, not Paul the apostle of the Resur-rection;—thus not St. Francis of Assisi but Karshish the open-minded Arab student stands entranced at first contact with the Christian faith, "The very God I think, Abib; dost thou think? So the All-Great were the All-Loving too."—

Now it is worthy of note that the poet wrote the first part of Saul at the age of 33, and made the addition which transformed it ten years later at the age of 43. Much insistence is laid in our discussions on Mr. Browning's opinions on this and that subject, an unreasonable insistence I sometimes think, seeing his vast sympathy embraces the standpoints of every sincere apologist for his creed even when the sincerity seems to shallower observers but a minimum element in the apology. It is as if we were to be irritated with Shakespeare because he fails to tell us whether he admires or despises his consummate knaves and fools. Very seldom does Mr. Browning lift the veil from the inner chamber of his own likes and dislikes, of his selected pre-ferences and opinions, but just now and then the veil flutters aside and we get a sanctioned glance into a reserve which should be hallowed in every man. And this biographical fact seems to me just such a fluttering aside of the veil. We are permitted to know by it that to the mature man, spiritually quickened as he must have been at that period of his life, his early conception of the poem grew crude and incomplete and his vision of the consolations of God expanded to salvation and immortality as alone competent to the need. And with that expansion comes joy. Other systems have each its striking virtue for note. Temperance, resignation, obedience, endurance, one and all of them are the watchwords of great philosophies, the sum of their wisdom projected by the experience of noble minds in contact with life's problems. Noble systems have grown out of Christianity, whose watchwords sum up the ethical teaching of Christ, while they claim to have advanced beyond need of Him and to have discovered that man is sufficient for his own salvation. Is there one of these, ancient or modern, that is not unspeakably sad?

What is the best message of Marcus Aurelius, surely the noblest seeker after God untaught by Christ? Temperance, endurance, resignation:—a great and beautiful message, but burdened with the pain of life and its transitoriness. Take the message of the Cyrenian and pursue a life of ever-varying sensation, form no ties, realise no obligations, be unhampered as the wind,—and find joy if you can. Take the graver, greater message of Epicurus. Men try it now-a-days, men with frail bodies and sensitive, captious, fastidious minds, and they pass as a caprice does and their life at the best seems to have been but a sigh. Take the systems of to-day which claim to teach better than Christ and at their best echo or develop His doctrines. Christ is not jealous that the seed He planted grows up into a mighty tree. Advance and growth are what He promised us and we will gladly take all that the thinkers of this century offer us and will thank Christ first for it. For without Him what is their best boon to the individual soul? A most mortal immortality, uncertain fame for the influential, for the rest of us oblivion. The very best in that kind is not the best possible for Mr. Browning. He sees the futility of a self-abnegation that is afflicted with the hopeless heroism of modern altruism. And in *Saul* as in a multitude of poems he teaches us that the individual is precious,—that life is but the avenue for each to immortality, the pledge of which is the "weakness in strength," the Emmanuel who trod it. For what pledge have they who, admitting God and rejecting his manifestation in Christ, still hope for immortality? Immortality is the atmosphere of the Divine Being, man has no claim to it, no organ in himself which can fit him to live and move and have his being in it. He has to learn of Christ, who has ascended up on high and ever liveth and who is the sufficient assurance for all ages, for Saul and for Cæsar, for Charlemagne and St. Bernard, for yesterday, to-day and for ever.

The appropriateness of Mr. Browning's selection of David to be both the actor in this episode and its narrator is emphasised by the historical fact that Christ came of the royal house of David and that His so coming was a national expectation and gave singular definiteness to such Messianic predictions as that of Zechariah : " At that day the house of David shall be as God, as the angel of the Lord before them."

The exceeding beauty of the close of this poem with its sanctification of all nature, gathering it up into the sphere of hallowed hope and expectation, tempts me to end by quoting it without further comment.

> " I know not too well how I found my way home in the night.
> There were witnesses, cohorts about me, to left and to right,
> Angels, powers, the unuttered, unseen, the alive, the aware :
> I repressed, I got through them as hardly, as strugglingly there,
> As a runner beset by the populace famished for news—
> Life or death. The whole earth was awakened, hell loosed with her crews ;
> And the stars of night beat with emotion, and tingled and shot
> Out in fire the strong pain of pent knowledge : but I fainted not
> For the Hand still impelled me at once and supported, suppressed
> All the tumult, and quenched it with quiet and holy behest,
> Till the rapture was shut in itself, and the earth sank to rest.
> Anon at the dawn, all that trouble had withered from earth—
> Not so much, but I saw it die out in the day's tender birth ;
> In the gathered intensity brought to the grey of the hills ;
> In the shuddering forests' held breath ; in the sudden wind-thrills ;
> In the startled wild beasts that bore off, each with eye sidling still
> Though averted with wonder and dread ; in the birds stiff and chill
> That rose heavily, as I approached them, made stupid with awe ;
> E'en the serpent that slid away silent,—he felt the new law.
> The same stared in the white humid faces upturned by the flowers ;
> The same worked in the heart of the cedar and moved the vine-bowers :
> And the little brooks witnessing murmured, persistent and low,
> With their obstinate, all but hushed voices—' E'en so, it is so ! ' "

ON BROWNING'S POEM "CRISTINA AND MONALDESCHI."

BY MRS. ALEXANDER IRELAND.

Read at the Eightieth Meeting of the Browning Society, Friday, February 27th, 1891.

Few characters in history present a more striking picture than does Cristina of Sweden, daughter of Gustavus Adolphus. The elements of her character were unique, tragic, bizarre, and culminated in the wildly romantic murder of the Marquis Monaldeschi under circumstances so astounding as to challenge belief, but that authentic records remain which leave no doubt as to the absolute details of the crime. Much has been written on the life of Cristina, but it was reserved for Mr. Browning to give us a poem on the subject which is almost hopelessly obscure to the uninitiated, whilst throbbing with intensest power to those who know.

It would be idle to enter here on any lengthy account of Cristina's remarkable childhood. In 1632, when his little child was but an infant, the brave and faithful Gustavus Adolphus fell on the battle-field of Lutzen. He had gone forth with unusual forebodings, and had given the most precise and careful instructions to his good friend Chancellor Oxenstiern regarding the whole plan of the education of this dear and only child, Cristina. Gloriously defending the religion that was dearer to him than life—namely, the Protestant faith, the devoted father passed away. His queen, the beautiful widowed Maria Eleonora of Brandenburg, impatient at her inability to interfere with the minute directions left for the education of her child, and in no way sympathizing with a plan which gave a boy's education to a girl, actually ran away from her

Y

responsibilities, and in disguise fled to Denmark, where after long years she died unregretted.   The only other female guardian left to the child, the Princess Katerina, sister of Gustavus, died prematurely while Cristina was yet very young.   The tutors and professors appointed by Oxenstiern taught their brilliant pupil much : she became highly accomplished.   She was also very hardy ; would rise at four, ride sixteen miles before breakfast, was often allowed to sleep all night in the open air, was never permitted to satisfy her hunger, and was thoroughly versed in Greek, Latin, French, German, English, Italian, and Spanish.   She had, indeed, a special Greek professor resident in the palace—much as other young ladies have a canary bird or a toy-terrier.   She was, withal, a true woman at heart, as her sad later history too plainly shews.   Wilful, passionate, rebellious, and perforce unfeminine, she suffered as only a woman *can* suffer.

In due time she had batches of royal suitors.   Prince Ulric of Denmark, the Elector Palatine, the Elector of Brandenburg, the Kings of Portugal and Spain, the King of the Romans, and her cousin Charles Gustavus, amongst others—but she rejected them all. She had no idea of binding herself by the marriage-tie, though the chancellor suggested it was desirable, and her people undoubtedly thought so too.   The position of Oxenstiern was certainly no sinecure.   His fatherly advices bored her terribly.   Cristina was a great correspondent, and was extremely independent.   She often appointed the hours of 4 or 5 A.M. for her audiences with foreign ambassadors or discourses with such men as Descartes and Saumares ; she would then go out hunting, and by ten o'clock would attend scientific lectures.

On October 24th, 1648, the Thirty Years' War came to an end, and peace was signed.   The Senate again urged Cristina to marry, and, to make an end of this annoyance, she resolved to abdicate.   Her successor, chosen by herself, was her cousin Charles Gustavus.   The formal and unusual ceremony of abdication took place in the Cathedral of Upsala in June 1654.   There was a great difficulty in finding anyone who would lift the crown from the golden-locked head of the beautiful young queen.   All the officers of state and the religious authorities were present.   The crown once removed, Cristina arose, after sitting for the last time on the silver throne, herself laid aside her robes of royal state, curtesyed to the prince, her successor, wished him well, and withdrew, leaving throne and kingdom without regret to set forth on her wild and capricious wandering. Other fetters beside those of royalty were thrown off by her when she crossed the little brook that divided Sweden from Denmark. With her triumphant words as to having *found liberty* at last, she saw not before her to what dark abyss that same liberty was to lead her. Picturesque, attractive, terribly human, dressed in manly costume, with one or two followers, she crossed Denmark and Germany, and went towards Rome. Inaccessible to counsel, she trusted no one, she gave confidence to no one: it was thus she had been taught. Impatience of restraint was undoubtedly one of her leading motives in the step she took, but there was a very much more powerful one behind it. Her abdication would have been more highly regarded had it not been followed by her change of religion. As a Roman Catholic she could not have held the Swedish sceptre. She now lost little time in publicly embracing the faith of Rome. Her moral course became so regrettable, that all her bright mental gifts could not redeem it, nor make of her a good and honourable woman. Yet we feel the deepest pity for her. She was received in Rome with great state by the religious authorities, and lost no time in appointing household officers exclusively Italian. Among these was the Marquis Monaldeschi, nominated "Master of the Horse." Cristina's own memoirs give a striking account of this Italian marquis. She describes him as "a gentleman of most handsome person and fine manners, who from the first moment reigned exclusively over my heart." "Italy," she says, "was a scene of enchantment to me when I met him there. I was penetrated, sunk in joy; all nature seemed the fairer for my happiness. The beautiful, proud Monaldeschi opened a new world to me! Could I, in this joy, remember my abjuration? Could I, unhappy one, have the least desire for God? But I was punished heavily for my impiety."

Indeed, the handsome, proud, wily Italian, for whom this lonely and strange nature felt so deep an attachment, proved a traitor and a scoundrel. Having taken every possible advantage of his position as "favourite," having reaped honours and riches, Monaldeschi wearied of his royal mistress and sought new attractions. It is, in fact, the closing scene of Queen Cristina's *liaison* with her Grand Equerry which inspired Browning to give us his splendid poem. The poet chooses the moment when Cristina's eyes were opened to the treachery of her lover; how her passion for him had been his "stock-in-trade" to amuse and interest a younger mistress in Rome.

From Rome, Cristina had proceeded to Fontainebleau, where the letters came into her hands which broke her life. There was a

certain Cardinal Azzolino not averse to supplanting Monaldeschi in
his influence on the queen. He had obtained possession of the whole
wretched and dangerous correspondence; he was the confessor of the
young Roman lady, and he used his power. The packet included
the queen's own letters to her lover—letters written in the fulness of
perfect trust, telling much that the unhappy lady could have told to
no other living being. Monaldeschi's letters to his young Roman
beauty made a jest, a mockery of the queen's exceeding fondness for
him. They were letters of unsparing and wounding ridicule; and
while acting thus, Monaldeschi had steadily adhered to the show of
unaltered attachment to the queen, and deep respect for his royal
mistress. Cristina's emotions on seeing the whole hateful, cowardly
treachery laid bare were doubtless maddening. She arranged an
interview with the marquis in the picture gallery in the Palace of
Fontainebleau. She was accompanied by an official of her Court,
and had at hand a priest from the neighbouring Convent of the
Maturins armed with copies of the letters which were to serve as
the death-warrant of the marquis. They had been placed by Cardinal
Azzolino in Cristina's hands through the medium of her "Major-
Domo" with the knowledge that the cardinal had already seen their
infamous contents. The *originals* she had on her own person. Added
to this, she had in the background her Captain of the Guard,
Sentinelli, with two other officers.

And now to Browning's poem. In the Galerie des Cerfs hung a
picture of François I.[1] and Diane de Poictiers, presumably the work
of Primatice, il Primatico, who had done much of the decoration in
the palace. To this picture the queen now led the marquis, pointing
out the motto on the frame—" Quis separabit ?"

And here Browning begins—

> " Ah, but how each loved each, Marquis!
> Here's the gallery they trod
> Both together, he her god,
> She his idol,—lend your rod,
> Chamberlain !—ay, there they are—' *Quis
> Separabit* ?'—plain those two
> Touching words come into view,
> Apposite for me and you !
>
> Since they witness to incessant
> Love like ours : King Francis, he—
> Diane the adored one, she—
> Prototypes of you and me."

---

[1] I believe the portrait is of Henri II.—F. J. F.

The crescent was the natural sign of Diane, but the salamander of François I. needs some explanation. As a bold, brave, and imperious youth, his father, to restrain his ardent nature, placed him at the age of thirteen in the care of a wise governor, Le Chevalier de Boissy, who, to express his tender and watchful care of his fiery-minded pupil, gave him for his device, or crest, the salamander, with the legend—" Nutrisco et extinguo (Je le nourris et je l'éteins)." This device of the salamander still exists on some of the old carvings and paintings at Fontainebleau.

With renewed sternness Cristina attacks her victim.

> " I—the woman ! See my habit,
> Ask my people ! Anyhow,
> Be we what we may, one vow
> Binds us, male or female. Now—
> Stand, Sir ! Read ! ' *Quis separabit* ! '"

It was true one vow had bound them. In the little ancient church of Avon, a village on the east side of the park of Fontainebleau, those two had stood, on a memorable evening, close to the *bénitier* in a *supreme* moment. Before them lay an ancient tombstone ; around them, the stillness of the church and the deepest happiness of life. And here, pointing to the marble slab at their feet, the marquis had vowed that as that grave kept a silence over the corpse which lay beneath, so would his love and trust hold fast the secret of Cristina's love to all eternity.

Now the woman's spirit was wounded to death. She was scorned, her pride outraged ; but she was a Queen and the man a subject, and she felt she must assert her dignity at least once more. The marquis doubtless tottered as he stood. " Kneel," she says—

> " Cure what giddiness you feel,
> This way. Do your senses reel !
> Not unlikely ! What rolls under !
> Yawning death in yon abyss
> Where the waters whirl and hiss,
> Round more frightful peaks than this."

But she will not release her victim yet. " Silent still ?" she says—

> " Why, pictures speak !—
> See, where Juno strikes Ixion,
> Primatice speaks plainly ! Pooh—
> Rather, Florentine Le Roux !
> I've lost head for who is who—
> So it swims and wanders ! Fie on
> What still proves me female ! Here,
> By the staircase !—for we near
> That dark ' Gallery of the Deer.' "

This was the final scene of the tragedy. A word as to the rival
painters, both of whom assisted in the decoration of the Palace of
Fontainebleau. François Primatice, otherwise Le Primatice, or il
Primatico, who died in 1570 at Bologna, was the rival of Maître Roux,
or " Le Roux ;" but Primatice was first in the field, and a terrible
jealousy arose between the two painters. Primatice was the pet pupil
of Giulio Romano. Rosso, who died in 1541, was a pupil of Michael
Angelo. Both were patronized by François I., and both contributed
largely to the magnificent decorations of the palace. Primatice had
been sent to Italy by the king, nominally to collect works of art ;
and it was only after Rosso's untimely death that he returned. Rosso
had ill-luck : he was only forty-five at the time of his death, and
poisoned himself from bitter remorse at having falsely accused his
friend Pellegrini. But to our death-scene. . . . .

Cristina now calls forth the priest and the assassins, having
granted herself the bitter pleasure of such personal revenge as was
possible for her, poor woman !

> " Friends, my four! You, Priest, confess him !
> I have judged the culprit there :
> Execute my sentence ! Care
> For no mail such cowards wear !
> Done, Priest ? Then, absolve and bless him !
> Now—you three, stab thick and fast,
> Deep and deeper ! Dead at last ?
> Thanks, friends—Father, thanks ! Aghast ? "
> " What one word of his confession
> Would you tell me, though I lured
> With that royal crown abjured
> Just because its bars immured
> Love too much ? Love burst compression,
> Fled free, finally confessed
> All its secrets to that breast
> Whence . . . . . let Avon tell the rest ! "

Let us note that in October 1657, Cristina already felt suspicious
of Monaldeschi. Keenly watching his actions, she had found him
guilty of a double perfidy, and had led him on to a conversation
touching a similar unfaithfulness. " What," the queen had said,
" does the man deserve who should so have betrayed a woman?"
" Instant death," said Monaldeschi, " 'twould be an act of justice."
" It is well," said she ; " I will remember your words." In a recently
published work on Cristina by F. W. Bain, B.A., a defence is made
for this murder of Monaldeschi. " The whole point," said the writer,
" turns on the legal aspect of the case ; how far had she a right to

exercise the power of life and death over the culprit?" And Mr. Bain goes on to state that, "By a special clause in the Act of Abdication, Cristina retained absolute and sovereign jurisdiction over her servants of all kinds." He therefore holds Cristina as morally justified. So far, so good. The only objection made by the French Court was that she ought not to have permitted the murder to take place at Fontainebleau.

Mr. Bain decides in favour of Cristina's action, and agrees with Leibnitz, who said: "All we can reproach the Queen of Sweden for, is that she had not sufficient respect to *the place* where she caused the execution to be performed." "Cristina," says Mr. Bain, "had, in fact, exactly the same right that a Court of Law has."

Few women would wish to take up that ground. It was as a woman and not as a legal client that she suffered. She made much noise in her day. Philosophy, Atheism, and Devotion by turns possessed her in excess; her nature lent itself to the tragedy as well as to the comedy of human life. She still attracts, fascinates, repels. Her own writings were powerful. Here are a few sentences from her "Aphorisms." "Fools," she says, "are more to be pitied than knaves." "The famous '*Know thyself*,' given out as the source of human wisdom, is only that of its misery." "Extraordinary merit is a crime never forgiven." "Genius is always a paradox to those who are without it."

Speaking of the murder of Monaldeschi, she wrote: "Poor women that we are, the details made me weep! That we should be so keen for vengeance, and then rain down our tears for the blood we ourselves have caused to be shed!" "I was on the point," she adds, "of casting myself at the feet of Father Le Bel, but restrained myself by my pride and my dignity. I did, however, by *way of reparation*, order an almost infinite number of masses to be said for the poor marquis. I had him buried in the church close to the *bénitier*, and instituted prayers for the repose of his soul. What agitation was mine! What a day of misfortune was that! And actually I was murmured at for this action, discussed, and complained of."

It was to Father Le Bel of the Monastery of the Maturins, presumably confessor to Queen Cristina [1] during her stay in Fontainebleau, that the copies of the fatal letters had been entrusted by the

---

[1] The actual narrative of Father Le Bel is to be found in a small, discoloured, vellum-bound book in the British Museum. It is one of three treatises there contained, and the book is catalogued as anonymous.

It was written November 6th, 1657, and translated into German in December

queen ; and his reliable narrative of the murder to which he was witness can be read in his own words. Four days after the copies of the letters had been handed to him, a messenger from the palace ordered Father Le Bel to the presence of the queen ; and now took place the final interview between the royal mistress and the Marquis Monaldeschi. He denying all knowledge of the contents of these copies, the queen produced the originals, and the doomed man, muttering something indistinctly, heard the three soldiers in attendance draw nearer with the clash of naked blades to despatch him. The queen withdrew somewhat, and her victim was left with the priest and the executioners. The unhappy man knelt down, laid his head on the priest's knees, made his last confession, and received absolution. It is too painful to dwell on the long and desperate struggle which ensued. Monaldeschi wore a heavy shirt of mail, which rendered it difficult to strike him effectually, but he was at length mercifully released at a quarter to four in the afternoon.

After this atrocious crime Cristina was compelled to leave France, and finally retired to Rome, giving herself up to her artistic tastes, science, chemistry, and idleness. Cardinal Azzolino was her confidential friend till death. Her theory of life had been that, as sovereign, she was responsible for her actions to no one, and this creed she faithfully carried out to the end. It is believed, however, that she had some wish to return to her own religion before her death, but she had no time. She died on April 19th, 1689, her epitaph, chosen by herself, being " Cristina lived sixty-three years." This is significant, and savours of defiance. Hers was a strange and a tragical life, a distorted human existence.

Browning's poem ends with splendid lines, in which the queen, while denouncing the shameful treachery of the man now lying dead

the same year. It contains a fine portrait of Cristina, which Mr. Bain has splendidly reproduced.

Cristina was herself an author. Amongst other works of hers is *L'Ouvrage de loisir* ; but by far the most important work of hers, which is also to be seen in the British Museum, is *Mémoires de ma vie. Dédiées à Dieu.* This was published in Paris by Dehay, in 1830. In it she says : " We *admire* strong characters : we ought rather to *pity* them ! " And perhaps she is right. The memoir is truly astounding. The light of the more " strong-minded woman " of to-day pales before the lurid revelations of this unhappy lady. We may add that the late Mr. Wilkie Collins, in a series of papers called, we believe, " Out-of-the-way Nooks in History," written for *Household Words*, gives a fine abstract of Father Le Bel's narrative. D'Alembert, who was always making " Réflexions " on every imaginable person and subject, judging by the eighteen ponderous volumes thereof in the British Museum, has freely eulogized Cristina in one of his effusions, and so have many other literary men.

before her, puts up one pitiful plea for her own conduct, sums up all her agony, and despair, and degradation in piercing expressions, which cleave the heart.

Nowhere (I think) has our beloved poet shown more wonderful treatment of a strikingly dramatic subject.

With regard to the much-vexed question of Cristina's legal position as to her commanded punishment of Count *Giovanni Rinaldo Monaldeschi*, I have made much research, and here give an extract from an undoubtedly reliable work, published at Bonn in 1837, on "Christina von Schweden und ihre Hof," von W. H. Grauert. This learned and carefully-prepared work, in three volumes, does not pronounce with certainty upon the point at issue, but it may be interesting to quote from it. Speaking of the assassination of the Count at Fontainebleau, the writer says :—[1]

" It made a painful impression. The Queen replied that she had the right to exercise jurisdiction over her servants at all times and in all places : that she was mistress of her will, and answerable to God only for her actions. The King of France, Louis XIV., was not merely giving her asylum and shelter—as to a prisoner or fugitive—he was entertaining her as a royal guest. Her intended action also was not without precedent. She took the Almighty to witness that she had cleansed her heart of all personal malice against the betrayer, and was only punishing a crime which, in its unexampled baseness, concerned the whole world.

"It is true that the suppliant had begged her either to let mercy outweigh right, or to transfer the whole case to a legal tribunal as an ordinary suit at law.

" ' What ?' she replied, ' am *I*, who have absolute sovereign rights over my subjects, thus to degrade myself ? to enter a suit and institute proceedings against a traitorous servant, of whose shameful acts of infidelity I hold the proofs in my hands ? written, too, and sealed by *himself* ! '

" ' It is true,' said the wretched man, ' but remember you are a prejudiced party.'

" It was after all," says Grauert, "a *woman* who devised and carried out a terrible death sentence, one that was executed without the shadow of customary judicial formalities.

" She was a Queen without a kingdom or sceptre who thus judged a subject and exercised a sovereign right.

[1] Vol. ii. pp. 118, 119, and following pages.

" The event took place in the country, and actually in the *royal residence* of a powerful foreign monarch, who was extending his kingly hospitality to the self-dethroned Queen of Sweden.

" The condemned man was also of noble family. The true and actual motive of this deed must remain always more or less shrouded in darkness. It certainly gave occasion to reports of a most dishonouring character. . . . .

" The French Court looked askance on a deed which had taken place at the Royal Castle of Fontainebleau *without official notification.*

" The refined French ladies, careful of open scandal, whose hostility had already been aroused by jealousy of Christina's attractions and accomplishments, loudly denounced what they regarded as mere reckless barbarity.

" Much curiosity was felt as to the Pope's actual knowledge of the facts, and the attitude he would assume with regard to the matter. . . . .

" Later on, Christina was openly charged with the deed. In 1668 the Swedish Government maintained this murder of Monaldeschi as a just reason for refusing her a residence in Sweden.

" Again, the same difficulty was urged in admitting her candidature for the throne of Poland (on the abdication of John Cassimir).

" The whole tissue of events was, indeed, so extraordinary that the case was dealt with as a *cause célèbre* in judicial records of the times, and argued by the highest authorities without absolute result.

" Two points present themselves to be dealt with separately, yet in their essence indissoluble : the question of *jurisdiction*, and, (shall we say ?) *propriety*—certainly the questions of *humanity* and *morality.*

" As to the first point two questions must be considered : (1) whether Christina, in spite of her abdication, still possessed judicial rights over her subjects, of whatever nationality ; (2) such rights being acknowledged her, could she legally exercise them in a foreign land where she was sojourning in the capacity of *guest* to the reigning monarch ?

" It has been largely assumed, and for the most part without formal debate, that Christina had forfeited such judicial rights on her abdication. In this case, the execution of Monaldeschi was simply a murder.

" This view may, however, be dismissed in regarding the fact that the Deed of Abdication specially reserved to Christina, by state covenant, the right to punish the misdeeds of the court, and of her personal attendants.

" This right she exercised, not only in the notorious case of Monaldeschi, but throughout her household, generally speaking.

" For she had only resigned the Swedish crown, and *not* her royal dignity and sovereignty.

" The inhabitants of territorial lands under her control were still compelled to take the oath of allegiance to her, under reserve only of the fealty due to king and country, thus rendering themselves open to the possibility of *lèse-majesté* (*crimen laesae majestatis*).

" Christina chose and dismissed her officials, maintained entire independence, and was responsible to no one."

This is the utmost extent of actual knowledge I can find on the subject of Cristina. Setting apart all *purely legal* right and wrong, the matter cannot fail to be a painful one, and specially so to a woman.

RICHARD CLAY AND SONS, LIMITED, LONDON AND BUNGAY.